Praise for *Sales Process Engineering* from Learning International, a highly respected international sales training firm.

Any organization can use the principles assembled in *Sales Process Engineering* to reduce the risks involved when changing or automating their sales process. Learning International strongly advocates the approach Dr. Selden describes.

—Ken Edwards
Vice President, Learning International

My research has taken me in search of the most effective sales principles all over the globe. This is one of the nicest collections of sales process improvement tools I've seen.

—Derwin Fox
Senior Vice President of Research and Development, Learning International

Our clients are going to be able to use the concepts of *Sales Process Engineering* to dramatically improve their sales performance. Learning International is committed to this approach.

—Debbie Qaqish
Training Manager, Learning International

Additional praise for *Sales Process Engineering*

Paul Selden is to be congratulated for his tireless efforts to advance the profession. *Sales Process Engineering* helps introduce a vast subject in a way that is easy to comprehend.

—William J. Latzko
Coauthor of *Four Days with Dr. Deming*

In my job I am always looking for ways to improve the sales process. Paul Selden is a pioneer in evaluating sales as a process. I recommend *Sales Process Engineering* to anyone who wants to improve their sales process, whether they be in sales, marketing, or customer service.

—Sean Mohan
Sales Automation Project Leader, Watlow Electric Manufacturing Company

Paul Selden's unique engineering approach to the sales process will help sales managers everywhere put down their bullwhips and pick up their pencils. The thoughts and applications Paul shares are based in the classics of TQM with a special focus on how salespeople and their managers can better manage their efforts and improve results.

—John J. Reimer
Executive Director, Pharmacia & Upjohn Animal Health

Sales Process Engineering launches a whole new way of looking at the sales process. This is the first book I've seen to connect the sales and marketing professional with modern schools of thought in process engineering—translated into their own language.

—Rick Newhauser
Chairman, Richard Allan Medical

As usual, Dr. Selden's material is comprehensive and thorough. It is always a pleasure to read his material. It opens new avenues of how we can change the way our salespeople sell, the way our company sells to its customers, and serves as a checkup as to how our entire sales process works.

—Alan Rowley
Sales Operation Manager, Shepherd's McGraw-Hill

Having worked both inside a Fortune 500 company and now as owner of my own business, I can say that the principles Paul Selden has put together are just as applicable for the small company, or the individual, as they are for large firms. *Sales Process Engineering* ties together a lot of conceptual and factual information in an easy-to-digest form.

—Rick Kehr
General Manager, Pres Kool Chevrolet

Sales Process Engineering

Also available from ASQ Quality Press

Sales Productivity Measurement
George A. Smith Jr.

The Sales Quality Audit
George A. Smith Jr.

Selling with Excellence: A Quality Approach for Sales Professionals
Larry A. McCloskey

Bringing Total Quality to Sales
Cas Welch and Pete Geissler

Applying Total Quality to Sales
Cas Welch and Pete Geissler

Mapping Work Processes
Dianne Galloway

To request a complimentary catalog of publications, call 800-248-1946.

Sales Process Engineering

A Personal Workshop

Paul H. Selden

ASQ Quality Press
Milwaukee, Wisconsin

Sales Processing Engineering: A Personal Workshop
Paul H. Selden

Library of Congress Cataloging-in-Publication Data
Selden, Paul H., 1951–
Sales process engineering: a personal workshop / Paul H. Selden.
p. cm.
Includes bibliographical references and index.
ISBN 0-87389-418-9 (alk. paper)
1. Selling—Data processing. 2. Marketing—Data processing.
I. Title.
HF438.35.S45 1997
658.8'00285—dc20 96-32071
CIP

10 9 8 7 6 5 4 3 2

ISBN 0-87389-357-3

Acquisitions Editor: Roger Holloway
Project Editor: Jeanne W. Bohn

ASQ Mission: To facilitate continuous improvement and increase customer satisfaction by identifying, communicating, and promoting the use of quality principles, concepts, and technologies; and thereby be recognized throughout the world as the leading authority on, and champion for, quality.

Attention: Schools and Corporations
ASQ Quality Press books, audiotapes, videotapes, and software are available at quantity discounts with bulk purchases for business, educational, or instructional use. For information, please contact ASQ Quality Press at 800-248-1946, or write to ASQ Quality Press, P.O. Box 3005, Milwaukee, WI 53201-3005.

For a free copy of the ASQ Quality Press Publications Catalog, including ASQ membership information, call 800-248-1946.

Printed in the United States of America

Printed on acid-free paper

Quality Press
611 East Wisconsin Avenue
Milwaukee, Wisconsin 53202

To Mary, Emily, Paul, and Erik

The word **"Quality"** means much more than the goodness or badness of a product. It refers to the *qualities* or *characteristics* of the thing or process being studied" [underscore added].

—Western Electric Co., *Statistical Quality Control Handbook*

[Applied behavior analysis] is the process of applying sometimes tentative principles of behavior to the improvement of specific behaviors, and simultaneously evaluating whether or not any changes noted are indeed attributable to the process of application—and if so, to what parts of that process [underscore added.]

—Donald M. Baer, Montrose M. Wolf, and Rodd R. Risley,
"Some Current Dimensions of Applied Behavior Analysis."

Contents

Preface

Sales process engineering is a subject about which much will be said and written in the years to come. Once imaginative readers understand the term, I think most will agree that the very concept will profoundly clarify—and change—the way we view sales, marketing, and customer service processes in our organizations. We will see much of our current approach as wasteful, inconvenient, low in quality, and yes, even tremendously disrespectful of many of the individuals involved. We will also have a much better idea how to make things better from a fact-based point of view.

I believe that a new cadre of professionals—sales process engineers—will dramatically improve the way sales, marketing, and customer service is conducted. As an individual deeply committed to bringing about sales process engineering as a professional discipline, I am naturally interested in seeing that the introduction to the subject be approachable—even fun. This book aims to provide such an introduction.

In trying to make a new topic come alive, an author can choose from many alternative styles. I have chosen to write as a playwright, creating the parts based on my experience in delivering this live workshop many times. In this regard the book owes a debt of gratitude to a style of writing common to stagecraft, but more particularly to William J. Latzko and David M. Saunders' excellent book *Four Days with Dr. Deming* (1995). Their work uses three voices—a narrator's, a workshop participant's, and that of W. Edwards Deming himself—to present Dr. Deming's philosophy of management in a very appealing way. *Sales Process Engineering: A Personal Workshop* uses Latzko and Saunders' style of placing the reader in the midst of a live workshop setting, as well.

In this workshop, the bold text represents that of a narrator (and part-time alter ego) conjured up to set the scene and provide variety. Thoughts of workshop participants are presented in italics (the same person throughout—the playwright's "everyman"—except where cumbersome). My comments to the group are presented within quotation marks in plain text. The book is subtitled *A Personal Workshop* because I hope the style draws the reader into feeling personally present, actively engaged as the workshop progresses.

One suggestion: Read a section or two at a sitting. Skip from topic to topic as each catches your interest. There is a lot here. Let the concepts soak in at your leisure.

As the reader will soon see, sales process engineering is a deep topic worthy of the most careful and thorough study. As you read on, I think you will find many connections and insights coming to mind, together with many practical applications. Rejoice in the personal discoveries you make. Welcome to a fascinating journey. Some will find in it a passionate, lifelong pursuit.

Who Should Read This Book

Anyone with an active intelligence whose livelihood depends on the success of sales, marketing, and customer service will be interested in participating in this personal workshop. Do you care about sales in your organization? Better questions may be, "Who doesn't?" or "Who shouldn't?" The audience for this book is wide.

It has been said, "Nothing moves without a sale." Whether this is true in a literal sense makes little difference. Many of us depend on the income our organizations acquire from sales. This being so, almost any thoughtful person will benefit from the ideas and practical techniques described in this book. We'll be helping our own personal well-being and increasing our own job security to the extent that we can help our firms correctly apply the concepts for competitive improvement contained here. For this reason alone, *Sales Process Engineering: A Personal Workshop* is must reading. Pass it on to a friend!

Better still, both the format and the content of this workshop can help restore a sense of fun and real excitement to the workplace. So much of what we do on a day-to-day basis is routine or, worse, frustrating. The tools provided in this easy-to-read book can return a practical sense of control over one's own results, and hence, over one's own destiny. The workshop sees the sales process as a fascinating puzzle, as if one were a character in one's own detective story. You are the detective. You can solve the case. This personal workshop gives you the equivalent of Sherlock Holmes' magnifying glass, plenty of encouragement, and carte blanche permission to help crack the code and unlock the mysteries involved with sales—your own and your organization's.

Sales, marketing, and customer service representatives who want to gain more control over their own destinies will find that this personal workshop gives them tools and insights for engineering their own results in a manner never before presented. *Sales Process Engineering* offers a set of methods almost everybody can use to ultimately improve their livelihoods and increase their own sense of personal satisfaction at the same time.

Leaders of automation, reengineering, and other process improvement efforts will find the specific techniques recommended in this workshop a welcome breath of fresh air in a field that could use a little change of perspective from the familiar advice. Unlike many approaches, *Sales Process Engineering: A Personal Workshop* will help you aim your improvements at more specific targets, systematically adjusting your processes and support systems to achieve more certain, more measurable results.

For consultants, teachers, and researchers actively studying and informing others about a wide variety of management philosophies, the information presented in this course is no less than nitroglycerin, pure dynamite. The personal workshop assembles concepts floating in the common parlance, such as reengineering, kaizen, total quality management, just-in-time, statistical process control, behavioral psychology, and the Theory of Constraints, among others, into a combination of ingredients possessing explosive practical potential, full of direct ideas for application.

Managers of sales, marketing, and customer service activities will find this book offers a feast of methods for bringing about both operational breakthroughs and ongoing improvement. The systematic approaches described here will better equip managers for working more effectively with external customers and, indeed, with all departments within a corporation, as well. For the most part, this text presumes that contemporary management knows what controls the likelihood of obtaining sales, gaining market share, and providing excellent service. The techniques discussed in this book provide a way to operationalize these variables and more reliably control the process of their delivery. A more predictable flow of work, fewer hassles, fewer brush fires, and a more fulfilling, less frustrating job will reward those who correctly follow the precepts presented.

Financial analysts and top financial officers should carefully review the sections of this workshop that discuss process modeling. If this workshop is correct in its assumptions, one of today's most popular approaches to financial modeling contains an inherent flaw. If not guarded against, this flaw adds great risk to many projection techniques in current use.

Senior management frequently needs to play the role of coach, mentor, inspirational leader, cheerleader, and organizational mediator all rolled into one. Implementing change requires leaders to repeat two simple phrases over and over: "This is what we need to do, and this is why we need to do it." A personal workshop provides managers with dozens of concrete examples to help strengthen their message and focus their vision at the same time.

Executives thinking about or who are now undertaking radical change in their organization should read this book before taking the plunge. Executives are often in the best position to see the need for change at a macro level. Fostering ownership of an action plan is one of the best possible ways to ensure its enthusiastic support. Sharing this workshop with the rest of the team members will help them construct the specific strategies and tactics necessary to bring about the overall corporate direction. The workshop also points out a serious structural flaw preventing sustained progress in most organizations, which only senior executives can correct.

It's also possible this book is not for you at all. You may already know and agree with everything you find in here. In that case, you might consider using this workshop as an orientation for someone you've just hired, for students, or for anyone else you know who would value a quick introduction to ideas and principles that might otherwise take years to learn.

The Future of Sales Process Engineering: An Interview with Dr. Joseph M. Juran

Joseph M. Juran is the Chairman Emeritus of The Juran Institute, recipient of Japan's Order of the Sacred Treasure, and author of many highly respected works in the field of quality engineering. Many of the principles of engineering found in this book, and much of my own personal inspiration during its preparation, were drawn from Dr. Juran's prolific and highly productive life's work. In many ways, Dr. Juran is the last living giant in his generation of great pioneering process- and quality-related engineers.

I met Dr. Juran during his highly attended "Last Word" tour and told him I was working on a long-term effort to apply many of the principles of quality and process engineering to the sales process. Now, having completed most of the manuscript, I wanted to get his thoughts on the subject of sales process engineering and its future.

Calling The Juran Institute many weeks earlier, I was gently and courteously cautioned that, at this time in his life, Dr. Juran grants very few interviews. Nevertheless, my request would be relayed. On the morning of Tuesday, April 9, the phone rang. Much to my surprise and delight, on the line was Laura Sutherland, Dr. Juran's assistant. I could hear the smile in her voice as she informed me that Dr. Juran was able to grant a brief interview; Dr. Juran was available—if I could take the call with him immediately. There was no time to gather notes. With great excitement at the chance to speak with one of the founding fathers of the quality movement, I plunged ahead.

Dr. Juran received no set of scripted questions in advance; he had only a thumbnail sketch of the topic. In spite of the relative novelty of the discipline of sales process engineering, Dr. Juran's responses were quick and his wit shone through right from the start. The exchange reveals much about the wisdom of this great man.

After a minute or two of preliminary greetings and remarks, the interview proceeded. Time was short, so my line of questioning was direct and to the point.

Dr. Selden: I appreciate your willingness to talk with me today.

Dr. Juran: Well, when you're 91 years old like I am and working on your memoirs, you'll not grant many interviews, either. There is a certain urgency at work!

Dr. Selden: I can imagine! That's a sense one feels when working on a worthy effort, regardless of age. I'll get right to the heart of the matter.

What are the most notable examples of the successful application of the principles of quality engineering in the sales process, considering that, by "sales process" we encompass sales, marketing, and customer service functions?

Dr. Juran: I'd look to the various companies that have won the Malcolm Baldrige [National Quality] Award. Many are manufacturing companies, but there are service companies, too. They should provide good examples.

Dr. Selden: Can there *be* a discipline of sales process engineering, in principle?

Dr. Juran: The key issues facing managers in sales are no different than those faced by managers in other disciplines. Sales managers say they face problems such as "It takes us too long . . . we're trying to reduce the time interval . . . we need to reduce the error rate." They want to know, "How do customers perceive us?" These issues are no different than those facing managers trying to improve in other fields. The systematic approaches to improvement are identical.

When you are designing a warehouse using the Pareto Principle, for example, you try to put things frequently ordered in a place where they are most accessible. You put those things that are not often needed elsewhere.

There should be no reason our familiar principles of quality and process engineering would not work in the sales process.

This does not mean that the people engaged in sales and marketing will not put up an argument as to why it can't be done. Often, people will say what they do is different! They'll say that but, of course, whether their field is really different is another matter.

Dr. Selden: As to the size of the opportunity for improvement, do you agree with the commonly cited figures that prior to improvement, the cost of failing to produce with quality is some 20 percent of sales in manufacturing and closer to 40 percent in service-related fields?

Dr. Juran: Those figures are often cited, but I'm not sure that they have been adequately researched lately. Just from my own experience, I'd say that in manufacturing, about one-third of what we engage in is in redoing what we've done before. I think the opportunity is just as great in service-related activities. The numbers would be different in businesses that had already undertaken rigorous actions to improve, of course.

Dr. Selden: Do you feel the sales process is worthy of such improvement?

Dr. Juran: Obviously! There should be plenty of room for improvement in the sales process. There is in almost any process.

We have time for one more question. Make it a good one!

Dr. Selden: Okay. To wrap up then, do you see any reason that would prevent development of a formal discipline of sales process engineering?

Dr. Juran: Sales process engineering could be a branch off the main tree of quality engineering; it could be a separate field. Time will tell.

The history or literature of manufacturing for quality, earlier in this century, was that there was no literature! Since my *Quality Control Handbook* was published in 1950, there has been a tremendous proliferation of specific applications in many fields. That's not to say that the first edition of that handbook was so terribly great, you understand. But there has been a huge jump in the number of fields that the principles have been applied to.

I can't see the stumbling blocks in this case—so early on, you never know. It is hard to say at this stage; that's for the future to decide.

I thanked Dr. Juran for his time and we said goodbye. In my mind's eye I pictured him going back to a cozy room full of books, notes, and photographs, working on his memoirs. Ninety-one years! What a rich and rewarding life.

When the interview was over, another visual image entered my thoughts. The image was clear and real, however others might judge it, so I do not hesitate to relay it now. In my mind's eye I could see a spark leaping from a burning fire—passing from one place to another. That's it. Just a little bit of flame leaping from a larger blaze as we, another generation, move ahead.

About the Author

In the late 1980s and early 1990s, Paul Selden, like many people, felt the United States slipping into a recession. Salespeople and marketing departments everywhere were facing tremendous burdens just trying to hold the line. At the same time, advancing technology made it possible for many companies to give their sales, marketing, and service personnel more and more computerized tools, often in the name of "sales force automation."

Paul became upset by what he saw. What was supposed to help increase individual productivity often turned into an increased burden. At the very time the recession was making it so difficult to sell anything, companies were demanding that their salespeople increase their quotas (do sales quotas ever go down?) while learning to use complicated new computer systems.

In the beginning, more often than not, the new computer systems provided little or no immediate tangible benefit for the people using them. Not only was the software prone to break down, the systems themselves seemed ill-conceived, with little or no direct link to reducing costs or increasing sales. As he traveled around the country on business, he reached a personal epiphany in the course of a single week.

Early that week Paul met with a well-known West Coast firm which had dedicated nearly two years of labor to find the right sales automation supplier. That effort ended with a massive request for proposal (RFP) issued to a dozen firms. With his background, Paul knew that only three suppliers could even begin to meet the criteria. He empathized with the other nine firms receiving this massive RFP. They would probably work tremendously hard to make themselves look as good as possible, yet waste all that time in the end.

On the East Coast later that same week, Paul met with a second Fortune 500 company about to implement sales force automation. A salesperson himself since he started his own large-scale computer training and documentation firm in 1978, Paul had seen huge increases in productivity and quality when computers were properly implemented. He had also seen tremendous failures, as well. His experience in sales, his professional experience with thousands of new computer users, and his formal education in behavioral psychology warned him that this second company's project had all the makings of a colossal failure. The new system was designed by one department. The majority of users would be from a different department—and none of the actual users had been asked for their input as the new system was being built. In essence, the new system was simply turning the sales force into a giant data-gathering mechanism for the marketing department. No benefit was being returned to the sales representatives themselves. It was a recipe for disaster—and all this in the midst of a recession.

These two experiences galvanized a broader sense of citizenship. Paul was at a time in his life when he could afford to return something back to the country. Paul had started his career as an entrepreneur and sales representative, "with a Chamber of Commerce directory in one hand, and a telephone in the other," as he often tells his audiences. Through selling, Paul had built his business into a corporation serving the country's largest firms. Concurrently, his work with the Ford Motor Company on its new just-in-time and process engineering approaches gave him the insight that automation, per se, contributed little by itself and could even be a handicap if not applied to an improved process.

In 1990, Paul provided funds to found a nonprofit professional association dedicated to helping everyone connected with sales process improvement efforts: staff, project leaders, and suppliers alike. The Sales Automation Association (recently named the Customer Relationship Management Association) is a place where all interested parties can openly share ideas about how to improve the sales, marketing, and customer service process. Throughout this period, Paul, a certified quality engineer and Ph.D. behavioral psychologist, has maintained membership and close ties with ASQC, an organization whose body of knowledge he drew on in preparation for his course on sales process engineering. He now divides his time between his personal businesses, consultation, and a schedule of active research, speaking, and volunteer work.

Note: Since the initial printing of this book, the Sales Automation Association has been renamed the Customer Relationship Management Association. Any reference to the SAA should be regarded as such.

Acknowledgments

It would not have been possible to prepare this book without assistance, encouragement, and inspiration drawn from a great many people. Throughout, I have tried to mention by name the many wonderful individuals who lent a generous hand. Extra thanks go to William Latzko, Hy Pitt, Tom Pyzdek, Dianne Ritter, and Shin Taguchi, who were especially helpful with their advice and insights. Special thanks to A. Blanton Godfrey and Laura Sutherland of The Juran Institute, and to Peggy Jennings of the American Supplier Institute, as well.

Where do you find people who believe in the worthiness of such a pioneering book? The answer provides interesting commentary. Other prospective publishers and agents for this book suggested that I "dumb it down" (their words). By happy contrast, ASQC thought "it's time for this book." Without the faith and encouragement of Jeannie Bohn, Roger Holloway, and Susan Westergard at ASQC Quality Press, there would be no book at all.

Thanks also to George Smith, fellow member and kindred spirit at the Sales Automation Association, for providing the kind of ongoing stimulation that comes from letting a colleague know that one is not alone. Long conversations and interesting discussions with David Bell, Chris Blatchly, Sheri Brown, George Columbo, Ken Compter, Kevin Duffy, Ken Edwards, Bill Fletcher, Ron Gilmore, Barton Goldenberg, Anne Greenan, Dave Hanaman, Dean Herington, Brian Jeffrey, Michael Marks, Tom McMullen, Karen Meyman, Tom Minero, Michael Penniman, Bev Powell, Debbie Qaqish, Larry Rider, Terrie Robb, Ron Schott, Paul Sheehan, Pam Spanjer, and John Wheeler helped round out the thoughts you see presented here, as well. Many individuals were kind enough to review and comment on early drafts of the book in manuscript form, including George Alland, Rick Kehr, Sean Mohan, Rick Newhauser, John Reimer, Alan Rowley, and Frank Smith. For many different reasons the following individuals, among many others, are owed a debt of gratitude: Vic Baglio, John Bell, Bob Bensen, Charlie Butler, Bill Byham, Mellissa Campagnelli, Brian Carroll, Tom Christenson, Earl Concors, Stevie Cote, Steve Daher, Jerry Decker, Julia Dorn, Dave Erdman, Chris Evanoff, Nancy Foncannon, Bill Gergel, Gerhard Gschwandtner, Si Gilman, John Gisler, Kerry Givens, Dale Gott, Terry Hansen, Bill Hoskens, Dick Houchard, Stanley Huber, Brad Huitema, Danny Hupp, Parris Jones, Jim Knapp, Ed Kutay, Ken Lally, Clark Lefurgy, Frank Liedel, Gordon Lodahl, Pete Luce, David Lyon, John MacKenzie, Richard Mallott, John Manoogian, Barbara Marko, Jim Martay, Larry Martin, Jack Michael, Paul Mountjoy, Ken Munch, Rob Murdoch, Ed Noe, John O'Brien, Mike Penn, Ed Ploor, Walther Prausnitz, Gary Price, Jean Puphal, Brent Richards, Victor Rocus, Charles Rose, John Ross, Don Schoenle, Matt Schomer, Jim Schott, Rebecca Steele, Mike Sullivan, Terry Taillard, Terri Takai, Thayer Taylor, Larry Theobald, Len Thornburg, Roger Ulrich, Tom Waldron, Vern Warren, Doug Watson, and Joan Wood. Credit is due to Brian Barnes for the line art portraits used throughout Days One and Two, and to Karen Wendt for her expert renderings of H. James Harrington and Eugene H. Melan. Credit is also due to Annette Wall, my production manager, for her patience, clarity, and sharp sense of design.

We stand on the edge of so many mysteries. Growing up, my mother received a gift that we kept in our living room. It was a small vase made by the Hopi. A painted ring and other designs encircled the vase. The ring stopped just short of a full circle. One day I noticed the gap and pointed it out to my mother. I said the gap looked like a mistake. She told me that no, it was not a mistake; the ring had intentionally not been completed. I asked why. On various occasions I heard two explanations. The first was that the gap provided a place to let spirits escape freely. The second explanation was that the artist did not want to make something so complete that the gods would mistake it for an attempt to create something perfect. This book reminds me of my mother's Hopi vase in many ways. Some gaps are intentional: In a survey course, one must simply stop somewhere. The reader needs to explore further to give meaning to the words. Some gaps are unintentional: I'm sure the reader will pick them out. And although the writing within these pages has an end, we stand on the edge of many mysteries. Our explorations, like the track of a ring being drawn on an ever-expanding globe, will never be complete.

Day One

A Collegial Introduction

It is 8 A.M., early for many seminars, yet some participants have been seated since 7:30 A.M. The elegant meeting room in this classic hotel is filled with a variety of men and women. Some are in casual attire; others are wearing formal business suits. There is a sense of growing anticipation. Dr. Selden warmly greets the audience.

"Welcome! In the next few days we'll be exploring the philosophies and tool sets surrounding the discipline of process engineering as it can be applied in sales, marketing, and customer service. These philosophies and tools have proven to be successful in other parts of business. I think we can learn from them.

"How many of you are in sales, marketing, or customer service? [A majority of participants raise their hands.] How many are in information management? [Many] I would guess quite a few of you are working on sales automation–related projects.

"It may surprise you that, trends notwithstanding and in spite of my role as the founder of the Sales Automation Association, I will hardly be talking to you about automation at all. Too many companies are applying automation without understanding its real purpose. Too many do not understand their own sales process. These companies will experience failure without learning why. If they succeed, they will not know how to repeat their success. Process comes first. Automation comes later. The emphasis for the next three days will be on understanding the process.

"Some of the ideas we talk about may be quite different and untraditional. I want us to feel we're in the right environment so that these ideas can be exchanged openly. A collegial atmosphere where open thought and free inquiry are permitted is best."

A recently reported survey by Coopers and Lybrand shows that the number of executives planning to increase their budgets for computer hardware and software has "more than doubled in the past five years" (Computers capture capital spending 1996).

Dr. Selden asks participants to introduce themselves to their immediate neighbors. He asks that they shake hands and share their name, position, and company background. He asks the group members what kind of personal expertise they may have in engineering, total quality management, or ISO 9000. He asks the participants to share their insights with each other as the seminar progresses.

100 Basket Weavers

"Today, the world of sales, marketing, and customer service reminds me of a roomful of 100 basket weavers. At the beginning of the day, they are exhorted by management to 'do your best.' At the end of the day, the baskets are packed up for delivery to the local market.

"Every day, the 20 most skillful basket weavers seem to have made the best baskets. Their baskets are the ones that sell. The good baskets fetch such a high price compared to the rest that overall, the entire group of basket weavers can afford to eat, buy shelter, and clothe themselves. Everyone is happy with the way things are.

"We're basket weavers!" Dr. Selden's voice rises. His hands gesture for emphasis. "Sitting on the floor, materials by our side. Each doing our own thing.

"In his book *Advanced Selling Strategies* (1995), Brian Tracy, the noted sales trainer, observed that 80 percent of all sales are made by 20 percent of the salespeople. Imagine those results plotted on a chart. I'll bet if we plotted the sales outcome of each rep from a modern company on a bar graph and held it up side-by-side with the sales generated by 100 basket weavers sitting in a room weaving baskets, the shape of the graphs would be practically identical."

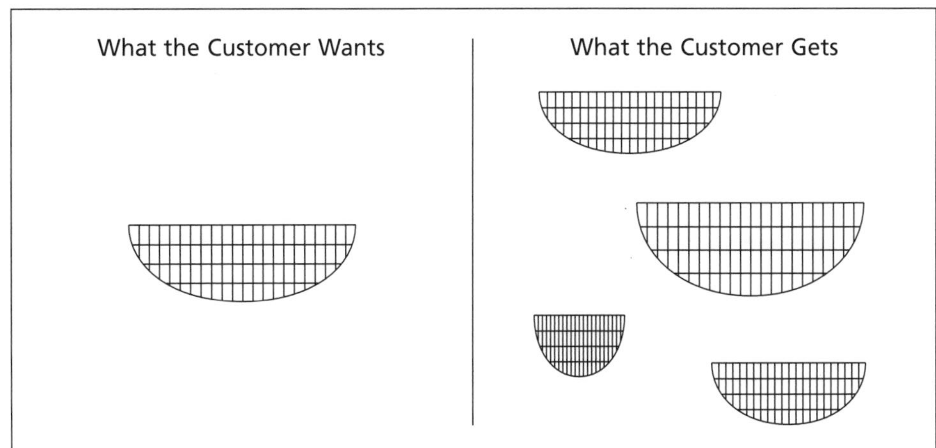

What Tracy says is true in my company. The majority of dollars are brought in by a minority of the reps. This is the twentieth century. We can put people on the moon, wipe out deadly diseases, and make systems that warn us of dangerous weather. Yet sales has advanced very little. Dr. Selden is comparing what we do with a primitive craft!

"Now, don't get me wrong. I admire artistry and respect individual craftsmanship a great deal. We need individual initiative, talent, pride, and motivation. We need the quest for personal excellence. We need to keep the best we know about sales as an art. But we need to advance our current understanding if we want to go beyond our current results. We're ready to advance further. Beyond a field where a handful of great basket weavers does most of the good work."

The Global Economy Is Driving Improvement

In 1975, the net trade balance between the United States and the rest of the world was $9 billion. As a producer, we sold that much more than we took in in foreign imports. In 1982, the United States became a net debtor nation and has not recovered since. In 1993, the United States bought $115 billion more from other countries than it sold to them. Winning a competition means being able to keep what you've got or win more, not lose it.

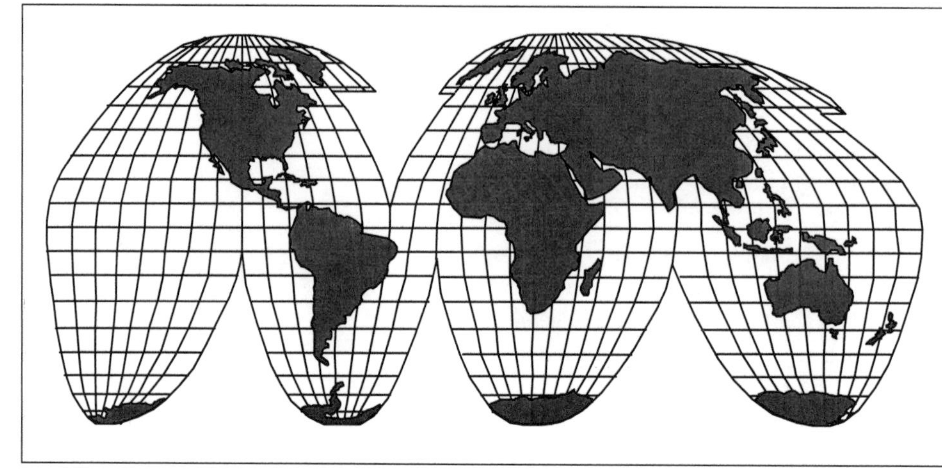

"Today companies are trying new approaches as never before—breaking the mold. Are they doing this because suddenly the ranks of corporate executives are filled with wild-eyed people who love risk, throwing caution to the winds, daring to be different? Executives are introducing change because they have no choice. If we don't improve, others will leave us watching their posteriors as they pass us by. That's not a pleasant view. Millions of shareholders don't like that view—it means their retirement funds are in jeopardy. Maybe that's why the tenure of the top executive seems shorter these days."

Dr. Selden is right. Things have changed so much in the last decade or two. Today it's not just the old familiar firm down the block we're competing with. It's firms on the other side of the globe whose people are fighting for a better way of life. They are working for a chance at better medicines for their people and decent housing. We're working for a color TV for the kid's bedroom. Who's going to work harder? The stakes are high.

"Executives have always had to get work done—through what?—through the well-managed efforts of other people. By definition. Who can afford a roomful of basket weavers where 80 percent of the work is done by 20 percent of the workforce?

"Top companies have already improved their physical production methods. Now they are turning their attention to sales, marketing, and customer service, an area that can consume as much as 16 percent (in electronics) to 45 percent (in pharmaceuticals) of the total corporate budget, according to *CFO* magazine (Lazere 1995). As executives and managers, as business owners, and as thinking, responsible employees, we must find a better sales process."

"Money Doesn't Grow on Trees"

"Is a basket weaving approach to sales acceptable? [Many shake their heads, no.] A basket weaving approach, where 20 percent of your weavers are producing 80 percent of your revenue, can work fine! Just two little requirements. One, you need to be the only basket weavers in town; and two, the town has to be short of baskets. Then, if people want baskets at all, they are forced to accept the services rendered by basket weavers who don't do their jobs very well. Sometimes customers get lucky and get good service; sometimes they don't. But they accept both good and bad because they have no choice. If you control a monopoly in a demand market, the customer has little choice but to accept the status quo, too.

"Look at the world around you. The Berlin Wall is down. The Soviet Union is no more. Communist China is producing huge quantities of goods for consumption by capitalists. How many more economies will we be competing against? Is this still a demand market? How many other basket weavers are competing against us? In an environment like this, it pays to equip your basket weavers with weaving looms! [The group laughs.] To stay even, we have to improve. To get ahead, the improvement must be even greater!"

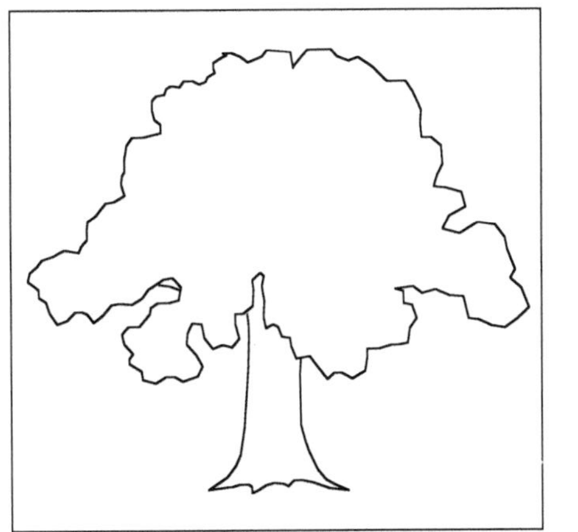

I wonder if our young people really appreciate how hard we adults have to work these days. Following World War II the United States had the majority of functioning factories in the developed world. Everyone else's were bombed out. We had a monopoly for close to a generation. I think that made us lax, complacent, and probably even arrogant. Then in the 1980s I remember the news stories warning that our quality was poor compared to foreign goods. Commentators talked about how our children might be the first generation in years that might have to get used to a lower standard of living. I could see the connection between a lack of quality, the potential for big layoffs, and eventual lower wages coming a mile away. Lots of people still griped about their paychecks, as if they were entitled to annual raises or bonuses without having to increase their own productivity in proportion. There's still too much of that something-for-nothing mentality. Now the chickens are coming home to roost.

The chickens may roost for a long time, too, if our kids don't learn what they need to compete in a world market. I just read that a study conducted at the University of Connecticut found that 47 percent of the nation's college seniors "could not calculate the perimeter of a room 65 feet wide and 35 feet long" (Associated Press 1996). I'm seeing too many statistics like that nowadays.

My parents grew up during the Great Depression. When I was young and would ask for a dime for a comic book or a quarter to go to the movies, my mother told me, "Money doesn't grow on trees." She'd give me a job to do around the house so I could earn my movie money. Money doesn't grow on trees. That old saying has a lot of truth in it. I wonder if enough families are helping their children understand. I wonder if we will help our children learn what they need, so our kids can enjoy a decent standard of living.

To Produce More with Fewer People

Dr. Selden states that a percentage of the world population, the United States was 5.1 percent in 1980. In 1994, the world's population had grown to 5.6 billion. The U.S. proportion of the world's population had dropped to 4.6 percent.

"Some people worry when they hear discussions about productivity. 'More work with less people? That's just a code word for layoffs!' they think. Some even sandbag efforts to improve. That's tiny thinking. The truth of it at a megatrend level is that the United States has less people than the rest of the world, and relative to the rest of the world, we have fewer and fewer people every day!

"So let's think about our 100 domestic basket weavers one last time. First, most of the sales volume is being produced by only 20 percent of our basket weavers. Second, foreign basket weavers are coming on-line. As each day passes, our band of 100 basket weavers is shrinking in proportion to the total number of competing basket weavers.

"The net result of this global equation is that we have two choices. First, we can work harder by working longer hours. Second, we can develop new ways to work so that all of our 100 people can produce baskets at the level of the top 20 percent. Who favors the first alternative? Anyone?"

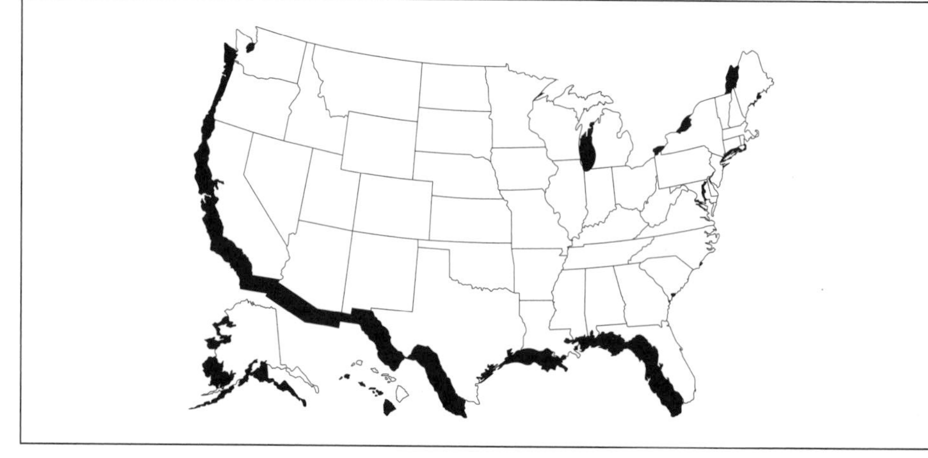

The image of the basket weavers is hitting me like a ton of bricks. Now I see where Dr. Selden is going with this. In the end, it's not a matter of increasing productivity so we can lay people off. We have to get the best from what we have—from all our people. In sales we have to find ways to reduce the gap between our low and high performers. The change in world population means we need both quality and quantity!

Compared to the United States, Japan puts in 40 percent more labor hours per capita. Both Germany and Japan invest more financial and physical capital than the United States, on a per capita basis (Lewis 1996). Relative to the rest of the world, a highly productive use of time and capital must be maintained by the United States in order to sustain its unparalleled standard of living.

Workshop Goals and Objectives

"Improving is a matter of survival. It's my contention that we've tried the basket weaving approach, and we need to do better. This workshop presents a different way."

Dr. Selden reviews the workshop goals and each day's objectives one by one. Both concepts and specific tools will be covered as an introduction to the discipline of sales process engineering as a whole.

"Techniques and know-how are important. It is just as important for me to leave you with a broader understanding. That understanding is that the sales process is a tangible something that can be described, drawn, measured, and examined, in an engineering-like fashion, and not just talked about in ill-defined metaphors and improved through 'secret' selling systems. That broad understanding has to work itself into the very fabric of your being so that you can look at sales in a more systematic way."

It seems that all the literature I've seen on the subject treats sales as an individual art of relationship building. I have stacks of books that talk about sales in terms of personal warfare, the art of love, or as a series of psychological tricks and magic phrases guaranteed to close a sale. Dr. Selden seems to be saying that there's more to it than that, something more tangible. Yet in my company, every time we've tried to approach the subject in those concrete terms, someone always interjects, "Sales is different. There are too many variables involved to treat sales as a science." The discussion always ends there. We go back to doing things as we've always done—basket weaving.

Main Goal

Grasp purpose of sales process engineering and begin to apply basic concepts and tools

Days One and Two

- Describe established schools of process engineering
- Apply concepts and tools to sales, marketing, and customer service

Day Three

- Understand fundamental nature of dynamic, interactive sales processes
- Learn objective ways to detect change and improvement
- Advise on strategic corporate direction supporting structural improvement

The Group's Top Concerns

"Obviously, an instructor has to have his or her own agenda and his or her own game plan before walking in the door. There wouldn't be a program, otherwise. Can you imagine an advertisement for a course whose description read, 'We'll cover whatever you want. Just pay your money and walk in the door.' [The group laughs at this image.]

"There are too many of you to ask for your individual expectations one by one. I want you to get used to working in teams—that will be a necessary skill when you get back to your jobs. And I want you to get to know each other."

Dr. Selden asks people to meet in small groups. They each are to introduce themselves, then choose a leader who will ask the others what their expectations are for the workshop. Recording their issues, the leader is to poll the group for their top shared expectation for the course. After time for discussion, Dr. Selden continues.

"You've heard my goals for the course. What did you come here hoping to receive? Let's hear your primary expectations."

Dr. Selden records each issue on a flip chart as the groups report.

- **How to convince representatives to try new approaches**
- **When to use specific techniques**
- **How to get ideas off the ground**
- **Proper uses for automation**
- **How to estimate costs and benefits**
- **How to get commitment from top management**
- **How to implement new approaches**

"I can't promise we'll have enough time to cover all of these in the detail you'd like, although I know that in the course of our regular agenda we'll cover many. As you see the opportunity to address an issue important to you, please ask."

Other Expectations?

- Ask as other issues arise during workshop
- We'll try to cover

Our Journey—Day One

"Now we enter the main body of work for the next two days. There's a lot of content to cover, so we'll be moving quickly. In our time together I can only acquaint you with the approaches and techniques involved and demonstrate their importance. I intend to point you to specific resources, so you can pursue any given topic in more depth later. We can't become engineers in one session, eh?"

I was hoping to learn as much as I can about this subject as quickly as possible. I only wish I could learn it all at once. Yet I guess I should realize that any topic that has true depth can't be mastered in one sitting. In that respect, I'm happy there seems to be something with true substance here. Depending on what we cover later, I guess I'll learn whether this is a subject matter worthy of long-term study.

Dr. Selden is pointing at the chart in front of the participants. It's a grid with people's names down the left. The center column is entitled "Philosophy." The right-hand column is entitled "Tools."

"This chart illustrates our journey for our first day. In the organization of topics, each of the names on the left is associated with the school of thought listed in the middle. On the far right, the column labeled 'Tools' lists 12 key process analysis and problem-solving tools in the order we'll be covering them. The tools themselves aren't

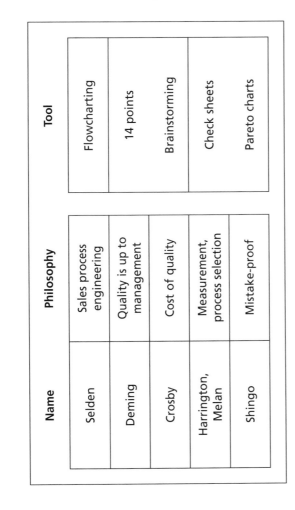

Name	Philosophy
Selden	Sales process engineering
Deming	Quality is up to management
Crosby	Cost of quality
Harrington, Melan	Measurement, process selection
Shingo	Mistake-proof

Tool
Flowcharting
14 points Brainstorming
Check sheets Pareto charts

associated with one process philosopher or another. Most of the people we'll discuss advocate using some or all of the tools listed."

Our Journey—Day Two

"Each of the individuals we'll cover has a somewhat unique personal philosophy of engineering, their own emphasis. One or two even seem to advocate their approaches to the exclusion of others. Some of the philosophers disagree with each other, sometimes in ways I personally find unprofessional. Some mock each other's ideas or make disparaging remarks about each other's ideas. I believe they all have something to say. Their contrasting points of view may stimulate us to think more creatively. The list represents a mini-curriculum on the subject of process engineering, in general."

Name	Philosophy	Tool
Hammer and Champy et al.	Reengineering	Run charts
Ohno	Just-in-time, industrial engineering	Histograms
Pavlov, Skinner	Behavioral engineering	Cause/effect diagrams Scatter plots
Juran	Quality planning, improvement, and control	SPC, systematic experimentation
Imai	Continuous improvement	Implementation sequence planning

Dr. Selden comments that he believes the Theory of Constraints, a philosophy associated with Dr. Eliyahu M. Goldratt, and the concepts and design of experiments techniques associated with Dr. Genichi Taguchi are also of great importance. Points related to these topics will be interwoven throughout the next three days.

"On our road map, you'll notice that my name is associated with sales process engineering. My philosophy is that the principles of process engineering can be used to further improve the sales, marketing, and customer service processes. This is my stake in the ground. I am willing to stand up and be counted along with others who are moving in this direction, to argue the point and defend my opinions publicly. I'm not trying to seem immodest by claiming to have invented anything new. My work is one of translation, application, teaching, and trying to build a professional discipline. My personal achievements do not match those of the venerable individuals whose names you see before you. But a field has to start somewhere; now it has a name under which many can work together. Together we'll grow the discipline, over time. History will judge our contributions."

"Tell us how you really feel," someone quips. The atmosphere Dr. Selden creates is both collegial and congenial.

"The pattern for this portion of the course will proceed something like this. For variety's sake we'll cover one or two of the leading process engineering thinkers, together with the approach most people attach to these philosophers' names. Then we'll cover one or two of the tools. Throughout, I'll ask you to think about what all this means in your own sales, marketing, or customer service situation. I'll offer examples of my own, too."

Signposts along the way will mark progress on the journey during the next two days of the program.

Different Perspectives, Same Animal

"Notice that I did not use the word *reengineering* in my description. The popular term *reengineering* is just one of the many philosophies we'll cover.

"This is also not a course on sales quality management, although I'll certainly be using the word *quality* many times.

"I've already said this is not a course on how to apply automation to the sales process, either.

"By the time we're done today, you'll see how all those elements fit into a very deep discipline that encompasses those specific pieces, and more.

"Have you ever thought that some of the management gurus around today are just like the proverbial blind men feeling an elephant? One touches the tail and declares it to be a snake. Another touches the legs and pronounces it to be a tree, and so on. The ones who pronounce their opinion as the only legitimate or worthwhile view, or who belittle others who are trying to advance the field as a whole—aren't they like the blind men in the proverb? I hope we'll see a bigger picture emerge.

"In the next few days your own understanding will expand to comprehend that we are, indeed, working with something big, something very powerful that has many parts."

Sales process engineering is not a fad. It is not a management panacea. To understand it requires an appreciation of many topics.

"That said, let's move on."

Part 1: Sales Process Engineering—A Conceptual Framework

> You've got to be careful if you don't know where you're going, because you might not get there.
>
> —*Yogi Berra*

Objectives

By the time we finish this topic you will be able to

- Define sales process engineering.
- Understand the goals and importance of sales process engineering.
- Outline major economic variables on which sales process engineering can have an impact.
- List typical problems encountered in the sales process.
- Better explain the key questions sales process engineering can answer.

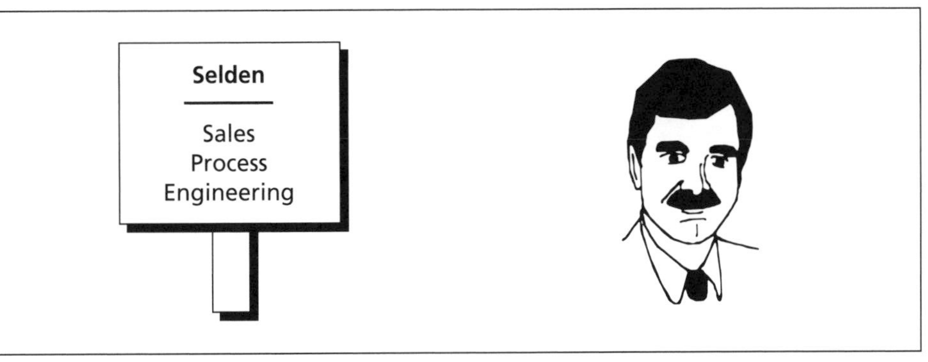

What Is a Process?

- Process: Any activity, or bounded group of interrelated work activities, that adds value to one or more inputs, and produces an output to an internal or external customer.

(Harrington 1991; Melan 1993)

[Note: Throughout this workshop, the word *sales* is used as a quick way to refer to an interrelated system of marketing, sales, and customer service processes whose collective output is sales.]

"To discuss a new discipline such as sales process engineering, we need to define what we are talking about. To do so helps expose any underlying assumptions that might either weaken or strengthen our case.

"Central to the definition of sales process engineering is the very word *process*. A process is any activity, or bounded group of interrelated activities, that adds value to one or more inputs and produces an output delivered to an internal or external customer. Note that a customer can either be internal or external. We produce many things for internal customers, as well as for external customers.

"With this definition in hand, we can now properly identify a process when we see one. Can anyone give me examples of processes in sales, marketing, and customer service?"

One fellow says, "Literature fulfillment." Another says, "Order processing." A few say, "Appointment setting." These people raised their hands fairly quickly. They've obviously thought about this before. I'm not sure our sales organization really has much of a process to speak of—at least not like an assembly line would. Our salespeople are basically left to do their own thing. We don't tell them how to do their jobs except for some orientation when they first start out.

"Let's see if the definition of *process* proves helpful—practical. We'd have a name for a process that didn't add value, wouldn't we? We'd be more likely to call it *unnecessary*, wouldn't we? What about a process that didn't produce what the internal customer needed? Wouldn't we now be able to identify that as *wasteful? Error-prone?* Immediately, our definition forces us to ask critical, pragmatic questions about what we are currently doing.

"Individual processes combine to form larger *systems*. For our purposes, we will be using the two terms—*system* and *process*—interchangeably. We are obviously concerned about how well our sales system is functioning, as a whole. I will often be using the term *process* in this larger sense."

The Fifth Discipline (1990) by Peter Senge at the Sloan Management School at MIT illustrates why it is important to be able to think in terms of processes and systems. According to Senge, _systems thinking_ is the fifth discipline that learning organizations will need to master to sustain their competitiveness in today's business environment. Public interest in Senge's work shows the extent to which the notion of process has entered the vernacular.

Is Sales a Process?

- Many people think *not!*
- Raises a big question:

Can sales ever be a process, in principle?

In any field, there are a number of fundamental assumptions one must acknowledge from the beginning. If one or more of these assumptions prove to be false, it calls into question the rest of the argument. For example, for hundreds of years prior to 1880, the world thought that one of the most fearful of all diseases, malaria, was caused by the foul air found near swamps. The very word *malaria* comes from the Italian words *mala* (bad), and *aria* (air). In 1890 the French physician Charles Louis Alphonse Laveran startled the world by discovering that malaria was caused by a tiny one-celled animal called a protozoan. Seventeen years later the British physician Ronald Ross found that this protozoan was transmitted by the anopheles mosquito, not by "bad air." These breakthroughs shifted the fight against malaria to that of using adequate screening and netting and to eradicating the mosquito and where it breeds (Asimov 1989). Once the original assumption for the cause of malaria was found false, real progress accelerated.

"Is sales a process? Many people think not. We'd better stop, right now, to ask the question of ourselves. If sales isn't a process we can all go home early."

I personally think one of the reasons so little progress has been made in the study of sales, marketing, and customer service as a process is that many people don't believe that sales is a real process in the first place. I've personally heard many people, even senior executives, say, "We really don't have a sales process." Is it possible that is our false assumption?

"Maybe the people who say that their company doesn't have a sales process are right. Maybe there's no such thing. Perhaps one of the reasons experts at process analysis have so little to say on the subject is that nothing *should* be said on the subject. It could be the wrong topic to apply the very concept of process to.

"So right away, we better raise the question. Is sales a process? If not, we better not waste our time studying it seriously, with ongoing commitment, with hard dollars, and with well-trained people. We'll just be wasting our resources."

Sales literature is filled with descriptions of sales as something practiced by magicians skilled at tricks, marketing as an art that can be passed on only by masters sharing their secrets. And customer service is often thought of in terms of the mysterious, knowing, Freudian-filled advice, such as "Love them to death."

In contrast with much of the traditional literature, this book treats sales as the measurable output of a process which can be studied and improved systematically—not as an assemblage of mysterious pieces and parts, not as a set of disjointed ingredients. For convenience, this process is referred to throughout this book as the "sales process." Understood in this way, the word sales refers to the output of a cross-functional system and should not be confused with a specific job title or single functional area. Such a view has the tremendous advantage of being able to study and improve the traditional "pieces and parts" as a unified whole.

Is Sales Exempt from the Law of Cause and Effect?

"If sales is not part of the universe of processes conforming to natural laws of cause and effect, what is the alternative? That selling is a supernatural activity, perhaps paranormal? Now, come on. That is blatantly absurd, regardless of how weird we think the marketing department is.

"Think for a moment. What would it really mean for sales to be exempt from the natural laws of *cause and effect?*"

This time I quickly speak up. I say that if sales were really exempt from the laws of cause and effect it would make attempts to manage the sales effort futile. Someone else joked in response that that would be good—if this were true, companies could save themselves a lot of money by letting all the do-nothing district managers go. That brings snorts of laughter from the group.

I wasn't totally sure where Dr. Selden was headed with all this discussion about the nature of what a process really is. Now I understand. If we admit that sales can be looked at as a process, we better be prepared to treat it with the same degree of seriousness and study it the way we do other important processes. We certainly do not treat sales in the same way as we treat the manufacturing process at our firm. I don't know any company that does. We're serious about sales, but I think we lack the study *part.*

A friend once told me about a top sales and marketing manager. The senior executive refused all attempts to define and train the salespeople in a specific method of selling.

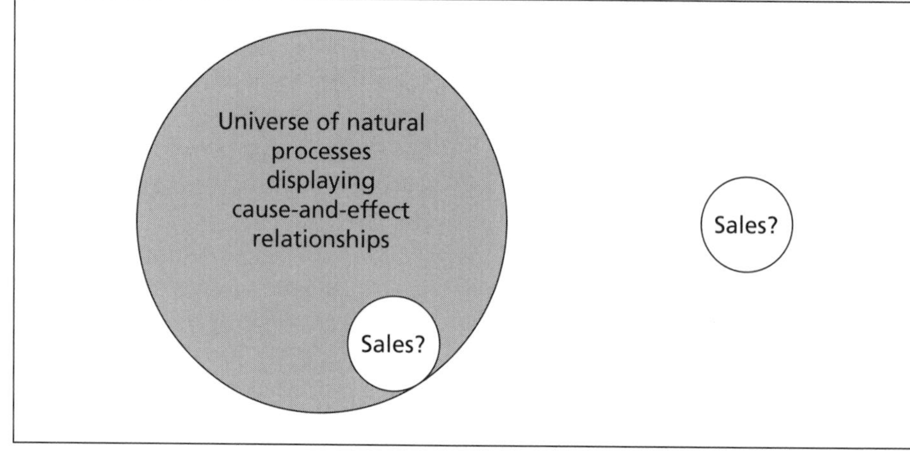

This refusal had to do with the executive's philosophy about individual responsibility. 'If we told them how to do it, the salespeople would blame the company and its methods if they failed to make quota. It's the reps' job to take responsibility for their own success, not ours,' the executive felt. With attitudes like this so prevalent, it's no wonder we haven't made more progress.

I say to the class that another part of the problem is that people disagree about what the causes are in sales and what effects they produce. In sales, every situation seems different. And things change so fast!

"We've already defined the word *process* as something that changes an input and transforms it into an output. Processes, in other words, obey the natural laws of cause and effect. The systematic study of causes and effects seems to describe the very essence of what it means to study processes. Whether we can control all of the causes at work in the sales process is a separate issue. How often situations repeat themselves is another issue. Systematic study will help us answer these important issues and not sweep them under the rug."

I bet that in most firms, people give up without even attempting to find the answers. They're too busy handling what's right in front of them.

Ballistic Systems

"For some time, people who have studied processes have found they fall into three general categories.

"The first type of process is a ballistic system, characterized by the absence of a feedback loop. The quality of the output depends entirely on the sort of inputs received and on the process itself. It's as if you shot an arrow in the air, but had no way of telling whether it hit the target or not. That's dangerous."

Dr. Selden says that's dangerous, yet we do it all the time. We continue to go to the same trade shows, year after year, and we don't know whether they are getting us what we need, or whether we should drop one and try another. We design new brochures in the name of giving things "a new look." We do get the new look—the physical appearance of the brochure changes. Do we get anything more than that? Much of the time I don't think we really know. I think we've got lots of ballistic systems in our company.

"Some people say their company has no sales process: their reps are lone rangers, doing their own thing. So long as the company makes a buck, it's up to each rep what to do and how to do it. I believe such people are looking only at their own single step in the total process; they are ignoring the fact that they get inputs from, and must deliver outputs to, other parts of the larger process.

"Please look at the next diagram carefully. I contend that most companies that claim they have no sales process probably actually operate as a series of semi-disconnected, ballistic process islands. Do you see how this might account for the tremendous variability and lack of coordination seen in the typical sales process?

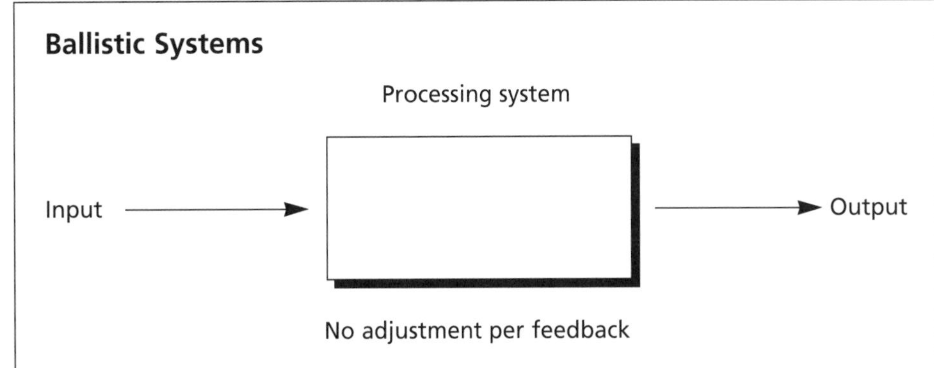

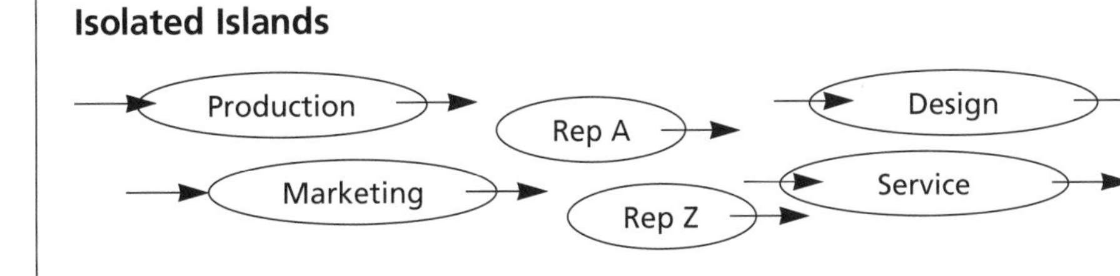

"In this type of process, the output achieved totally depends on the quality of the inputs and the quality of each processor, namely, the rep! Such a process can be economically viable, but that's hardly the point. Such systems produce tremendous waste, probably harming the environment and placing incredible stress on the people involved, including the customer!

"Companies like this remind me of a *Mad Magazine* I once read as a kid. In one of its movie parodies, the leader of a commando unit briefs his troops, saying, 'The plan is, we'll have no plan. That way we won't get stuck with a plan that doesn't work!'"

Engineers such as Monden (1983) describe problems associated with the isolated island work flow, together with other processing patterns to avoid.

Guided Systems

"A guided system adjusts itself based on feedback received."

In a feedback loop, the sensor reads the current state of the output. The comparator compares the current output with a target value and sends this information to an actuator, which triggers the appropriate adjustment to the process or the inputs involved.

"A feedback loop needs five parts: a sensor, a target setting, a comparator, an actuator, and signal transmission devices that connect the elements (Juran 1988). If one of those elements is missing, it cannot function properly."

Dr. Selden asks the group members to think of processes in their sales, marketing, and service processes where guided systems have been set up.

We have plenty of them. Our target settings are our sales goals. Our sensors and transmission devices are the computers that pick up our monthly booked sales. They print out reports the sales managers receive. The managers are both the comparators and the actuators. They compare the booked sales with the monthly quotas and let the reps know how they are doing. They coach and encourage the reps to do something different. That pattern is repeated up the line. But come to think of it, there's little, if any, immediate feedback loop to even permit detecting whether an adjustment is really made.

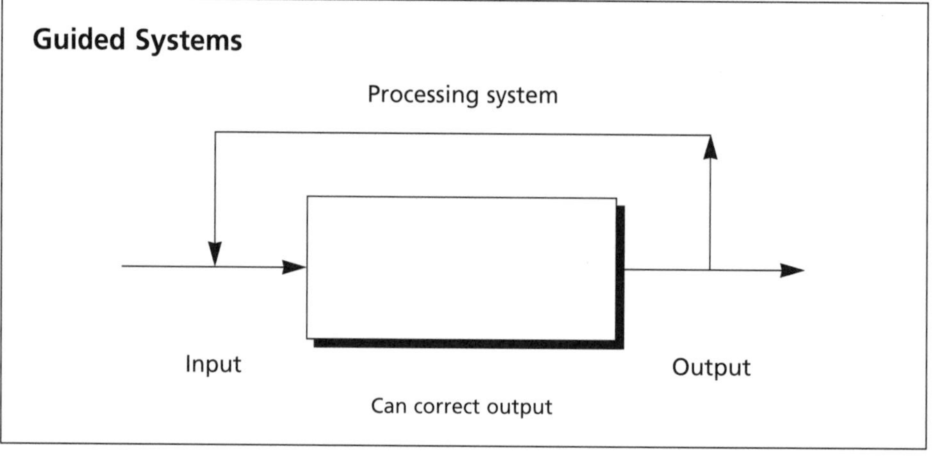

"In sales and marketing, 99 percent of our truly active feedback loops are attached to the end result of a long series of events, aren't they? The end result is the sale itself. Think for a moment. This means we only know about how we're doing after it is too late to do anything about it! Can you think of any other important aspect related to commerce, where huge sums of money and people's livelihoods are at stake, where we only bother to seriously detect and adjust what's happening *after* it has already happened?

"Imagine that you are in a cockpit of a plane, where all the forward windows are blocked. The only instrument you have is a rearview mirror. Who wants to board this flight? Step forward.

"Look at the illustration! [Dr. Selden's voice rises emphatically.] You can talk all you want about improvement, and you can sprinkle your business conversations all you like with the word *process* to impress and amaze your friends and coworkers. This simple diagram shows you are not serious about any of it unless those feedback loops are in place. It is a physical impossibility! Without feedback loops you have a ballistic system, characterized in practice by people who shoot off one great idea after another like bullets in the dark."

Adaptive Systems

"An adaptive system not only can adjust its output, it connects a feedback loop to customers. Dale Brethower (1972) points out that the entire goal of the system adjusts to meet what helps the customer meet his or her goals. If the customer's needs change, the processing system shifts to meet the new output requirements. Notice how this diagram graphically illustrates the mechanisms necessary to what is termed *consultative selling* work in practice. A consultative salesperson needs a knowledge of the customer's goals and business needs and must possess the ability to adjust solutions proposed accordingly."

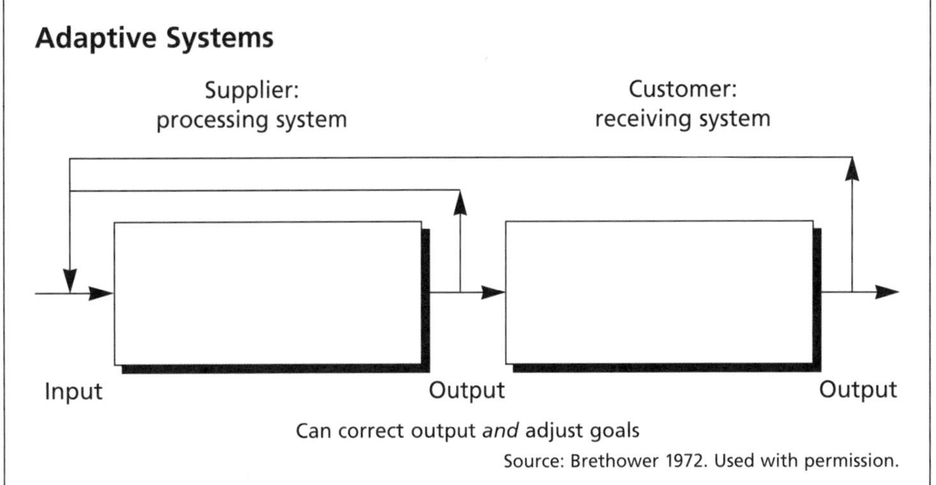

Source: Brethower 1972. Used with permission.

Wow. This is what our product designers and manufacturing people are so excited about these days. They send out survey after survey and interview customers right and left to get their feedback on product designs and how well they are satisfied with their purchases. In sales and marketing, I'm not sure we even want to hear their answers. I think we fear that if they spoke up, all we would hear are complaints.

"Distinguishing between these processes is not just an idle exercise. The drawings of boxes and lines may seem simple. The concepts are easy to understand, but the implications are powerful. If you need an adaptive system, you better not have set up a ballistic system. All the components must physically be in place. Feedback loops must be working, or the process will not perform successfully. Period! All you'll have are nice sounding words. 'We are consultative in our sales approach.' Ha! It's not possible unless the proper feedback loops are in place and functioning well. The good news is that since so few of your competitors probably do this, think of the opportunity you'd have if you put real effort into it!

"Several things are missing from this particular diagram—and almost all such illustrations—that we will need to understand and map out in order to develop a picture of a robust sales process. I'll underscore one point now, since I brought it to your attention before. The results of much of our sales and marketing efforts are known only because we attach feedback loops to the end result: sales. Sales is one of the outcome variables produced by our sales process. If the government didn't require us to pay taxes, and if the Securities and Exchange Commission didn't require reporting to shareholders, we might not even report sales!

"What is missing, not only in the drawing but also in many of our sales processes, is a feedback loop attached to the process itself, to process variables and to the inputs. Attaching feedback to process variables lets us adjust the process *before* the outcome variable is generated. This gives our airplane a window, an altimeter, and so on. It's easier to tell where you will end up if you know where you are going along the way."

Much of the early research on the effects of feedback on human behavior comes from a field called *behavioral psychology.*

Key Definition: Sales

"We've already talked about the meaning of the word *process.* If we are to clarify the work of sales process engineering, we better also look at the meaning of a word we're more familiar with: *sales.* Do we really understand the term?

"My dictionary defines sales as involving the exchange of title to goods or services for valuable consideration. Does this sound okay to you? [Most nod their heads, yes.] This same dictionary also defines the word *sell* as, 'to deliver in violation of duty, trust, or loyalty: to betray.'

"I think we in the profession had better look very closely at these definitions. They color our own assumptions. They certainly reflect a popular conception of what sales and marketing is all about. Do any of you know someone who would find the very thought of going into sales anathema?

"I find a problem with the traditional definitions. Exchanging a title is a discrete event—a one-time, single occurrence. Once the deal is done, it's over. The classic definition of sales may fit a strictly legal interpretation, but it strengthens the old image of selling as an act of betrayal: the rep's job is to take the money and run.

"Nowadays that is not what typically happens, any more than doctors apply leeches if you are sick. The classic, legal definition misses the concept of sales as a process. It also focuses attention on the outcome of the sales process and draws attention away from the other important elements.

"The old definition also misses the concept that securing *repeat* sales is an important aim of that process. Once we've made our first sale to a particular customer, our objective must shift to that of obtaining repeat sales with that customer, or we have nothing left except to start all over with someone new. Look at the numbers in your own company. I think you'll find that selling to new customers is a very expensive proposition.

"As bad as the old definitions are, they do, however, focus us on our subject. When I speak of sales, marketing, and customer service as being part of a larger sales process, I mean to include any function connected with securing a new or repeat sale, primarily focused on actions where a supplier has direct personal contact with a customer. In some businesses, installation plays a role, for example. Throughout this workshop, all these functions are summarized by the single word *sales* to remind ourselves of the output these functions are supposed to deliver to a company: income from new and repeat sales."

- Sales: Exchange of title to goods or services for valuable consideration
- Old view: too focused on discrete, one-time transaction
- New view: must include repeat sales and entire process, not just single exchange

Sales as a Process

"It's time to move beyond abstract concepts. How can we visualize sales as a process? Take a look at a typical business-to-business sales process, as an example. If your business sells to other businesses, your process may differ in the particulars. If you are in retailing or the catalog business, your process may be quite different. A company selling to distributors may focus on influencing large end-users to order from an intermediate supplier. Pharmaceutical marketing involves influencing prescribing preferences, but does not usually involve direct selling to a physician. The example I'm illustrating just gives us a place to begin; it doesn't assume that the same person or company executes each step."

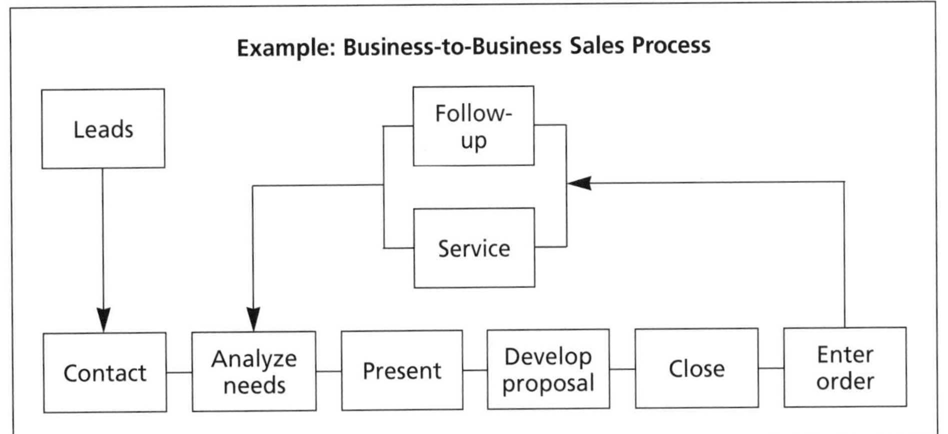

At the top left in the illustration, leads come in from various sources. These may be responses to magazine ads in the form of lists. They may arrive in the form of a name received from another customer or a friend or in the form of a letter written to the company inquiring about its products and services. In general, lead (or *demand*) generation is the job of the marketing department found in larger firms.

Typically, some form of contact follows next. In the world of business-to-business selling for high-ticket items, the initial greetings may quickly turn into a more specific discussion about the particular needs a prospective customer has. In certain circumstances, this needs analysis may be quite detailed, especially where product alternatives are many and their applications are complex and diverse.

If all goes well during the needs analysis, the salesperson may now present a set of alternative solutions that fill the potential customer's needs. Selecting the right solution from a list of many potential alternatives often requires a great deal of skill.

The rep may then be asked to submit a formal bid or quote, which requires someone to develop a proposal. In some businesses, proposals can be quite complex. Bids submitted on multimillion-dollar projects can span dozens, even hundreds, of pages.

Once a proposal is developed, a formal presentation or close often follows. Impressions made as objections to the proposal are raised and answered and can influence the decision to buy. In complex sales, the sales rep may never see all the people influencing the purchase.

If the proposal is accepted, it's time to enter the order so that the appropriate service, delivery, installation, and billing can take place. There is often extensive follow-up to see that all went well.

"I strongly suggest you pick up a guide such as *Mapping Work Processes* by Dianne Galloway (1994) to help you chart your own process. Her guide is easy to follow. Even a simple process map can surface problem areas that were previously hidden."

Key Characteristics of Engineering

- Engineering: Systematic application of scientific and mathematical principles to achieve practical ends
- Empirical approach to problem solving
- Use of tests to verify assumptions, operating limits
- Use of quantitative and qualitative specifications to guide development
- Systematic approach
- Use of available math and science tools
- Conservative, especially in matters of safety and health

"Let's look at the last word in our definition: *engineering*. I don't mind the dictionary's classic definition of the word. Engineering is defined as the use of scientific and mathematical principles to achieve practical ends.

"Most of us are familiar with what sales, marketing, and service people do. What about engineers? What words come to mind when you think of the word *engineer?* What do engineers do? What is their job like?"

Different people speak up. "Design," one person says. Another says, "Scientific." Another says, "Systematic." "Measurement." "Process oriented."

"These are all fair descriptions. Do these words describe the mind-set of the typical salesperson in your firm?" [This image seems to amuse the participants.]

"Good salespeople probably do possess these characteristics, by the way. In fact, the most successful sales, marketing, and customer service people I've met are very methodical. But many of our sales cultures do not support a climate conducive to sales process *engineering*.

"Relative to most salespeople, the typical engineer is more *empirical*. Salespeople tend to rely more on intuition. Engineers rely on *tests*.

"Circle the word *quantitative* in your copy of the slides I've passed out [see illustration] to emphasize it relative to the word *qualitative*. In sales, much of our training advice is qualitative in nature. 'Be consultative.' 'Help your customers.' 'Sales involves consulting.' 'Build relationships.' 'Sales is like war, it's like making love,' we describe. 'Sales involves a funnel, sales involves a pipeline.' Any of these descriptions may be fine as far as they go, but something's missing. We have to get beyond metaphors if we are to have engineering. As sales process engineers, we must employ quantitative analysis, together with descriptive analysis.

"Engineering is also *conservative*, especially when it comes to matters of *safety* and *health*. In today's sales environment that goal is not as far-fetched as you might think, either from the supplier's or the customer's point of view.

"The stresses we put on today's sales rep would not be tolerated in many modern factories. Today's salesperson often works in an environment filled with fear, uncertainty, lack of instruction, and conflicting orders. The biggest danger may be to a salesperson's moral and spiritual health, if you will, whenever this environment encourages promising more than can be delivered. This degrades a person's integrity and the good name of the firm, as well.

"And although great strides have been made, risks to the customer are still present, as well, more often in terms of simple lack of promised performance if not in terms of direct jeopardy of safety and health. Part of our job as engineers will be to reduce these dangers to our own people and to the customers in our sales process.

"One of our goals will be to improve performance without increasing employee burnout. Our job is to increase benefits and reduce dangers to the customer, as well. Ours is a *noble* pursuit."

What Is Sales Process Engineering?

Sales process engineering is the systematic application of scientific and mathematical principles to better serve the practical goals of a particular sales process (Selden 1994b).

- Sales process engineering is the systematic application of scientific and mathematical principles to better serve the practical goals of a particular sales process.

- The Sales Automation Association is leading the long-term effort to develop sales process engineering as an engineering discipline.

"We've talked about what each of the words in the definition mean. The discipline concerns itself not just with securing an initial sale to a customer, but also with what it takes to secure ongoing sales. Its emphasis is on marketing, sales, and service: portions of the business cycle not normally focused on in ISO 9000, the international standards for operating a world-class, quality-oriented business.

"The discipline looks at the entire sales process, not just its outcome in terms of dollars sold. This means sales process engineers will be examining inputs to the process and the specific subprocesses and operations that work upon those inputs, too. Getting the input and within-process variables right is a necessary precondition for getting the output variables right, in a cause-and-effect view of the world.

"Notice the word *particular.* The complete definition recognizes and implies there are likely to be very different sales processes in different organizations. The definition does not lay out a quest for the one perfect process, any more than a mechanical design engineer sets out to design one perfect engine. The definition does not exclude other parts of a company, but it does provide an emphasis to help offset the historic emphasis on manufacturing, design, and assembly.

"Finally, the definition requires us to pursue *practical* ends using the tools and systematic approaches of an engineer. Though we are interested in process inputs and process functionality, the engineer wants to achieve practical outcomes.

"Now we can look squarely at the power found when we put the definition together. A good definition should point us in the right direction by suggesting positive approaches and lines of inquiry. Our definition does so. A good definition also tells us when we're on the wrong track. Our definition tells us that we should be skeptical of any effort claiming to employ sales process engineering that doesn't use the tools and principles of *math* and *science.* We'll not believe the seriousness with which an organization is pursuing the matter if the effort is not *systematic.* We'll blow the whistle if no specific goal is set forth and if that goal cannot plausibly be linked to obtaining customers and securing repeat sales. We'll know the project has nothing to do with process engineering if the boundaries of inquiry do not encompass a process or portion of a process."

Some authors imply that most customer preference for a product is dictated by factors built in at the design and production stage of a product's life. While true in some cases, this emphasis ignores the entire service sector and cases where products are almost identical. In the latter cases, the marketing, sales, and customer service functions provide the key differentiation. In such cases the sales process is worth examining with greater vigor than in the past. See, for example, the *Wall Street Journal* article "Marketing Plays a Bigger Role in Distinguishing PCs" (Carlton 1995).

Even though this sounds a bit theoretical, I'm glad we set out our assumptions and definitions up-front. I can already see that our process is missing important elements—such as feedback loops—that all processes need to function well. Already I can see that our current approach to sales focuses too much on a single transaction. And I agree that although we have lots of numbers in sales, they don't support an engineering-like approach to quantitative analysis.

Underlying Assumptions

Defining sales process engineering exposes the concept to legitimate scrutiny. "Can it work?" is one question. "Is the very idea sound?" is another. "Getting consistently superior results at the least cost is best done through creative sales process engineering" is an assertion resting on at least five basic assumptions. There may be others as yet unstated. These five assumptions are the following:

1. Sales can be thought of as a process, and that process can be controlled in useful ways. This assumption rests on the premise that sales outcomes obey principles of cause and effect.

2. Systematic inquiry into the sales process—raising questions and solving problems step-by-step—is not only possible, but desirable. This assumption rests on history, which, during the past 300 years, has shown that tremendous advances occur when people use scientific and engineering-like approaches.

3. Until sales process engineering develops its own uniquely effective tools, we should be able to borrow existing mathematical and scientific tools and methods from other disciplines. Some may work very well. This assumption has not been thoroughly tested.

4. Sales process engineering rests on the assumption that simply talking about a problem and finding a solution on paper will not be sufficient. Engineering is not passive. It does not merely sit back in a corner and gather statistics. Engineers must act on knowledge gained to improve performance, or the nature of competition and natural process drift means that things will actually decline.

5. Once implemented, processes tend to degrade and drift over time. Therefore, engineers must actively hold gains achieved through proper management and control. Maintenance and ongoing improvement will always be required to remain competitive and because customer needs change.

> ### Underlying Assumptions
>
> Getting consistently superior results at the least cost is best done through creative sales process engineering.
>
> - Sales is a process that can be controlled.
> - Improving the process involves answers to key questions—solving problems—which is best carried out systematically.
> - Until unique approaches are developed, tools will be borrowed from other disciplines.
> - Progress requires *acting* on knowledge gained.
> - Holding the gain requires *active* maintenance and ongoing improvement.

"For those who still scoff and question whether sales process engineering is worth pursuing, I suggest the following test. (1) Over the next three days, count and tally how many times a technique you are already successfully using is mentioned. (2) Look at your tally, then ask yourself, 'Would putting all these pieces and parts into a more unified, more coherent, and more systematically focused whole be even more effective?' (3) Then ask yourself if, during the course of these three days, you have been able to refute any of the explicit underlying assumptions we just covered from a logical, scientific, or mathematical basis.

"If your own experience tells you it should work, and you can't refute the assumptions, you will have validated the discipline. Fair enough? Let's move on."

Principle of Customer Identity

"What is the goal of sales process engineering? On the way to improving a sales process, there will be difficulties. These must be surmounted to reach the goal. We'll overcome these difficulties with a joyful heart, though, knowing that our goals are noble and in the highest traditions of service.

"For all of us who have a sense of duty and a sense of obligation to do our best, practicing our craft will be a fulfilling experience. Those working in sales process engineering will receive tremendous personal satisfaction as the journey is made.

"For those of us who are trying our best to follow the golden rule, sales process engineering offers a way to express our faith on a daily basis. Why? Because of the principle of customer identity.

"To improve a sales process means better serving our customers. At the very least, we will attempt to satisfy their requirements; even better is to go beyond mere satisfaction and aim for unexpected delight."

Dr. Selden comments that recognizing the principle of the customer helps us break down barriers that traditionally exist between our sales, marketing, and customer service departments, as well. The principle gives the sales process engineer and everyone else working within the system a sense of tighter camaraderie. This makes for an emotional and spiritual sense of fulfillment. It also has a practical effect which Dr. Selden says he'll explain later when he discusses the concept of *specifications.*

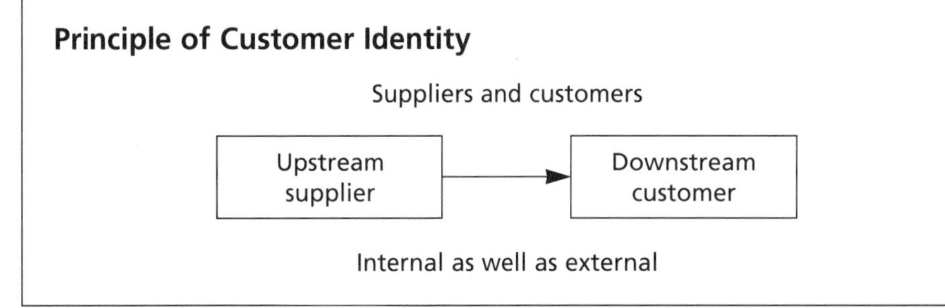

"The principle of customer identity states that whoever receives the output of a process is the customer for that process. Each subsequent downstream process is the customer for the preceding process upstream. Further, whether explicitly stated or not, each customer has a set of requirements for the input from the preceding process. Helping customers articulate their requirements, agreeing on them, and setting up a method for fulfilling these requirements is one of the key missions of everyone within an organization. This is a tremendously liberating concept. It frees us to do the right thing professionally, counteracting short-term pressures to make a sale regardless of the customer's best interests.

"In sales, marketing, and service we are used to thinking of our customers as external to the organization. Be sure to include internal customers, too."

Sales process engineering suggests an optimistic solution to thinkers like Lester C. Thurow (1996), who in *The Future of Capitalism* wonders whether selfish avarice may push capitalistic societies into a bleak future. The sales process cannot function if the customer—our neighbor—is ignored. Sales process engineering supports the contention of Rand Corp. senior social scientist Francis Fukuyama (1995), who argues in his book *Trust: The Social Virtues & the Creation of Prosperity* that how we behave as a community with respect to one another is a predictor of economic success.

Customer Satisfaction and Delight

"Let's think for a moment about who our customers are and consider their requirements. I'll jot your ideas down as you mention them.

"Who are your customers, and what are their requirements?"

Dr. Selden lists ideas on flip charts as participants offer them.

"Even if we took the time to conduct voice of the customer interviews internally and externally, I don't think the list would be much more accurate. You've given us the equivalent of a very thorough and expensive survey in the space of a 15-minute discussion."

Customer Satisfaction and Delight

- Giving customers what they want
  - —External customers
  - —Top executives
  - —Sales management
  - —Sales reps
  - —Marketing/service
  - —Other internal staffs
- Giving companies the ability to stay in business
  - —Capital from investors
  - —Less regulatory burden

External Customers
- *Quality*
- *Timely delivery*
- *Availability and selection*
- *Honest advice*
- *Low price*

Management
- *Ability to spot performance deficiencies*
- *Ability to train quickly and effectively*
- *Ability to motivate good performance*

Marketing
- *Increasing demand*
- *Market share and equity*
- *Image and prestige*
- *Complaint reduction*

Sales
- *Commissions*
- *Reduce hassles*
- *Less paperwork*

Top Executives
- *Profitability*
- *Return on investment*
- *Shareholder dividends*
- *Investment capital*
- *Reduced regulatory burden*

Internal Staffs
- *Meeting deadlines*
- *Staying within budget*
- *Meeting project objectives*

Customer Service
- *Prompt answers/solutions*
- *Thoroughness*
- *Accurate order information*

Finding ways to meet or exceed customer requirements is a great way to get people on your side. It reduces the politics and posturing often associated with changing a way of doing business. A sales process engineer aims to make people's lives easier, not to usurp their power or territory.

Tune the Process to Meet Specific Goals

"We're spending so much time on the basics because the basics are not always obvious, or people would not foul them up so royally and with such great regularity! One mistake I see over and over is that companies do not do a thorough job of process analysis prior to deciding they should 'automate.' The Sales Automation Association, or SAA, warns against that approach. It is clear that automation will be involved in most contemporary efforts at sales process improvement. I strongly suggest you become familiar with the SAA's approach regardless of what stage you are in. Keep the goals we've just discussed in mind if you want your effort to succeed. If you are having trouble it's very likely you failed to tune the process to meet a specific goal right from the start."

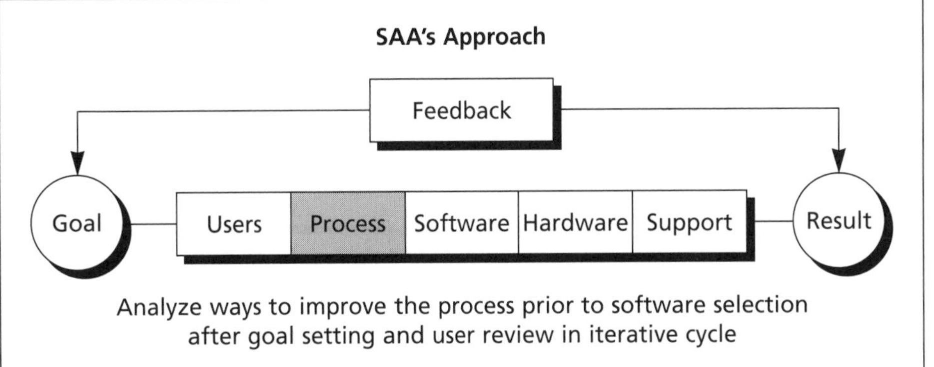

The SAA recommends that companies embarking on a sales process improvement effort start by setting a specific, measurable *goal* aimed at meeting or exceeding customer requirements. The goal can be set high as a deliberate challenge, or it can be arrived at following careful analysis of what can realistically be achieved.

The reaction of people or *users* directly involved with the process should be solicited early, so their comments can be taken into account. Their input is helpful for another reason: They know where process problems currently exist. Their observations can save time during the analysis phase.

***Process analysis* follows to confirm ideas received from others, but also to help generate a broader, more fact-based view of the process as a whole. All these steps are iterative: Input received at each new step may alter previous thinking.**

Nonautomated process changes and tools will likely play a key part in process improvement. *Software* may support the effort, but it must be selected only after the first three steps have been completed. This helps ensure that the automation supports the improved process and not the other way around. Select sufficient *hardware* to run the software.

Regardless of the changes involved, proper training and ongoing *support* is essential. *Results* must be monitored, and a *feedback* loop must be set up for those steering the project so they can improve it.

In my company we put the cart before the horse time after time. We start with the hardware—"I want laptops for our reps!" someone says—so most of our attention is focused on finding software our reps can use on it. We develop or buy software without much discussion with the reps to see what they really want. Since getting the software and hardware to work together is usually so tough, a few weeks before launching the system we run out of budget for any decent kind of support. Not only that, since the people running the project are usually more technically adept, they don't put themselves in the shoes of new users, so they forget about training until the eleventh hour. Then there's a mad dash to slap something together so we don't miss our deadlines. The system is taught at the level of keystrokes, not from the point of view of how to use a tool to get the job done. Of course, no one is collecting data on whether the actual overall performance metrics have improved. When the boss asks, "Is the new system working?" everyone scrambles around to find whatever stories make themselves look good.

Standing on the Edge of a New Frontier

Before Dr. Selden formally announces a break, an unexpected muse launches him into an animated commentary.

"Listen! You might conclude that progress in thinking about processes and their characteristics in other fields, such as in manufacturing, means that we already know about sales, marketing, and service from a process point of view. The frequently cited failures in sales automation (Selden 1996) and reengineering (Davenport 1995) should warn us how little we really know.

"This is a new field! Thinkers contributing to the advancement of sales process engineering are true pioneers. The principles have not been fully explored and translated into the language of sales, marketing, and customer service. You can confirm this yourself by browsing through books published on process improvement, process management, and the like. When you leaf though the books you'll find that 99 percent of the examples and discussion is from a manufacturing or assembly point of view. Sales, marketing, and customer service are usually relegated to a one-page list of how the concepts apply to 'other' areas. After discussing at great length all the steps associated with making a product, the topics of most interest to us in this room are lumped into a tiny box on their charts, labeled 'distribution.' As if the only thing you had to do after making a widget is pass it off the back of a truck to an eager throng clamoring for your wonderful creations. Ha!

- Most texts on quality, process improvement, and reengineering only lightly cover sales.
- Mainly talk about marketing and primarily in connection with customer problems.
- But are a *great* source of information we can translate into our terms.
- They help us think about the *process as a whole.*
- Makes the entire field an exciting new frontier for pioneering work.

"Distribution! The image of sales and marketing as distribution is from some 1930s movie. Newsboys in tweed caps standing on street corners early in the morning.

"Yet, let's give credit where credit is due! Process engineering has worked fairly well. Maybe the process engineers are on to something but just haven't translated it into our language. Maybe there haven't been many people in sales who have spoken the language of process engineering, either. That's beginning to change.

"Speaking of giving proper credit, some so-called sales gurus haven't helped matters any. Now, I don't fault anyone who gets excited about a method they've found that works well. It's just that at times, I get this sneaking suspicion that some people promote their own approach as totally unique when in fact they know they got their methods elsewhere and fail to properly credit their sources. This means serious students can't doublecheck and fully explore the knowledge that may already exist. The drive to seem new and totally unique tends to make such books sound like just another opinion or fad. Deliberately failing to acknowledge the work of others also discourages people from coming forward with good ideas, for fear their thoughts won't be given due credit. I applaud the professional courtesy of those who are helping to map out our professional journey by properly referencing their sources. Sharing sources helps all of us who wish to blaze a trail.

"Okay, I got that off my chest. Let's take a 15-minute break."

Some of the contemporary pioneers in sales process engineering whose writings are gaining attention are Barton Goldenberg (1996), Thomas Siebel and Michael Malone (1996), Larry McCloskey (1995), George Smith (1995), Cas Welch and Pete Geissler (1995), George Columbo (1994), Timothy McMahon (1994), Allan J. Magrath (1993), and Todd C. Scofield and Donald R. Shaw (1992).

Reflections on the Status Quo During Break

In our firm, I wouldn't say that we've ever really tried sales process engineering in the full sense Dr. Selden is speaking of. It's not to say our managers aren't smart or don't care. They do. Our top people in sales and marketing are committed individuals who work very hard. They've given their lives to the company. Yet, I think most seem to have inherited a system that usually demands their full attention just to keep the status quo going. Not only that, having achieved so much personally, their natural sense of self-worth and dignity might get in the way of listening to other ideas. The standard by which they judge things seems to be whether it fits their own way for getting things done, not a standard that looks at the process itself and asks whether the new idea would be better. There are a lot of vested interests in maintaining things basically as they are.

In our company, gains in sales usually come from new product launches or occasional windfalls, not from fundamental improvements in how we sell. We don't have anyone devoted to studying this subject, either. We have a team of people studying how automation can be used in sales, marketing, and service, but the team's focus seems to be on the computers and not on the sales process the computers are supposed to improve. We are coming up with lots of great ideas for how software could be used, but how do we separate bells, whistles, and fluff from the substance that can really pay off? I know for a fact the project leader is only doing this part time on top of all the other duties rightsizing has left us with. How can this be called systematic?

We have systematic people in our firm, I know that. The marketing research department has some great analysts. Our engineers really know their stuff. Our managers in sales are great at time management and working within the system; so are our top salespeople. I've talked to our top salespeople. They're very organized. They have to be to sell the amount they do.

If this is so, why do we end up with so many hit-or-miss efforts? Even our so-called strategic thrusts don't survive when the executive who sponsored it takes a new position. We have no organizational structure to survive and remember what worked and what didn't work. That's completely different than our engineering group. Executives come and go, but the engineers have a structure that somehow sustains their efforts to improve in spite of everything else.

Tool 1: The Flowchart

The break ends, and Dr. Selden changes pace by presenting the first of the 12 tools to be discussed.

"Now that we've defined what we mean by sales process engineering, let's move on to the first formal tool in the engineering arsenal we'll learn today: the flowchart. Stay with me. We'll be focusing on its application in the sales process, not on an abstract set of instructions.

"Flowcharting is a familiar tool to use, and a great place to start when first trying to understand your process. This illustration maps out a portion of a telemarketing process having to do with screening leads. In this company, incoming names—reply card responses gathered by a publisher in response to an advertisement—are surveyed in a brief telephone call to determine whether they are sufficiently qualified as a potential customer or not. If they are qualified, the lead is passed on to the sales rep for further follow-up. If not qualified, the lead is put on what this company calls a *referral plan* to an allied division that may be more likely to help the potential customer.

"Flowcharting is so easy to use that many people feel no further discussion is required. Yet there is something on this chart that is not on 99 percent of the sales-related process flowcharts you've seen in the past. Does anybody see it? [No one raises his or her hand.]

"It's right in the middle. The diamond. Information processing people would call this a *decision diamond*. Yes, the diamond symbolizes a decision, but it's much more than that. As sales process engineers we're going to call it a *specification*. Please write that word next to the diamond: *specification*.

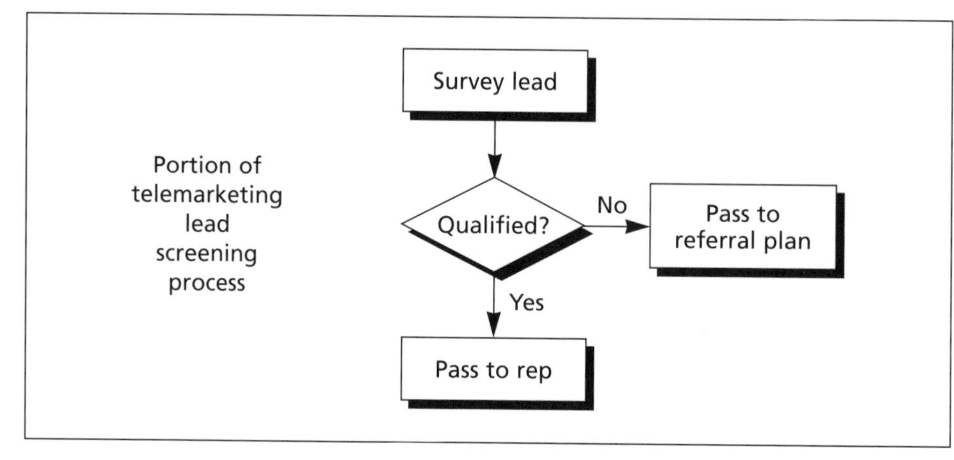

"In sales and marketing we have failed to insist—probably because we've failed to even recognize the need—that each upstream supplier deliver to its downstream customer an output that meets an explicit specification.

"Information processing people take it for granted that the computer will handle decisions automatically. But in sales and marketing we have a tremendous problem. We have little or no written specifications. How many of those leads must be qualified each week? What constitutes the test for qualification? Many sales, marketing, and customer service operations don't know the answer to questions like these because the very concept of specifications is foreign."

The ultimate set of specifications is held by our external customers. Failing to meet external customer specifications means failure to secure orders. This explains the critical importance of listening to the customer and understanding customers' needs.

Flowcharting Instructions

Dr. Selden reviews the instructions for flowcharting, commenting as he goes.

"A flowchart is a picture of the steps in a process. Drawing a flowchart helps you begin to understand your current system and how it currently performs. From there you can better spot opportunities for improvement. Just because a tool is simple doesn't mean it's trivial. Nuts and bolts are simple, but their usefulness is far from trivial.

"Some people say their sales reps do not follow a process, good, bad, or otherwise. The people who say this may not know how to flowchart. They may not have studied the situation. At the very least, the salesperson is part of a larger process and is almost always responsible for an output, such as a sale. The inputs might be products, services, customer names, brochures, training in sales presentations, and so forth. What the salesperson does with the inputs to create the sale may not be as routine as a flowchart would suggest, but both inputs and outputs can certainly be studied with an eye to improvement. The 'solo producer' kind of arrangement is found in factories where individuals or small teams are responsible for assembling final units. Process engineers such as Monden call this an *isolated island layout,* which has advantages and disadvantages you can study on your own. Even in this situation, there is advice you can give your reps. As Hubert Humphrey, chairman of the World Marketing Alliance says, 'Find out who's doing the best and copy them!'"

In my company, it's not that there is no process, it's that everyone seems to have his or her own way of doing things. We probably have 50 different ways to do the same thing. Our salespeople are cowboys. I guess that gets back to the basket weaving situation Dr. Selden described to us at the very beginning.

"A variation of the flowchart often used is called a *functional flowchart.* In a functional flowchart the different departments involved are often listed in columns, and the process steps cross from column to column as the department responsible for performing that step changes.

Before finalizing flowcharts, a handy way to facilitate group interaction is to stick Post-it® notes to a wall, documenting the process. Tipping a square Post-it® note sideways turns it into a diamond shape. Modern computerized flowcharting tools can also be used, projecting the image so everyone can see it. Your work is documented as you go.

"Be sure to define the boundaries of the process you are studying with the help of people who really know the process as it stands. That way the scope of your effort is made manageable, and you may uncover hidden problems with the ownership of what happens in the 'white space' between different processes. One simple drawing may reveal that no one has really accepted ownership for a critical part of the flow.

"Each process box must have definite inputs and outputs attached to it. Making sure the inputs and outputs are clearly defined provides a starting point for obtaining agreement on the specifications that should be attached to each.

- Flowchart: picture of steps in a process
- Variation: functional flowchart (shows ownership of steps)
- Common symbols: diamond (decisions) and rectangles (procedures); many others
- Define boundaries of process
- Assemble true experts in flow to diagram
- Each block needs definite input from previous operation
- Each block should deliver output to next step downstream

"Let me share a story with you. I once worked with a snack food company, helping to design a systematic program for its 10,000 route salespeople. One of its sharp marketing people flowcharted the entire sales process, outlining all the steps and how they depended on one another. We built these concepts into a rigorous training curriculum. The company, Frito-Lay, has done rather well. Its largest competitor, a rather well-known firm, recently threw in the towel."

Breaking a link in a process chain is dangerous. Engineers use the concept of redundancy—fail-safe and parallel systems—to provide a backup mechanism for processes that fail in service. They use the concept of building in a safety factor—400 percent to 500 percent factors are not uncommon—and engineering a system to withstand large unanticipated stress, as well.

Checkpoint: Flowcharting Exercise

Dr. Selden assigns an exercise to the group, saying that it's time to get to work. He breaks the large group into pairs, sharing our results. We're supposed to work fast, taking a look at our larger sales, marketing, and service process—whatever we're most familiar with—and breaking it into five to seven main subprocesses. He insists we draw diamonds between the major blocks to leave room for specifications, even if we don't know what to list as our specifications.

I have a little trouble getting started. Where should I begin? Our sales reps are cowboys—independent. I don't think they follow a process, per se, but I guess they do get inputs. We give them price lists, promotional offers, catalogs, and training. They are assigned a territory. They have customers. We let them know when new prospective customers enter their territory or inquire about our services. So I suppose that they do get leads. That would be marketing's responsibility. Marketing is responsible for the promotional offers; they set up catalogs and price lists, too. Those would be outputs from marketing, which the sales group receives as inputs. I'll draw a diamond between those outputs from marketing and sales. Sales doesn't set clear specifications for what marketing delivers. Marketing just does its own thing based on informal input.

Okay, I guess a little of what I've drawn looks somewhat like a process, at least between marketing and sales. I don't know enough about marketing to draw the inputs. I guess they have discussions with the product developers about new products, but that's not my area, so I'll just put a question mark there. I wish our marketing head was here.

The reps themselves do make presentations, when they judge it proper. On a fairly regular basis, management orients the reps to special promotions and urges them to sell those deals when a promotion is running. Reps also meet with clients and assess their needs, and they also make recommendations. They write up orders and see that they are processed, following through with the client if there are any problems.

Now that I look back at the picture of the business-to-business sales process Dr. Selden projected earlier, I guess maybe it describes things fairly well, in a general way. I'll redraw it with the decision diamonds he asked for.

It astounds me that we never thought to set numeric specifications for these major steps before, but we haven't. Dr. Selden said that if we think a step is important enough to draw as a box, it's important enough to set specifications for its inputs and outputs.

Bottlenecks: A Main Process Enemy

"You have visualized sales as a process with a *flow.* The flow includes marketing, sales, and service. The process may need to rely on other departments within an organization too. Credit, accounting, design, and development or manufacturing are involved. If this is so, principles that apply to *flow* in other situations may apply in the sales process, too.

"There are many types of sales processes. Some apply to consumer packaged goods, others to business-to-business, and others to retail. Each needs to be mapped differently.

"Consider the business-to-business sales process we explored earlier. General demand is stimulated by marketing and leads are received. Individual customer needs are analyzed and orders are closed by sales. Orders are entered by customer service. But who asks what their own internal customers require in order for them to do their job? Once work leaves a department, it's usually someone else's problem. Who checks to see if the specifications were met? There's a formal term for this phenomenon, by the way. It's called *over-the-wall engineering.*"

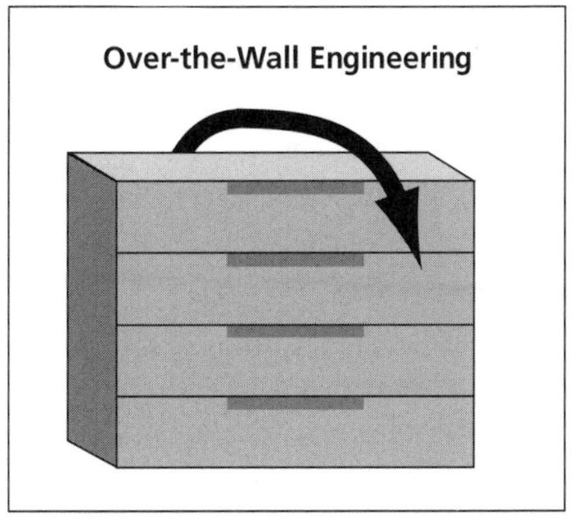

In our company, we don't really view sales as a connected process. We don't count the other departments, because each does its own thing. Each constantly feuds with the other. Whenever a marketing program flops, marketing blames sales for lack of execution. We blame marketing for coming up with crazy ideas sales can't carry out in the first place. Service is always pointing its finger at sales for getting customer orders wrong. Someone should draw the whole process for the department heads to show them what we are trying to accomplish as a complete system.

"Once we see that sales is a process, we can look at and learn from rules that apply to other processes. Have any of you read *The Goal* (1992) by Eliyahu Goldratt?" asks Dr. Selden. "It's a fascinating instructional fable about the head of a troubled manufacturing plant. He's also about to lose his wife because worries about the plant are affecting his marriage. In the book, the hero learns a rule. If you learn this rule, you'll learn to fight a major enemy in all processes.

"Look at this figure, and write down the rule: *The output of a process is limited to that of its most restrictive constraint.*

"Until you find and relieve that bottleneck, most of the capability of the sales process is wasted!"

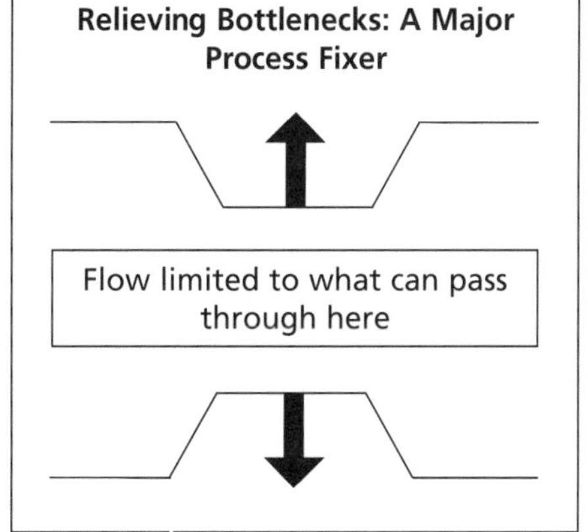

Stimulating Our Powers of Observation

Dr. Selden holds out his hand as if he is grasping a small object. He asks the group members to close their eyes and relax. He asks participants to think back in time to when they were in grade school.

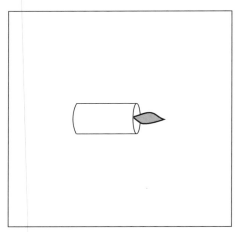

"Imagine I'm holding a candle. When I was in junior high school, my seventh grade science teacher issued candles to us—one per desk, with a book of matches and a saucer. He asked us to put the candle in the saucer, light the candle, and look at it.

"An engineer must be a good observer. If we are going to be sales process engineers, we must practice being observant. Close your eyes. Picture that candle burning. What do you see? Tell me the obvious. Nothing is too simple to mention."

I have my eyes closed, picturing the candle. Should I mention that I see a flame? That the candle is white?

One person in the group breaks the ice. She points out that the candle is shaped like a cylinder. Another person says he observes that the candle has a wick, and that he sees a flame at the end of the wick.

I raise my hand and say that the candle feels waxy and is soft enough to scratch with my fingernail. I feel a little silly for mentioning something so obvious, but at least I said what was on my mind.

"When we looked at the burning candle, our teacher told us that it was possible to record more than 100 observations about a simple burning candle. He made me think. My classmates had only observed some 20 or 30 characteristics.

- The height of the candle
- Its color
- The fact there was melted wax in a puddle on top

"In fact, I remember feeling clever that we noted particles circulating in a pattern within the melted wax on top. Sharp observers. [The class chuckles at this self-deprecating image.]

"Now I need you to look at something else and tell me what you see."

Dr. Selden goes to the flip chart and draws a pair of wavy lines on the paper. They are roughly parallel.

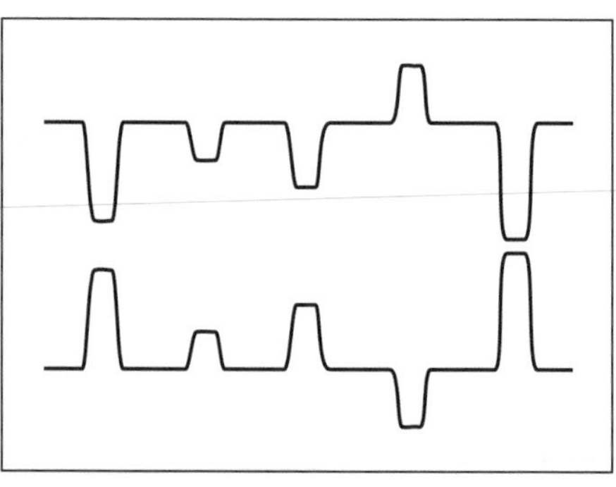

Lessons of a Wavy Pipeline

"These lines are meant to represent what we often call the *sales pipeline.* Typically, people draw the sales pipeline as a smooth pipe, like a water line. That's not how it really is, is it? [Heads nod in agreement.]

"Look at this pipeline. Imagine sales leads entering at the left. At the right, the output is closed sales. Now, thinking back to our candle experiment, I want you to tell me what you observe here. Tell me the obvious."

Now this is getting good. He's right. People often draw the sales pipeline as if it had no obstructions. That hides the real situation. I want to mention this, but I'll wait to hear what other people say first. There's a long pause. People seem afraid to say anything. Maybe people don't want to mention the obvious. Dr. Selden asks for ideas even if a point seems simple.

A young man speaks up. He says that the lines are wavy. Another fellow says that there appear to be bottlenecks in the line, a point we covered earlier.

"Bottlenecks are a main process enemy," Dr. Selden reminds the class.

A woman speaks up, saying that some of the bottlenecks are bigger than others. The class members seem to be running out of ideas.

Many ideas are going through my head. I tell the class that, in my company, we have no idea where our bottlenecks even are. We won't be able to improve our processes until they are identified.

"Let's see what else we can squeeze out of this picture. Another observation is that the pipe seems to have an average diameter, from which the bottlenecks deviate. Do you also see that there is a bump about two-thirds down the pipeline, where the pipe actually seems larger than the average? The capacity for flow is a coin with two sides. There are bottlenecks; the other side of the coin is that in other parts, there is overcapacity.

"I'll give you a name for another process enemy: *suboptimization.* Suboptimization occurs when parts of the pipeline haven't been engineered with a view to what will maximize throughput of the whole system. This occurs when part of a process is improved or built far beyond the capacity of

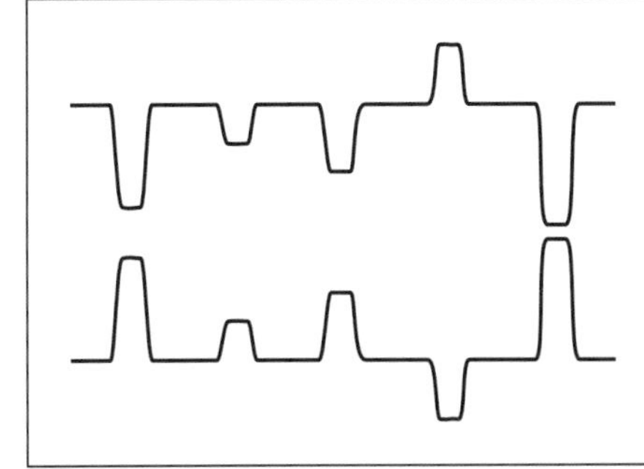

the rest of the system to supply it or to use what it produces.

"How do you suppose a system gets built like this? [Dr. Selden's normally calm voice is booming. He shouts at the class.] It's because one part of the system doesn't talk to the other! The parts are decoupled from one another, like isolated islands, each doing its own thing without regard for how local processes impact the system as a whole! [He stabs at the bottlenecks.] The sales department doesn't discuss its specifications with marketing! And service doesn't tell anyone else what's going wrong! There is no sales process engineering!"

Causes of Low Sales

In the early 1980s, manufacturers found themselves in trouble. An inventory of unsold goods formed a millstone around industry's neck. Maintenance to prevent deterioration in storage and other carrying costs mounted.

Executives asked manufacturing, "Why do we have this inventory?" The answer took many forms. "We need extra on hand in case we don't make enough good ones to ship." "We need a stockpile in case our suppliers don't deliver in time." "We need to work ahead of orders in case of a strike." "We can't drop our inventory—we'd be at risk of all the problems in our process," came the inevitable reply. In other words, a sea of inventory was used to buffer the ship of manufacturing from the many rocks and shoals found in the process.

We can raise a similar question of sales, marketing, and service. Rephrased, it might go like this: "What do we use to buffer our sales process from problems?" Searching our soul, we might admit that sales, marketing, and service also rely on a sea of people, time, and an inventory of work in process (prospects and customers at various stages of the sales pipeline) to buffer problems. Our logic goes, "Because there are many poor prospects in any given batch of leads, if one person can call 100 prospects and obtain one sale, we need three salespeople and 300 prospects if we want three sales. If one service person can solve 20 customer delivery and claims problems per day, we will need two service people to handle 40 customer problems per day."

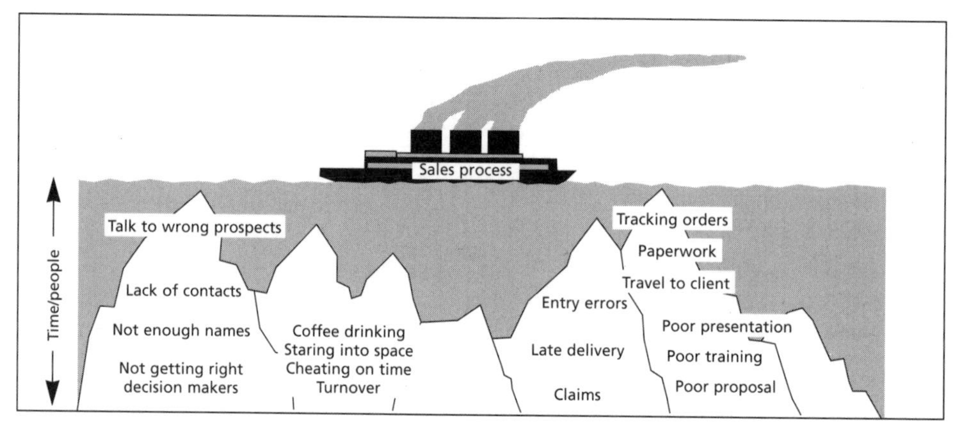

There are hundreds of legitimate sounding answers to the question of why so many people, so much time, and so many prospects are found in the sales process. "We need all the people, and things take so long, and we need so many prospects and customers because we have to talk with the wrong prospects and we aren't getting to the decision makers. We have to travel. There's so much paperwork." We accept these problems as beyond control, which can be solved only by adding time and more people.

During the early 1980s, top executives sometimes found they could not motivate their people to change unless they cut the space for inventory storage and work in process in half, sometimes literally in the form of a new chain link fence, or by rejecting entire shipments from suppliers if the quality was poor. They reasoned, "If underlying problems exist in our manufacturing process, when we drop the inventory level, the problems will be exposed on the surface. From there, why don't we just face the problems head on and eliminate them one by one? If we adopt a philosophy of continuous improvement, we will tackle the obvious problems, drop the inventory level again, expose new problems, tackle those, and so on, until we reach the level actually required." It turns out that solving the process problems had the effect of lowering costs and improving customer satisfaction as well. Can we apply these lessons to the sales process?

A sales process engineer must relentlessly attack the rocks and shoals found in the sales process. That attack must be ongoing and untiring. In doing so, benefits in quality, cost, and customer satisfaction will be realized, as well.

The *Guide to Implementing Sales Automation* (Selden 1994c), from which this illustration was taken, contains tables that describe strategies and tactics for addressing the specific rocks and shoals listed in the figure.

Does Innovation Come Easy?

"Will attacking these sales process problems be easy? Let me share a story with you.

"Thomas Edison once said, 'I shall make electricity so cheap that only the rich can afford to burn candles.' When is the last time you lit a candle in your home? He must have had his skeptics, but look in your own homes now. Candles are reserved for birthdays, anniversaries, romance—special occasions!

"Sales process engineering will lead us to similar great innovations. But let's remember, what we accept as commonplace now does not come easy.

"How many trials do you think it took Edison to come up with a filament for the lightbulb? One that would glow with the right kind of intensity and not burn up?"

The class offers some guesses. One says 100 trials, another says 500. There is silence. Finally, another guesses, 1000 trials.

"It took some *6000* trials! Now that is being systematic. It's also a lesson—an engineer should not give up. Just think if you were to apply the lessons of our wavy pipeline in your own company, to your own sales process."

Thomas Edison not only developed the lightbulb, he built a power company so people could have the electricity to use lightbulbs in their homes.

The telephone served as a similar innovation, changing the sales process by reducing the need for physical travel and increasing the speed of communication.

> I shall make electricity so cheap that only the rich can afford to burn candles.
>
> —*Thomas Edison*

Today in sales, the Internet, wireless data transmission, electronic order processing, electronic data interchange, inexpensive video conferencing systems, broad band cabling, and the like are providing similar technological underpinnings for a new generation of radical sales process improvements. How many trials will it take to make these technologies fully practical?

As a change of pace, Dr. Selden goes on to humorously recount the course of innovation, pegging the date for the first known reference to sales process engineering to be 1991.

"Which of you will be the bringer of light to your company?"

I know Dr. Selden is trying to inspire us. I can see that some of the ideas we're discussing are simple and uncomplicated. But it seems many other innovations are simple, like the plow. Some are more complicated, like the loom or the computer.

I'd love to be able to come back after a seminar like this and really do some innovative things. I'd love to be the one to lead the charge. I need to learn more before I'm comfortable, though. Sales process engineering can't be as simple as just mapping our process and eliminating bottlenecks, can it?

- Wheel and axle: circa 3400 B.C.
- Plow: circa 2900 B.C.
- Athenian democracy: circa 800 B.C.
- Printing press with moveable type: 1451
- Electric battery: 1800
- Jacquard's loom: 1805
- Indoor water closet: 1872
- Electronic computer: 1943
- Sales process engineering: 1991? (first known reference)

In *Virtual Selling*, a forceful review of ideas for improving the sales process, authors Thomas Siebel and Michael Malone (1996) write, "the conversion of every qualified lead into a satisfied and ongoing customer—is as realistic and salubrious a goal for the Informed Sales Force as Six Sigma quality is for manufacturing lines."

Caveats

Dr. Selden points out realistic difficulties that will face early practitioners of sales process engineering.

"We're about to cover some extremely powerful tools. We'll be learning approaches to process engineering that have revolutionized the workplace wherever else they've been properly applied.

"But we must not let ourselves get carried away. This is the first time many of the tools and ideas we're about to cover have been translated for use in the sales process. Many have not been tested to the degree they will be 10 years from now. The entire field is so young. A body of knowledge for sales process engineering has only been agreed upon recently, so how can practitioners have been trained in any quantity? A certification process is in its infancy.

"What this means is that as of now, there is no cookie cutter approach or any simple pattern to follow for sure results. In any particular case, the success of the approach will depend on the situation and on a combination of the skill of the practitioner and the tools chosen for the job. Let's not get carried away with the idea that learning this material guarantees instant fame and fortune."

Difficulties Facing Early Practitioners

- Systematic study is advancing
- Application of approaches relatively untested
- Body of knowledge only recently agreed upon
- Practitioners have yet to be trained in quantity

Therefore, actual utility and results in practice depend on knowledge, creativity, and ingenuity of practitioner and specific situation—which can be expected to vary widely in the beginning.

This course is unlike any other sales and marketing course I've taken. Others have promised results, guaranteed them. This sounds more like real life.

This field is so new. If I pursue this, I can be a pioneer in every sense of the word—including having to watch out for arrows in my back. There are going to be some people who don't like to have their power threatened by someone with a different way of looking at things. There are a lot of vested interests in preserving the status quo. We may go up blind alleys. I don't want to take hits for failing. Creating the right climate is going to be important.

But I don't think being systematic about sales process improvement is as risky as some other things I've seen companies do these days. The greatest risk I've seen with the seat-of-the-pants approach we take now is the risk of a cascading financial disaster. I've talked with far too many of my peers at other companies spending millions of dollars on so-called sales, marketing, and customer service improvement efforts who seem unable to genuinely articulate what the benefit of their so-called improvements will be. Their biggest risk isn't that their project dollars will be wasted. It's in shutting down their whole company if their new methods alienate their customers or employees. The old approach is so willy-nilly and so hazardous. The sad part is they aren't even aware of it. Dr. Selden is urging caution, but I think sales process engineering will shelter far more risk than it exposes.

Sources of Revenue and Expense

"Now let's talk about the good news: increased profitability. A sales process engineer will increase revenue and reduce expense systematically, from a cause-and-effect point of view. An accounting point of view might lay out these variables on a spreadsheet. Some of you might not like to divert attention from all this good information about process behavior to talk about money. The two are quite connected. A business process needs inputs, and one of these is money. Process engineers like to view things graphically to highlight the causal relationships involved.

"If profit is a critical process outcome, as engineers we must ask ourselves, 'What variables do we need to change in order to improve profit?' We'll find that profit is comprised of a number of factors. It follows we must focus on the causal variables that affect profits.

"Sources of income include ordinary sales of products and services. They may also include income from royalties and licensing arrangements, rentals, interest, and so on. Holding the rest constant, increasing any of these variables increases profit in an absolute sense and as a ratio of income to expense.

"Sources of expense include labor, materials, tools, and facilities. Holding the rest constant, decreasing the variables that add to cost increases profits in the same manner.

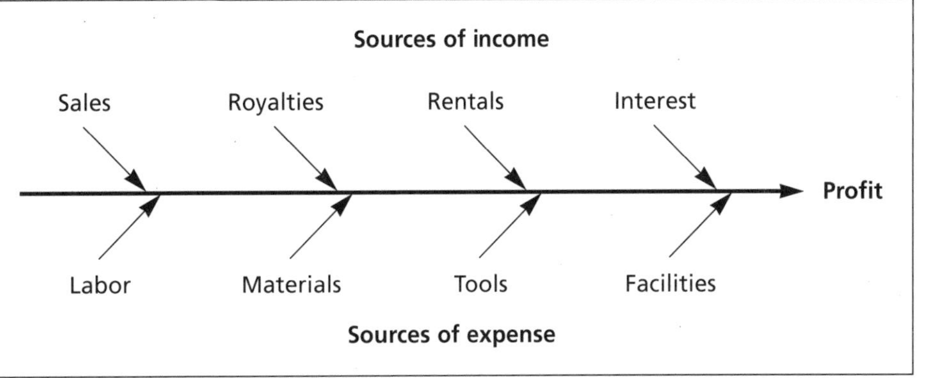

"The interesting thing is that although these relationships are well-known from an accounting point of view, the implications are not always acted on in sales.

"Take facilities, for instance. Companies often invest great sums of money on brick and mortar to house salespeople's desks and telephones when, in fact, the salespeople themselves are not even supposed to be in the office except for a very small percent of the time. Salespeople are supposed to be with clients. Only recently have some very large firms eliminated such permanent facilities for their salespeople, achieving dramatic expense reductions in the process. Even though some of these relationships may seem obvious once considered, sales process engineering can force them to the surface where they can be directly examined, perhaps for the first time."

Compaq, IBM, Lotus Development, Perkin-Elmer, and many others have virtually eliminated the need for salespeople to report to a fixed office. Mobile computing technology lets salespeople send and receive communications, receive schedules, and conduct almost all their normal business while on the road or working out of an office in their own home. Independent sales representatives from firms such as Avon, Amway, and Tupperware have worked in this type of environment for years, even without the high technology support in the home.

Financial Targets for Improving the Sales Process

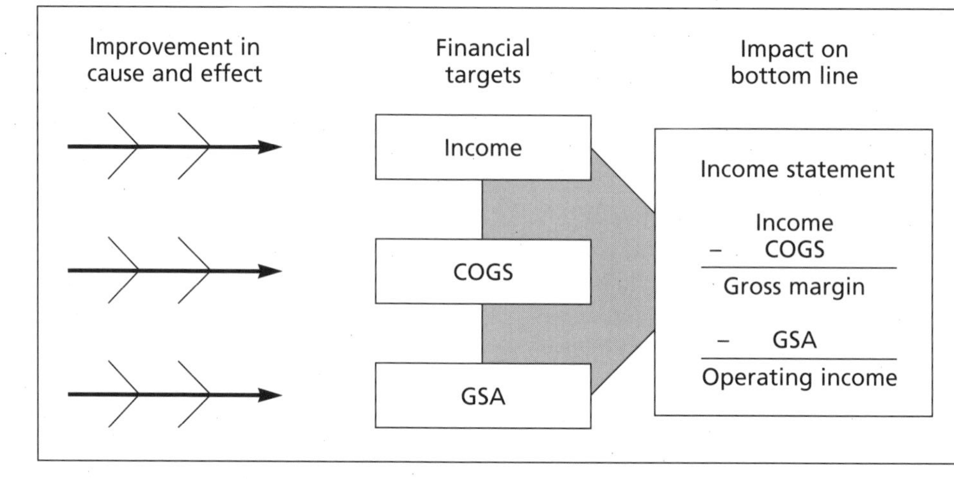

"None of what I've said is to take anything away from the field of accounting. Accounting's world view is highly optimized around a function having to do with financial, tax, and traditional management reporting, which is not designed to pinpoint opportunities to improve processes, per se. The process view of accounting is a relative newcomer, as the breakthrough work of Cooper and Kaplan on activity-based costing in 1988 and the analysis of throughput costing by Noreen, Smith, and Mackey in 1995 testifies.

"Sales process engineers must understand the world of accounting in order to do their jobs. The financial goals of sales process engineering must be understood clearly.

"Claims are frequently made that various changes in the sales, marketing, and customer service functions will improve the bottom line. The sales process engineer must be able to show which item or items on the income statement such changes will improve, and demonstrate the causal relationships involved.

"I've been told that the illustration you see here is the first time the relationship between process changes—on the left—and the bottom line—has been so clearly illustrated. Understand the implications and you will greatly sharpen the focus of your efforts."

The income statement is a company's major financial scorecard. With respect to variables under control of most sales, marketing, and customer service processes, an income statement is composed of three main variables: income; the cost of goods sold, or COGS; and general, sales, and administrative (GSA) expense. Income received by a corporation does not flow directly to the bottom line. Out of every $100 received in income, often some $80 is directly paid to the company's suppliers and internal production areas. This $80 is what is known as the cost of goods sold. The difference between income and the cost of goods sold is called the *gross margin.* An additional $8 to $9 is paid in the form of expenses for general overhead, sales expenses, and administrative costs—GSA. Subtracting GSA from the gross margin leaves what is known as *operating income.* Operating income is normally under control of normal operations; it's the scorecard for the company's main line of business. Out of $100 of income taken in, the average large company only gets to keep between $11 and $12 in operating income. Normally, actions related to the sale or acquisition of stocks, bonds, and facilities and the effects of taxes are not within the control of ordinary operations, yet these items affect the final bottom line, or profit after taxes, but are not a fair measure of typical sales process improvement efforts.

"Sad to say, even prominent speakers make statements such as, 'You can pay for $3000 of sales automation just by selling an extra $3000.' Bill Griffis of Standard and Poor's Compustat estimates that in large companies, operating income is only $11.25 for every $100 of sales. This means that a company gets to keep only $337.50 for every $3000 in sales. How does $337.50 pay for $3000 of hardware and software?

"Don't make the same mistake with your process analysis. In the long run a company needs to keep more than it spends. Faulty analysis can lead to the catastrophic engineering failure we call bankruptcy."

Executives' New View of Profit

In manufacturing arenas, the executive's view of how profit is made has shifted radically since the early 1980s. In the early 1980s, recession and consumer resistance to an endless march of price hikes meant that price increases could no longer be imposed to cover up rampant increases in manufacturing costs. Consumers were too price sensitive. A new view, associated with Japanese just-in-time manufacturing leaders such as Taaichi Ohno, head of Toyota, was that in the face of price ceilings, profit could be achieved only through cost reduction.

Ohno pointed out, among other things, that in Japan the cost of labor and raw materials is about the same as in other parts of the world. The price Japan can charge for goods sold overseas is limited by competitive pressures and consumer price sensitivity. The only difference, Ohno pointed out, is in the *methods* Japanese manufacturers use within their overall process.

American business has learned that changes in process methods can simultaneously produce high quality at low cost. The old way of thinking, that high quality can be achieved only at high cost, is rapidly being replaced by the new views. Doing business on a world-class level demands nothing less.

- Old view: Selling price = Cost + Profit
  —Price could be increased to cover costs
- New view: Profit = Selling price – Cost
  —Margin hard to increase; cost must be reduced to make a profit

"American executives went to Japan by the plane load during the 1980s to learn how changes in methods and processes could help achieve both higher quality and the lower cost structures necessary to stay profitable.

"Sales process engineering will be helped by top executives' increased awareness that improved processes are a great—perhaps the best—way to increase profits. On one hand, since total cost is the sum of *necessary* plus *unnecessary* expenses, sales process engineers will help management reduce costs by eliminating unnecessary work expenses and procedures.

On the other hand, the new executive view of how to make a profit is often so focused on cost reduction that serious efforts to study and increase *sales*—which will also be part of the sales process engineer's job—may receive a lukewarm or skeptical greeting. Some executives are certain about what to do to cut costs, but much less certain about how to increase sales. This kind of reception has a chilling effect on legitimate engineering efforts aimed at a goal of systematically increasing income. Techniques aimed at increasing customer delight offer plenty of room for process improvement, but may or may not reduce internal costs. Sales enhancement requires a different mind-set than a strict cost-cutting mentality usually brings to the table.

"The day I stop receiving mailed invitations for events that took place *last* week is the day I'll know there is little room left for improvement in marketing."

Top 10 Sales Process Opportunities—Selden

Dr. Selden offers 10 concrete opportunities for sales improvement. He states that these are every bit as tangible as opportunities to cut cost.

"Where, specifically, is sales process engineering likely to increase profit? As the next few days continue, you'll be coming up with many answers to that question yourself.

"Having begged the question, I don't want to keep you in suspense. What discrete parts of the sales process might yield to a focused improvement effort? Let me suggest 10 that come to mind, in rough order of the chart I presented earlier describing a business-to-business sales process. This list is based on conversations I've had with hundreds of people who I've interacted with in my courses. I've seen these problems reflected in personal observations gained in working with my own clients over the past two decades. This list is not meant to be scientific; your opportunities may be quite different, but these are a great place to start looking.

"The first problem is marketing's failure to find and capitalize on existing information. Marketing often has more data about its customers than it realizes. It may be hidden in accounts payable, customer service, sales, and in other areas of the company. Such data can be a real gold mine if used to improve product design, track customer retention and satisfaction trends, and properly target mailings and special promotions."

In their excellent book *The One to One Future* (1993), Peppers and Rogers tell the story of a small Midwest florist who sends previous customers a postcard to remind them of approaching birthdays, what they previously ordered, and how to repeat the order.

"The second problem is insufficient qualification of leads prior to passing them on to sales. For some reason, few people in management think this is a problem, probably because, as my enthusiastic colleague Gil Cargill says, '*Round here* we've always done it this way.' [Dr. Selden sweeps his arms in a circle like a windmill.] Salespeople themselves say calling on leads straight from the typical prospect list is a waste of their time. It drives them crazy. This gets at the issue of specifications. If the quality of leads was considered as part of the specifications in the overall sales process in the same way the quality of incoming parts was in the manufacturing process, many batches of leads would be rejected outright as simply unacceptable and shipped back to the supplier at the supplier's expense.

"The third problem is the blind use of field sales personnel to perform all types of customer contact. Some salespeople do everything from literature fulfillment to technical estimation to installation to handling service calls. Is this the most cost-effective use of field salespeople? Can we off-load some of these tasks to less expensive personnel who might actually be more adept at these tasks than the field salesperson? Can we eliminate the need for some of these tasks entirely?"

"The fourth problem is the absence of presentation impact analysis. We often don't know what percentage of presentations convert into sales or opportunities to propose or to go further with a client. How can we determine if presentations need to be improved when we don't even know what their impact is? How can we determine whether a new presentation is better than a previous one? Can we quantify how adept our people are at making presentations?"

Sales Process Problems—Selden

1. Failure of marketing to find and capitalize on existing information
2. Insufficient qualification of leads prior to passing to sales
3. Blind use of field sales to perform all types of contact
4. Absence of presentation impact analysis

Top 10 Sa[illegible] Opportunities—Selden (cont'd.)

"The fift[illegible]om-ple[illegible]r [illegible] solutions re[illegible] percentage of tha[illegible] lower-than-desired qual[illegible] needs analysis results in extra co[illegible] tional information needs to be gathered la[illegible] or in the form of returns and other indices of poor customer satisfaction.

"The sixth problem is pricing policies and systems for complex items. I've seen more than one company whose salespeople set discounts on products without regard to costs, often selling goods below costs. Other approaches are so convoluted that pricing and correct configuration of complex items is susceptible to a high degree of error. In the end, we don't know how truly profitable a particular line of business is.

"The seventh problem is labor-intensive and error-prone quote and proposal generation. An industrial engineer would find, on examining this portion of the sales process, that most of the labor involved is pure motion, with almost no creative value added. This is a very expensive process, relative to the alternatives. Proposals accumulate errors made earlier in the process, just as toxins build up in the food chain.

"The eighth problem is a lack of ability to understand and adjust the sales close to true customer motivations. Not knowing why a customer might approve or reject our proposals, or who the people influencing a [illegible]ale truly are, leads to waste and lower-than-[illegible]irable ratios of proposals delivered to [illegible]osals accepted.

[illegible] ninth problem is in order process-[illegible]ng or poorly communicated order-[illegible]mation leads to mis-shipments, [illegible]k, and a host of service problems. As [illegible]ammer and Champy (1993) pointed out, this one area represents a rich opportunity for improvement. As we have seen, there are many others.

"The tenth problem is one that cuts across the entire sales process and that is perhaps the greatest of all: broken implicit and explicit service commitments. The current structure of salespeople's jobs is such that they sometimes overpromise and underdeliver. To the extent this can be prevented, companies—and the individuals who work within them—will be better able to live up to their moral obligations and the golden rule. Our sales, marketing, and customer service processes should be designed to make it a virtual certainty that we treat the customer as we ourselves would wish to be treated. We'd be head and shoulders above the competition.

"Fixing or preventing these problems represent major opportunities for sales process improvement."

Sales Process Problems—Selden (cont'd.)

5. Nonuniform and incomplete customer needs analysis
6. Pricing policies and systems for complex items
7. Labor-intensive quote and proposal generation
8. Lack of ability to understand and adjust close to true customer motivations
9. Order processing errors and waste
10. Broken implicit and explicit service commitments

The top three things customers expect from suppliers in North America, Europe, and Japan are (1) "A supplier organization that can be trusted," (2) "A salesperson who is honest," and (3) "A salesperson who keeps promises" (Corcoran et al. 1995).

Key Sales Process Questions

Dr. Selden draws the attention of the class to an illustration at the front of the room. On the big screen is a set of connected ovals representing existing disciplines that sales process engineering will draw from. He remarks that an interdisciplinary approach will be necessary to answer essential questions about the sales process. Dr. Selden points out that these disciplines are already highly respected by most top executives. It's their application to the sales process that feels somewhat new and unfamiliar.

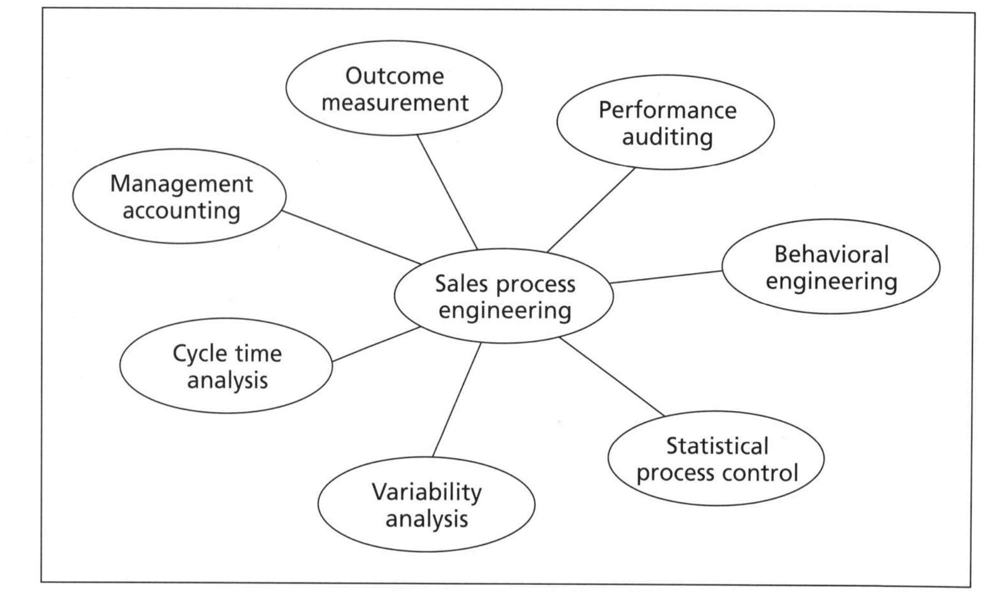

"You are away from the office and the ringing phones. You are in a meditative frame of mind.

"Look at the process flowchart you drew a moment ago. If you could ask questions of that process, and have it answer, what would you ask it? What would you need to know to really understand the process you have drawn?"

Different people in the room speak up. Dr Selden ties their questions to the disciplines connected with sales process engineering.

"*What are we producing?*"

"That is connected to disciplines associated with measurement and performance auditing. Good."

"*How much time is it taking?*"

"That is what we study using techniques associated with cycle time analysis. Excellent."

"*What does it cost?*"

"Of course. Good. That is where management accounting comes in. We'd better not go broke thinking that we are improving things."

"*Is our process producing consistent results?*"

"Ah. For someone to ask that in sales and marketing is unusual. Often all we seem to care about is whether we made quota by the end of each quarter. But consistency is important too. This is where statistical process control and variability analysis fit in.

"Allow me to put one question in the kitty myself. The importance will be clearer later. The question is, are we prompting and rewarding the desired buying and selling behaviors? We are dealing with human behavior in addition to process behavior. This is where behavioral engineering comes into play."

Key Sales Process Questions (cont'd.)

These questions seem to cut to the heart of things. I don't think our company has a handle on them. As Dr. Selden said in the beginning, the minute we acknowledge that sales is a process, we must treat the sales process as a subject for serious study.

Right now we have lots of information, but the way it's organized is not from the point of view of looking at our process as a process, from a macro-level. Our views seem to focus on the final output, in the form of fairly gross sales figures. Revenue is just one of the outputs of the process. Information having to do with customer retention, causal relationships, expenses connected with each input, and the quality of in-process outputs and inputs all seems to be lacking. We don't even know who our most profitable customers are, and why. How can we do the right thing when we don't even know when we're doing things right?

I do know we are in a constant state of fighting brush fires. We respond to problems that command our immediate attention, such as personnel problems, unusually low sales, or a request from top management or marketing to do one thing or another. We seem to be doing that kind of thing all the time. What I'm afraid of is that we're just fighting the symptoms of what may be a larger problem.

These process-oriented questions seem to be getting at the kind of information we need to make true headway. If we keep looking at the picture in the same way we've always been viewing it, we'll keep getting the same old results.

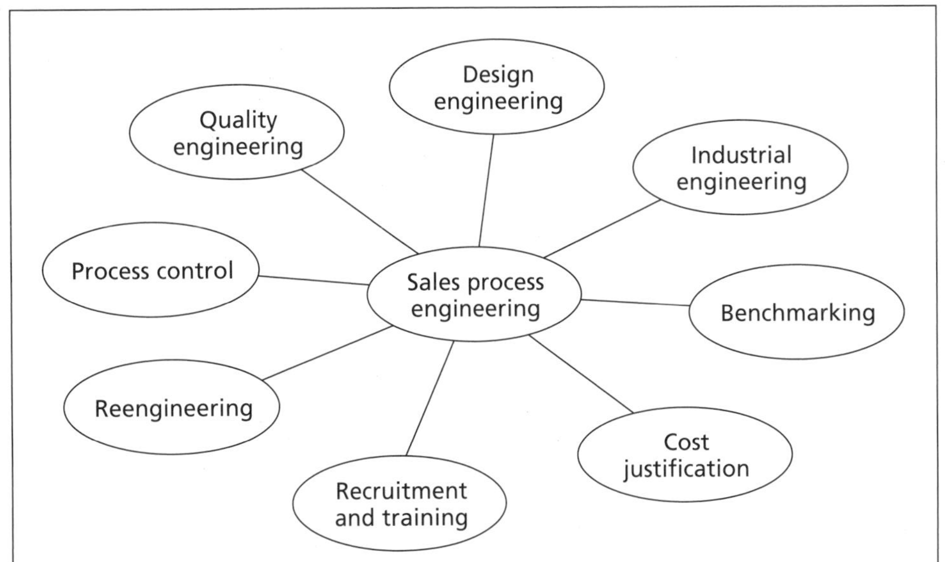

Dr. Selden puts up another illustration, showing how other disciplines relate to sales process engineering. He asks if the topics spur additional questions about the sales, marketing, and service process. A number of people seem to be receiving insights, and their questions are being voiced in an excited manner.

"Are we meeting our customer's specifications and expectations?"

"Good—quality engineering and process control can help us find out."

"Are there further ways to satisfy or delight the customer?"

"Excellent—that is what marketing and design engineering are always asking."

"Is anyone doing better than we are?"

"We'd better find out, to serve as motivation and an index of how competitive we really are. That's the province of benchmarking."

"How could we do it better?"

"Industrial engineering provides the techniques, and reengineering provides the inspiration to ask this question, too."

"Can our people do it?"

"This is where serious attention has to be given to personnel recruitment and training."

"Is it worth it to close the gap?"

"We need to study cost justification to avoid overspending on solutions."

Discrete Scope May Be Only One Available, or Best!

"To complete our overview of sales process engineering fundamentals, I'd like to point out that engineers do not always get to work on an entire process. So don't be overwhelmed by all these questions. An entire process doesn't always need total overhaul. Remember the illustration about bottlenecks! One pinpointed change may increase flow through the entire system!

"The gauge diagrammed at point D receives the entire contribution of a variety of upstream operations, from points A through D. If a sales process engineer was only given the resources to deal with the operation between points A and B, it is entirely possible that problems in operations between points B and C or C and D will prevent improvement from showing up when measured at point D. Unless the segment between A and B is the system's greatest constraint, an engineer given the ability only to affect the operation between points A and B should not be judged by the whole system's outcome at point D. This implies room for economy when setting up process gauges, as well.

"In the beginning, engineers may only have the opportunity to impact discrete portions of the process. As they are honing their skills, they must not feel bad about results that fail to appear on the bottom line. As we have discussed, unseen bottlenecks elsewhere in the process may be responsible for a lack of overall results. Therefore, an engineer charged with improving overall operating income should try to obtain the largest view of the process possible. If this is not possible for some reason, operating income may not change in spite of success in more discrete portions. However, success in discrete portions will help build confidence and encourage work on the rest of the process when that becomes possible."

Gauge and Judge Impact Where Appropriate

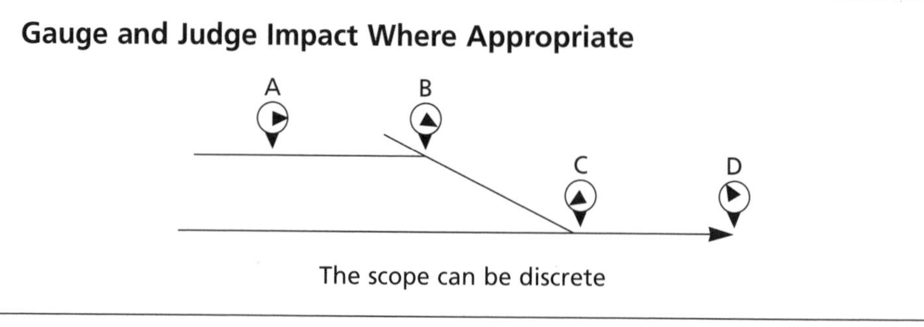

The scope can be discrete

I'm glad Dr. Selden is covering this financial information. Our company has a sales and marketing-related automation effort going. The project leaders are always saying that it should have a bottom-line effect, but I don't think I've clearly heard where it will be. I don't think I've heard which part of the sales, marketing, and customer service process it will affect or if it is aimed at the entire process.

To me, this is completing the realistic picture Dr. Selden is painting of how the top executives' view of economics fits in with sales process engineering.

Being able to speak in the same financial language as executives and the controller's office is going to make it easier to target our efforts at improvements that people will pay attention to. I had no real appreciation for how much people involved with engineering dwelt on operating income. Maybe I've over-stereotyped them as a bunch of propeller-heads, only interested in gadgets and gizmos. For some reason, the concept of engineering is striking me as more real-world than before, not some abstract effort. It's grounded in accomplishing tangible business goals.

I'm also glad Dr. Selden pointed out that working on one part of an effort doesn't mean there will be an inevitable improvement in the bottom line as a whole. After all, one manager could spend what another saves! That doesn't mean that no savings occurred!

Part 2: Solving Process Problems

Yogi: Where are you?

Joe: Some guy says to tell you I'm at the library.

Yogi: Oh, you ain't too far, just a couple of blocks. Only don't go that way, come this way.

—*Yogi Berra (on the phone to a lost Joe Garagiola)*

Objectives

By the time we finish this topic you will be able to

- Identify who in an organization can control a major source of process problems.
- List two types of variables controlling any process.
- Describe an all-purpose process improvement sequence.
- Match major problem-solving tools to stages of a process improvement effort.

Established Disciplines Agree on a Key Point

"We're going to cover established schools of thought pertaining to process engineering, translating and applying many of their commonly agreed on principles to the sales, marketing, and service arenas.

"Some of the schools of thought we'll survey include the Theory of Constraints, total quality management, just-in-time, continuous improvement, business reengineering, process analysis and management, behavioral psychology, and others. We've already touched on some of these, including the Theory of Constraints.

"As I've studied these approaches, many echo common agreement. You'll see how these threads of agreement interweave throughout the day. We must underscore one point of agreement, right from the beginning. It serves as a foundation.

"The concept is this. Within a system, only 15 percent to 20 percent of the problems found within that system are due to the performance of individuals within it. The remaining 80 percent to 85 percent of the problems are built into the very nature of the system itself. These are structural problems. This means that the majority of reps or service personnel working within the system do not have the authority or resources to change structural problems.

"Salespeople, for example, do not set list prices. They do not decide which products to add to the company's line. They do not set credit policies. They do not define their own territories. They don't create the company's four-color glossy marketing brochures. They are given these structural parameters and, for the most part, reps are told to work within them."

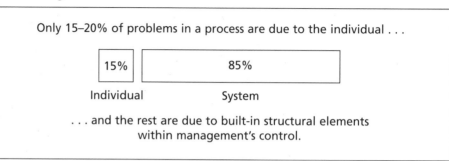

Only 15–20% of problems in a process are due to the individual . . .

15%	85%
Individual	System

. . . and the rest are due to built-in structural elements within management's control.

A sudden flash of insight washes over me. The entire emphasis of my company's training, and most of our funding to improve sales, has been focused on the behavior of individual reps. We hold them completely responsible for our sales outcomes. It's their feet we hold to the fire. I wonder how much we'd gain if we spent the same energy looking more closely at the structural elements?

In fact, it's worse than this. We ignore input from the field that we don't want to hear. Our reps, and even our truck drivers, recently told us that our company's decision to change the shape of its containers would make it harder for the customers to use and store one of our products. This input was completely ignored. Only after we lost an entire percent in market share was the original container returned.

"Structural elements are within management's control. So engineers point out that it is management's responsibility to work on structural problems built into the system. By and large, managers get the kind of results they do because of the processes on which the company is built."

The sales process engineer will almost never examine the performance of individual representatives in the same way his or her managers do—as a way to spot individuals who are "misbehaving." The sales process engineer will not be a super-manager policing the beat. The sales process engineer will, by and large, work on major structural issues. The sales process engineer will find ways to spot and remove obstacles preventing superior performance. The sales process engineer will find ways to raise the platform on which everyone can stand.

Two Types of Problems

Understanding cause and effect is at the heart of being able to improve a process. Major thinkers in the process improvement movement have identified two types of problems in a system that hold back improvement: *sporadic* and *chronic*.

Sporadic problems are like a stop sign in the middle of the road. They stand out and bring things to a halt. Sporadic problems are so obvious that existing feedback systems can detect them. Ordinary, day-to-day troubleshooting procedures can pinpoint what happened. The problem might even be fixed on the spot with some sort of emergency action. Preventive measures can often reduce the chances the problem will recur in the future.

"Process engineers speak of sporadic and chronic problems in a system. A sporadic problem is easy to see when it occurs. In marketing, an example of a sporadic cause for low attendance at an event might be that the invitations were mailed late. We can tell when this occurs. The mailing date was written on our calendar. It's staring us in the face. Troubleshooting is easy. Let's say the reason the date was missed was that the brochure was not ready in time. Immediately fixing the problem is possible: We'll send the material first class instead of bulk mail. In the end the invitations may be received earlier than otherwise. Preventing the problem in the future is easy: We'll make sure we start work on the brochure earlier. Managers spend a lot of time fighting this type of brush fire."

- Sporadic problems: feedback detects, then troubleshooting, fixing, and preventing reduces chance of recurrence
- Chronic problems: ordinary feedback not sufficient, must change very nature of process or inputs; careful diagnosis, remedy testing, and implementation needed

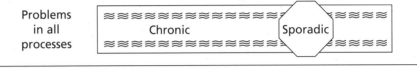

Chronic problems are built into the system itself. These are illustrated as ruts in the road. Chronic problems are so accepted as part of the way things are done that they are not usually picked up by ordinary feedback loops. For chronic problems to improve, the very nature of the system must be altered. The process or the inputs must be changed. Since such a fundamental change may lead to inadvertent disruption elsewhere, any such redesign must be well thought through. The causes of the problems experienced must be understood before one rushes in with a so-called solution. Some of the most pernicious chronic sources of process problems are *policies* that no one thinks to question. Of couse, some policies are quite essential. That is why, in the case of chronic problems, testing the remedy and its implementation must be more systematic, often due to the novelty of the attempt, the risks involved, and the need to offset any vested interests in the status quo.

"In the case of marketing efforts, chronic problems prevent us from doing better, *even once all the sporadic problems have been fixed or prevented.* Our current lineup of special events might only appeal to a limited market, no matter how great our brochures or how timely our mailings are. Thinking up new events, lining up speakers, and securing meeting rooms all take time and incur risks that must be carefully thought out. And if our entire firm was devoted to marketing just that one type of event, we might never even dream of changing what we do so in such a radical manner. Like buggy whip makers, we might watch as attendance evaporates.

"If you understand the difference between sporadic and chronic sources of problems, you'll see why people such as Michael Hammer say that in order to get radical improvement one must usually completely change the existing system, and not just tinker with it. A lot of people say Hammer is just popularizing something we already know and have already studied in more depth before. Yet his basic recognition that to get fundamental change requires getting at the chronic sources of our performance problems is correct."

Problem-Solving Tools: Juran's Sequence

"As our friend Yogi Berra showed earlier, it's important to have a sense of direction when trying to reach a destination. I promised you earlier that I'd give you a set of steps right up-front that sales process engineers can use to tackle their sales, marketing, and customer service problems. As I do so, I'll also try to identify where the specific tools we'll be learning fit into the sequence. Learning how to use process troubleshooting and improvement tools is one thing. Knowing when to use each is important, too. To a large extent, our workshop will cover the tools in the order I'm about to mention them. Those of you with a high need for structure will appreciate that. [Dr. Selden makes this last remark with a big smile on his face.]

"That said, what is a reasonable way to go about improving things? One set of well-established recommendations, that will work for either sporadic or chronic causes, has been proven time and time again. A fellow by the name of Joseph M. Juran drew this up years ago. The steps I'm about to discuss were covered in The Juran Institute's workbook series entitled "Quality Improvement Tools" (Plsek and Onnias 1989). If you ever get lost and aren't sure what to do next, turn to this set of steps. They'll help you find your way again.

"The first step is to list and prioritize your problems. It's likely you can't tackle everything at once. Assigning a priority gets the order in which you'll do things out in the open. Tools that help you do this are the flowcharting techniques we've already covered, plus brainstorming and Pareto charting.

"The second step is to define the project and the team that'll be working on it. This can be done through brainstorming and by executive decision.

"Third, you'll analyze the symptoms of the problem, trying to list the undesirable effects associated with what you're observing. Again, flowcharting and Pareto charting will come in handy here.

"Fourth, it's time to formulate theories of what is causing events to happen as they are. Ideas can be generated through brainstorming, but we'll also be using the more structured techniques associated with cause-and-effect diagramming.

Dr. Selden comments that up through step 4, individuals' opinions, ideas, and intuition play a large part in the problem-solving sequence. In steps 5–12, empirical data begin to play a much larger role.

"In the fifth step it's time to test our theories. We need to find out what is causing things to turn out as they are and see whether our hunches are correct. In step 5, flowcharting and Pareto charting still have a place, but the techniques associated with histograms, scatter plots, run charts, and even experimental design play a much greater role. We can argue all day long about what is causing things to happen, but until we test it more systematically, everything we say is just theory. In the world of reality, you can't prove something just by arguing about it. This is where the modern spirit of fact-based management comes into play.

"The tests you perform on your cause-and-effect theories will help you to isolate root causes of sales, marketing, and service problems. Lack of sales and high costs are effects, not the cause itself. So in step 6, you'll be identifying the root causes using techniques such as flowcharting, Pareto charting, histograms, and scatter plots."

Juran's 12-Step Problem-Solving Sequence

1. List and prioritize problems (flowchart, Pareto chart, brainstorm).
2. Define project and team (brainstorm, executive decision).
3. Analyze symptoms (flowchart, Pareto chart).
4. Formulate theories of causes (brainstorm, cause-and-effect diagrams).
5. Test theories (flowchart, Pareto chart, histograms, scatter plots, run charts, experimental design).
6. Identify root causes (flowchart, Pareto chart, histograms, scatter plots).

Problem-Solving Tools: Juran's Sequence (cont'd.)

"To some of you the emphasis on a fact-based approach still probably sounds a bit foreign. Powerful people in an organization often say, 'Because I say it is so, therefore it's true.' Do you know people like that? Opinion does not always equal reality, and therein lies a danger. As we've learned many times in the history of science, not only is opinion often not true, it's dangerous because it prevents more fruitful lines of inquiry.

"Relying on conventional wisdom can lead to a failure to investigate and understand how things really work. Who knows how many people were injured as a result of a failure to systematically explore the causes of malaria, prevented by fatalistic attitudes and the popular notion that it was caused by 'bad air?' How many companies suffer because a high percent of their decisions rely on similar false, untested opinions, outmoded policy, and fatalistic attitudes?"

The theory of spontaneous generation, propounded since Aristotle, held that animate beings could arise from inanimate objects. Frogs were said to spontaneously generate from river mud. Maggots were said to spontaneously generate from meat.

It wasn't until 1670 that the theory of spontaneous generation was discredited by Francesco Redi. In an elegantly simple experiment, Redi demonstrated that the maggots hatched from eggs too tiny to see. The eggs themselves were deposited in rotting, uncovered meat by flies.

Juran's 12-Step Problem-Solving Sequence (cont'd.)

7. Consider alternative solutions (flowcharts, brainstorming, cause-and-effect diagrams).
8. Design solutions and controls (flow diagrams, histograms, scatter plots, run charts, SPC).
9. Address resistance to change (brainstorming, implementation plans).
10. Implement solutions and controls.
11. Check performance (Pareto charts, histograms, run charts, SPC).
12. Monitor control system.

"Facts are important. So step 7 requires us to explore alternative solutions. The solution we've seized on as our early favorite may be more cumbersome or expensive than others we haven't explored. Flowcharts, brainstorming, and cause-and-effect diagrams can help us uncover viable alternatives.

"In step 8 we'll design our solutions and control systems to make sure they are being followed. Flowcharts, histograms, and scatter plots are useful here, but we'll also be observing the outcomes using run charts and making sure the results are holding steady by means of statistical process control (SPC) techniques. Such ideas may sound foreign, but if people with little formal education can use SPC to achieve amazing results in our factories, so can we in sales, marketing, and customer service.

"People tend to resist things they aren't familiar with, so in step 9 we'll explicitly address resistance to change. Brainstorming can help, but so can systematic implementation plans.

"In step 10 we'll implement the solutions and controls, using the techniques already discussed.

"Then, in step 11 we'll check the actual performance obtained using tools such as our Pareto charts, histograms, run charts, and SPC.

"Finally, to hold the gains we'll monitor the control systems we've set in place and adjust as needed."

Dr. Selden reiterates that he is presenting Dr. Juran's approach up-front so people don't lose sight of an overall method as they learn the more specific philosophies and tools.

Directions Can Be Helpful

Dr. Selden comments that a true master of sales process engineering will know more than just how to follow a set of step-by-step instructions in cookbook fashion. Blindly following instructions without understanding the body of knowledge behind them can be dangerous.

Yet Dr. Selden differs from some public speakers who seem to look down on people or who intimidate an audience that doesn't know the "exact" right questions to ask or who are looking for a set of steps they can use to get started.

Dr. Selden feels there is a great deal of value in being able to suggest a place to start and a general direction to head. He says that at the foundation of knowledge is the ability to discern and articulate patterns. When one person first discovers a pattern, others can follow it more easily.

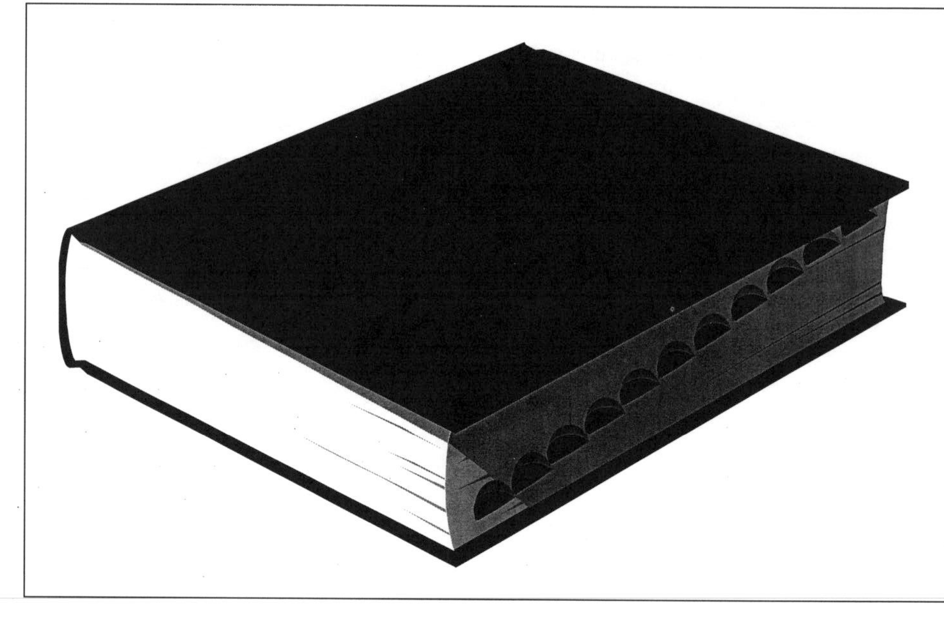

Dr. Selden Points to Further Sources

Dr. Selden comments that one of his favorite guides to the process improvement tools used at each step of Dr. Juran's 12-step problem-solving sequence is *The Memory Jogger II* (Brassard and Ritter 1994). Its handy, pocket-sized format makes it easy to carry in a briefcase or similar organizer. Another pocket-sized favorite mentioned by Dr. Selden is Thomas Pyzdek's *Pocket Guide to Quality Tools* (1994). Dr. Selden publicly thanks Diane Ritter and Tom Pyzdek for providing him with a sounding board as he was translating several of the more difficult concepts into sales, marketing, and customer service examples.

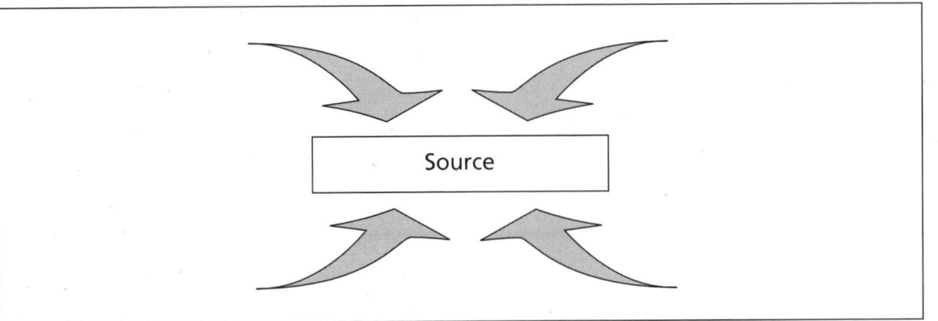

"Why am I acknowledging all these resources? Shouldn't I envy other people's knowledge? No! I'm grateful for the trail they blazed! They helped me get where I wanted to go sooner! I'm making an explicit point that bears repeating. There is already a rich literature filled with references to the tools and techniques we're covering. I'm deliberately going to teach you approaches already well proven and tested and supported by a great depth of research and reference work. Their use in sales, marketing, and service processes is just beginning, though, which makes this area all the more exciting to the early pioneers.

"I could have come up with my own terms for all these tools, or recast the language into some unique, special jargon. I won't do you the disservice. I'm not a self-improvement guru appealing to a mass audience. This is engineering we're talking about—not a 'secret' method only I have discovered! I refuse to talk down to you. More than that, I want you to be able to refer back to more complete sources when you're ready. I want you to leave here with plenty of links back to the great body of work that already exists.

"I want to give credit where credit is due! That rewards everyone for their hard work and encourages further advancement. Why do you think scientists name bugs after their discoverer? Would you want to devote your life to finding bugs unless you could name one after you? [The audience laughs at this.]

"I've done my best to translate the approaches we're about to learn into terms directly applicable to sales, marketing, and service functions. I'll warn you right off the bat that my few examples may not be enough. Give me your help in making the points. Please share your insights and examples as we go along."

Dr. Selden's approach is so unlike others in sales and marketing. So much of the literature is filled with special, "previously unknown" systems for selling claimed by some expert to be the correct way to look at things, or the seven steps to follow, with nothing other than their own experience or authority to back it up. After you've been around for a while, you learn to recognize the fragrant odor of baloney, but the constant need to filter does get annoying. I like the way Dr. Selden is linking this material to well understood and agreed-upon techniques we can learn more about on our own.

Intuition vs. Fact Finding in Process Engineering

"Before we break for lunch I want to leave you with an image that sums up the spirit of everything we've covered so far. Please listen carefully.

"Creativity is wonderful. In his book *The Dragons of Eden,* Carl Sagan (1978) wrote eloquently about how insights, formed on the creative left side of our brain, are often marvelously on target. Yet advances made by science since the 1800s have shown the need to combine creativity—the 'aha' experience achieved through insight—with the evidence that comes from showing that what you think is real. After the 'aha' we get from creativity, we need the 'I can show it' from evidence. Both are necessary."

Opinion is notoriously unreliable and misguided. In *A Mathematician Reads the Newspaper* (1995), John Allen Paulos cites predispositions we are all susceptible to, including (1) "availability error . . . a strong disposition to make judgments or evaluations in light of the first thing that comes to mind;" (2) the halo effect, which is "the tendency to judge a person or a group in terms of one salient characteristic;" and (3) the anchoring effect, which is the tendency to skew current estimates in the direction of originally mentioned numbers, however erroneous the initial figures might be. The tendency for better-informed and more skillful junior practitioners to show deference to ill-informed senior members of a group is well understood by medical doctors and aircraft pilots.

Even though some of the points made in the last 15 minutes have gone by kind of fast, this one really makes sense. Creativity is great, and we need it. But we've already got too many opinions in our company and no clear way to test their merit. Everyone has lots of ideas about what our problems are; we have no shortage of people with theories. That's good. Dr. Selden is saying that belief gives us direction. Our problem is that once the boss or some of the more vocal members of our team say, "This is the way it's going to be," we need a way to see whether that approach leaves us any better off or not. I think if someone were assigned to finding out what pays off and what doesn't, in a systematic way, we'd be further ahead in the long run. That systematic approach pays off in our product research and development area; I don't know why it wouldn't work in sales, marketing, and service.

"Let's look at specific examples of common beliefs in our profession. In sales, we're told that the way to sell is to make friends with the customer. That's probably true. But is a positive customer relationship the only thing that contributes to a sale? Is 'relationship selling' the single magic potion that will cure all ills? From all the books that have been written on that subject alone, you might think so. If we stop inquiry there, we'll lose sales when it comes time to make a complex sale involving decision makers we can't even meet.

"Let's take another 'magic bullet' theory popular in sales, namely, that salespeople must be 'consultants.' That's also true in some circumstances, especially where the customer is facing a complicated set of choices regarding product or service selection. Yet how many firms have gone to the trouble to construct a set of systematic needs analysis questions that reps must ask in order to find out customers' true needs? Sometimes it seems we're willing to mouth the words, but not as quick to engineer the structure to make the good ideas happen.

"In sales and marketing, all too often we do not move beyond talk and buzzwords. An engineer must move into a deeper exploration of what works and what doesn't, and in what quantity, and under what circumstances. Beyond the 'I think' to the 'I can show.'"

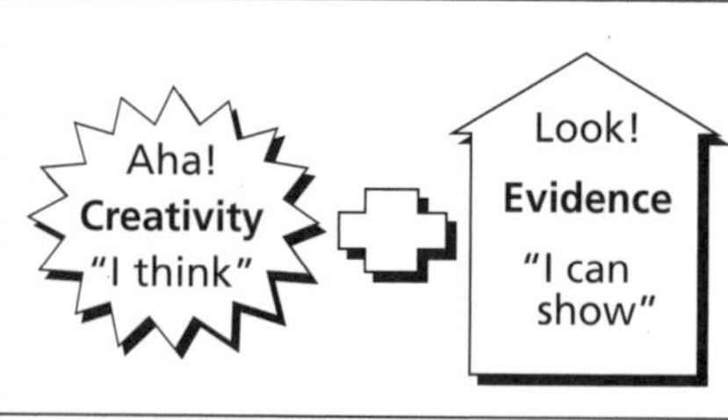

- Brainstorming and creativity are both desired and necessary when generating theories.
- From there, setting priorities and testing of theories *must* involve observations.

Noon Break

Many people are talking about the morning's session in the halls on the way to lunch. Even though the morning's session was just an overview, it has stimulated a lot of thought.

Conversations range from what companies are doing with automation to bottlenecks in the sales process to how best to raise executive awareness of the issues involved. People are remarking on the relative lack of specifications within the sales process, as compared with the emphasis on specifications for the final sales volumes desired.

The idea that sales, marketing, and service need to work together and with the rest of the company in a coordinated fashion seems to be giving people permission to look at their goals in a more cooperative fashion. The concept of over-the-wall engineering is clearly a refreshing one to the group, one they can identify with.

The illustration about bottlenecks seems to have fired the group's imagination. So has the illustration linking variables in the sales process to the income statement. Linking improvement efforts to specific financial outcomes has powerful implications.

Some of the discussion is about competition based on price, and how cost reduction is necessary to preserve margins in that scenario. There is consensus that prices can be reliably increased only by continuously developing innovative, distinctly different goods and services.

Another idea voiced is that funding for improvement efforts should be easy to find. "Just draw it from the wasted funds that are already being spent," one person says.

Some of the group members are concerned whether increasing efficiency means reducing the size of a sales force. There is genuine human concern about losing jobs as a result of improvement efforts. Others voice an implicit faith that with improvement comes greater job opportunity, not less, keeping in mind the message Dr. Selden drove home in his opening remarks. To stay competitive on a global scale in the face of a declining proportion the United States occupies compared with the world population means that everybody needs to work, and that everybody needs to be as productive as possible—achieving their full potential.

"But Everyone Is Different"

After lunch, Dr. Selden picks up several important threads from the morning's session before returning to his agenda. He remarks that the shift from intuition-based management to a balanced approach that more strongly emphasizes facts and systematic research will represent a difficult cultural transition for some firms. He wants to let the concept sink in. He asks for comments.

One individual is obviously troubled by the discussion of the need for a systematic analysis of sales as a process. The gentleman says in agitated excitement, "But how do you address the issue that in sales everybody has their own style, different personalities, their own way of doing things, and different ways of following processes? How can this be standardized?"

"The fact that people with entirely different styles and personalities can be consistently successful suggests that there is a common factor at work that is less obvious than outward appearances seem to indicate.

"I've interviewed top salespeople in a number of firms. Each differed from the other in many ways. Some were plain looking, others were attractive. Some were serious and smiled infrequently; others were more friendly. Some were older; others were younger. Some wore expensive watches. Others dressed more plainly. As you say, their styles and personalities were entirely different. The only thing they had in common is that they were all well off!

"But you know something? When I asked them all what the secret of their success was, they all said the same thing: They all did what they said they were going to do. They honored their commitments. They were methodical. Many different words describe the common factor, but it amounts to the same behaviors. Do what you say, and say what you do.

"I also asked them, from what they knew of their fellow reps, what seemed to characterize reps in the bottom 10 percent of the heap? Their remarks struck me. The top reps would laugh and say things like, 'The ones on the bottom don't get out of bed when the alarm clock rings.' 'They don't get back to customers when they say they're going to.' Again, common factors seemed evident: low rates of sales activity and failure to follow through on their commitments. Failure to stick to the plan.

"To sum up, I think standardization is already in place for the most successful reps. Some factors may not be important to standardize. In the cases I've seen, trying to standardize personalities or individual styles would not be as useful as standardizing ways to be consistent in honoring promises made to the customer or ways to support high rates of sales-related activities.

"The job of the sales process engineer is to devise systems and methods so that the useful standardization is supported and made more certain, and so that waste is reduced."

Part of the sales process engineer's job will involve devising ways to more tightly couple verbal behavior to the physical "deed," designing and building systems in such a way that they make execution of important individual behaviors much more certain. For example, systems that allow instant stock availability checking will tend to decrease the verbal behavior of promising what can't be delivered.

Focus on Structural Improvements

Another member of the group comments. She says, "Are the improvements aimed at the top 20 percent of our reps, anyway? What they are doing is working. What the bottom 20 percent of the reps are doing is not working. Their brand of individuality, or their lack of standardization, if you will, isn't helping them or the company. It seems that anything we can do for them will be better."

Dr. Selden tells a story.

"The focus of what is to be improved is important. Have you ever been in New York City or Chicago or one of the other big cities during a holiday? At each street corner there is a wall of people facing each other, just waiting for the light to change so they can cross. On one side is a solid mass of people, and on the other side, another solid mass. It seems impossible for the two groups to exchange street corners without any injuries. Yet when the light changes, everyone seems to make it through the crowd and to the other side. There's no real confusion. Collisions are rare! No one has to guide each individual as they cross. Traffic engineers don't try to intervene at that level, do they?"

The lightbulbs are really turning on for me now. Individuals make small, personal adjustments as they cross a street. Traffic engineers have devised a larger framework that supports and controls behavior more or less automatically, for the good of all. The engineers don't try to dictate whether particular people should dodge right or left as they manuever across the street. Respect for others and for the law instilled from childhood take care of the individual behavior. Police are there to take care if things really get out of hand. Engineers work at a macro level to prevent confusion and problems and to preserve public health, convenience, and well-being.

"Let's not scare ourselves into a lack of progress by thinking our focus is to erase all differences between people. That won't be possible or necessary. On the other hand, what must be more uniform—like making it more certain that people walk into intersections only when traffic clears—should be made easier to do, using curbs, lights, and signs. Our focus will be on structures that help the 80 percent perform like the top 20 percent. Our curbs, lights, and signs will likely take the form of structures such as automated teller machines, needs analysis forms, electronic order replenishment systems, and policies that let customer service reps send $2 replacement parts on their own authority without having to fill out $20 of approval request paperwork."

Another member of the audience comments. "I just wanted to support your observations about standardization with my own example. My company, a large consumer products firm, has many divisions. Each division thought it had already standardized its sales approach. In every case, each time one of the less standardized divisions has gone ahead and installed a more uniform process, its performance improved further."

Our Understanding Lags by About 200 Years

Dr. Selden is obviously excited by the group's comments. He has the kind of personality where his enthusiasm doesn't take much to ignite. He breaks into another animated story, jolting the group with his initial statement.

"The sales, marketing, and service professions lag other major disciplines by about 200 years."

That really gets my attention. Most of us, including myself, feel that we're not that bad off. We're making a living, so how can we be that far behind?

"In the late 1700s the French medical profession held a view that for each different disease, each different patient might manifest totally different symptoms, even if the cause of the disease was the same. They held that Jane's symptoms for the same disease that John had, for example, could be completely different. In this situation, where the doctors believed that everybody's situation was so different, physicians tended to treat each patient as the patient requested. The key to a physician's personal success usually lay in his bedside manner—in his relationship with the patient. At that time, the death rate in Parisian hospitals was 59 percent. Read James Burke's *The Day the Universe Changed* (1995) if you think I'm making this up.

"This approach changed when it became clear, though systematic observation and the practical use of statistics, that common symptoms often had common causes. Doctors found they could diagnose disease without even consulting patients, just by examining their urine or by listening to their heart or lungs."

The public health detectives who found the solution to the last major cholera epidemic in London used a method nearly identical to Juran's problem-solving sequence to isolate the source of the outbreak. They used comparative analysis of data to trace the source of the epidemic to a public well placed dangerously close to a septic system. In 1854, John Snow confirmed the theory that cholera was spread by contamination of food and water supplies with fecal matter. Deaths fell dramatically after he prevented the use of just one contaminated well. London controlled further outbreaks when it instituted the preventive measure of sand filters in the water supply system.

"Are there parallels to the French medical profession in the 1700s with what we practice today? Think about it. Don't many of our managers hold that conditions are so dissimilar in each sales situation that systematic study is of little use at all? Yet don't these same managers often pursue the holy grail of the single magic sales bullet? The medical profession used to go from cure to cure like that, too. Blood letting, water cures, and even walking 'barefoot in wet grass' were popular crazes in their day. We're not too far from that same stage, are we? There's room for tremendous advancement.

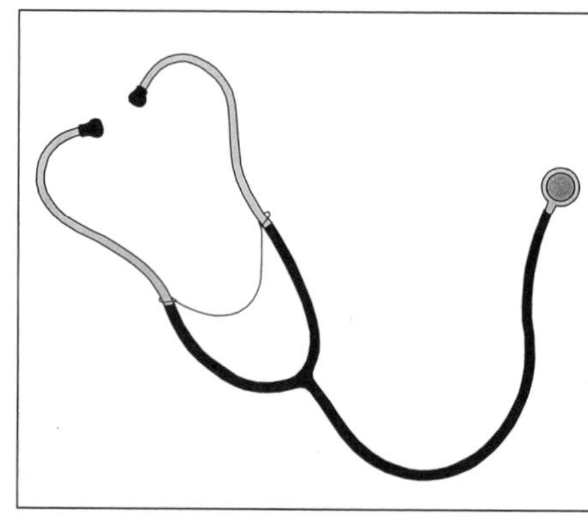

Our profession would benefit greatly just by following the physician's precept, 'First, do no harm.'

"Bankers use well-tested, simple formulas to assess a company's overall financial health prior to making a loan. Sales process engineers should be able to assess a company's sales process by using several key diagnostic tools, too. What will be our stethoscope of the future? Factories use process control stations to visualize and adjust what's happening on the line. We can too."

Part 3: Established Process Schools and Tools

> If you ask me anything I don't know, I'm not going to answer.
>
> —*Yogi Berra to a radio broadcaster before an interview*

Objectives

By the time we finish this topic you will be able to

- See how the established schools of process engineering can be applied to sales process improvement.
- Apply major problem-solving tools to practical situations.

W. Edwards Deming

W. Edwards Deming (1900–1993), author of *Out of the Crisis* (1986) and a number of books on statistics, achieved a lifetime of accomplishments. Dr. Deming received his Ph.D. in physics from Yale University. Early on, he studied with Walter A. Shewhart (inventor of statistical process control at Bell Labs). In 1940 Dr. Deming helped pioneer sampling techniques while working for the U.S. Census Bureau. In 1946 Dr. Deming left the Census Bureau to strike out on his own, opening his own consulting practice. Well-known for his understanding of how statistics can be applied in practical settings, Dr. Deming gained a reputation for his achievements in Japan following World War II where he aided in Japan's post-war reconstruction effort. His efforts had such a profound impact on the Japanese economy and their philosophy of manufacturing with quality that in 1951, the Japanese named their most prestigious award for quality after Dr. Deming, entitling it the Deming Prize.

Today Dr. Deming is remembered as someone who, for years, tried to deliver his message of quality improvement to the United States. He went largely ignored for 30 years. Interest in Dr. Deming's message awakened in the United States in the 1980s, when it became clear that his approaches and teaching had helped the Japanese establish superiority in many arenas, enabling their products to capture huge market shares in almost every field they entered.

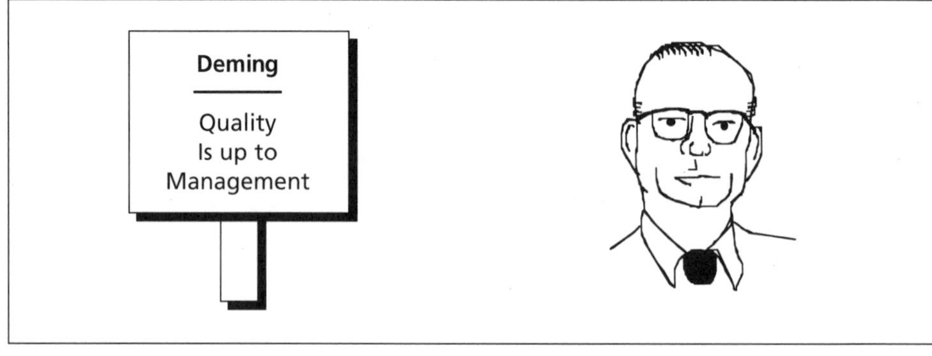

Interest in Dr. Deming's techniques and philosophies has resurfaced in the 1990s as the United States, assisted by organizations he helped found, such as ASQC, is redoubling its effort to take world leadership again.

Prior to continuing, Dr. Selden mentions to the group that the topics about to be covered will be at an overview level. Each is the subject of many books and days of coursework in its own right. He points out that he doesn't have all the answers or know all there is to know about the topics that follow and asks for people in the group to contribute to the discussion at any time. He says that he may be like Yogi Berra in that he may not be able to answer all the questions that come up, but he does promise to ask for the participants' help.

W. Edwards Deming (1900–1993)

- Author, *Out of the Crisis*
- Ph.D. in physics, Yale
- Studied with Walter A. Shewhart (SPC inventor at Bell Labs)
- 1940: Helped pioneer sampling in U.S. Census
- 1946: Left census bureau for consulting practice
- Aided post–World War II Japan reconstruction
- 1951: Deming Prize established

The PDCA Cycle

Deming is known for advocating a four-step program for improving any process, which he called the plan-do-check-act (PDCA) cycle, or Shewhart cycle (after its originator). As with many powerful approaches, the cycle is easy to describe, yet has tremendous impact when applied.

The four steps are as follows:

- ***Plan.* Study a process and think of ways it can be improved. Form a team of people associated with the process. Determine whether additional data or testing are needed.**
- ***Do.* Perform the testing or make the change. It's better to do this on a small scale first.**
- ***Check.* Observe what happens.**
- ***Act.* Determine what was learned. If needed, repeat the testing. Watch for any side effects. Act on the difference between what you expected and what occurred.**

Once the cycle has been completed, repeat it. Each time the PDCA cycle is repeated, the process is further fine-tuned. When the process finally achieves stability, shift the attention to another process.

Improving processes is a never-ending activity. In practice, the repeating cycle of PDCA is actually an upward spiral. Through each loop, the potential for improvement—elevated performance—exists. The PDCA cycle is never finished, because the market is always changing: The competition is always improving, and customer needs are always changing.

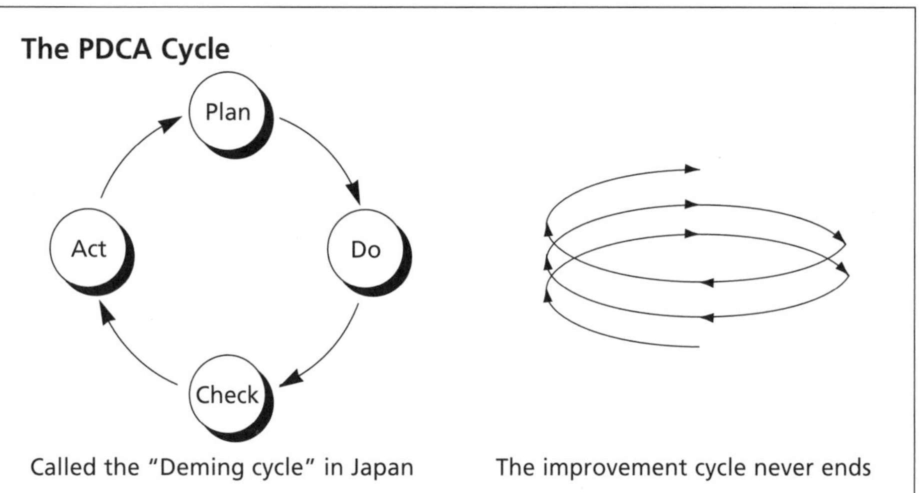

Called the "Deming cycle" in Japan

The improvement cycle never ends

"The PDCA cycle—plan, do, check, act—underlies modern efforts to improve processes, whether in terms of their quality, speed, cost, or any other important variable. Many of us think of the cycle as being so intuitively correct that we make the mistake of imagining we are following it in our approaches to sales. We are not. Look at the diagrams and think for a moment. What often seems to be missing in our current efforts?"

Dr. Selden pauses for a moment. No one responds. I raise my hand and say, with more hesitation in my voice than I care to admit, "I think we're missing the 'check' and 'act' parts of the cycle. We have lots of great plans about how we should approach customers and how our marketing programs should look and work. Our company is big on planning. We implement our plans. We aren't bad at the 'do' part. We spend a lot of money training people. Our management is aggressive at making sure our people deliver the message and coordinate our programs with our customers. But the amount of checking and acting on the difference between what we planned and what we obtained is weak. That part is all seat of the pants.

"Many times, when our results are not exactly what we'd hoped, we go into a kind of collective stupor. We sweep it under the rug as fast as we can instead of really learning from our mistakes. We're afraid to admit failure. The amount of actual thoughtful checking is almost nil, compared to the amount we spend on planning and doing. I'm not sure we even have a way to learn from what we've done." When I finish talking, I look around. People are nodding their heads in agreement.

Tool 2: Deming's 14 Points

"My outline of names and philosophies identifies Dr. Deming with the concept that an organization's quality, productivity, and competitiveness are primarily up to its management. Management controls most of the structure that determines the eventual performance outcomes. Much of upper management in the United States has been trained in what Dr. Deming's 14 points mean in manufacturing. If you can link your process improvement goals in sales, marketing, and customer service to Dr. Deming's ideas, your managers may listen to you more closely. It's a language they may already speak.

"Dr. Deming outlined a method of management. Some call the approach his 14 points and others call it his 14 obligations. Just as the other tools we are covering—such as flowcharting—address ways to solve performance problems, I am calling Deming's 14 points a tool. We need to use this tool to provide the organizational culture in which process improvement can flourish. Dr. Deming's ideas are a set of policy tools.

"As we cover the 14 points that comprise Dr. Deming's famous management method, we'll dwell on those that seem more controversial and hard to apply in the sales process. The rest we can more readily understand, so they require less discussion."

Point 1: Create constancy of purpose for the improvement of products and service.

"Even though in sales and marketing our aim may be to make money, only the U.S. Mint can do so directly. You can only do so by being innovative, through research, improvement, and constant maintenance of what is working. We must always be looking to the future, developing long-term plans and ways to stay in business."

Point 2: Adopt the new philosophy.

"Deming stressed that we need to pursue quality with a passion and with zeal. We need to fully understand that to the extent quality problems exist, we are not as productive as we think. In manufacturing it's easier to understand. If we produce 20 pieces in four hours, it seems on the surface that our productivity is five pieces per hour. We now realize that if four of the 20 pieces are bad, our true productivity is only four pieces per hour. Nowadays, manufacturers readily acknowledge that it's cheaper to increase productivity by increasing quality than by producing more pieces.

"But a funny thing happens to us in sales and marketing. We can work the math, but we don't want to accept the conclusion. We voice opinions that a salesperson 'needs' to talk with 10 prospects in order to hit the one good one, as though this ratio were an immutable law of nature.

"We often measure rep productivity in terms of sales activities per day or week. What would happen to our thinking if we counted only the amount of good outputs achieved in a period of time? To adopt the new philosophy means zealously reducing poor quality in sales and marketing. Traditional thinking locks us into the path we've always been on."

Oh boy, the implications of this would really shake us up. Our management has always held the idea that a rep should call on four prospects per day. Every time we even ask the question about whether it's better to call on four and have one good conversation or to call on three and have two good conversations, we get looked at as if we are from Mars. Management likes to hang onto the security blanket of contact counts.

1. Create constancy of purpose for improvement of products and service.
2. Adopt the new philosophy.

Deming's 14 Points (cont'd.)

Point 3: Cease dependence on mass inspection

"Rather than inspecting out bad quality, we must learn to build in quality. We may never be able to eliminate inspection entirely, but we shouldn't rely on it alone. Is this a foreign concept in sales? If we adopted this one principle alone, how much further ahead we'd be! Of 20 newly hired salespeople, we often fire two, three, or more for failing to sell up to our specifications. Deming says we should be looking to find ways to reduce this sort of harmful variation in the first place, rather than waiting for trouble to happen, then weeding out the failures."

Point 4: End the practice of awarding business on price tag alone.

"Price tags are so misleading. We should base our cost metrics on parameters related to the long-term value provided—the cost of ownership *plus* the initial purchase price—rather than simple initial purchase price. The cheapest often isn't the best bargain.

"Our salespeople must learn this principle and use it in their customer presentations. If a competitor sells Brand X for $100, and ours is sold for $110, which is cheaper? If the cost of ownership for Brand X due to its lack of reliability, shorter service life, and consumption of more expensive supplies is $50 per year more than our product, which is cheaper? After one year, Brand X costs $40 more to own. Purchasing agents at many

> 3. Cease dependence on mass inspection.
> 4. End the practice of awarding business on price tag alone.

companies have been trained to think in these terms. Our sales and marketing people need to take advantage of this knowledge. Our business focus and customer presentations need to incorporate these insights."

Dr. Selden writes an example on the board.

True cost = Initial purchase price (IPP) + Cost of ownership (COO)

Brand X = $100 (10% cheaper IPP!) + $50 (COO) = $150

Our product = $110 (more expensive?) + $0 = $110 (the real winner!)

"Let's take another example. Oftentimes, marketers place ads on the basis of a cost per reader metric alone. That's their measure of productivity. Let's say the decision is whether to spend $10,000 to reach an audience of 200,000 readers, where only 1000 of those readers has a use for the product, versus spending $2000 to reach 2000 readers, half of whom are potential consumers. Many advertising people figure that the cost per reader in the first instance is only 5 cents, versus $1 per reader in the second case. What is the real cost of reaching the true consumer?

Dr. Selden writes the math on the board to clarify this point.

Magazine A

$$\frac{\$10{,}000}{200{,}000 \text{ readers}} = \$.05 \text{ per reader}$$

(cheaper?)

Magazine B

$$\frac{\$2{,}000}{2{,}000 \text{ readers}} = \$1 \text{ per reader}$$

(a poorer deal?)

versus

Magazine A

$$\frac{\$10{,}000}{1{,}000 \text{ buyers}} = \$10 \text{ per buyer}$$

Magazine B

$$\frac{\$2{,}000}{1{,}000 \text{ buyers}} = \$2 \text{ per buyer}$$

(the real winner!)

> **Figuring long-term value also applies to the concept of the lifetime value (LTV) of a customer. Peppers and Rogers (1993) provide many illustrations of how one can use LTV to determine what type of customer is most worth pursuing—or even which is worth "firing!"**

An Electronic Edge

"Today's electronic systems can put the entire history of your company's interaction with a customer at the fingertips of the customer's purchasing agents at many progressive firms. They know your quality records, fill rates, pricing, complaint records, everything. They can compare these records with your competitor's records.

"Against this backdrop, how are you going to compete unless your systems provide similar information to your reps to allow them to be equally progressive?

"Your reps need to have everything your company has done, including complementary design work, extra engineering services, and beyond-warranty repair records—in short, everything that has value that reduces the cost of owning your products—to help present your side of the story.

"In a fact-based world your people need to be able to answer facts with facts, including historical details pertaining to the relationship that address the issue of the lifetime relationship and the true costs of doing business with a customer."

That last observation really has me thinking. An analogy just came to mind, and I can't shake it. In the Ptolemaic view of the universe, the earth was at the center of everything. Copernicus put the sun in the center. In the Newtonian view, both sun and Earth are part of a vast universe, all in motion. Our old views of selling tended to put the rep, or supplier, at the center, didn't they? There is a very strong bias now to put the customer in the most prominent position, isn't there? Is that where our view of sales process engineering will come to rest? It seems that we may come to see both supplier and customer as part of a larger universe, too.

As practiced, customers use automated systems to help suppliers live up to their best intentions to follow the golden rule. The reverse is true as well. Sad to say, the customer is not always right; some are downright dishonest.

Anyone familiar with the surveillance systems in Las Vegas and modern retail stores understands that not all customers have learned that following the golden rule is in their own best interest. In other words, a certain percentage of people cheat, lie, and steal. Some customers try to press suppliers into making one-sided deals not in the supplier's best interest.

Technology supporting the sales process from the supplier's point of view is just as essential as technology focused on supporting the customer's point of view.

Deming's 14 Points (cont'd.)

Point 5: Improve constantly and forever the system of production and service.

Dr. Deming taught that effort spent in designing the fundamental systems for delivering products and service was repaid many times over. Quality must be built in at the design stage of each important contributor: products, services, and the processes that create them. Both innovation and improvement are needed. Dr. Deming was adamant about this point, which he credited to Dr. Joseph Juran.

Point 6: Institute training and retraining.

Without proper skills, a process cannot be followed, and the money spent on structural improvements and innovations will not pay off. Dr. Deming advocated training in a systematic fashion, but only up to the point where further training had no additional benefit. Dr. Deming suggested using statistical control charting to quantitatively detect when this learning plateau occurred. Up until the point of no additional benefit, training should be continued.

"The application of Dr. Deming's sixth point in sales is obvious, and the value of sales training, per se, is well recognized. How could we further improve? Think about this. Most sales training is delivered as a one-time event. People are trained. At 5 P.M., class is over. Too often, changes in actual sales performance are not monitored following training to determine whether any impact was achieved, so remedial training cannot be a matter of course. In too many companies I've seen, sales trainers actually *resist* attempts to observe whether specific in-class training relates to changes in performance on the job! This attitude ensures an environment of continued ignorance where dodging responsibility for performance improvement is accepted as tradition. The tradition is zealously guarded. Attempts to change are openly resisted or sandbagged. In an environment such as this, the sales training that works versus the training that doesn't work can never be discovered."

Point 7: Institute leadership.

Dr. Deming places the responsibility for finding and removing barriers to improvement squarely on the shoulders of management. A leader must know the job well enough to take initiative when it is called for and must be able to create an environment in which people are willing to work together toward continuous improvement.

"Half the reps will always have a lower sales volume than the other half—and will therefore fall below the median in sales volume—by definition. A true leader must recognize that this means the real job is to improve the entire system to close the gap between high and low performers and to raise the median. Beating up those below the median is not just disrespectful—it's wasteful. How can this be leadership?"

> 5. Improve constantly and forever the system of production and service.
> 6. Institute training and retraining.
> 7. Institute leadership.

I'm afraid many of our managers wouldn't know what to do with their time if they didn't view their job as "kicking behind and taking names." Our people's opinion of management as a whole isn't that great, either, I'm afraid. It's not just at our company. The other day I was at a dinner party. The fellow I sat next to said he thought that "99 percent of American managers are 'retired in place'—not enthusiastic or engaged in their own business." I was shocked. Can that be true?

Deming's 14 Points (cont'd.)

Point 8: Drive out fear.

"Most people in sales and marketing live with the constant fear of personal failure, as an inborn trait. A personal drive to succeed is often a healthy thing. But some fear is not at all helpful. If fear prevents a person from acknowledging personal mistakes, questioning traditional approaches, or pointing out problems and bad results, valuable opportunities to improve may never surface. Blaming people makes them afraid to point out problems and opportunities for improvement. Management's job in sales, marketing, and service is to drive out this type of fear in the organization. Management must create a climate in which opportunities and problems can be openly examined, corrected, and prevented."

Another light just went on. This must be one reason why, in Japan, suggestion systems seem to work so well. In fact, I've heard that in Japan, coming up with ways to improve is not only encouraged, but expected. In sales I've seen a lot of managers shrug their shoulders when they get suggestions. They often treat ideas as mere complaints and dismiss them. How many opportunities do we waste each year in this way?

An interesting perspective on a phenomenon dubbed "organizationally induced helplessness" may be found in articles by Richard F. Kankus and Robert D. Cavalier (1995), and by Roger McGrath Jr. (1994). In their fact-filled article "Putting Fear to Flight," Beth Sulzer-Azaroff and Dwight Harshbarger (1995) discuss how positive reinforcement can be used both to improve performance and reduce fear at the same time.

Point 9: Break down barriers between staff areas.

Processes within a company cross departments. Too often these departments are suspicious and at odds with each other. A new approach, called *concurrent engineering,* brings all departments responsible for the ultimate outcome together to agree on what each must do, prior to doing it.

"Do your marketing departments consult with sales to determine the quality of leads their ads generate? How many times does sales phone in an order with incomplete information, leaving the service department to ask a customer what was meant? How often does service communicate with product design and marketing to let them know what the complaints, problems, and ideas are? Dr. Deming recommends breaking down walls between staff areas and focusing all our efforts on a unified set of goals."

Dr. Selden touched on this point earlier. If each department sets mutually agreed on specifications for its outputs based on the end goal for the entire system, it would give everyone more tangible objectives to shoot for. I wonder if our current corporate culture could support such a sharp focus?

8. Drive out fear.
9. Break down barriers between staff areas.

Deming's 14 Points (cont'd.)

Point 10: Eliminate slogans, exhortations, and targets for the workforce.

"People in sales look at Dr. Deming's recommendation to eliminate slogans, exhortations, and targets for the workforce as nonsensical. 'What could he possibly mean by this? We have to have slogans in marketing!' we say.

"In Dr. Deming's work with many industries, he found that typically, nothing of substance supported all the signs and banners proclaiming goals like 'zero defects.' In many cases, management seemed to think that just putting up a poster would somehow dramatically change results. Dr. Deming believed that most people try to do a good job already. Just being told to 'do better' is superficial, even insulting. The same goes for arbitrarily raising quotas and targets."

In sales and marketing we're used to thinking of slogans, exhortations, and targets as motivational. That's our culture. But I think I'm getting the idea. If we simply urge people to sell more without giving them the tools and structure to do so, there's no concrete reason to expect any real improvement, no matter how catchy the slogan.

Point 11: Eliminate numerical quotas.

"Of all the points Dr. Deming raised, point 11 seems to cause the most problems with sales and marketing people. The idea of eliminating numerical quotas seems so contrary to what we're used to. Let me tell you a story. You'll instantly understand.

"In the old Soviet Union, a truck factory was given a quota to produce a certain number of trucks. It did so, and was pleased to announce to the central committee that the plant met quota. The plant did not report, however, that in order to meet quota, the trucks went off the end of the line with only three wheels. Does that ever happen in sales?"

"Instantly understand" is right. Last year, my company met its very ambitious sales goals. We had a big party to celebrate. This year, we found that our victory was an illusion. Many of the orders were discounted so heavily we won't make any money on them. Others were sold to customers we're finding to be poor credit risks. Still others were mysteriously cancelled after the first of the year, and we're wondering if customers were even serious or not. In a few cases, we may be dealing with outright fraud: phony signatures, fake purchase orders. I could go on. It was a disaster. Slogans? "Anything to get the sale" seems to have been our operative slogan last year.

10. Eliminate slogans, exhortations, and targets for the workforce.
11. Eliminate numerical quotas.

Deming's 14 Points (cont'd.)

Point 12: Remove barriers to pride of workmanship.

Dr. Deming taught that people want to feel good about the quality of work they do. One of the greatest things managers can do for their people is to remove barriers that make it impossible to take natural pride in a job well done. Misguided supervisors with a "just ship it" attitude, faulty equipment, defective materials, and a poor process all conspire to rob people of dignity and pride in their work.

Point 13: Institute a vigorous program of education and retraining.

A profound humanitarian at heart, Dr. Deming believed that a company should prepare its people to perform work they may need to carry out in the future. Point 7, concerning training and retraining, has to do with providing specific job skills necessary to perform today's job. Point 13 has to do with encouraging lifelong learning and training aimed at the jobs of the future. Dr. Deming insisted that people not lose their jobs if quality improvement rendered some work unnecessary.

Point 14: Take action to accomplish the transformation.

Since processes cross departmental boundaries, Dr. Deming said that cross-functional teams need to mobilize in order to achieve results. Dr. Deming felt that change had to come from within for the results to be lasting. An outside master of the principles could assist, but the transformation had to be brought about by people inside the firm.

Dr. Deming believed it important for a broad base of people to possess the necessary process improvement tools, concepts, and skills. This would allow them to improve the system at their level and make intelligent contributions as they participated in the necessary teams. Once a critical mass was reached, the transformation could be achieved.

Above all, action must take place. It's no good just to talk about improvement. Through the four-step plan-do-check-act cycle, an organization can always be moving ahead. Without action, that won't happen.

12. Remove barriers to pride of workmanship.
13. Institute a vigorous program of education and retraining.
14. Take action to accomplish the transformation.

"As you can see, Dr. Deming's 14 points are a policy-level tool management can use to create the right climate for positive changes. The 14 points are wonderfully humane and respectful of the individuals working in the system. At the same time, they encourage a relentless pursuit of improvement."

Obstacle—Neglect of Long-Range Planning

Deming taught that there are seven "deadly diseases" afflicting modern companies. The interested reader should review excellent books such as *Four Days with Dr. Deming* (1995) by William J. Latzko and David M. Saunders and *The Deming Management Method* (1986) by Mary Walton for more detailed information about Dr. Deming's philosophy. Dr. Deming also highlighted a number of specific obstacles to transforming the culture of an organization standing in the way of improvement.

Dr. Selden continues, discussing how the obstacles might apply in the sales, marketing, and customer service arenas.

"Dr. Deming taught many important things as part of his management method. Let's cover five of the obstacles to transforming the culture of an organization before continuing our journey today.

Neglect of long-range planning and transformation.

"The top U.S. companies spend, on the average, close to 4 percent of every dollar in sales on research and development. How many of those R&D dollars are aimed at systematically improving the sales and marketing processes? How many people in sales, marketing, and customer service are trained in R&D methodologies? What dedicated department is in place to carry out the necessary cross-departmental research necessary to improve the sales process as a whole? Who is conducting the R&D that will tell us the specific factors that cause sales to happen? Do we know the extent of our poor quality? In a hypercompetitive, global economy, how much guesswork can we afford? Tradition can be a mighty expensive luxury these days.

"Companies would do well to apply the lessons they have learned in product and manufacturing process R&D to their sales, marketing, and service processes in a company. Until a structure for doing so is set in place, our efforts will be hit or miss, regardless of the glowing language we use to describe what we're doing. Hit or miss equals risk. Risk you could be sheltering is not only dumb, it's foolhardy."

My company spends money here and there on market analysis, database construction, corporate intelligence, automation, and all the rest. The budgets probably add up to millions of dollars. But it strikes me that each of the efforts marches to its own drummer.

- Neglect of long-range planning and transformation

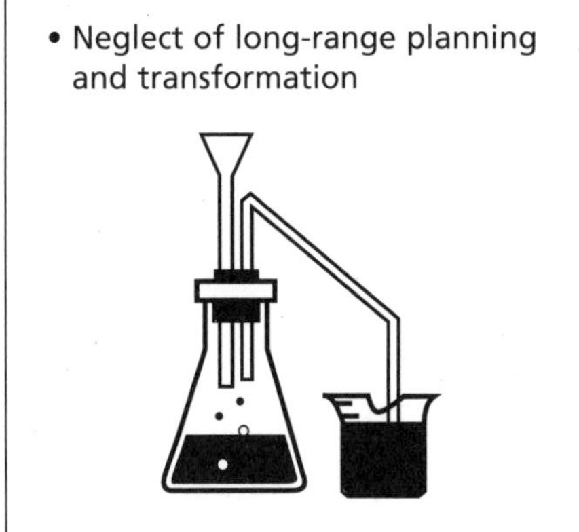

There is little or no coordination between these areas. There is no long-term game plan guiding these individuals and these projects. Dr. Selden's right about something else. Even if we wanted to create a dedicated department of sales process improvement, we really don't have a group of individuals skilled enough in the sales process engineering concepts and tools to proceed in anything resembling an orderly course of study. Maybe that's one of the long-term transformations we should be investing in.

Obstacle—Automation Will Transform Industry

- The supposition that solving problems, automation, gadgets, and new machinery will transform industry

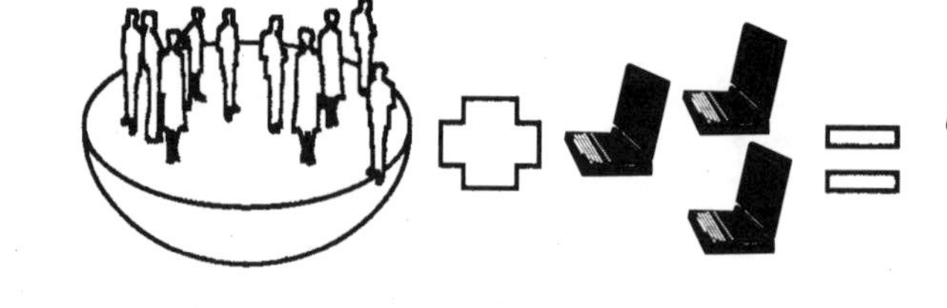

"I'll share a story with you that seems to be repeated every day. I often hear this story from people in my other workshops.

"A top executive is sitting in the first-class section of a plane. He is sitting next to a sales executive working on a laptop. The top exec asks, 'What are you working on?' They get into a conversation about the laptop and the software running on it. 'How do you like it?' the exec asks. The sales exec explains how great the e-mail is, and so forth. When the top exec gets back to the office he declares that all his sales reps shall have laptops, and he forms an automation team, telling them to get it done within two months. Sound familiar?

"Whenever I think of this story I get the visual image of people in one bowl, computers in another. Mix, shake, and stir. Instant solution. Think it's going to work? [Dr. Selden's voice rises.] No! Not without understanding the process!

"Let me relay another story. An older gentleman came up to me at a conference the other day. This gentleman was quite successful. As we talked, I came to understand that he had owned his own small business for many years, had traveled the world, and had amassed considerable wealth. A smart fellow in almost every respect—except when it came to understanding his sales process and how it related to automation. He asked me, 'What kind of automation should I get my salespeople?' I replied I couldn't tell him off the top of my head, and I asked him what part of his sales process was causing him the most trouble. He replied, 'Well, I want to know what my people are doing out there. The other day I had to go over to my rep's house and get him out of bed at 10 A.M. because he was late for an appointment.'

"I told him flat out that if he knew that kind of problem was going on with his own eyes, automation would not help him see it any better or deliver the necessary consequences for poor performance any more immediately. I suggested he hold off on automation until he was ready to enforce discipline as a manager.

"This is how most people go wrong in their sales and marketing automation programs. I just wish the mistakes weren't so costly." [A knowing murmur ripples through the audience.]

Dr. Selden is making a lot of sense. Every process is different. Even if they are following the same steps on paper, different companies have different bottlenecks. I guess you apply a tool only if it is going to relieve your own specific bottlenecks. Copying what someone else is doing is dangerous and expensive.

Obstacle—Blaming the Workforce for Problems

"Even after people say they understand the principles of process engineering, some clearly still don't get it. Even after this class, I will still hear some of you say things like, 'So the purpose of what we're doing is to help management to spot the below-average performers quicker.'

"No!

"First, the engineer is not as likely to be interested in the performance of any specific individual as in identifying and making structural changes that improve the overall output of the entire system. The top 10 opportunities for improving the sales process mainly involve things the rep on the line can't easily change. They are in management's court.

"Second, the nature of variation is such that there will always be differences in individual performance due entirely to random, natural causes. Someone will always perform below average, just by chance."

Percent of problems known by each group is estimated as follows (Mazie 1995, 102):

- **Top management: 4%**
- **Supervisors: 74%**
- **Workers: 100%**

This is striking home. We tell our salespeople to work as a team and blame them when they don't. It's our own fault.

The company's commission structure rewards them for individual behavior, and our sales contests permit only a handful of main winners. We're telling them to cooperate, but rewarding them when they compete against each other. Then we wonder why they don't share information and their most creative, successful approaches.

The same goes for telling them to cooperate between divisions and blaming them when they don't. Or telling marketing, sales, and service to cooperate with each other, and again, blaming them when they seem to behave in their own self-interest.

Obstacle—Quality by Inspection

"Too often, companies produce 100 widgets then inspect them all to weed out the bad ones. The 20 that aren't good are rejected. That leaves 80 good ones, but the money was spent to produce 100 good ones. If you build in quality from the start, the waste, rework, scrap, and warranty work associated with rejects, and the need for quality by inspection, are greatly reduced.

"By the way, Dr. Deming never said that all inspection could entirely be eliminated. Where preventive or mistake-proofing systems have not been installed and quality is below the specific standard, heavy inspection—100 percent—and sorting is a vital necessity to prevent bad products from reaching the customer.

"Here's a thought-provoking question. What is it that sales, marketing, and customer service produces? What is it that we or the customer reject? Where can we build in quality so that the number of rejects is reduced?"

Dr. Selden pauses to see if anyone has ideas. Someone says, "Customers accept or reject proposals." Another says, "Prospects accept or decline the chance to meet for a personal presentation." Another comments, "Readers accept a coupon and use it, or not." Dr. Selden is clearly excited by the participants' ideas.

"That's what we're talking about! The trick is to find what will build in the chances for acceptance from the start so that at the moment of inspection, an acceptable outcome is more likely. Traditional management can afford to say, 'Well, there's nothing we can do about it.' That's complacency! The sales process engineer cannot afford this attitude. Our job is to do something about it."

Obstacle—Inadequate Testing of Prototypes

"If ever there was an obstacle standing in the way of structural progress in sales, marketing, and service, it is the lack of adequate testing of prototypes. It may sound odd for me to place such emphasis on this, but think about it for a moment. Many companies don't even have labs in which new approaches can be tested before they are released. A top manager says, 'It looks good to me, let's go with it.' Suddenly 100 reps are the guinea pigs for an approach that is completely untested in any mature and responsible sense of the word.

"I'm not talking about the excellent market testing that some companies are well-known for. Let me give you some examples of what I'm referring to.

"We've got companies shifting their entire sales force from cross selling across an entire product line, to product category selling, to vertical market segmentation, and back again. We've got others moving from a single rep approach to team selling. Others going from a classic hierarchical, pyramidal management structure to a totally empowered, flat organization. Still others are adopting new technology. I ask you: How many companies systematically test these new approaches prior to whole-scale adoption? Testing the old way versus the new way, working out the bugs, piloting, then releasing it to the rest of the company?

"Earlier I was talking in the hallway to a gentleman from a Fortune 500 company. He has to decide which software to buy. I could tell he hadn't even determined the business goals he wanted the software to accomplish. He just wanted 'automation.' He's going to be making what I call the classic back-of-the-cereal-box comparison. 'Well, this one has X set of features, and the other has Y set,' he'll say. His analysis will have nothing to do with whether either X or Y features help him meet his company's business goals. He may never prototype against that issue at all. He'll miss the forest for the trees. The entire agenda for the discussion is which list of features is more appealing. Which 'costs less' per rep. That's the mentality.

"Prototyping shouldn't focus and test to see whether Feature X is jazzier than Feature Y. Test to see which accomplishes the goal."

"Dr. Deming speaks of other obstacles we face in transforming our way of management. Be sure to pick up a copy of one of the books I've mentioned for a more complete picture, the next time you get a chance. By the way, for those of you who want to be sales process engineers, that assignment is mandatory."

Discussion

"Before we conclude our discussion about Dr. Deming, let me ask you this. Have any of your firms already embraced the Deming approach, and what have you found?"

A woman in the audience comments. "My company has gone through the whole process in the last seven years. Overall, it has been extremely helpful. But one thing we haven't been able to do is completely drive out the fear. I'm not sure that's possible in a corporation of our size. Managers are responsible for the overall results. Managers are always under pressure."

Dr. Selden responds. "We need people to be unafraid of pointing out problems, to be able to admit mistakes. Should people be completely unafraid of doing a bad job if they know how to do the right thing, when they possess the tools, and all other conditions are proper? No. Dr. Deming asks us to drive out the kind of fear that keeps us from working effectively to improve."

A gentleman stands up. He says, "I'm from one of the Big Three automakers. In the 1980s we decided to adopt Dr. Deming's approach. It's produced excellent results. We use concurrent engineering, we've adopted a nonadversarial relationship with our unions, and we have instituted tremendous internal training efforts. I don't think we'd still be competitive if we hadn't employed Dr. Deming's management philosophy. In marketing, we're pursuing a vigorous voice of the customer approach. I'm usually surrounded by manufacturing types when we talk about Dr. Deming's principles. This discussion has given me even more ideas of how we can move ahead in sales and marketing."

The woman who first spoke continues her story. "We've gone through the Deming process, team building, knocking down barriers, and all of that. But the president of the company has a desk that sits right under an air conditioning vent. He's cold, so he asks for the thermostat to be turned up. No one has the nerve to tell him that the rest of us are sweating."

"Does that mean that the Deming process hasn't worked so far, or does it mean it hasn't gone far enough? It sounds like you'd like the fear to be reduced further and to extend to more personal matters. By the way, I'll tell everyone here how to become a millionaire. Listen closely. [Dr. Selden's voice drops to a stage whisper.] Solve the gender gap in heating and air conditioning."

My take-away from this discussion is that we need to eliminate fear, at least to the point where we're not producing three-wheeled trucks. We want to eliminate the unhealthy fear that leads salespeople to write falsified purchase orders to meet unrealistically high quotas. We need to provide a climate where people can raise, discuss, and solve problems—and work out how to take advantage of opportunities to improve—more openly than in the past.

Philip B. Crosby

Philip B. Crosby will probably best be remembered for his popular and forceful articulation of the concept that quality doesn't cost, it pays. As vice president of quality at ITT, Crosby's "Zero Defects: Do It Right the First Time" programs helped save $720 million in one year.

In 1979, coincident with the publication of his immensely popular book *Quality Is Free* (1979), Crosby struck out on his own to found Philip Crosby Associates, a consulting and training firm located in Winter Garden, Florida. Since then his firm has trained thousands of managers in "the art of making quality certain."

Crosby's work outlines a specific methodology managers can follow to make top managers aware of the financial impact of improving quality. His clear writing style and ability to turn a memorable phrase helped make Crosby one of the best known quality advocates during the 1980s.

"Crosby's ability to turn a phrase has led to a classic case of resentment and professional sniping, in my opinion. If you read between the lines, you may conclude that Deming's vehement objection to slogans stems, in part, from Crosby's memorable exhortation to "do it right the first time." I don't know if that's a fair conclusion or not. What I do know is that for a while in the 1980s, Crosby's sayings were on the lips of almost every manufacturing manager in America. Long-time proponents of process improvement, many of whom were more technically adept, had to watch in the wings while Crosby stood in the limelight during the 1980s. Professional jealousy is a reality in any field.

"Let's expose and then quickly set aside the main controversy before moving into the solid work Crosby has done. Crosby's zero defects program had a tagline, 'Do it right the first time.' Worded in the imperative voice, this phrase tends to stick in the craw. Everybody knows there are many activities that one cannot possibly do right the first time. There is no way I could sit at the piano and play Beethoven's Moonlight Sonata correctly the first time. Prototype rockets crash all the time. You have to be permitted to fail at certain activities in the short term, or attempting long-term progress is discouraged. However, the phrase does serve as a catchy target for our continuous improvement efforts.

"Now let's turn to more substantive matters associated with Philip Crosby's work."

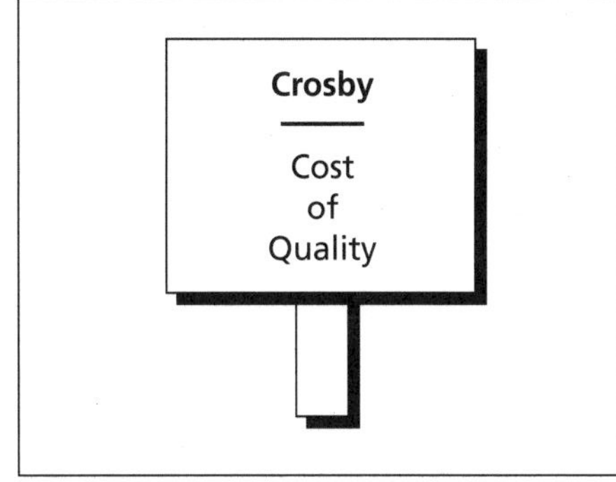

Philip B. Crosby

- Author, *Quality Is Free* and *Quality Without Tears*
- Vice president of quality at ITT—14 years
- Active as consultant since 1979
- CEO, Philip Crosby Associates Inc. in Winter Garden, Florida
- Popularizer
- Well-known for pithy sayings such as "Do it right the first time, every time"

Quality Is Free

Crosby's landmark book *Quality Is Free* (1979) contains the essential elements of his teachings, including his own 14-step instructions, complete with plenty of examples, on how to form and maintain an internal quality improvement team.

Much of the book explains and helps the reader calculate what is known as the *cost of quality*, or COQ. COQ is defined as the cost of doing things wrong. If one defines what is wrong as the lack of conformance to an agreed upon standard, an objective measure of quality becomes possible. With this definition in hand, one can begin to use accounting procedures to attach costs to quality failures, quantifying the opportunity for improvement.

The figure we'll arrive at is shocking. Crosby estimates that in manufacturing industries, 20 percent of total revenue is consumed by costs associated with doing things wrong. In service industries, he puts the figure at closer to 40 percent.

"Not too long ago, I was presenting the concept of cost of quality in a private seminar held in Chicago. I was speaking before a group of large-scale distributors of hardware goods. Their collective income from sales was in the billions of dollars. I could see them shaking their heads and talking amongst themselves as I described costs associated with poor quality. I stopped my presentation and asked, 'What are you all whispering about? Let me in on it.'

Crosby on the Cost of Quality

- Explicit instructions on forming corrective action teams: 14 steps
- Estimates that 20% of all manufacturing, 40% of service revenue spent on cost of poor quality
- Target: COQ should only be 2.5% of sales
- Points out that each $1 saved through reduction of poor quality yields $1 profit, as target approached
- "What costs money is not doing things right the first time"
- Cost of quality: failure, inspection, prevention

Someone from the group replied that they were talking about an internal study they had recently completed. The study found that 52 percent of their costs in the service area came from doing things wrong: claims, returns, allowances, and so on. Fifty-two percent. They understood the value of improving!

"Crosby says the total cost of quality should be closer to 2.5 percent of sales—not 40 percent. Why do I highlight the 40 percent? Well, we know that sales is not manufacturing. Sales, marketing, and customer service clearly possess the characteristics of a service type of operation. Interestingly enough, Deming pointed out that only 14 out of 100 jobs in the country are directly involved in making something concrete. In other words, that 40 percent figure probably applies to us."

Dr. Michael LeBeouf (1989) points out that businesses with low service quality lose 2 percent per year in market share, as contrasted with companies with high service quality, which gain 6 percent per year in market share.

"Is it better to earn a dollar or save a dollar? It's frequently better to save a dollar. A dollar saved is a dollar extra on the bottom line. If you earn a dollar, you have to subtract the cost of operations from it before it hits the bottom line. Many companies are lucky if even 10 cents of every dollar sold goes to the bottom line before taxes. What costs money is not doing things right the first time."

Typical Costs of Quality

The cost of quality (COQ) can be broken into three components: costs associated with outright failure, costs associated with inspection, and costs of preventive measures.

Failure costs are attached to things that fail to conform to requirements. Crosby points out that failure costs may include public relations, redesign, rework, scrap, warranty, service, and litigation, among others.

Costs associated with inspection include, among others, performance audits, supplier audits, receiving inspection and testing, status measurement, and reporting.

Prevention costs include, among others, planning and training, and preventive maintenance. See *Principles of Quality Costs* (Campanella 1990) for complete lists of contemporary definitions and items associated with the cost of quality.

"Costs associated with nonconformance may be considered wasteful. The aim should be to eliminate them. Quality is not just improved for its own sake. The goal is to increase profits.

"Prior to improvement, costs associated with failure can amount to 70 percent of the total cost of poor quality. That's 14 percent of sales in a company whose cost of poor quality is running at 20 percent of revenue. Returns, rejects, warranty, and service work can easily consume that much. Inspection costs in an environment such as this tend to be heavy. Inspectors and managers spend their time—and the company's money—weeding out bad parts so they don't get shipped to the customer. The costs of this appraisal type of activity can consume the other 30 percent, 6 percent of sales in a typical manufacturing firm. Frequently, little or nothing is spent on quality planning or training: less than 1 percent to 2 percent.

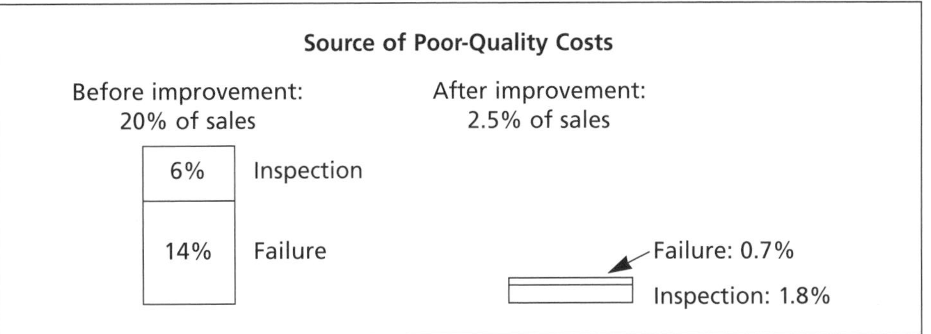

Crosby says that companies should strive to achieve a point where failure costs consume no more than 0.7 percent of sales; he allocates 1.8 percent for inspection.

"Now please don't make the same mistake some companies did in the 1980s. After hearing Crosby's lectures, some execs went back and fired all their inspectors! Need I mention that these same executives did not first improve their processes to the point where inspection was unnecessary?"

Bill Latzko (1996) cautions that cutting the cost of poor quality must be done carefully. For example, a step that looks "unessential" may in fact be necessary to preserve good customer relations and sustain sales. As with any other management accounting tool, COQ must be used properly.

"To achieve these improvements, it is necessary to invest more in prevention. Companies have often found the return on their investment in this area to be 200 percent or more, leading to a profitability increase of between 5 percent to 10 percent of sales. At these levels, the pursuit of quality becomes just as important as the pursuit of a company's main line of business."

Carlton Shuffleburger of the U.S. Postal Service (USPS 1993) reports that after the USPS improved the quality of its sales presentations, $5 million in incremental revenue came from the region using the new presentation.

Tool 3: Brainstorming

"Before we discuss how to apply Crosby's ideas in the sales process, I want to introduce another process improvement tool: brainstorming. We're familiar with brainstorming. You may have watched an experienced facilitator lead a brainstorming session. Perhaps you have already received training in this tool.

"I need to teach you how to use the brainstorming tool yourself. If you lead a sales process improvement effort, you'll use this tool over and over again.

"Brainstorming falls on the creativity side, the idea side, the 'I think' side of our earlier illustration. You can use brainstorming prior to looking for harder evidence.

"Start by picking a neutral issue in order to get the group warmed up. For example, if I asked you, 'Why won't the car start?' some of your ideas might be the following:

- The battery is dead!
- The car is out of gas!
- We're in the wrong car!
- I forgot the keys!
- There's water in the gas line!
- A piston is seized!
- There's no oil!
- I'm using the wrong key!
- There's a potato up my tail pipe!

[Laughter]

> Neutral issue: Why won't the car start?
>
> - Battery dead!
> - Out of gas!
> - In wrong car!
> - Forgot keys!
> - Water in gas line!
> - Piston seized!
> - No oil!
> - Wrong key!
> - Potato up tailpipe!

"That last one isn't so far-fetched. If any of you saw Eddie Murphy in *Beverly Hills Cop,* you know what I mean. Plugging the exhaust prevents air from being drawn into the carburetor. No go."

Brainstorming: Instructions

- Brainstorming: voicing, listing ideas in group
- No criticism permitted; no censorship
- Unconventional, wacky, outrageous ideas encouraged
- Expanding, combining, adding to ideas encouraged
- Capture many ideas in short time
- Warm up with neutral ideas and exampled of discouraging comments to avoid
- Explain issue involved clearly; use facilitator
- Analysis may be next, but is separate

Brainstorming involves voicing and listing people's ideas in a group setting. Brainstorming is a great way to capture many ideas in a short period of time. Use a facilitator. The facilitator must stay upbeat and encouraging and be diplomatic, but firm enough to prevent people from criticizing each other's ideas.

The facilitator writes down ideas using the original wording as much as possible. Flip charts, white boards, or computer projection systems may be used. Computer projection makes it easier to sort and communicate later on, as do white boards with built-in copy systems.

As mentioned previously, the facilitator should warm up the group with a neutral idea or issue.

Then the facilitator should explain the pertinent issue in clear terms so that everyone understands what is being asked of him or her.

Criticism of ideas is not permitted—no censorship. The facilitator must remind the group that snide remarks or judging an idea are forbidden.

The facilitator should present examples of discouraging comments the group should avoid making, such as "That's ridiculous" or "That will never work."

Unconventional, wacky, wild, and outrageous ideas are encouraged. Things people never thought of before may lead to a solution or breakthrough.

Expanding on other people's ideas, combining two or more ideas, and adding to ideas is encouraged. People often say, "My idea was already taken." Encourage people to put a new twist on things or to repeat an idea already offered in a different way.

To encourage ideas from group members who may be shy, a valid approach is to ask everyone, in turn, for one idea. The facilitator requests ideas until all have been written down.

Analysis of people's ideas may be a next step, but it is a separate step. Do not try to filter ideas during the brainstorming portion of the session. Save that for later.

Checkpoint: Brainstorming

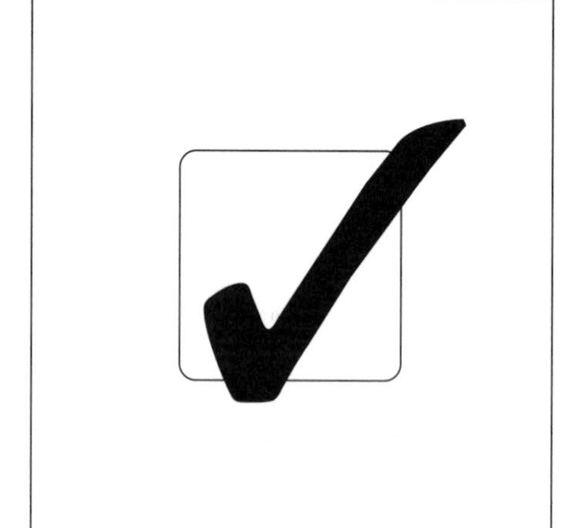

"Let's see whether this is making sense. I'd like your input as to whether these concepts can be applied to your own practical situation.

"First, I want to call a volunteer from the audience to be the facilitator for a brainstorming session. This will warm us up for Exercise Two, where I'll find out whether you can apply some of the concepts we've learned—and how clear my explanations have been!"

Pete, a manager of a sales improvement project spanning many divisions, volunteers. Dr. Selden privately coaches him for a few minutes and asks the audience to give Pete a hand for volunteering.

Pete introduces the group to the brainstorming session, starting with a neutral topic, as coached. Pete says, "A burglar alarm went off in a house. What may have caused it?" The group offers a variety of ideas.

- **Short in the wire**
- **Burglar in the house**
- **Cat walked through the infrared beam**
- **Lightning set it off**
- **Forgot the code**
- **Didn't know alarm was on**

At this point Pete calls on one of the participants who was obviously wanting to say something. The participant says the idea he had was already chosen. Pete encourages him to build on that idea and maybe put a twist on it.

The participant replies in a rush of thought, "Well, maybe the owner accidently put in the wrong code, or a baseball broke the window, or the power went off and set off a low-battery alarm."

At this point the audience breaks out in smiles. With the right atmosphere, the ideas can really pour out.

Brainstorming Applications of Dr. Deming's Ideas

Dr. Selden asks the group to applaud Pete's work as a facilitator and asks for another volunteer. Joan, an information systems director for a medical supply firm, steps up. Dr. Selden asks for the audience to applaud. He coaches her in the next formal exercise.

Joan introduces the exercise, asking the group to brainstorm how Dr. Deming's 14-point program could be applied in sales and marketing. The group has no trouble coming up with ideas.

"The principle about eliminating numerical quotas—you've got to drive by quality, not just getting the box out the door. It's got to be a combination. When they are desperate, our people will sell anything just to make their numbers, whether the customer really needs it or not."

"Everything applies here—but especially Deming's principle about creating constancy of purpose. Our departments seem to have their own agendas, and I don't think we're all aimed at the same thing. Sales will sell to make its numbers, but that sometimes puts an extra burden on customer service if the wrong products are sold. We should have a more unified view, probably aimed at overall profitability and growth, not just at the top line."

"I think we undertrain our people on concepts related to quality. For example, sales presentations are a big thing in my company. I don't think anyone in marketing or sales pays real attention to the results of our presentations to see whether one presentation is better than another, or to see whether the group needs more training in presentation delivery."

"The point regarding breaking down the barriers between staff areas really hits home with me. Communication between design and sales is very poor. If sales knows what customers like or don't like, why do we have to wait until we see customer service problems before anyone seems to notice? We should be more proactive."

"Driving out fear hits home with me. In my company we have so much fingerpointing, fanny covering, and blame dodging it's a miracle anything gets done at all. If sales reps don't make their numbers, they blame marketing. If a marketing campaign doesn't work, marketing blames sales. Service blames everyone else for the complaints they get, but secretly I don't think they want a solution because problems are job security for them."

Additional Brainstorming Exercise

- Management obstacles
- Cost of quality

Brainstorming the Cost of (Poor) Quality

Many ideas were generated with that last exercise. Dr. Selden now asks the group to applaud Joan's work as a facilitator, asking for another volunteer. Don, a vice president of marketing and sales for a well-known insurance company, comes forward. The audience, obviously enjoying itself, applauds him spontaneously. Dr. Selden prepares Don for his role.

Don asks the group members to think of specific costs entailed by poor quality in particular parts of their entire sales process. He stresses the need to suggest and guess at specific numerical amounts such as dollars or in percentages. After some hesitation, again, the ideas pour out rapidly.

"Not knowing customer contract pricing is probably costing us about 20 percent of our total customer service labor, with having to look up pricing and in correcting misapplied pricing. I have no idea what the cost is in customer dissatisfaction, but it's there, too."

"Order entry errors cost my company the service of one full-time person. With all expenses figured in, I bet that's $40,000 to $50,000 per year."

"Our sales people don't always follow up on issues that arise after the sale. I think that results in about 50 percent of our total order cancellation rate. That maybe adds up to $500,000 per year."

Typical Cost of (Poor) Quality as Percent of Sales

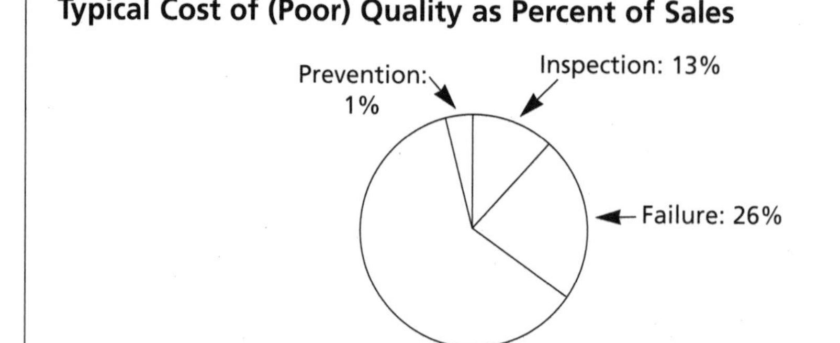

"Our salespeople probably fail to pursue at least 10 percent to 20 percent of the sales leads they are given. Assuming their judgment not to follow up leads is at least half justified, that still leaves a gap of 5 percent to 10 percent in potential sales revenue that we're missing."

"Our failure to find out a customer's true needs early on probably results in wasting about 30 percent of the total customer follow-up time we expend after our first presentation."

"In my company, failing to find customers' true needs is costing us about $5000 in service calls to reinstall and change the complex equipment they order on every third order we sell."

Dr. Selden offers a personal example, saying he is illustrating the need for leaders to model frank objectivity in their own business matters.

"We probably waste about $500 in postage and labor to purge and correct bad addresses on every $2500 we spend on mass mailing, overall. Not only that, our last mailing went out late. We probably lost revenue because people weren't able to schedule the workshop at the last minute. If my own fear of criticism wasn't driven out, I might not be as open to hearing about or dealing with such problems."

Guesses Can Be a First Step

"Do you see what we've done? This is very exciting. In the last few minutes, we created some guesses about how our sales process is performing.

"Brainstorming is an excellent way to generate an initial set of ideas about where to begin your sales process improvement and engineering efforts. In the absence of more concrete data, brainstorming gives you a place to start. You'll find more specific answers through inquiry, as you move from the 'I think' to the 'I can show.'"

Dr. Selden draws another diagram, using a few of the figures participants have provided to illustrate how poor quality affects the process.

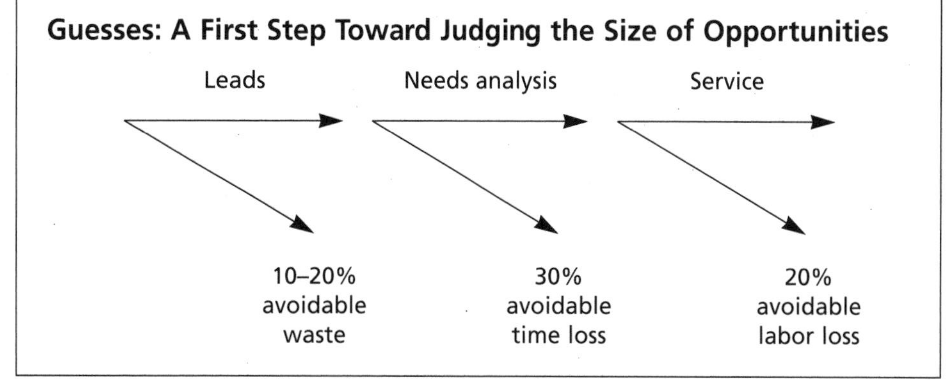

"In this view of the sales process, we can see how you've applied your theories or hypotheses about where your process is failing to perform to specific parts of the sales process. Quantification underscores the magnitude of our opportunities to improve. Graphing where the losses occur makes them even more tangible."

Afternoon break is called.

Thoughts on Deming and Crosby

I think I'm getting the drift of this. Some of Dr. Deming's ideas are going to take a while to sink in, but I'm glad we covered them. I know they are important, and I can see how they can help management set the right climate for improvement.

Crosby's concepts really make a lot of sense to me. I guess what Dr. Selden was saying before break was that before an idea is confirmed, all it can be is an assumption. But ideas give you a place to start. Whether a true number is 5 percent, 10 percent, or 20 percent, $200,000 or $1,500,000 in the beginning, I don't think it matters so much. Just being specific could give us a place to start, and it could put us in the frame of mind to confirm our assumptions or hypotheses in a more specific way.

The motivation is very clear. We're pursuing a hidden pot of gold, buried in our organizations in the form of waste, poor quality, and a host of other opportunities.

Process Analysis and Management Basics

Dr. H. James Harrington spent 40 years with IBM prior to starting his own firm. He has served as chairman of the board for ASQC and is currently the international quality advisor for Ernst & Young, LLP.

"Jim Harrington is someone I would call a consultant's consultant. If you haven't got his book *Business Process Improvement* (1991), I suggest you get it. The book summarizes a lifetime of experience."

H. James Harrington   Eugene H. Melan

Eugene H. Melan worked for many years at IBM prior to becoming a visiting associate professor of business at Marist College. His book *Process Management* (1993) was one of the first of the contemporary works to survey techniques associated with process analysis from a business point of view.

Process Analysis and Management Basics

- *Business Process Improvement*[SM]—James Harrington
- *Process Management*—Eugene Melan

Harrington's Objectives of Business Process Improvement

Dr. Harrington suggests that we should be interested in three different measures.

• Effectiveness: producing desired results. This was discussed earlier in terms of meeting specifications.

• Efficiency: minimizing the resources used to achieve those results. Earlier, this was discussed in terms of reducing costs and improving cycle time.

• Adaptability: increasing the ability to meet changing customer and business needs. This refers to the ability of an organization to be flexible and quick to change methods that may have been very effective and efficient in their day, but are no longer meeting customers' needs.

Engineers stuck for places to look for opportunities to improve can use lists such as provided by Dr. Harrington as self-explanatory idea starters. Ultimately, all might be important, but some efforts may justifiably focus on one or two.

Objectives

- Increase effectiveness—producing desired results
- Increased efficiency—minimizing resources
- Increase adaptability—increasing ability to meet changing customer and business needs

Effectiveness Measures

- Appearance
- Timeliness
- Accuracy
- Performance
- Reliability
- Usability
- Serviceability
- Durability
- Cost
- Responsiveness
- Adaptability
- Dependability

(Harrington 1991)

Efficiency Measures

Value added is the difference between the original cost of an item and what it is now worth to the customer. From the customer's perspective, the only real value added (sometimes abbreviated RVA) is the cost or time it takes to perform just those activities essential to the production of what has been specified or expected. Storage, time spent waiting, and transportation, for example, usually do not contribute to actual value from the customer's perspective and should be minimized. Customers don't want to pay for a supplier's inefficiency.

Harrington reports that non–value-added activities often consume 95 percent of the total cycle time in production. World-class operations regularly reduce non–value-added cycle time to 10 percent or less of the total cycle time.

"About seven years ago, the vice president of information systems at a very large Detroit bearing manufacturer told me that prior to improvement, one of its bearings could 'sit' for an entire year in storage. The average time to make that product, sell it, and ship it, combined, was less than a day. Wait time is one of the most costly items in any process."

Efficiency Measures

- Processing time, cycle time
- Resources expended per unit output
- Value-added cost per unit of output
- Percentage of value-added time
- Poor-quality cost
- Wait time per unit

(Harrington 1991)

Adaptability Measures

"Effectiveness and efficiency more or less speak for themselves. Why should we be interested in adaptability?"

Dr. Harrington looks for opportunities to improve adaptability in measures such as

- **Time to process special requests**
- **Percent of special requests turned down**
- **Percent of time special requests are escalated**

Adaptability, as defined by Dr. Harrington, is a measure of an organization's flexibility and ability to respond to situations that are out of the ordinary.

In the sales context we might think of "special requests" as special orders or special customer requirements that vary significantly from the average. The longer it takes to process special orders, or if special needs cannot be met and orders get turned away, to that extent the process is less adaptable.

The "percent of time special requests are escalated" is defined as how often the initial person discussing matters with a customer must refer the customer to other departments or to management for resolution. An organization that empowers the individual at the initial point of customer contact with the ability and tools to address customer needs directly is more adaptable than one that does not.

I'm trying not to be overwhelmed by this list of measures. We can pick and choose what we need. In fact, the list is inspiring me that we can measure things we didn't consider to be measurable before. Sometimes I think that because we don't have data-based sensors on items in our sales process, personal opinion and survey results become our de facto, prevailing sensor. I'm becoming less happy with those traditional sorts of measures the more I think about them.

> **Adaptability Measures**
> - Time to process special requests
> - Percent of special requests turned down
> - Percent of time special requests are escalated
>
> (Harrington 1991)

How to Measure

Since much of sales, marketing, and customer service involves human behavior, sales process engineers should become familiar with techniques for behavioral measurement. Measurement is a necessary step in moving from "I think" to "I can show." Books by Brown (1982), Connellan (1978), Gilbert (1978), and Miller (1978) discuss many behavioral measurement techniques in a simple, clear manner.

Although he is not a behavioral psychologist, Dr. Harrington devotes much of his book *Business Process Improvement* (1991) to issues related to measurement. Since this is such an important subject, a brief summary is in order while Harrington's work is being discussed. Harrington discusses these techniques as related to cycle time, but they are applicable to many types of other measures, as well (see especially pp. 124–125).

Process End Point

The outputs of a sales process, such as invoices, receipts, register tallies, inventory counts, and so forth, can be measured.

Controlled Experimentation

Discrete samples can be tracked and studied as they make their way through a process. One of the most clever and amusing examples of this technique is told when an industrial engineer became frustrated by top management's skepticism of the time-motion data he was turning in to the company's order processing department. To break through management's refusal to understand in a light-hearted way, the engineer persuaded a vice president to pin an order to his necktie and physically walk the order through the process. The VP's skepticism turned to enlightenment as he found himself shuffled back and forth between all the individuals handling the order and as he waited for long time periods at each station!

Historical Research

Company plans, announcements, and data already collected can be used to compare intended results versus actual outcomes.

Scientific Analysis

In many cases it will be necessary to break the process into major components, or operations, to understand where difficulties and opportunities for improvement can be found. It may be necessary to measure inputs to a process and to develop measures of what is happening inside a process, as well.

How to Measure

- At process end point
  - —Outputs
- Controlled experimentation
  - —Following trail of sample through process
- Historical research
  - —Plans, announcements
- Scientific analysis
  - —Breakdown by component

The Importance of Visual Representation

"I like this chart from Harrington because it tells what might otherwise be a complicated story in an elegant, graphical fashion. You might be able to use a chart like this in support of your efforts.

"The vertical axis shows the cost of placing an order for office supplies in dollars. That's right, it costs this company almost $600 to order what might only be a $25 item!

"The horizontal axis shows the cycle time it took for each step to be performed. From the time the user recognized a need for the typical office supply item, it took close to 37 days to receive it.

"The biggest cost was in finding suppliers; the biggest delays were at the requisitioning, ordering, and receiving stages.

"You might try charting aspects of your sales process in this fashion and see what you find. The visual impact of how your sales process is performing can be a powerful persuader."

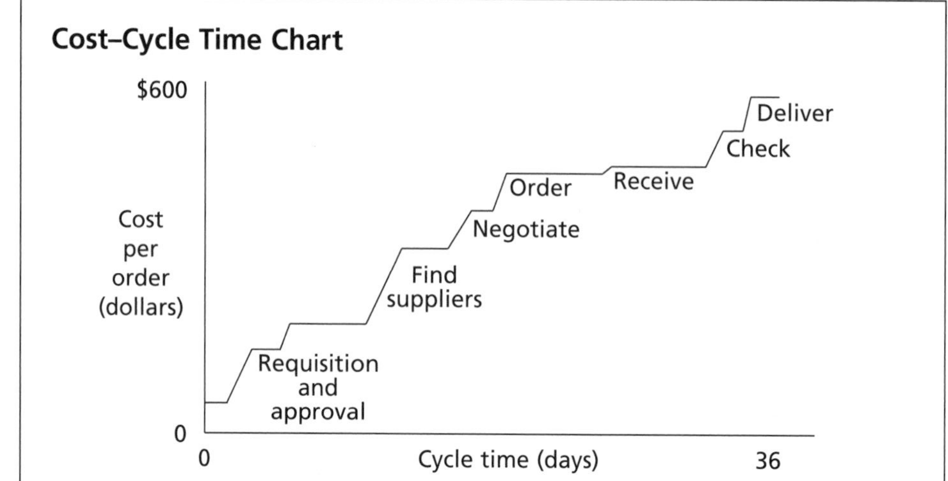

Source: H. James Harrington, *Business Process Improvement* (New York: McGraw-Hill), 1991. Used with permission of The McGraw-Hill Companies.

Selecting a Process to Improve

"The decision of which process to improve, once measurements have been taken, is not a trivial one. A number of factors enter into the ultimate decision. To my knowledge there is no universally agreed-on method for simplifying the choices.

"Dr. Harrington suggests making the decision at the executive level, based on a number of factors. To quote him,

- Customer impact: How much does the customer care?
- Changeability index: Can you fix it?
- Performance status: How broken is it?
- Business impact: How important is it to the business?
- Work impact: What resources are available?

"Believe me, I'm not trying to confuse you with a long list of potential measures and choices. Dr. Harrington offers one of the clearest descriptions of how to tackle the issue of 'Where do I begin?' It's important that you understand the alternatives."

Prioritizing Opportunities to Improve

- Customer impact: How much does the customer care?
- Ease of changing: Can you fix it?
- Current performance: How bad is it?
- Business impact: How important is it to us?
- Resources: What will it take to improve

(Harrington 1991)

This is setting off another round of reflection as I listen. My company uses a rational approach to decision making in some cases, but I think a lot of the time the manager with the strongest feelings about an issue wins the argument. Knowing that there are dimensions we can apply to process improvement decisions is a step forward for me.

In my company, the most rational approach we've used in the past has been to divide a page on a flip chart in half, list the "pros" involved in the decision on one side and the "cons" on the other. That approach seems to rely heavily on a consensus management approach. Consensus may be okay in some fields, but I like this emphasis on a systematic approach to gathering facts.

Different process engineers address the issue of prioritization in different ways. For example, proponents of just-in-time suggest looking for obvious process bottlenecks. In *Theory of Constraints*, Eliyahu M. Goldratt (1990) advocates reviewing system constraints in a larger context, even to the extent of viewing management policies as a potential constraint.

Process Selection—Melan

Melan suggests using one or more of the following criteria to decide which business process to improve.

- **Management judgment and preference**
- **Customer complaints**
- **Employee complaints**
- **Perceived importance and criticality**
- **Effect on customer satisfaction**
- **Random selection**
- **Process size and cost (Melan 1993, 150)**

"Melan's list of process selection approaches is fairly self-explanatory. Certainly, management judgment plays a part. The second and third items on the list are important, too. What customers and employees have to say is certainly an excellent source of input. The comment about random selection makes sense if no other more pressing factor is present. Many decisions have no right answer in an absolute sense or are unanswerable due to a lack of perfect knowledge. I suppose they might just as well be made by flipping a coin. At least forward motion occurs.

"I think the future holds other, more systematic approaches for us. After all, if we can draw a picture of a wavy pipeline, why can't we use a tool such as that, or others still more quantitative and compelling, to help us make decisions about what is happening and what needs to be improved in a process?"

That's a tool I wish we had now: some sort of combination of diagrams and measurements that could tell us what we need to improve and that avoids subobtimizing or making one part of the process better at the expense of the others.

Process Selection—Melan

- Management judgment and preference
- Customer complaints
- Employee complaints
- Perceived importance and criticality
- Effect on customer satisfaction
- Random selection
- Process size and cost

(Melan 1993)

AT&T's Pareto Priority Index

Dr. Selden writes a formula on the white board. He urges the participants to write it down, saying it is not part of the regular course materials.

"I think the future of sales process engineering has to lie in the direction of more precise quantitative analysis and decision-making tools. Historically, that's simply how disciplines progress, whether we like it or not.

"The formula I've written on the board, drawn from Juran and Gryna's excellent book *Quality Planning and Analysis* (1993), is a step in the direction of more quantitative tools. The formula is easy to work through once you understand what it means. Apparently, AT&T has used this approach for many years.

"Simply put, the Pareto priority index (PPI) multiplies the savings anticipated from a project by the chance that it will be successful. This number is divided by the figure obtained when multiplying the project's total cost by the number of years it will take to implement. The word *Pareto* is used to describe the procedure of ranking the scores from greatest to least.

$$\text{PPI} = \frac{\text{Savings} \times \text{Probability of success}}{\text{Cost} \times \text{Time to complete (years)}}$$

"Let's say we have two sales process improvement efforts that we're sure will yield a savings because each is focused on relieving bottlenecks of roughly equal concern.

"Project A, an approach to improve the speed and accuracy with which proposals are generated, should yield a savings of $100,000, have a probability of success of 80 percent, a cost to implement of $40,000, and a time to implement of one year.

"Project B, an approach to improve order entry speed and accuracy, is projected to yield a savings of $200,000, have a probability of success of 60 percent, a cost to implement of $100,000, and a time to implement of a year and a half.

"Working through the equations, Project A has a PPI of 2.0 and Project B has a PPI of 0.8. If only one project could be carried out at a time, Project A should be selected first. Just watch out so this whole exercise doesn't result in suboptimization.

"The PPI provides us with a consistent yardstick that combines qualitative and quantitative dimensions. Whether or not the PPI formula is the 'best' way to look at things is almost secondary at this stage of our profession. The fact that such a formula forces you to openly examine issues concerning payback, cost, timing, and the chances of success is even more important."

Shigeo Shingo

Shigeo Shingo (1909–1990) was one of the great contributors to engineering. Trained as a mechanical engineer, his ideas and techniques influenced industrial, quality, and process engineering worldwide, especially in the manufacturing and assembly-related industries where he spent so much of his life.

Dr. Shingo had the genius for being able to look at a mechanical operation and, within a few minutes, figure out a way to improve it greatly at very little cost—"mistake-proofing" it. An example of this concept in action is the familiar stop attached to a depth gauge on a drill press to physically prevent drilling too deeply. Shingo's many books, including *Zero Quality Control* (1986), contain hundreds of well-illustrated examples of such mistake-proofing (in Japanese, *poka-yoke*) devices. His other great contribution is in the area known as *single-minute exchange of die* (SMED).

A practical man, Dr. Shingo once said there were many types of engineers, but only one amounted to anything: the improvement engineer who got things done. The other types were either busy in meetings talking about problems (the table engineer), looking through catalogs for pre-fab solutions to problems (the catalog engineer), or saying no to potential solutions (the nyet engineer).

Relatively unsung in western circles, Dr. Shingo's influence among those "in the know" is great. Awarding Shingo an honorary doctorate, the University of Utah's School of Management established the Shingo Prize for Manufacturing Excellence in his honor. Dr. Shingo has been credited for co-inventing Toyota's JIT production system and for developing a revolutionary system for flexible manufacturing changeovers (SMED).

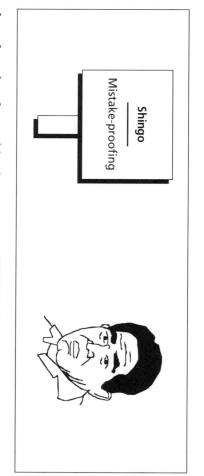

SMED

In stamping presses, changing a die from one to another used to take up to 36 hours. In the meantime, the line was stopped. Production income was lost. Dr. Shingo figured a way to execute die changes in less than a minute. The techniques are available to anyone reading his books.

In sales, the principles underlying the SMED technique can be applied in a variety of changeover situations: reps changing territories; new product orientations; the time it takes new reps to come up to speed, react to competitive product introductions, react to negative publicity—anything that requires a change in direction. Modern sales automation, coupled with the principles of SMED, could revolutionize contemporary sales process engineering. As a case in point, Gary Engle from John Fluke Manufacturing has said, "We were able to demonstrate with this data-based sales information, when a salesperson left the company we had dramatically reduced turnover lag time from six months to just one week" (Fleschner 1993).

Shigeo Shingo (1909–1990)

- Author, *Zero Quality Control,* many others
- Co-inventor of JIT at Toyota
- Mechanical engineer
- Responsible for many technical and conceptual breakthroughs
- Best known for mistake-proofing (poka-yoke) and single-minute exchange of die (SMED) techniques

Zero Quality Control

"Shingo's ideas are tremendously important to us in sales, marketing, and customer service. In the next few minutes I'd like to share with you some of the underlying rationale—that took him decades to realize and articulate—before I describe more about his poka-yoke techniques. Shingo's ideas also show how, at the philosophical level, many of these engineers like to challenge each other's thinking.

"What does this phrase *zero quality control* mean? It almost sounds like a bad translation, after all the work that has been done in the name of quality control.

"Shingo observed that companies adapting quality control philosophies seemed to emphasize inspection of results as a way to tell whether the system was functioning properly. Goods would be produced, and, through sampling-based inspection techniques, the proportion of those goods meeting specification was determined. Out-of-specification products were found. Statistics were used to make predictions about what the rest of a batch looked like.

"Shingo challenged the wisdom of practicing quality control at this level. In essence, he asked, 'With this approach, aren't a certain number of errors still going to make it through the system? Aren't you almost viewing a certain number of errors as inevitable, even acceptable?'

Doing Away with Quality "Control"

- Quality control
  - —Emphasis on inspection
  - —Use of sampling to facilitate inspection
  - —Statistics used to generalize back to population
  - —Errors still get through, almost accepted as inevitable
- Major shortcomings of quality control
  - —If error is found, still requires fixing
  - —Internal or external, price of fixing is high
- Solution: Eliminate need for quality control via 100% source inspection or automatic prevention of the cause of the defect

"To Dr. Shingo, the old quality control approach fell short. If errors are found, they still must be fixed. Whether caught before or after they reach the customer, the cost of fixing errors is much more than the cost of doing things right.

"A colleague, Kathy Barton, who works for General Electric, once commented that GE had found the cost of correcting mistakes to be some 10 times the cost of doing things correctly in the first place. This isn't surprising. Just consider what it costs to bring back a customer after you've lost him or her to the competition.

"Shingo's solution was to eliminate the need for this type of quality control—to reduce it to zero—by instituting techniques for automatically inspecting 100 percent of the parts under construction at the source of their initial construction or assembly and by automatically preventing the defect from occurring. He called this type of inspection *100 percent source inspection* and he called this type of prevention technique *mistake-proofing*. Whether you can replace quality control in all situations or not, the concept of automatically eliminating the need for quality control, where possible, is powerful."

Poka-Yoke Example

The previous illustration shows how mistake-proofing is used to prevent poorly formed widgets from creeping into downstream operations. (It assumes the group making the widgets is trying to improve as well, but does not take its perfection for granted!)

The specification calls for a widget 10 cm tall, ±0.5 cm.

Relying on old-style quality control alone, we might sample five items every hour. The mean height and range of the sampled items would be charted. Finding a sample that was out of control would mean a tedious process of inspecting all the parts that had been produced in that lot, sorting them out, and so forth.

In the illustration, the first gate is set at 10.6 cm. Items too tall are caught and shunted aside before they enter the production stream. The next gate is set at 9.5 cm. Items too short pass underneath into a "too short" bin. Those just right are caught and shunted into a production line, for use. Manual inspection is eliminated; quality control charts are eliminated. Only 100 percent good parts enter production.

Companies such as FedEx use a similar system to scan bar-coded ZIP destinations and automatically shunt packages into the proper conveyor prior to containerization. Spiegel/Eddie Bauer's warehouse management system allows tracking garments along 40 miles of hanging rails (Voss 1996).

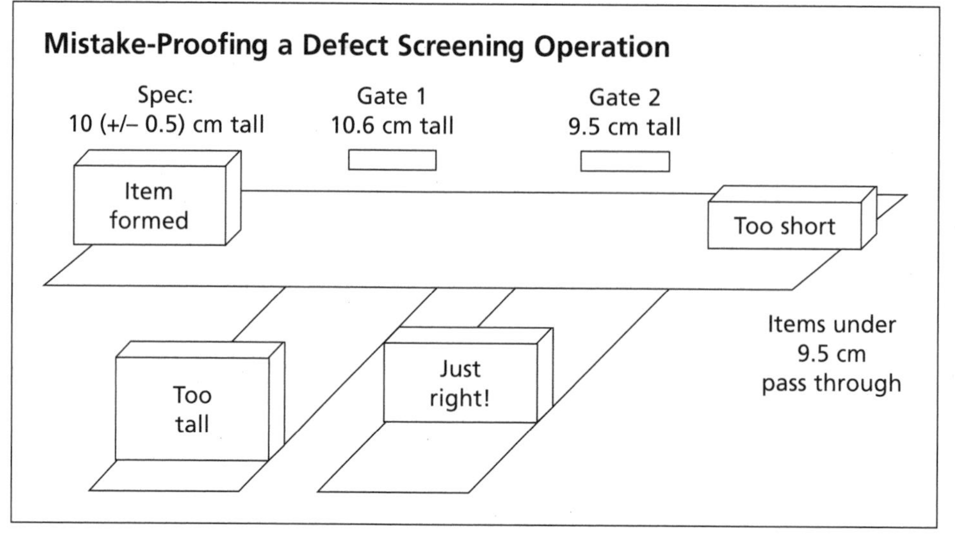

"In sales, it's easy to think of ways the concept of poka-yoke can be applied. Computer firms such as Dell do an incredible amount of business over the phone. Hundreds of people sit at phones, helping customers match the type of computer they want with a wide array of options available.

"Prior to instituting an electronic configuration system, customer service reps taking the orders had to rely on paper, intracompany bulletins, and catalogs to help them piece together, say, whether a particular fax-modem could be ordered to go on a computer of a particular speed, with a particular sized hard drive. The rate of obsolescence alone made it very difficult for the customer service people to correctly combine all the options in a fully compatible fashion.

"With their electronic configuration system, customer service reps are physically prevented from setting up a computer incorrectly. Once the model is picked, the system limits the number of options available. As each new option is selected, only options that are compatible with everything else selected up to that point remain."

ITT Fluid Technology Corp. uses sales configuration systems to increase the accuracy of its pump, valve, and fluid handling equipment and price bids at the same time (Farnum 1995).

Four Bases for Zero Quality Control System

Dr. Shingo states that there are four basic concepts to his approach. We have already covered two, namely, using automatic devices to inspect 100 percent of the time and implementing ways to automatically prevent defects at the source using mistake-proofing. Third, he states that when problems occur, corrective action must occur as quickly as possible, and fourth, that mistake-proofing techniques should be used to help eliminate human error, too.

"The schematic diagram illustrates one way that Dr. Shingo's ideas can be combined and applied to customer needs analysis and proposal generation portions of the sales process."

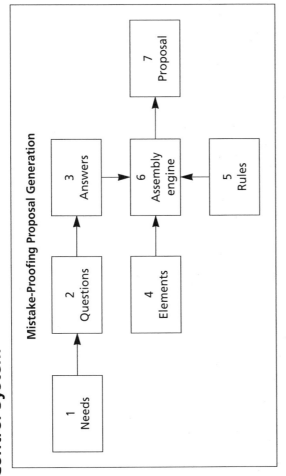

Mistake-Proofing Proposal Generation

1 Needs → 2 Questions → 3 Answers → 6 Assembly engine
4 Elements → 6 Assembly engine
5 Rules → 6 Assembly engine
6 Assembly engine → 7 Proposal

> **In *Virtual Selling*, Thomas Siebel and Michael Malone (1996) state that in an up-to-date sales process, "the presentation, configuration, and close are the same thing" (p. 199).**

"On the left, customer needs (at 1) are assessed using a set of systematic needs analysis questions (2). These questions, derived from the company's most skillful individuals, would either be written down or computerized to prevent less skillful salespeople from forgetting what to ask or look for. Having the questions written down makes it easier to train and easier to use as a checklist so nothing is forgotten.

"Elements (4) of a company's most successful proposals—pricing formulas, descriptive language, and so forth—are kept as discrete building blocks. Using the elements and styles correlated with the highest percentage of successful proposals in different situations reduces the chances of customer rejection.

"Rules (5) governing under what conditions a particular element should appear in a proposal, based on the pattern of answers (3) to the needs analysis questions, are also established beforehand. The company's most qualified people are the ones asked to create the rules. Making the rules explicit makes it easier to train people how to assemble the proposals and reduces variation between experts and novices in the company.

"The final step in foolproofing is using a computer 'engine' (6) that uses the rules, automatically looks at the answers, and automatically selects and assembles the correct proposal elements into a finished proposal (7). Such systems are commercially available. A company not possessing an automated assembly engine can still perform this last step manually, albeit more slowly and with a greater chance for error.

"Think about ways to mistake-proof wherever you are. Never look at a problem in your marketing, sales, or service approach without thinking of ways to prevent it from occurring in the first place."

Tool 4: The Check Sheet

That last idea alone could probably save my company a ton of money—and make our customers a lot happier, too. Our quotation process allows too many mistakes to occur. It takes a long time to train a rep until he or she can do a decent proposal. I think even the skillful ones sometimes shortchange the company, just to close the sale. Dr. Selden is plowing ahead like a freight train. I'll have to revisit some of my lecture notes later.

"The tool we're going to look at now is one of the simplest ways to begin using data to help improve the sales process. The tool is called a *check sheet.*

"To illustrate the tool, I've taken a problem that drives salespeople and their managers crazy—losing bids. Let's say your company realizes that knowing why you lost a bid is one of the first steps toward systematically improving your sales process—and your sales, as well. Let's say you begin a program of systematically surveying clients who reject your proposals to find out why they turn you down."

"Using a check sheet, you make a tally of all the reasons you hear about, spanning the first and second quarters of the year.

Reasons Bids Were Rejected

Problem	Quarter		
	First	Second	Total
Terms	///	//	5
Solution not right	~~////~~ ////	~~////~~ //	16
Cost/benefit low or absent	~~////~~ /	////	10
Delivery unsatisfactory	~~////~~ /	~~////~~ /	12
Total	24	19	43

"As the illustration shows, out of 24 bids rejected in the first quarter, three were rejected primarily because of the terms offered. The overall solution proposed was not to their liking nine times. They rejected bids six times because they felt the benefits they'd be getting relative to the costs involved to be low, or the cost/benefit analysis wasn't there at all. Six times, they felt something about the delivery of what you proposed was unsatisfactory. In the second quarter, the terms were unacceptable twice, the solution was unsatisfactory seven times, the cost/benefit appeal was low or entirely absent four times, and delivery was unsatisfactory six times. The totals on the right keep overall score of how many times each reason was cited.

"From here, a check sheet such as this offers many directions to go. The cost of adjusting your terms, for example, might be very slight compared to the fact that apparently more than one out of 10 proposals was rejected for that reason. Increasing sales by 10 percent just by adjusting terms sounds like a good potential opportunity to me. Devising a new way to state the cost/benefit analysis, or doing a better job at matching solutions to customer needs, might all be within the control of sales and marketing."

The Most Important Specification to Know

That last example is triggering some great insights for me. The most important specifications to know are probably not even our internal process specifications. The place to start may be our customer's specification.

All our internal specifications must ultimately aim at meeting a final "inspection" by our customer. We'll waste everything up to that point if what we offer doesn't meet that final test. If we spend $5 million on our sales effort, but close only 10 percent of our deals, technically, maybe Crosby would say that we've wasted up to 90 percent of our $5 million: $4,500,000. That's a big source of funding for any improvement efforts we might launch, I'd guess. The biggest obstacle I'll face when I look at a number like that is getting people to believe that part of the $4.5 million is an unnecessary expense. Our attitude is that it's a cost of doing business.

I've drawn a diagram in my notebook that Dr. Selden's last example and earlier comments about customer specifications have driven home. It's three boxes with a decision diamond in between.

I think it'd be important to keep in mind that one of our own sales process specifications should be that our offer meets the customer's specifications in a way superior to the competitor's offer, so I've drawn in a box to represent the competitor, too. After all, on many deals a competitor is likely to be presenting its offer, too.

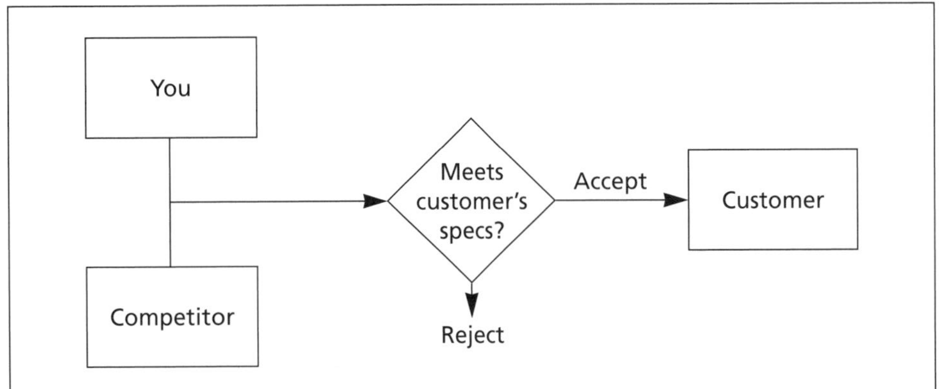

I bet companies that listen to their customers' spoken or unstated specifications can achieve a real advantage in the marketplace. I read a recent example of this in a leading consumer magazine (Big pickups 1996). It turns out that in the market for vehicles in the United States, surprisingly enough, the best-selling product isn't a car at all—it's a pickup truck. The article said that among the big pickups, the Ford F-series has been a best-seller for years and years. Part of the reason for this must be what I've heard Ford calls its ongoing commitment to "listening to the voice of the customer." This shows up in hundreds of ways. Ford's models now sport a passenger-side third door as a standard option. In competitive makes, the third door is an extra-cost option or not available at all. It just struck me. The advantage wouldn't be sustained if the act itself of looking for the customer's specifications wasn't sustained!

The diagram shows things in a static way, but I think real life is more dynamic than this. A proposal that presents a superior operational solution may fail to meet the customer's needs from an economic point of view. Not only that, variables beyond my control may be present, such as another decision maker entering the picture at the last minute.

Yet when all is said and done, we should be able to detect a pattern of some sort and work on improving that pattern, either all at once or little by little. The thing is to start somewhere and improve.

"Don't ever make the mistake of thinking that buildings, computers, consultants, or even employees are your company's greatest assets. Every company's greatest asset is its customers, because without customers there is no company. It's that simple" (LeBoeuf 1989).

Check Sheets: Instructions

Check sheets are simple tallies of the frequency an event occurs over a specified time period. The event might be a behavior such as answering a complaint, a physical object such as an invoice, or an event of some sort such as a new product release.

What will be counted must be defined exactly. There will usually be some ambiguity and disagreement, which must be minimized. The goal is that the person making the tallies counts the same thing in the same way, from day to day, and that different people count the same thing in the same way. Don't let a fear of imprecision stop you from gathering facts—some degree of variation is inevitable and unpreventable.

Starting out, decide on the time period over which the observations should occur.

Use a form with plenty of space and clear labels. Make it easy to use and understand.

Collect the data routinely and honestly. Don't shortchange the engineering value of what you are doing by censoring your records.

Allow time to collect the information. Data collection has a price, as do activities that consume time. If you've decided that there's a big enough payoff for counting in the first place, be sure to set the time aside to do it. Fortunately, check sheets are easy enough to mark, so it should take relatively little time to note when something occurs.

Until you have data, all you have is someone's guess. Check sheets are a great way to begin moving from opinion to fact.

- Check sheet: tally of event frequencies or occurrence
- Define exactly what will be counted
- Decide on time period
- Simple way to begin moving from opinion to fact
- Use form with plenty of space, clear labels
- Collect data consistently and honestly
- Allow time for collection

It's hard to explain, but I feel like I'm entering the second stage of a rocket launch, or the point just as a plane is taking off the ground. All of a sudden I'm seeing practical ways that data can enter into the discussions we have in the office.

This is not just some abstract discussion about how quality is good for you or how you can break the customer service function into steps and flowchart it. For some reason, this simple discussion about using check sheets is making everything real, taking it out of the realm of theory. This is great stuff. And at this stage, it's so simple. I wonder what the next generation of sales process engineering will cover?

Tool 5: The Pareto Chart

"We talked about AT&T's Pareto priority index earlier, in the context of deciding which improvement effort to work on first. Now we'll take a more formal look at Pareto charting as part of our process engineering tool kit. The Pareto chart takes data from any source and displays them in graphic form, ranking the frequency of occurrence of a variable in order of magnitude.

"In this example we're looking at the order entry part of the sales, marketing, and customer service process. In many businesses, order entry can be tremendously labor intensive. In the organizations I've worked with, some 20 percent of all orders submitted may contain an error, either through commission or omission. I've talked with other consultants who have seen order processing error rates as high as 98 percent!

"Errors of omission may be costly to correct. Salespeople faxing in orders to customer service from the field sometimes skip key information, such as shipping methods or units of measure. Should it go regular ground or by air? Does the customer want 10 items or 10 cartons? In situations where a rep's catalog contains thousands of possible items, each of which may have a separate count per carton, what the rep takes as an order quantity might not fall on the right

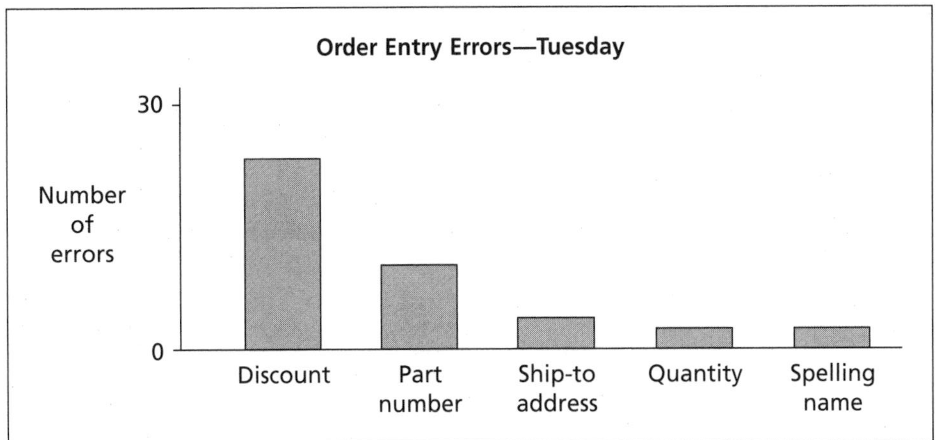

break—the customer wants 15 items, but the items come packed 18 to a carton. The rep phones an order for 15 into the service desk, and the customer service rep has to 'up' the order to the correct carton size. Depending on the relationship with the customer, explaining the difference between what was ordered versus what was shipped and telephone tag may eat up more time and money. The order desk may add mistakes of its own. The long and short of it is that order entry and processing is often filled with opportunities to improve.

"In the example in front of you, we're ranking order entry errors by frequency. In this case, the company has the greatest problem with misapplied discounts. A rep might promise a 5 percent discount, but fail to write it on the order. When it gets to the order desk, what does the customer service rep do? Grants no discount. Resulting in what? Claims and customer dissatisfaction. Customers were not receiving the discounts their long-term contract called for, reps were applying 'most favorable customer' discounts to orders that didn't warrant them, a rep serving one part of a company wasn't giving the same discount as a rep serving the other, and so forth.

"Next, in order of frequency, were errors concerning part numbers, ship-to addresses, quantities, and customer names."

Pareto Charts: Instructions

The Pareto chart is named after Vilfredo Pareto (1848–1923), an Italian economist. Pareto found that in many cases, approximately 80 percent of the wealth was held by some 20 percent of the population. Extending his research, Pareto discovered that this sort of relationship held in other natural phenomena.

A Pareto chart is a bar graph of known causes, displayed left to right in order of the observed magnitude of each cause.

The vertical axis represents frequency. Along the horizontal axis run labels representing what each of the bars stand for.

The height of the bars represents the observed magnitude.

In the 1950s Juran noted that in many cases regarding process engineering, a "vital few" factors often account for the main effect noted; the remaining factors Juran dubbed the "useful many."

Pareto charts are useful for deciding where to begin a project. Often a vital few events or causes account for the majority of the problems observed, thus suggesting a natural place to start.

Sometimes another vertical axis is added on the right. This axis represents the cumulative percentage of the total cases accounted for, through each of the bars charted. Above each bar, a point represents the cumulative percentage. The points are connected with a line.

- Pareto chart: Plot or list known causes in order of their observed magnitude on graph or table (usually bar graph)
- Based on widely applicable relationship explored by Vilfredo Pareto (1848–1923)
- Large number of effects usually accounted for by small number of causes (ratio often 80/20)
- Height of bars represents observed magnitude
- Useful for prioritizing where to begin a project

Checkpoint: Check Sheets

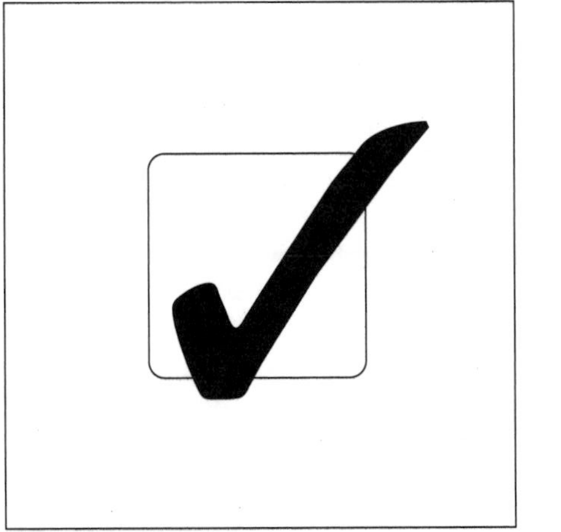

Dr. Selden asks the group members to work on an exercise to cement their understanding of the check sheet and Pareto charting techniques.

First, he reminds the group that check sheets can be used as a simple way to collect quantitative process data. Next, he asks the group members to suggest a portion of their sales process where they are experiencing a problem. He asks for some ideas.

One woman says that in her company incorrect pricing is a problem. Another woman says that she will be focusing on order entry errors. A fellow in the back states he should be looking more deeply into the quality of the sales presentations made. Another says his group should look more closely at the number of leads generated from ad campaigns.

Dr. Selden writes the main words on the board so that everyone can see them.

- **Incorrect pricing**
- **Order entry errors**
- **Quality of sales presentations**
- **Number of leads**

Dr. Selden then asks the group as a whole what type of data they would capture for each variable, using check sheets to tally the data.

"What might we count, surrounding the issue of incorrect pricing and the others?"

The woman who had the idea related to pricing says she will be counting the reasons for incorrect pricing: wrong discount rates, incorrect contract codes, order quantity errors, order entry errors, and incomplete specification of complex items.

The woman who mentioned order entry errors says she would sort the tallies into two categories: either missing or incorrect information.

The fellow who mentioned the quality of sales presentations says his company uses a seven-dimension sales presentation scoring system, which managers complete as they observe reps and file historically. He says he's going to collate and tally those.

The man focusing on sales leads says he's going to tally how many leads come in by the source of the lead, using historical data where possible.

Checkpoint: Pareto Charts

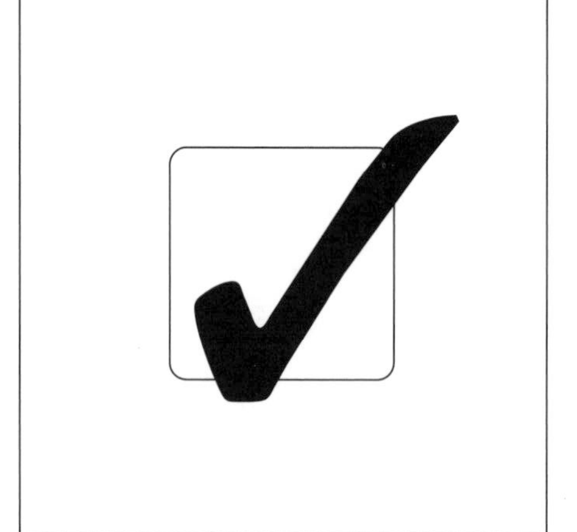

"Now I want us to get a little practice using the Pareto charting tool. We'll be using it to help decide which process improvement idea would have the greatest impact on cost.

"But Pareto charts don't work unless you have something of substance to graph. So here's what I want you to do. First, we're going to brainstorm ways mistake-proofing could improve your sales process. These should be serious enough to warrant follow-up after this workshop. Any ideas? I'll jot down the first five on the board."

The group is quiet for a moment or two, then participants pour out many ideas.

"An insurance agent could use an electronic claim check system to pull up the type of claim being made to see whether that was on the customer's policy, rather than manually receiving a claim, investigating it, and then later finding out that the item being claimed wasn't insured."

"How about making it a rule that follow-up calls must be scheduled at the time of the initial call, rather than waiting until later and trying to set something up by phone?"

"We could try setting up an electronic catalog in our own customer's place of business so that the customer could place orders electronically."

"I think equipping reps with laptops that would take orders electronically, prompting them for all necessary information before submitting it, would work."

"We could make product selection rules explicit in the form of a decision-making aid such as a flowchart, so reps could recommend the right product instead of relying only on their personal experience."

"These are great ideas!" Dr. Selden observes. "Now let's pretend that within your company, each of these ideas had actually been submitted in a brainstorming session. Using Pareto charting, please use your imagination to assess the potential each idea has for reducing cost, and graph the savings for each mistake-proofing technique in order of magnitude. For the next five minutes I'd like you to do just that. Force yourself to make estimates and rank the potential savings for each idea by size. If any of you come up with more than $1 million in savings per year, for any given idea, please raise your hand."

Within minutes, a few hands go up.

"Wonderful! These are thought starters of what the data might be. There's big money hidden in these opportunities. As an engineer, your job is to get real data to confirm these estimates and act accordingly."

Our Journey—Day One

Dr. Selden again posts his road map of the journey for Day One. He calls a break for the day, saying that tonight there is no homework assignment.

Name	Philosophy	Tool
Selden	Sales process engineering	Flowcharting
Deming	Quality is up to management	14 points
Crosby	Cost of quality	Brainstorming
Harrington, Melan	Measurement, process selection	Check sheets
Shingo	Mistake-proofing	Pareto charts

I'm starting to see the logic in what we're doing a lot more clearly. At the beginning of the course, it all seemed a hodgepodge of names, philosophies, and tools.

Beginning with the big picture in mind was appropriate. The meaning of "I think" versus "I can show" stands out loud and clear now. Engineering is an empty word if you can't balance ideas with facts—and measurements. That's almost an attitudinal change that management must model and support, from the top down, and I guess that's the meaning of much of Dr. Deming's teachings.

Once the organization realizes there is opportunity for improvement, there's a need to pinpoint those areas, size them up, and make some reasonable decisions about where to begin. That's where Crosby, Harrington, and Melan fit in for me.

I had never heard of Shingo before today, but of course I've heard of 'fool-proofing.' Somehow, put in the light of mistake-proofing, the idea seems a lot more tangible. There are lots of places I'd like to try it in my company. Even creating checklists could help us remember to do things we tend to forget. And though we weren't able to cover it well, I'm going to check out those sources on the single-minute exchange of die Dr. Selden referenced. We do a lot of changeovers in marketing, sales, and customer service, and I never thought there was a method to improve changeover time in such a systematic way before.

I like the conceptual framework the individuals provide, but I also like the specific tools we're covering: Flowcharting might help us uncover bottlenecks, the 14 points give us specific management ideas for creating a climate conducive to improvement, and brainstorming is a great way to generate ideas—the "I thinks." The check sheets and Pareto charts make it easier to look for hard data and use data intelligently to arrive at the "I can shows." Even if we can't always find it, I think the discipline involved will help us improve, if nothing else.

I had heard of some of the individuals and techniques before coming here today, but I've never studied them with an eye to how their principles apply to the sales process. The context Dr. Selden is placing them in is great. I feel like we're taking parts off the shelf and assembling some kind of powerful machine as we go along. I'll be better oriented going into tomorrow's session.

Day Two

Our Journey—Day Two

Dr. Selden welcomes the class again, chatting with some of the early arrivals until 8 A.M.

After recapping the previous day's topics and discussing lingering questions and issues, the topics for Day Two are displayed.

Just as with Day One, Day Two's topics are a mixture of established schools of thought and tools. Many of the names displayed are new to the group.

Our Journey—Day Two

Name	Philosophy	Tool
Hammer and Champy et al.	Reengineering	Run charts
Ohno	Just-in-time, industrial engineering	Histograms
Pavlov, Skinner	Behavioral engineering	Cause/effect diagrams Scatter plots
Juran	Quality planning, improvement, and control	SPC, systematic experimentation
Imai	Continuous improvement	Implementation sequence planning

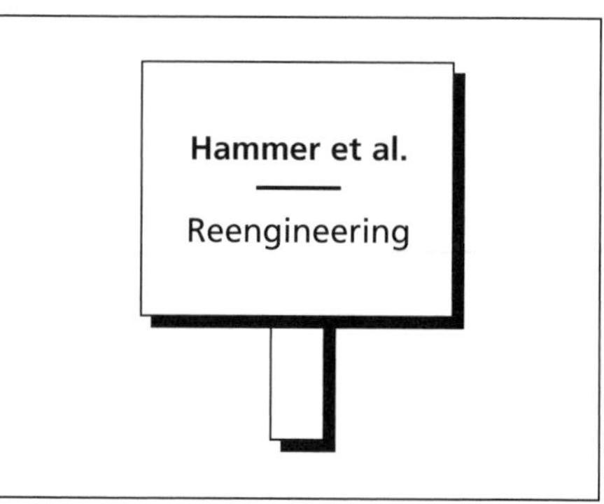

The Reengineering School: Breaking the Mold

"In the past few years, one of the most hotly debated approaches to management has been that of reengineering. The reengineers are like the early impressionists were in their day: considered wild beasts by those clinging to the past, brilliant innovators by those ready for a fresh approach. There is no question that the premise underlying reengineering needs to be understood if one is to practice sales process engineering.

"A lot of people think that the concept of reengineering starts and ends with the work of Michael Hammer and James Champy. That's not so. I need to make you aware there are other works on the subject by a number of respected individuals, even more than we will be able to cover today.

"Out of curiosity, I wonder who has actually read Hammer and Champy's book *Reengineering the Corporation* (1993)."

About a fifth of the attendees hands go up.

"What did you think of it?"

Comments from the participants are all over the map.

"It was pretty high level."

"I think it helped give our senior executives something to point at and say, 'I'm going to do something.'"

"I thought the ideas were very thought provoking; they helped us to think of some new approaches to the ways we do business."

Reengineering's Main Points of Emphasis

- *Reengineering the Corporation*—Michael Hammer and James Champy
- *The Reengineering Revolution*—Michael Hammer and Steven A. Stanton
- *Reengineering*—V. Daniel Hunt
- *Reengineering Your Business*—Daniel Morris and Joel Brandon
- *Business Process Reengineering*—Henry Johansson, Patrick McHugh, John Pendlebury, and William Wheeler

"I don't think the companies doing reengineering really thought through the consequences of what they were doing."

"You can see that people's opinions of reengineering are mixed, just as they are about any of the philosophies we cover. You should read Hammer and Champy's book, and many of the others, as well, to see what they have to say for yourself.

"I'll cover the highlights. Let's move on!"

Chronic Problems Require Breakthrough Solutions

Problem

Outdated organizations aren't able to

- **Serve customers the way customers like**
- **Respond quickly to competitive pressures**
- **Adapt to today's pace of change**

Solution

Reengineering is "the fundamental rethinking and radical redesign of business processes to achieve dramatic improvements in critical, contemporary measures of performance, such as cost, quality, service, and speed" (Hammer and Champy 1993, 32).

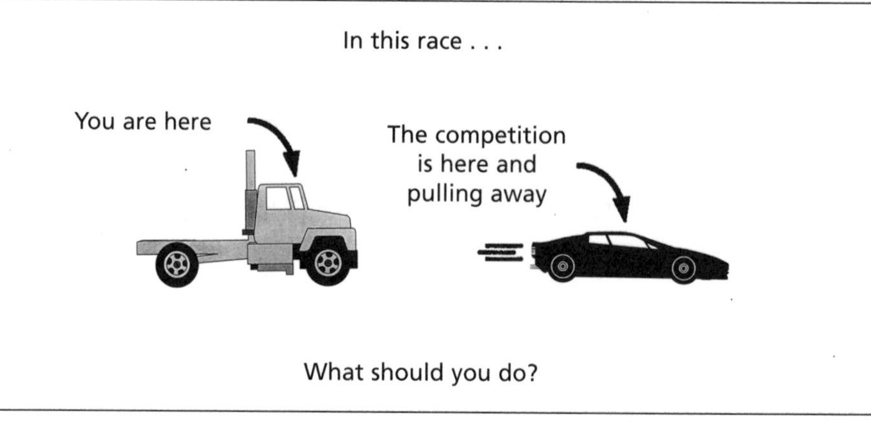
In this race . . .
You are here
The competition is here and pulling away
What should you do?

Dr. Selden projects a slide. In it, a tractor from an 18-wheeler is losing a race against a high-speed sports car.

"*Reengineering* is a word used to label what you must do if you are in the truck.

"You are losing the race. Going as fast as you can won't help. The truck can't go fast enough. Making small changes in how you corner won't help. The race car is far too maneuverable for small changes in how you steer to make enough difference.

"For the clever marketing types in the audience, the answer is no, let's say you can't convince the judges to switch the race to one having to do with hauling capacity.

"And for the clever political types in the audience, the answer is no, let's say you can't enact legislation to require drivers to all go 55 miles per hour.

"What is the solution? You must change vehicles entirely. When the race isn't even close, or when the competition is so far ahead that small changes won't work, only a complete change—a radical change—in the way things are done can hope to restore competitiveness.

"In my earlier days, management trainers used the metaphor of a car stuck in sand. Pushing the gas pedal harder doesn't help, it just digs you in deeper. In some cases, only a structural process change will do. Whether you call it *reengineering, redesign, reinvention, revitalization, innovation,* or *leap frogging* doesn't matter. In all of these cases we're talking about a change that breaks so much with the past that it is discontinuous. It's starting entirely fresh rather than patching up the old."

Characteristics of a Reengineered Process

"*Reengineering the Corporation* is an excellent read, one of the truly interesting and compelling business books of the decade (Hammer and Champy 1993). Its power to shake complacent executives of failing companies out of their lethargy is a chief merit of the book.

"In their book, Hammer and Champy do not publish credentials that say they are licensed or certified engineers. Their book does not list a specific step-by-step approach for implementing radical change. It only contains one principle. No quantitative formulae are presented.

"Instead, like patient zoologists in the field, the authors have noted characteristics that appear to be common to organizations that have successfully implemented radical structural change.

"Perhaps the most salient point they make is this: Companies successful at reengineering have found places where technology or new processes make it possible for one person, newly trained as more of a generalist, to perform the work of multiple specialists. By doing so they've eliminated process steps, together with error- and delay-inducing handoffs between people.

"The emphasis on technology's role in reengineering is not surprising. James Champy is chairman of CSC Index, a division of Computer Sciences Corporation, and part of a rare modern breed of seasoned businesspeople who also understand this relatively new tool called the *computer*."

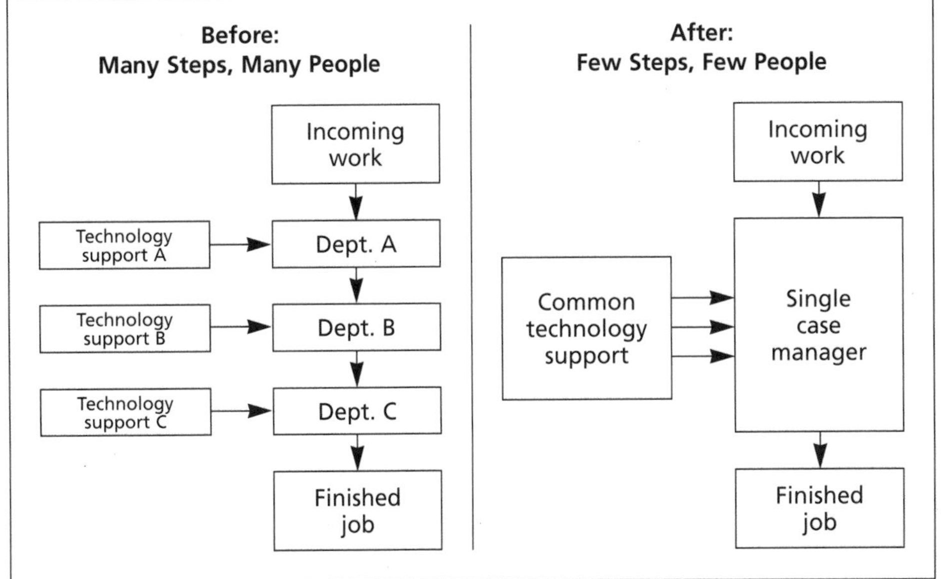

Example: Ford Motor Company

In the mid-1980s, Ford Motor Company had approximately 500 people processing its accounts payable. Ford noticed that Mazda's accounts payables department had only five people. Though the volume of work at Mazda was less, Mazda's process enabled each person to handle far more suppliers and payments on a per-person basis than Ford's group.

Ford's solution was to eliminate the need for its central accounts payable staff to physically match supplier invoices and records of goods logged in at the receiving dock to the original purchase order for the goods. Ford did so by implementing an information management system that allowed receiving clerks to call up the original purchase order as goods were unloaded and check off items received right on the spot. The computer automatically authorized payment for properly matched items. The result was a tripling in efficiency. Ford decreased its central accounts payable staff to about 150 people. Dr. Selden's firm documented the new approach and trained Ford's people how to use it.

Different Authors, Different Emphases

"From an engineering point of view, increasing efficiency (or productivity) means increasing the output one person can generate. As one aim of engineering, that's a simple fact, and no one seems to quarrel with it too much.

"However, Michael Hammer and James Champy will forever face the wrath of humanists (and many engineers) everywhere, and not just out of envy. They state only one principle in their book, and, lest I be accused of hyperbole, I will quote it for you directly. Their principle is that 'as few people as possible should be involved in the performance of a process' (Hammer and Champy 1993, 144). Making personnel reduction the apparent target of your efforts is not guaranteed to make friends." [Grim laughter ripples through the audience.]

Having read their book myself, it seems there's a lesson for engineers here somewhere. It sounds like Hammer and Champy were simply stating the classic definition of increasing efficiency, but in a different way. If increased efficiency means one person can generate more than before, then it is also true that you will need fewer people to generate the same output as before. Their blunt "if you want to make an omelette, you've got to break some eggs" point of view regarding what to do with people who can't adapt to change also probably didn't endear them to many.

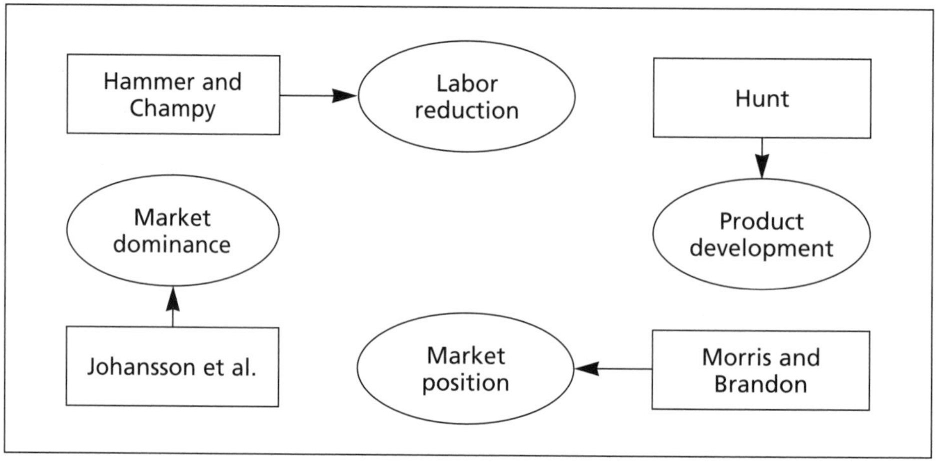

Hammer and Champy → Labor reduction
Hunt → Product development
Johansson et al. → Market dominance
Morris and Brandon → Market position

"Other authors suggest that reengineering be employed to reach distinctly different goals. As my audience, I don't want you to leave with the mistaken idea that reengineering is used only to achieve personnel reductions. A quick look at a few additional authors should help us understand the elephant and not just its trunk.

"Hunt advocates the use of reengineering to achieve improvements in product development (1993). His rationale is simple: companies are following an overall long-term strategy of high quality, and product quality plays a key part of that goal.

"Morris and Brandon emphasize how to use reengineering to achieve superior market positioning (1993). They recommend explicitly tying department goals to corporate goals. This provides a nice guideline for the typical engineer, who often works on a less-than-companywide scale.

"Johansson, McHugh, Pendlebury, and Wheeler recommend aiming the reengineering effort at market dominance through superior quality, service, cycle time, and cost (Johansson et al. 1993). Their message is that to be truly superior, one must grow the market and reduce costs.

"A business is like a living organism comprised of many organs. All must work well together to achieve the greatest vigor. A sales process engineer must understand this."

Just-in-Time: Ohno

Taiichi Ohno (1912–1990), an industrial engineer, is often called the father of just-in-time (JIT) and the kanban system of work processing. Ohno was trained as an industrial engineer and rose to prominence within Toyota as he applied his techniques first to one department, then another, spreading his methods and philosophies as the results became clear.

Even after he had risen to one of the pinnacles of the modern industrial society as executive vice president of Toyota, Ohno never lost his love for sharing the knowledge he had acquired over a lifetime of successful experience. Ohno worked closely with the Japan Management Association, often presenting seminars about the Toyota system of production. Toyota is widely regarded as Japan's leading manufacturer by the Japanese themselves. Both Shigeo Shingo (1986) and Yasuhiro Monden (1993) have written clear and valuable texts on Toyota's production system, as has the Japan Management Association (1989) itself.

The results of the JIT approach are often astonishing, by any yardstick. The foreword of the book *Kanban: Just-in-Time at Toyota* (Japan Management Association 1989) cites the example of Omark Industries, a U.S. firm that applied JIT concepts. Within several years, Omark found it was, in many cases, able to

- Reduce lead times from 12 weeks to four days.

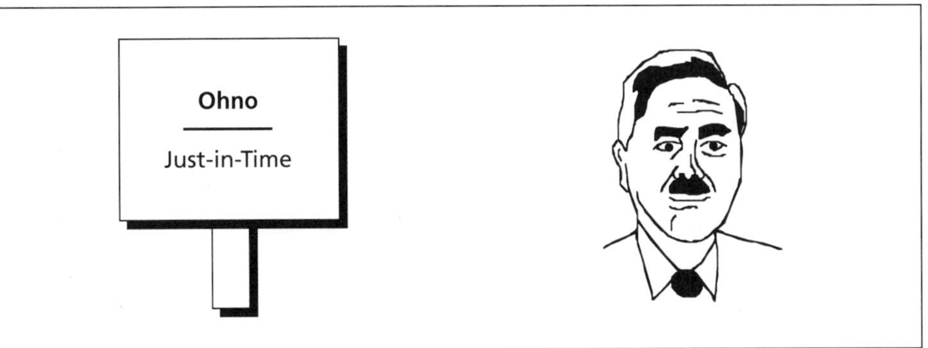

- Reduce setup times during changeovers from eight hours to one minute four seconds.
- Reduce work sitting in process queues and storage by 50 percent.
- Free up space available by up to 40 percent.

JIT means delivering exactly what is needed in the right quantity and the right quality, just in time for when it is needed. In sales, JIT principles are being applied every day. Companies like Perkin-Elmer have eliminated the use of office space for sales people by equipping them with mobile computing tools that allow reps to get the information they need without going into a central office. Telemarketing firms have adopted technology that reduces nonwork time to the bare minimum, tripling the number of contacts per day per person from a typical average of 25 to 30 up to 75 to 90.

The work involved in translating the principles of JIT into the sales, marketing, and service arenas is in its infancy. The texts and authors cited above should be studied by serious students to aid in this translation.

Taiichi Ohno (1912–1990)

- Vice president, Toyota Motors
- Toyota: Regarded as leader by Japanese themselves
- Father of kanban and JIT
- Industrial engineer
- Omark Industries (United States)
  - —Lead time: reduced from 12 weeks to 4 days
  - —Setup time: reduced from 8 hours to 1 minute 4 seconds
  - —Work in process: reduced 50%
  - —Floor space: Increased 30% to 40%

DAY TWO

Characteristics of a Just-In-Time System

JIT is a "pull demand" system where process suppliers produce nothing until an internal order is placed for it. Strictly speaking, nothing is produced until it is ordered, so nothing is produced in advance of its need. Everything is produced and delivered just in time for use by the process that placed the order. Nothing is produced first, then pushed through—no ticket for Item A, no production for Item A. In JIT, orders are signalled by means of a card called a *kanban,* often a simple paper ticket or an empty tray.

Firm customer orders and market forecasts serve as the initial trigger for an order, so reducing cycle time is critical. In the illustration, Lots A and B have already been sold and shipped. Lot C has been sold and is about to be shipped. Lot D is being completed. The more quickly an order can be filled, the less work in process, the lower the cycle time, and the less overall cost consumed.

For just-in-time to work, a number of positive practices must be set in place.

Respect for employees is utmost. To feel good about their work, people need to aim at high standards and have a clear sense of direction. Independence is required: An employee spotting a serious defect is empowered to stop the entire line to focus attention and action. Teamwork is a must: Workers are not pitted against each other, and management is not adversarial.

With JIT, automation is used rationally, only after other process changes have been studied and set in place. Automation is often more expensive and harder to change—once set up—than other improvements. When done right, people do not touch an automated process unless something goes wrong. One person can oversee many processes at once; only "emergencies" need attention.

Finally, to reduce both internal work queues and stockpiles of finished work and to keep cycle times as short as possible, work is done in short, not long, runs. Small, custom-tailored batches are processed, requiring frequent, fast setup changes. Flexibility is not just allowed; it is expected. As needs change, workers must be able to perform a variety of jobs with excellence. Timing is critical. Operations and deliveries must take place exactly when needed.

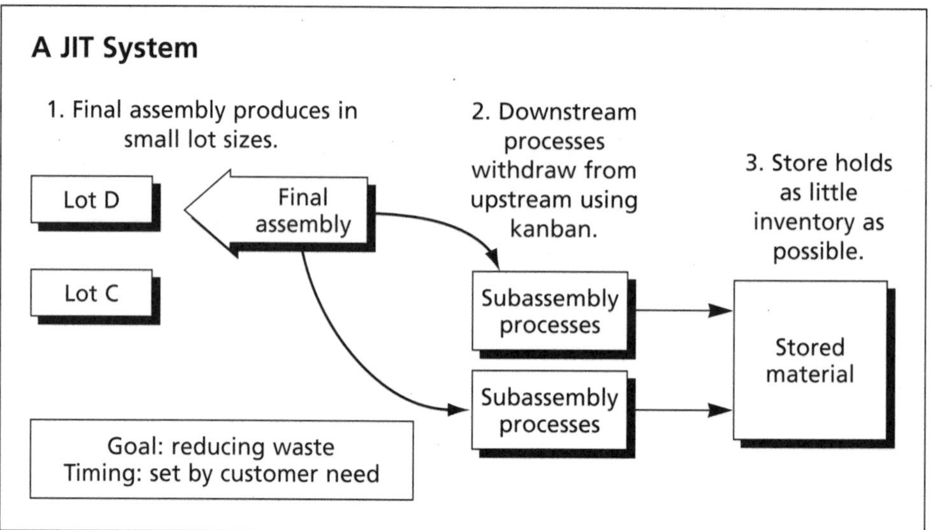
A JIT System
1. Final assembly produces in small lot sizes.
Lot D
Lot C
Final assembly
2. Downstream processes withdraw from upstream using kanban.
Subassembly processes
Subassembly processes
3. Store holds as little inventory as possible.
Stored material
Goal: reducing waste
Timing: set by customer need

Blue Jeans and JIT

The idea for just-in-time was inspired when Taiichi Ohno observed an American supermarket. Customers came to the shelf to withdraw what they needed. Shelves were restocked based on what was withdrawn.

A global garment maker of popular jeans now uses an electronic inventory system to help determine the quantity of each specific item to allocate to each of its retail stores. The system uses actual sales data obtained from electronic cash registers at each store to customize the quantity shipped to actual demand. Prior to installing the system, allocations were divided equally among stores, without considering demand. The system also allows customers to custom-order jeans to their individual measurements.

JIT in Sales, Marketing, and Service

"Almost any situation where a sales or service rep is visiting a site just to check inventory and replenish stock could use a JIT approach to cut travel time. Nalco Chemical, a billion dollar specialty chemical firm, has attached sensors to feed bins in its customer locations. The sensors automatically call the sales rep when stocks are low or when the process itself is in danger of going out of control. Replenishment supplies are ordered just in time. And the rep also knows, in many cases before the customer's own engineers, how well the process is performing. Now that's service."

This session is moving so fast, it's hard to absorb all the ideas going through my head. JIT principles could give us so many ideas for improvement.

If marketing could let us know when our customer's fiscal year ended, we could time our sales calls to the time of year our customers' planning and budgeting cycle is most receptive to new ideas.

In the insurance business, the rep should be able to generate alternative proposals right on the spot, when the customer is most ready to purchase. They should be able to compare the advantages of our approach with the competition using concrete data rather than words.

In real estate, how much transportation time could be saved by letting customers plug in their own preferences and letting a computer pull up pictures of a house? I bet digital cameras, large hard drives, the Internet, and recordable CD-ROM disks are making that possible right now.

Major appliance makers could send coupons to customers good for purchases of their next product, before the useful life of their current appliance was over. How many customers would repurchase? It's a lot easier to keep a customer than to secure one in the first place.

"In the diagram I've drawn, notice the arrows as they point to the rise in need in situations A and B. The interval for sensing changes in demand is critical! The pre-set interval was able to detect an increase in demand A, in time to make the sale. In situation B the supplier was either too early or too late to get the order."

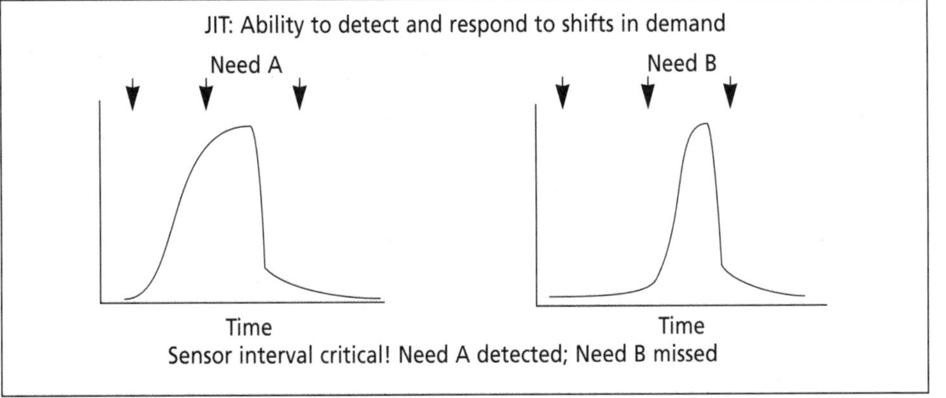

Sensor interval critical! Need A detected; Need B missed

"[W]e've determined that in the industry, on average, products turn every 36–48 months. . . . At the beginning of that cycle, our sales professionals call on existing customers once a quarter. . . . In the later stages . . . [w]e've determined that the typical sales cycle for copiers is about 30 days, so that's why we schedule calls [more] frequently—to make sure we're in their offices somewhere during that cycle," recently stated Murray Martin, president, Pitney Bowes copier division. During the past five years, Pitney Bowes has seen customer loyalty increase 50 percent (Fleschner 1996b).

JIT and the Teen Driver

A national insurance company uses a database of young teens and their parents to generate customized, mass mail solicitations for auto insurance just before they are first eligible for their license.

DAY TWO

True Cost: Very Small

"Nowadays it's often hard enough to hold your price, let alone increase it. It's not always the salesperson's fault. There are cases when a buyer says, 'Well, Brand X is the same as yours in market appeal, function, and form. Your price is the same. Why should I buy yours?'

"In hypercompetitive markets, with a great variety of high-quality goods chasing the same dollar, prices are almost impossible to increase. Just the opposite occurs. In some cases, sophisticated large-scale buyers either dictate the price in a 'take it or leave it' fashion, or they expect decreasing prices.

"So how can a business make money? These days competitors have roughly equal access to labor and raw materials. In world markets, labor and raw materials pricing is largely equivalent. In fact, U.S. labor is now a relatively decent bargain compared to the world market. Ohno says that in the future, profitability will come mainly from the methods used: by improving and driving costs out of internal processes. I'd add that profits can also come through introducing new and better products that face *less* competition, but let's stick with Ohno's thinking for now."

The true cost in any process is very small. There's a saying at Toyota, "The true cost is only the size of a plum seed" (Japan Management Association 1989, 7). There's usually a lot of waste in any given process.

- True cost = Total cost – Unnecessary costs
- True labor (work) = Total labor – Wasted motion
- True cycle time = Total time – Waste – Wait

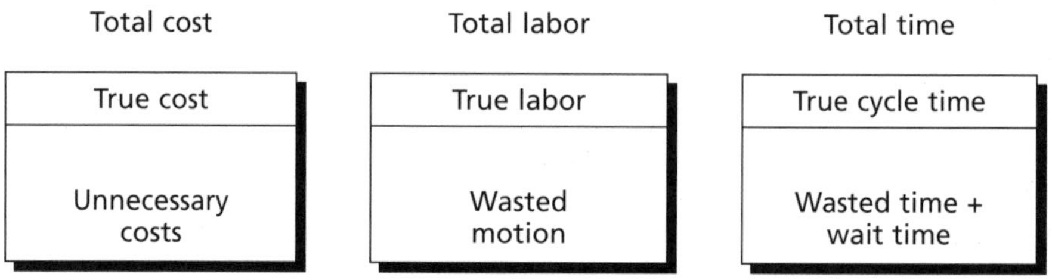

Total cost	Total labor	Total time
True cost	True labor	True cycle time
Unnecessary costs	Wasted motion	Wasted time + wait time

"Do you want to increase sales by 10 percent? Move meetings to Saturdays, ask reps to use Sundays for travel time, and insist that all paperwork be done after hours. What a great way to improve sales! Work 10 percent more hours, and sales should go up 10 percent! Is that an improvement? No! Society suffers when people are asked to work to the exclusion of all else. Our childrens' schooling suffers. Marriages break up. Delinquency rises. That's eating your seed corn."

The wrong way to increase output is by increasing the workload. That just adds labor time, but it doesn't eliminate the wasted motion.

"Waste must be eliminated for improvement and rationalization to take place. But that does not mean time saved should be wasted. Time saved must be converted into useful work, or people will invent new wasted motions in order to avoid boredom and to look busy. Holding hours of labor constant, if total output per person does not increase, you may have traded one waste for another."

Dr. Selden is answering an objection I've heard from upper management about our sales automation. The execs joke that the reps will just use the time saved for golf.

Seven Sources of Waste

An article in the *Wall Street Journal* reported that results of a five-year study showed that nearly three out of four leads went unanswered. Only one in eight generated a follow-up call. The average time for a brochure to arrive was 58 days. The average time for a follow-up call was 89 days (Gibson 1993).

"JIT texts stress that to deliver things just in time, we need to eliminate all forms of waste in a process. Eliminate the waste, and now only the truly useful work remains.

"The texts are in near universal agreement on where specific sources of waste can be found. I'm going to recite them one by one. As I do, I want you to think to yourselves. Jot down examples of waste in your sales process as you think of them.

Types of Waste

1. Overproducing (the worst offense)
2. Waiting—time on hand (easy to spot)
3. Transporting
4. Process problems
5. Unnecessary stock on hand
6. Unnecessary motion
7. Producing defective goods

"The first type of waste is that of *overproduction*. Your immediate reaction may be, 'Hey, what's so bad about selling too much?' That's not all it means. Overproduction means getting too far ahead of the next process in line. Think to yourself what that might mean, and jot down some ideas."

Overproduction. Who says you can't sell too much? Backorders are so long on some of our items, it's killing production, and that's going to hurt quality and our reputation. And though it's trivial compared to our other problems, our marketing department consistently orders thousands more brochures than we ever use.

"The second type of waste is *waiting*, or having time on hand. Fortunately, wait time is easy to spot."

We wait a lot in sales. We wait in airports. We wait in waiting rooms! Cell phones and laptops have helped to reduce dead wait time.

"The third type of waste is *transportation*. It adds no value, but consumes time."

Bingo. Sounds like windshield time to me. Each hour I'm in a car is an hour I'm not selling. I could save an hour or two each day if I didn't have to stop by the office. We're using video conferencing to link overseas sales and U.S. engineering. It seems to be working well. Maybe we should try it more.

"The fourth type of waste is *process goof ups*, pure and simple."

I'm jotting down "order entry errors" on that one. I bet I spend 10 percent of my time just checking to see if my client's paperwork is entered correctly.

"The fifth type of waste is that of *unnecessary stock on hand:* too much inventory or work in process."

Though the manufacturing terms get in the way a bit, I think I can translate. Our engineers can't keep up with the backlog of estimates our sales and marketing group has created. The backlog represents work in process we've paid for, but can't capitalize on. So does any lead we haven't called on.

"The sixth type of waste is *unnecessary motion*."

Does that ever hit a sore spot. I wonder whether our call reports fall into that category? And our proposals—it seems that I'm forever hunting through old ones trying to find just the right magic words to use. How much of that hunting, cutting, and pasting could be eliminated?

"The seventh type of waste is *producing defective goods*."

That one is obvious. I wonder what we'd find if we ever classified our advertisements, sales presentations, customer needs analysis sessions, and the like on a scale of one to 10? I don't even think we know what kind of defects we produce in sales and marketing. I don't think we know how to surface the waste we have and how to quantify it.

Waste Reduction Challenge

"The people I've talked to who have seriously tried to improve quality and reduce waste in their firms find that they can't do it all at once. Shooting for a 90 percent improvement in one year is more than most organizations can handle even when intentions are good.

"The books I've read and the people I've talked with say it's best to start with a goal of cutting waste in half during the first year. In the following year, the new goal is to cut the remaining level of waste in half, and so on, each year, for four or five years. At the end of that time the waste is almost gone."

Our company has gone through so many supposedly instant miracle cures, it's a joke. We never stick with anything long enough to get even a 50 percent improvement. I like this long-horizon view. We're less likely to become discouraged.

"As you learn more about JIT, you may come across a story about the man in the white cap. Most factories have a man in the white cap. Most sales and marketing departments do, too.

"In the factory, the man in the white cap is the fellow who listens to a cantankerous machine for a few minutes. No one else can fix it. He turns a dial, hits a certain spot with his hammer, and *voilà*, all is smooth and wonderful. A magician. Everyone respects his skill. Yet if you ask him how production can be increased from 800 to 1000 per day, he'll say, 'It's impossible. You better outsource it.'

"We have our men in white caps in sales and marketing, too. They are wizards at what they do. Put them in front of a customer, and you'll have a sale in no time. Yet if you ask them whether it's possible for the average rep to find five new clients each quarter, they'll say, 'It's impossible. Better hire more reps.'

"These men in white caps are great at what they do. Yet they are incapable of looking at the process as a whole to see where it can be improved.

"There are men in white caps in management, too. They are great with their people, but don't look at the structure to see what holds back overall improvement.

"A real leader respects the skill of the men in white caps but understands that skills regarding process innovation are a separate matter.

"I predict that part of managers' jobs in the future will be to work on process improvement activities within their domain, as well as on their 'normal' job."

Waste Reduction Challenge

- Reduce to *half* current level, then
- Cut it again by *half*, then
- Cut it in *half* again, then
- Reduce the remainder by *half*

Improving Efficiency Has Limits

"We now have enough clues to answer a question that the industrial engineers working on JIT answered long ago. Let's see if I can pose it clearly.

"The question is this: If efficiency, or productivity, is defined as the output divided by the number of employees, as in

$$\frac{\text{Output}}{\text{Number of employees}},$$

for example,

$$\frac{\text{1000 orders}}{\text{100 reps}},$$

should we always focus on increasing the total output of the 100 reps, so that now, for example, 100 reps book 1500 orders? Assume the order size is constant.

"Before you answer, let's look at our familiar bottleneck diagram."

Dr. Selden leafs back through his flip charts. When he gets to the bottleneck diagram, he draws three arrows to indicate the amount of output an improved system might be capable of. He explains that the position of the arrows is arbitrary; he could draw longer or shorter arrows to represent the new output capability at any level.

"Where do you want to set our new target at: A, B, or C?"

I think people are afraid to answer. This seems like one of those trick questions facilitators are always embarrassing the audience with. Finally, someone speaks up. The answer offered is that the "B" level seems to be correct, because that seems to be where the diameter of the pipe would be without obstructions or suboptimization.

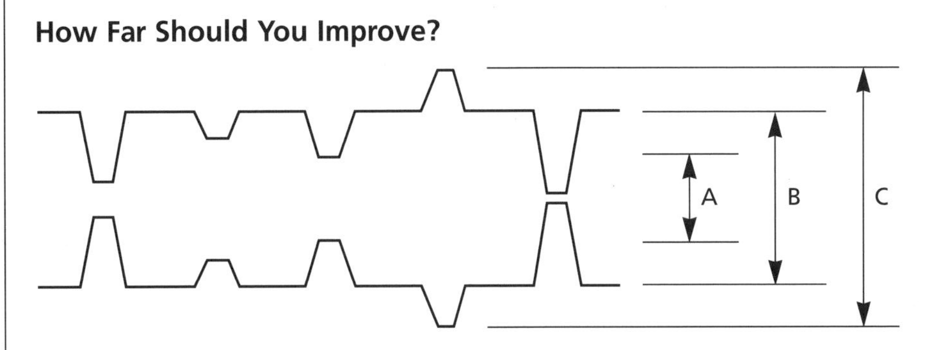

Dr. Selden responds.

"The answer is, 'It depends on what your market can absorb and what you can properly service!' It does no good to increase sales output to 1500 if there is no market for the extra deals. The proponents of JIT point out that in good times it may work to keep the number of employees the same and book 1500 orders. But in bad times the market may not even be able to absorb the original 1000 orders. That's why many chief financial officers, trained in the JIT way of thinking during previous recessions, are very skeptical of any so-called project aimed at increasing efficiency that promises absolute increases in sales. Look at the equation. You can either increase efficiency by holding output constant or by reducing the number of employees required.

"This issue must be carefully thought through before wild claims are made."

Unlike the auto industry, which may find doubling the number of vehicles sold per rep unrealistic, the market for many new goods and services is nowhere near saturation. At Bock Pharmacal, a niche pharmaceuticals maker, productivity (gross sales per rep) increased from $137,000 in 1990 to $378,000 in 1995 (Fleschner 1996a) as overall sales volume increased as well.

The Value of Speed

"America's foremost reconnaissance jet, the SR71 Blackbird, flew so fast—faster than three and a half times the speed of sound—that it was often able to fly into and out of enemy missile range more quickly than the enemy could detect its presence and react. Even if antiaircraft missiles were fired, the Blackbird could outrun them, leaving them far behind."

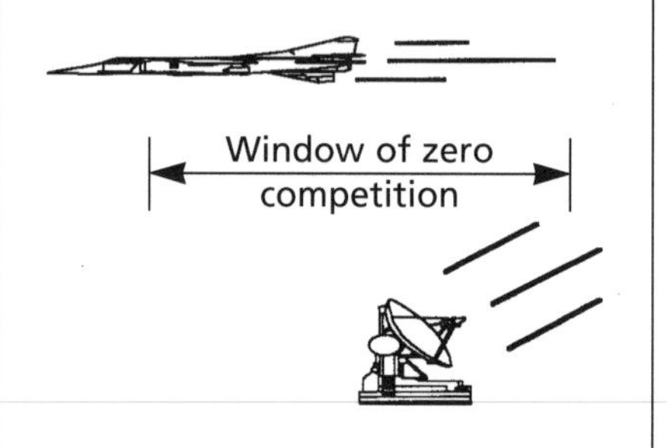

"Speed is a competitive advantage in itself. Speed directly reduces your window of exposure to risk. Whether the relationship is linear or otherwise, you can imagine if the window of exposure to risk is half as long, the risk of disruption is reduced, perhaps by half. That's one reason why sailors like to make quick passages over cruising grounds known to be stormy.

"In the marketplace, improvements in speed can be looked at from the point of view of cycle time reduction. Being faster to offer an improved product—reducing the cycle time from concept to customer—yields a competitive advantage. The shorter the time a new concept is first conceived to when it first reaches the customer, the less time a competitor has to beat us to the punch. Being first to market offers a window of zero competition, when no competitor is in the field to challenge your bid for customer attention and sales.

"In the minivan market, Chrysler enjoyed years of sales before competitive products became available. Pharmaceutical firms first to get FDA approval reap tremendous advantages.

"Reducing cycle time can greatly improve forecasting accuracy, as well. Same-day orders are a sure thing. Events projected to happen exactly 52 weeks from now tend not to happen just as planned. The less time an order or potential order spends in the process as a whole, the more accurate the forecast—the entire system benefits. Schedules are smoother. Costs go down."

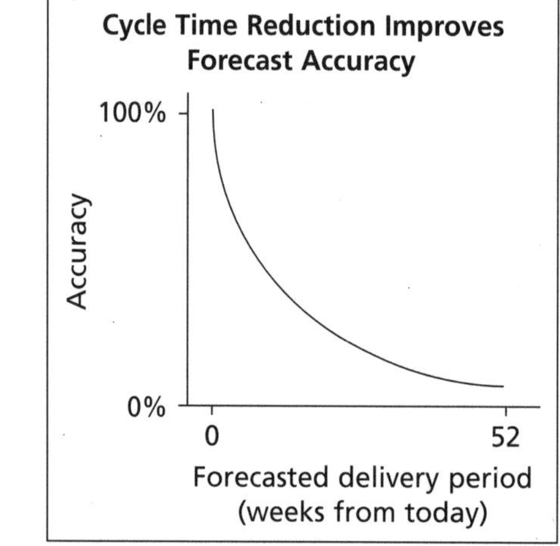

In their thought-provoking book *The 22 Immutable Laws of Marketing* (1993), Al Ries and Jack Trout underscore the importance of speed when they declare that with respect to getting to the market with a new product, "It's better to be first than it is to be better." They ask, "(1) What's the name of the first person to fly the Atlantic Ocean solo? Charles Lindbergh, right? (2) What's the name of the second person to fly the Atlantic Ocean solo? Not so easy to remember, is it?" They go on to ask the name of the second person to land on the moon, the second president of the United States, and so forth—all more difficult to name than the first.

Statements such as Ries and Trout's are worded in a way likely to repel single-minded proponents of quality. "Is it ever 'better' not to be 'better?'" they might ask. From yet another point of view, scientists and engineers know that increasing speed in real-life processes eventually produces chaotic turbulence. Viewers of Lucille Ball's TV show enjoyed this phenomenon watching Lucy and her friend Vivian working in a candy factory. They spilled box after box when the production line sped up past a certain point. What will make sales process engineering such an interesting field is the lively conflict that takes place at the intersection of different disciplines and opinions—and its resolution in the world of fact.

Tool 6: The Run Chart

"Concepts associated with JIT are great for giving us direction and ideas. Now we need to look at another tool to help us quantify the opportunities we have: run charts.

"The example I've projected illustrates a plot of the frequency of customer inquiries we've received, by month, over the course of a year. Run charts make trends, peaks, and valleys easy to spot. In this case, inquiries peak in May and September and really drop over the summer, then again toward the holidays in December. In number-oriented businesses such as fulfillment houses and catalog operations, such a chart would help guide our staffing decisions, among other things. It also points out the need for alternative inquiry generation approaches or products to keep demand high during the off months.

"My well-versed colleague Robert Obermayer speaks at many conferences on the subject of lead generation and its connection with sales. The first question he asks when given an assignment to increase sales is, 'What is your lead generation plan?' He understands the connection between leads and sales. The chief obstacle he faces is in companies where marketing and sales do not work together in a coordinated way. Departments like that miss opportunities to capitalize on what the other is doing. Their view of sales as a process is immature."

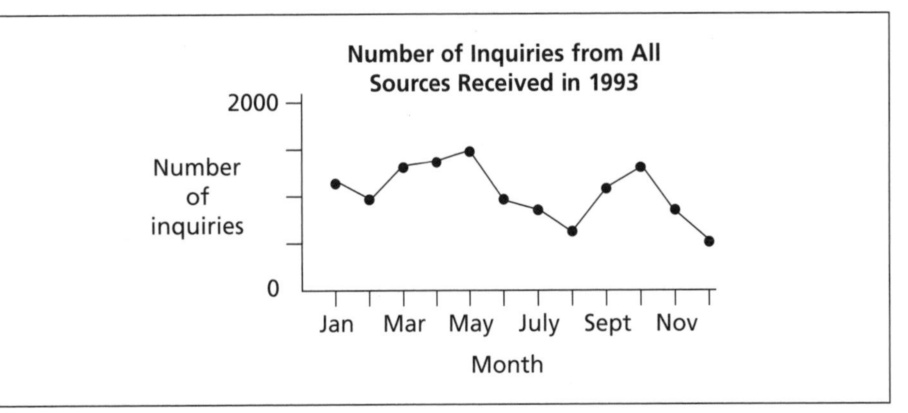

Run Charts: Instructions

Run charts normally plot measures of frequency and other dimensions over time. Percentages, averages, ranges, and standard deviations can also be recorded.

Run charts are often used to plot tangible results or output. They are extremely simple to construct.

Since run charts record data over time, they are very helpful in revealing trends.

To form a run chart, mark equal intervals of time along the horizontal axis. Gradations for the measurement of interest are marked along the vertical axis. Plot the points in sequence and connect the dots. To begin using the run chart in an engineering frame of mind, immediately investigate any point that falls outside of properly set specifications. Take preventive and corrective action as appropriate.

All processes vary to a greater or lesser extent, just due to chance variation. However, from a statistical point of view it is extremely unlikely that in a plot of nine to 20 points, five or more points would either consecutively increase or consecutively decrease just due to chance alone. In a plot of 21 to 100 points, it is extremely unlikely that six or more points would increase or decrease consecutively. Knowing this can help you determine whether a process change you deliberately made is having an effect, or whether the results found might be just due to chance variation. Thomas Pyzdek's *Pocket Guide to Quality Tools* (1994) offers further guidelines on how to use run charts to spot statistically significant trend changes.

A drawback of run charts is that they don't fully show whether any given point falls within the normal swings found in the process involved.

- Run chart: plot of measurements over time
- Often used to plot results or output
- Extremely simple; helpful in seeing trends
- Connect the data points; plot in sequence
- When plotting nine to 20 points, five or more points consecutively increasing or decreasing is probably not due to chance; plotting 21 to 100 points, six or more highly unlikely
- Drawback: doesn't fully show if change is within normal process tendency

This engineering mind-set is contagious. In the previous example, I guess if my specification called for a minimum number of 700 leads per month in order to ensure smooth operations, I would have to immediately jump on the results for August and December and ask whether I should do anything about them or not.

Tool 7: The Histogram

"Now let's look at the seventh tool, the histogram. The histogram plots how many times something is found, in order of dimension. Histograms reveal the central tendency and dispersion of the data under study.

"This example illustrates one of the most important metrics I feel we can look at in the early stages of sales process engineering: yield. In this sense, yield is no different than the concept of crop yield or the yield of computer chips in a batch of silicon wafers.

"The graph here illustrates the yield of appointments set compared to the number of leads received as inputs. Roughly speaking, out of 100 leads, let's say we get a certain number of appointments."

The concept of yield can be applied at any process stage, as long as the numbers are countable and obtainable. Out of a 100 appointments, a certain number of opportunities to submit a firm proposal result. Out of 100 proposals submitted, a certain number of closed sales is obtained. Yield can be used as one quantitative measure of the quality of a subprocess. The lower the quality of the operation and its inputs, the lower the yield of the output.

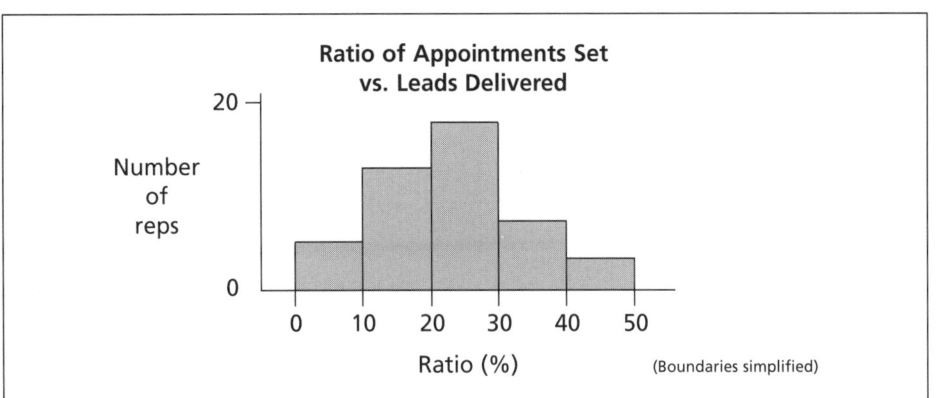

"In the graph above, we've plotted the performance distribution of the company's 50 reps. I've graphed how many reps in this company have a particular 'appointment yield' so far this year. The data are grouped into bins large enough to allow the shape of the distribution to appear. Here we've defined the appointment yield as a ratio equal to the number of appointments set divided by the number of sales leads received. Always be careful as to the specific formulas and operations by which you define any metrics you use. Otherwise, long-term comparisons will be difficult to make or be invalid.

"In this example, almost 20 of the reps seem to be able to turn about 20 to 30 out of every 100 leads they get into appointments. Very few of the reps achieve yields at the 40 percent to 50 percent levels. If your process specification required all reps to achieve a yield of between 20 percent to 60 percent, a histogram immediately displays the type of gap you're facing."

"Ninety-two percent of all salespersons [give up] without asking for the order a fifth time. Sixty percent of all customers say 'no' four times before saying 'yes'" (LeBoeuf 1989).

Histograms: Instructions

A histogram graphs the frequency distribution of items measured. Histograms visually reveal the variation or dispersion of the items as well as their central tendency.

Histograms are often represented as bar graphs, but line graphs are also used. The histogram clusters data that otherwise could be plotted as a continuous curve.

The shape of a histogram may be skewed to one side or another, or it may be exponentially shaped. In many processes, the performance yields a bell-shaped curve. So many processes in nature are bell-shaped that bell-shaped distributions are often referred to as *normal* distributions.

Histograms may also be bimodal, or multipeaked, with the peaks in different locations. Bimodal distributions serve as a clue that the data come from different sources, or different processes, such as from different sales territories, or include widely different product lines. Juran and Gryna's *Quality Planning and Analysis* contains many insightful examples of how to interpret different-shaped histograms (1993, 189–192).

- Histogram: Graph depicting frequency distribution of items measured
- Illustrations variation and central tendency
- Curve can be skewed or exponentially shaped, but many processes normally distributed
- Clusters data that could be plotted in continuous curve
- Less than 50 data points: 5–7 classes; 50 to 100: 6–10; 100–250: 7–12; 250+: 10–20
- Divide total range by number of classes to get interval of each class; tally and plot frequencies

To create a histogram, group the data into classes of equal intervals. A rule of thumb when setting up the histogram is that with fewer than 50 data points, the data should be divided into five to seven classes. If there are 50 to 100 points, six to 10 classes are appropriate. With 100 to 250 points, seven to 12 classes should be used; and with more than 250 data points, 10 to 20 classes.

Once you have the number of classes in mind, figure the size of the class, or its interval. To do this, subtract the highest data point from the lowest (say, $50 - 0 = 50$) and divide the result by the number of classes you've picked (for example, 50 divided by five classes equals a class size of 10). Class boundaries must be mutually exclusive. In our example, we would only use the boundaries of zero, 10, 20, 30, 40, and 50 if none of the data fell on those exact points. Adjust class boundaries to ensure that no data points fall exactly on the interval boundary. Brassard and Ritter's *The Memory Jogger II* offers further useful information (1994, 65–75).

Reflections

The class pauses for a brief mid-morning break. Following the break, Dr. Selden asks for comments and questions before the next exercise begins.

Others begin commenting. I'm afraid I only half tune in because another insight leaps to mind and I'm off thinking to myself again.

Seeing the histogram triggered a thought. In sales management we often focus on the personalities, attitudes, and charisma of the reps. If a rep is at the lower end of the range, we managers naturally focus on that particular rep's "problem." The entire improvement effort can be mired in stern talks, defensiveness, and vague or not-so-vague threats.

It seems most of the efforts of middle sales management are focused on maintenance or on putting out brush fires. Maybe that will never change. Maybe that's the job of day-to-day management. Maybe a structural change will just create a new set of brush fires to deal with. Whose job will it be to be a sales process engineer?

I can see that the engineering approach would be different—much more dispassionate. Seeing the chart of all the reps at once puts things in perspective. As engineers, I think we'd try to design a structural solution that probably isn't aimed at any one particular rep at all. The solution is more likely to elevate the performance of all reps or to change the shape of the distribution. Since the element we'd usually work on is structural, not individual, we're more likely to be interested in tangible elements in the sales process and not someone's state of mind. The tangible elements might be the materials used in a sales presentation, training, the script involved in a telemarketing call, a decision-making tool, or possibly some aspect of automation everyone could use.

In our company we're always focused on how the reps will be more productive. I guess one structural change we've already made is to group our customers by the volume of their orders. Because their hourly wage is so much less than a rep in the field, telemarketers and customer service reps are used to working with customers whose volume with us is small. Field sales personnel are reserved for larger accounts.

***Telemarketing* magazine reports that growth in firms specializing in telemarketing has ranged from between 53 percent and 728 percent (Tehrani 1995).**

Still, I'm also wondering whether we should be putting so much emphasis on the rep when we think about our improvement efforts. Maybe the next frontier is to map things out, starting with the customer and how the customer would prefer doing business with us.

See *High Performance Sales Organizations* for examples of how to map what Learning International calls the *customer relationship process* (Corcoran et al. 1995).

Checkpoint: Run Charts

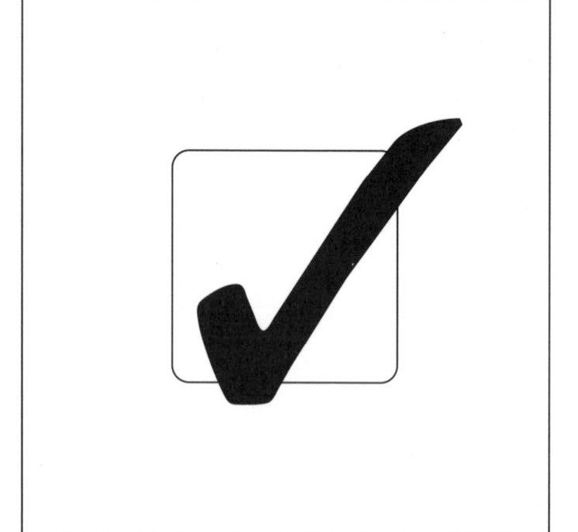

Dr. Selden introduces another exercise, remarking that it's time to see whether the philosophies and tools are sinking in. His concern that we absorb the ideas instead of just passively listening to them is evident. It's as if all of us were his personal protégés. It's clear that some are thirsting to learn more than others. His care stands out, regardless of how much everyone is buying into this.

"It's time to see whether you really understand how we might apply run charts to our sales process engineering efforts. I want to do that in the context of how the general concept of reengineering might be applied, as well.

"Reengineering requires you to think of how things might be very different from the way they are today. This requires creativity. It's much easier to look at the way things are than to think of inventions.

"Here's what I want you to do. First, split into pairs with your neighbor. One of you describe your current sales process and the major steps you employ in it that cause your company problems. Then, as a pair, brainstorm how some of those steps might be completely eliminated or ways the work could be combined into one position. Perhaps you'll need to introduce some form of automation to make that possible. Briefly jot down how life looks before and after the change.

"Then, draw a blank run chart. Put dimensions along the horizontal and vertical axis that could be used to track the impact of your process design change. In a few minutes I'll ask you to share your ideas."

The group is silent for a moment. Then it's obvious lightbulbs are turning on, because people are writing furiously. After a while, Dr. Selden asks for two volunteers to share their notes.

One man raises his hand. "Our firm is an international clothing maker. A rep meets with a buyer. They work out rough designs and fabrics. Sketches are written up on a special form, and the numbers related to the quantity of a potential order—the sizes, colors, and everything else involved—are jotted down. That form is faxed to our Asian manufacturing site for confirmation on availability of production. The form is also faxed to our pricing department to establish the bid. Pricing passes the form to credit once the dollars are figured. It takes about three weeks to get an answer to our prospective customer. We want to computerize the entire design system so that once the design is set, pricing is figured right on the screen, together with credit approval. Simultaneously, we want the potential job to be relayed straight to our manufacturer's scheduling system for immediate or 24-hour notice of timing. We want to print the proposal on demand and be able to enter the order electronically, all from virtually the same screen. If the right databases were available, this should be doable. Our run chart will plot the approximate total hours worked, per order, in our pricing and credit departments. I'd imagine the hours would go down once the system was installed."

A woman raises her hand. "Our company uses a lot of reps who are, as you've mentioned earlier, order takers/delivery reps for 90 percent of their time and sales reps for 10 percent. It takes a lot of time in the store to fill out the stocking tickets. Much of the reps' time is spent taking inventory. Our reengineering idea was to switch over the delivery side to professional delivery people in the case of the larger stores that use scanners at the checkout. The actual inventory counting would be done by the scanner data. That data would automatically trigger the replenishment order. Full-time loading personnel would handle loading the delivery trucks, perhaps even assisted by an automated warehousing and picking system. The higher-priced sales specialists would focus all of their time on sales, using data models of the store layout to suggest product arrangement and profit-enhancing ideas to the retailer. The rep would turn into more of a consultant. We might gain efficiency, but I think it would also help us gain market dominance. The run chart would plot shelf space allocated to our products over time."

Checkpoint: JIT and Histograms

"These are excellent, bold ideas. That's what reengineering is all about: process innovation. Remember, big changes entail big risks. I urge you to test your ideas in some form of pilot prior to implementing them. Proponents of just-in-time approaches, on the other hand, advocate improvements—even if they are small. Smaller changes usually involve less risk. If something doesn't work, it can more easily be reversed. In this next exercise we'll focus on JIT."

Dr. Selden explains the exercise. He asks people to work in pairs again. He asks people to think about their processes, this time focusing on where they think waste occurs. He suggests using any of the seven categories outlined earlier as idea-starters: overproduction, waiting, and so forth. He asks that the teams jot down their comments about waste, then draw a histogram that could be used to capture data about that part of the process. He does not ask for solutions to the problem this time, only for ways to measure waste using a histogram. When he calls for volunteers, many ideas are offered, including the following:

- **The amount of time orders sit in a queue**
- **Order size**
- **Time to produce a proposal**
- **Time spent in cars/on planes over a seven-day period**
- **Closing ratios: the percentage of orders booked versus proposed**

"The interesting thing about engineering is we don't need to beat our chests about how novel or how great our insights and solutions are. We're probably working on things people talked about and knew something about to begin with. The difference with using a fact-based approach is that engineers know how to use data to help tackle problems systematically. The data can serve as an incentive to pursue solutions more doggedly or to find ways to help meet specifications more certainly. Notice also that what we've covered so far does not require difficult statistics. We've used few formulas. Yet we've covered practical ways of moving from a theory-based to a fact-based approach."

Exercises

- Reengineering and run charts
- JIT and histograms

Behavioral Engineering

"It's time to shift gears. In this next section we'll review the work of two eminent behavioral scientists: Ivan Pavlov and B. F. Skinner. The reason for studying behavioral principles as they relate to sales process engineering will soon be clear."

Ivan Pavlov

Ivan Pavlov (1849–1936), the noted Russian physiologist, was perhaps best known for his discovery of the conditioned reflex. In modern times his fame for this discovery overshadows the work that won him the Nobel prize in 1904 for physiology/medicine.

Pavlov's discovery of the conditioned reflex came when he was studying the digestive system of dogs. His assistants would spray meat powder into a dog's mouth. The dog reflexively salivated in response. The amount of saliva would be measured. After a number of experiences, or trials, with the meat powder, Pavlov noticed that the dogs were salivating before the powder was sprayed. In fact, the dogs began to salivate the moment they saw the white lab-coated assistants approaching. The salivation reflex in response to the sight of the lab assistants had been conditioned or learned.

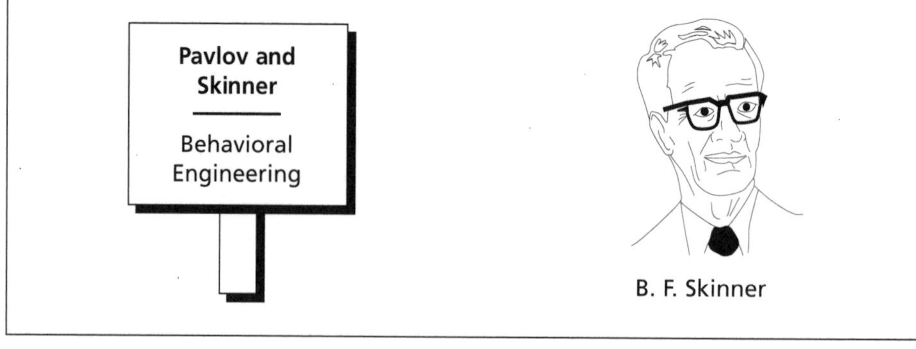

B. F. Skinner

B. F. Skinner

B. F. Skinner (1904–1992) is perhaps the best known modern psychologist. His work spanned many years and included a number of best-selling books including *Walden II* (1948), *Science and Human Behavior* (1953), and *Beyond Freedom and Dignity* (1971).

He achieved notoriety because his work questioned the established views of psychology, much of which were based on the work of Sigmund Freud. Freud postulated that much of human behavior was controlled by hidden, inner mechanisms that could not be directly observed. Skinner challenged this view, declaring Freud's constructs to be unscientific and unnecessary as an explanation of human behavior. Skinner held that much of human behavior could easily be accounted for as the result of observable events that followed behavior (such as reinforcement or punishment) and stimuli that came before the behavior (cues called *discriminative stimuli*). Skinner based his conclusions on controlled experiments that are replicated in labs across the country every day. Skinner's work primarily focused on the rate, or frequency, of learned responding (operant responding).

What Supplies the Energy in a Sales Process?

"The law of inertia states that a body in motion will tend to stay in motion, and a body at rest tends to stay at rest. If that is so, sales process engineers must ask, 'What supplies the energy to cause movement in a sales process?'

"Perhaps we had better remember what it is that we are moving, in a sales process, before we answer that question. It may help to illustrate the situation.

"When dealing with inanimate objects, we can put objects on a motor-driven conveyor belt. The objects will be passed along at a certain speed. The electricity driving the motor supplies the energy.

"Inanimate objects must have energy applied to them. They are, after all, inanimate. A stone contains no means of self-propulsion, self-regulation, or self-adjustment. Inanimate objects have no need to propagate the species.

"So when we're dealing with people, some of our more familiar process cause-and-effect analyses begin to fall short.

"Why is that? Think about it. In sales, we cannot literally put people on a conveyor belt to move them from one process stage to another: from lead to appointment, to presentation to close. They would object! They would want to escape! People don't like being forced! If they didn't like what you are doing, they'd call the police!" [The group chuckles at the image of people struggling on a conveyor belt.]

Inanimate Objects Must Have Energy Applied to Them

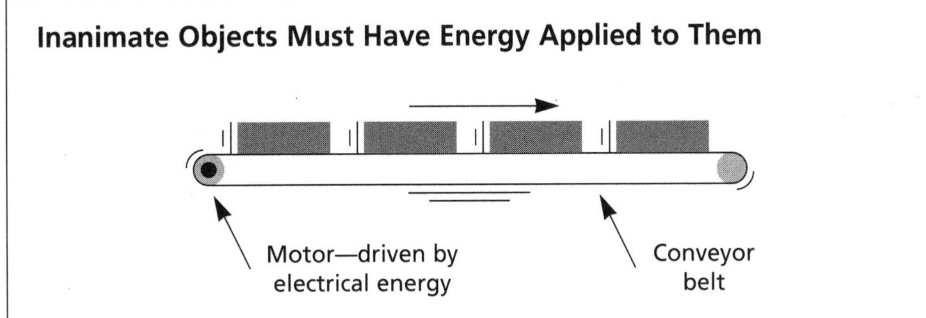

Mechanical Process Analysis Tools Fall Short

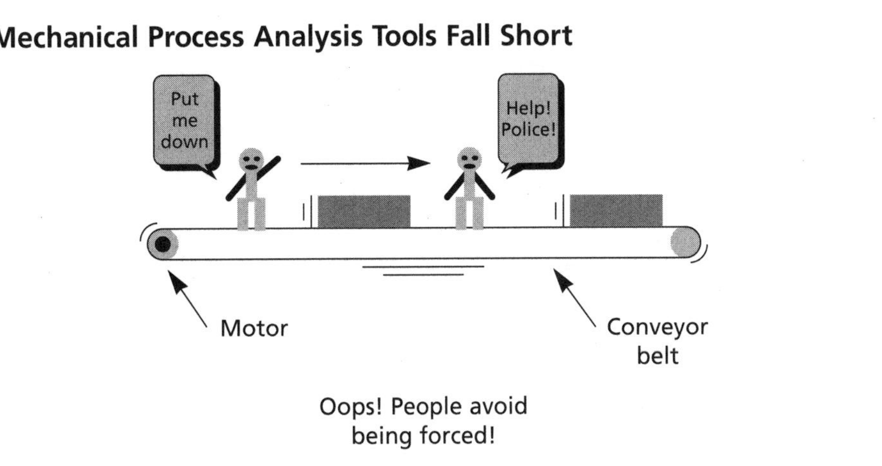

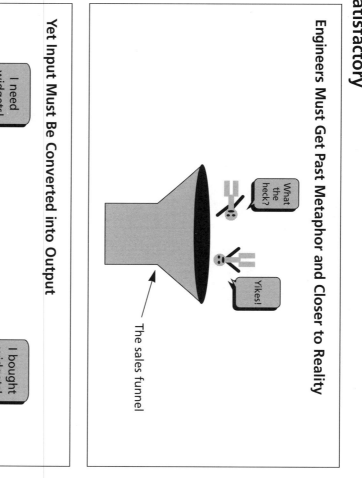

Even the Sales Funnel Is Unsatisfactory

"Even the familiar sales funnel is unsatisfactory. I was raised on the idea that sales is like a funnel. Suspects fall into the top, and as you do your work, they turn into prospects, then into customers as they come out the bottom. Fewer and fewer remain at each level. We know the story.

"Yet the power of this image breaks down when we try to use it for anything but a rudimentary motivational metaphor.

"Look! Do we literally drop people into the top of a funnel? The very metaphor of a funnel is inappropriate. What do funnels do? How do they actually perform? In reality, isn't a funnel designed to transfer whatever is put in the top into another container without spilling anything? Isn't that why we use funnels?

"If I tried to use a sales funnel to pour oil into my outboard engine's fuel tank, what would happen? I'd wind up spilling most of the oil all over the place!

"So we need to move closer to reality. Management can speak poetry. Engineers must deal with reality.

"The reality when we are dealing with biological beings is that although inputs need to be converted into outputs, different laws are at work. In the sales process, a person expresses a need for widgets at one end. A sequence of events occurs and converts that input into an output: a customer who has bought the widgets."

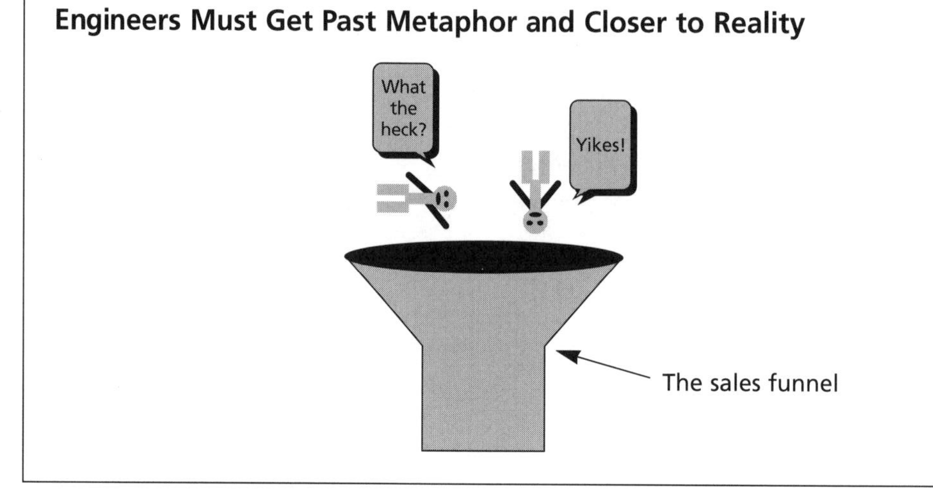

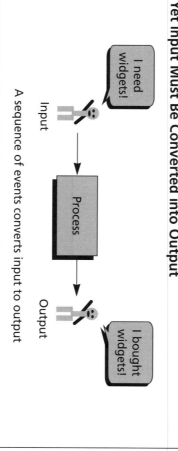

What Causes Behavior Within a Process?

"When experienced salespeople are first exposed to the concepts of how engineering may be applied to the sales, marketing, and service processes, their reaction is often skeptical. 'Well, we're dealing with people, not machines and tangible widgets.' Aside from the fact that many elements of the sales process deal with machines—computers, automobiles, airplanes, and telephones—and tangible widgets—such as advertisements, telemarketing scripts, product packaging, and lead lists—these experienced salespeople have a point. There's a big difference between people and inanimate objects.

"Up until now, many of the principles we've been covering could obviously be applied to inanimate objects. Inanimate objects obey the laws of physics, chemistry, and the like. The law of inertia states that an object will tend to stay at rest unless energy is applied to it and so on.

"Now we are dealing with objects that are very much animated—people. We have to ask ourselves: What known principles apply to animate objects? Well, animate beings follow the laws of chemistry and physics, as well. If a person steps off the Leaning Tower of Pisa, the forces of gravity apply to that individual, whether he likes it or not. But, as people, we are also biological beings as well as physical ones, and we follow a second general set of laws: those that apply to biological organisms.

Inanimate objects

- Subject to principles of physics, chemistry, etc.
- Example: Law of inertia applies to inanimate objects—unless energy applied, no motion occurs

Animate beings

- Organic beings subject to two sets of laws
- Biological plus physical
- Example: Law of survival, propagation of species, genetics, nutrition, learning

"Biological principles include the law of survival, the need to propagate the species, genetic principles, laws pertaining to cellular growth, learned behavior, and so on.

"Does the observation that 'we're dealing with people, not machines,' mean that the variables dealing with people can't be studied? Sometimes when I hear that comment, I think that is the intent of the speaker. 'Harumph—well, this deals with people, so it's hopeless to pursue the matter further.' What's the point of training our people, if that's the case? Of course we think behavior can be changed, and of course we're familiar with many positive, acceptable ways to do so.

"Instead of dropping the matter because we're 'dealing with people,' let's pursue it as proper engineers and see what we find from a constructive point of view."

What Supplies the Motive Force in the Sales Process?

"So we're back to our original question. Now that we see the situation more clearly, I think we're in a better position to answer it. What supplies the motive force in the sales process? Ultimately, the answer must be found in *biological* causes.

"Since we are working with human behavior, the motive force must lie in the biological variables responsible for controlling behavior. In the hallway earlier, someone briefly mentioned the importance of compensation systems in controlling behavior. As sales process engineers, we'll not only need to study how automation can change behavior, we'll also need to be aware of how variables such as compensation plans affect behavior. Our field of view needs to be quite wide."

In his article "Sales Success—When the Price Is Right," Don Rice (1996) cites a study involving the impact of pricing on behavior. When the price for work gloves was set to 37 cents, they sold poorly. The price was increased to 39 cents and the gloves sold like hotcakes.

We will ultimately need to study how the personnel selection process, job objectives, the goals set, and the type of feedback people receive regarding their progress toward the goals have an impact on behavior.

"Many biological variables are beyond our control. We are born with a set of genes. I am not going to try to out-jump Michael Jordon. Each person is built differently from the next. The type of nervous system we are born with and our visual acuity, among other biological features, set a natural bandwidth that we learn to operate within.

"Many variables that have an impact on behavior are within our control, however, especially those related to learned behavior. And even our biological platforms can be augmented or changed. I can't see infrared, but with a special scope or photographic paper, I can see an infrared representation. I'm not seven feet tall, but I can climb a ladder and reach even higher. My judgment is fairly intact now, but give me an adult beverage or two and the picture may alter somewhat."

- Motive force in sales process ultimately stems from biological causes
- Principle is to control variables responsible for desired behavior
- Many biological variables beyond our control
- Many are within control, especially those having to do with learned behavior

Types of Processes That Control Human Behavior

Reflexive Conditioning

Yum! I'm hungry! That picture makes my mouth water!

Burger!

Paired stimulus controls reflexive response

Conditioning Process

Unconditioned stimulus (burger) → Reflex (salivation)

\+

Conditioned stimulus (picture of burger) → Reflex (salivation)

"In this survey course it's my job to cover the two primary processes that actually control human behavior: reflexive and operant conditioning. Let's see how these principles, even though it may be at a very simple level, are relevant to sales process engineering. We need to get at the issue of what really supplies the motive force in our sales processes, at a level that goes beyond metaphors like the sales funnel and that take us closer to reality.

"We employ reflexive conditioning all the time, especially when we're working with advertising. Remember your psychology classes? We pair a new stimulus with a stimulus that already evokes a reflexive response such as salivation—advertisers translate the word *salivation* into the phrase *mouth watering*, by the way—so that in the future, the new stimulus evokes the reflexive response by itself. Many commercials are written as comedy. Why? Because laughter feels good. Marketers want to pair their products with feeling good.

"Skeptical? Unimportant? I tell you what: Let's take some completely arbitrary images—a crown, a pair of golden arches, and a nattily attired Southern gentleman with white hair and a white goatee to match. These images have already acquired the ability to evoke internal feelings of their own. The crown evokes an image of royalty, power, superiority. The color gold evokes warmth, security, and value, while the curve of the paired arches may evoke a soft, gentle, even feminine form of supportiveness. The Southern gentleman is kindly, grandfatherly, wealthy looking, and clean. Maybe this nice, kindly looking man will give a good little boy or girl a treat if we pay him a visit.

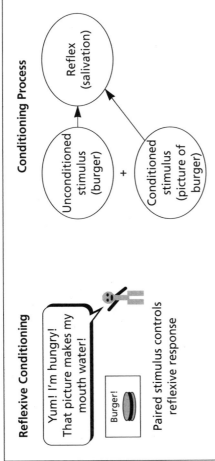

"Now all we have to do is repeatedly pair these attractive stimuli with an image of something that already makes your mouth water: say, a broiling burger, or a hamburger heaping with lettuce and a special, savory sauce, or some delicious-looking fried chicken and a few corporate names. Repeat thousands of times over a lifetime. This is a recipe for effective advertising. When we see the crown, or the arches, or the Southern gentleman, suddenly our mouth is likely to water. Especially if it's been four or five hours since we've last eaten!

"I'll not do you the disservice of being disingenuous. Effective advertising is designed to set up reflexive responses. Any advertisement or logo paired with food, which does less than evoke a favorable reflexive response, has a less-than-satisfactory yield. The response targeted in any given ad may not necessarily be the salivary response, by the way. The response may be a smile, a sexual tingle, a feeling of comfort, or some other reflex. If the marketer is successful at this stage, the next type of conditioning is easier to achieve: operant conditioning, especially concerning the behaviors of *approach* and *purchase*.

Learned Behavior

Learned behavior is acquired through interaction with the environment. One difference between humans and other organisms is that a great deal of human behavior is learned, whereas animals seem to display a greater proportion of instinctive behavior.

Scientists refer to learned behavior as *operant* or *instrumental*. The terms refer to the fact that operant behavior operates on the environment around us and that the behavior is instrumental in achieving what looks to be a purpose.

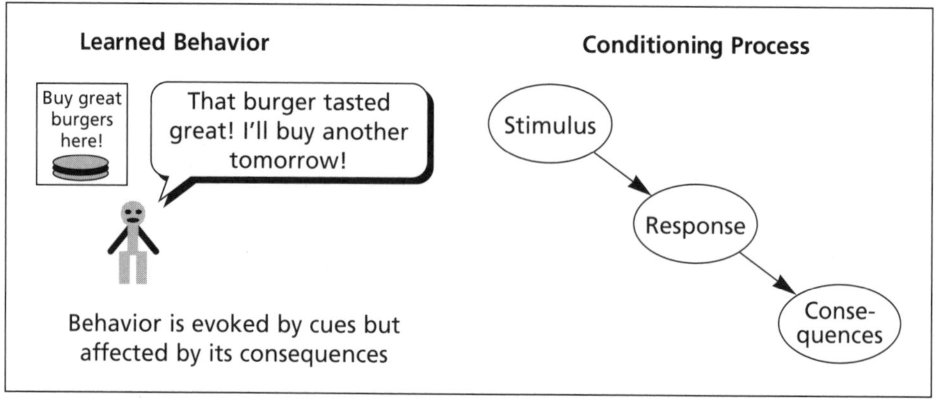
Learned Behavior
Buy great burgers here!
That burger tasted great! I'll buy another tomorrow!
Behavior is evoked by cues but affected by its consequences
Conditioning Process
Stimulus
Response
Conse-quences

"There's another form of behavior: that which is entirely learned through experience. Let's look at the conditioning sequence for learned behavior. First, you may see a sign of some sort or you may be asked to do something. Behavioral scientists call this stimulus an *antecedent* or *discriminative* stimulus or cue. If you perform the response and a reinforcing consequence follows, you'll tend to repeat that behavior again. The power of the discriminative stimulus to elicit that behavior is strengthed, too.

"We see this relationship all the time in sales, marketing, and service settings. For example, let's say you're hungry. Most of us can relate to this. You see a sign for a restaurant you've never been to before. You stop in. The meal is delicious and the service is great. You're now more likely to eat at that restaurant again in the future, aren't you? The relationship is probabilistic: the tendency to go there again has been strengthened, but the relationship is not one to one. As long as you have a choice, you won't go to the new restaurant *every* time you're hungry. Your tendency to go there again in the future has simply increased; the relationship is not absolute, it's simply more probable.

"Now let's say you go to that restaurant again and the food is wonderful a second time. This further strengthens the frequency of your behavior. In the real world, if you went there a third time and for the third time in a row you had a delightful meal, what would happen? This would become one of your favorite restaurants, wouldn't it? It's hard to find an affordable restaurant that consistently offers delicious food and good service.

"The interesting thing is that you'll tend to repeat behavior that is reinforced, even if no clear discriminative stimulus preceded it. In the example above, the sign itself meant little to you the first time you went to the restaurant. Let's say no one told you to go there. You just went because you were hungry, and other choices weren't available. When the sequence is repeated over and over, however, the sign comes to take on the power to elicit your behavior all by itself. If you see that same sign in a different city, you'll be more likely to stop by that new restaurant than otherwise, even though you'd never eaten at that particular restaurant before."

Consumer Behavior and Service Consistency

This is fascinating. I have always been interested in human behavior, just as much as or more than anything of a more mechanical nature. What strikes me about this part of the presentation is it's obvious to me that human behavior can be viewed from the perspective of cause and effect. This is not a black art. I've heard that market researchers in consumer packaged goods have studied consumer shopping behavior in a super-scientific way. I understand they mock up stores and observe live supermarkets to observe what aisles customers are most likely to walk down, where the ideal display height for snack items is, and what kind of packaging is most likely to be chosen.

That restaurant story we just heard is pretty apt. As I think about it, I guess it also illustrates the converse point, too. If the food wasn't good the first time I wouldn't go back. I have lots of other options to choose from in my town these days. It used to be that we only had a couple of decent restaurants. Now we've got tons of them.

That point Dr. Selden just made about the restaurant sign in the other city was interesting, too, and the power a sign develops to prompt my "stopping in" behavior. That must be what chains and franchise operations of all sorts are capitalizing on: the power of a brand to attract approach behavior. I wonder what would happen if the restaurant in the other city didn't serve a meal that was equal to the standards I'd come to expect from the first restaurant? Would that reduce the strength of the sign's ability to prompt my "stopping in" behavior elsewhere? I bet it would. I guess that is something important for a business to look into. Especially if it had invested a lot in its signs and brand image. I think that's a point Dr. Selden has been trying to make. A lot of money is at stake, and this whole business is worth pursuing more systematically.

My eye lights on a histogram I'd drawn earlier. Oh boy. I didn't really get all Dr. Selden's emphasis on the importance of reducing variability before. Suddenly it's hitting me like a flash. We absolutely must reinforce customer buying behavior to ensure a high rate of repeat purchases. Any variability there would kill us.

If we punish the customer's behavior in one location, we might wipe out the beneficial effects we gained by reinforcing that purchase behavior in the first location. I bet that's why companies like McDonalds invest so much in their service training and procedure manuals! People are individuals, but consistent delivery is critical!

Contingencies of Reinforcement

The relationship between stimuli, responses, and consequences may be more or less obvious. What may not be obvious is that the relationship between these variables—the cues, behavior, and consequences are a collective set comprising *contingencies of reinforcement*—has been extensively mapped out in hundreds of research experiments over the past century. (See, for example, the *Journal of the Experimental Analysis of Behavior.*) Response rate, latency, duration, probability, shape, and force have all been explored as a function of variables such as the type of cue that precedes it and the nature of the consequence that follows it (Honig 1966).

Contingencies of reinforcement have been well explored in laboratory settings. What excites pioneers in sales process engineering is that application of the principles discovered in practical settings is far from well documented. Further adding to the engineering challenge, the work in practical settings is often complex. Instinctive, reflexive, and instrumental behavior can occur simultaneously. Moreover, not all the variables involved can be controlled. Research into so-called chaos theory encourages us to believe that broad patterns and trends should be discernable, nevertheless (Gleick 1987).

From a quantitative point of view, behavioral science has advanced far beyond the point of simply describing reflexive and learned behavior. The frequency of behavior can be controlled, for example, by changing the schedule with which reinforcement is delivered. The results are highly illuminating.

When food is delivered to an animal each time it presses a bar, the schedule of reinforcement is called a continuous reinforcement frequency schedule. The slope of the cumulative response curve in such a case is charted on the lower right.

When reinforcement is delivered only when a fixed ratio of responses have been emitted—say, one food pellet for every three responses—the rate of response increases. This slope is plotted in the middle.

If reinforcement is delivered on a variable schedule—say, sometimes after one response, sometimes after 20 responses, and everywhere in between—the response rate is highest of all. Notice the similarity to how slot machines pay off.

Dr. Selden asks the group members if they can think of obvious examples of how reinforcement is used in sales, marketing, and service situations. After a moment or two, hands go up.

"What about when cereal makers offer coupons worth cents off the next purchase, in specially marked boxes?" someone asks.

"Wouldn't the lottery-like games offered by some fast-food places be an example?" offers another.

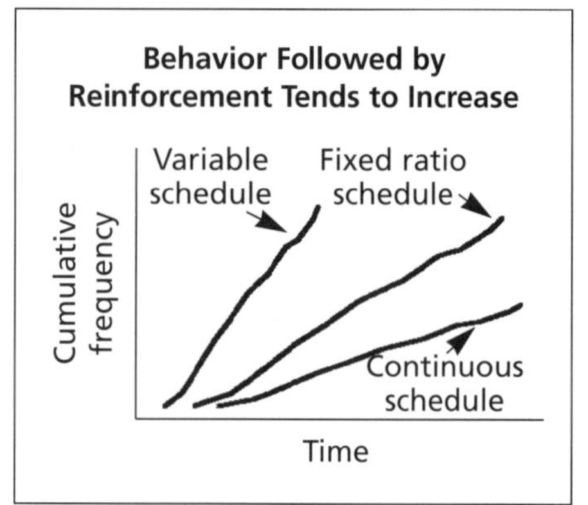

"How about frequent flyer miles given for each dollar purchased using certain credit cards?"

"Aren't commission schedules used that way?"

"What about sending a prompt free replacement for something that breaks?"

"Excellent examples. You'll see them all around you. That last one is something I can really identify with. I've recently had excellent dealings with Coleman, Rubbermaid, Bausch & Lomb, and Cross in terms of getting quick replacements. These are huge operations, but they give service like the friendly store down the block.

"By the way, when behavior is first being established, the longer the delay between the response and when reinforcement takes place, the lower the frequency of the behavior. That's why, as a general rule of thumb, it's so important to reduce cycle times so that the difference between when a customer expects something and when you deliver it is as close to zero as possible."

Stimulus Generalization

"So much of this seminar is devoted to the *mechanical* principles of process engineering, I feel it is important to balance the presentation with examples of *behavioral* principles we sales process engineers need to be aware of. Should I continue with a few more behavioral principles, or should I skip ahead? [The group urges him to go on.]

"The nature of the discriminative stimulus that precedes, or sets the occasion for, reinforcement comes to acquire the power to control behavior, as well. Please look at this slide carefully. Let's say a pure orange light is always illuminated during times when a bar press will release food. When another light—red, reddish-orange, yellowish-orange, or yellow—is lit, pressing a bar has no effect. After learning this relationship, a typical frequency of responding in the presence of the different lights is charted. Notice that most of the responses occur when the orange light is on. But just as interesting is the fact that responding generalizes to lights most similar in color to the orange, even though those relationships never involved reinforcement.

"Do you see why companies have to protect their logo and brand names with such vigor? Even the shape of the package is critical. Think of a soft drink bottle shape, for example. Do any stand out?" [Many of the participants nod their heads in agreement.]

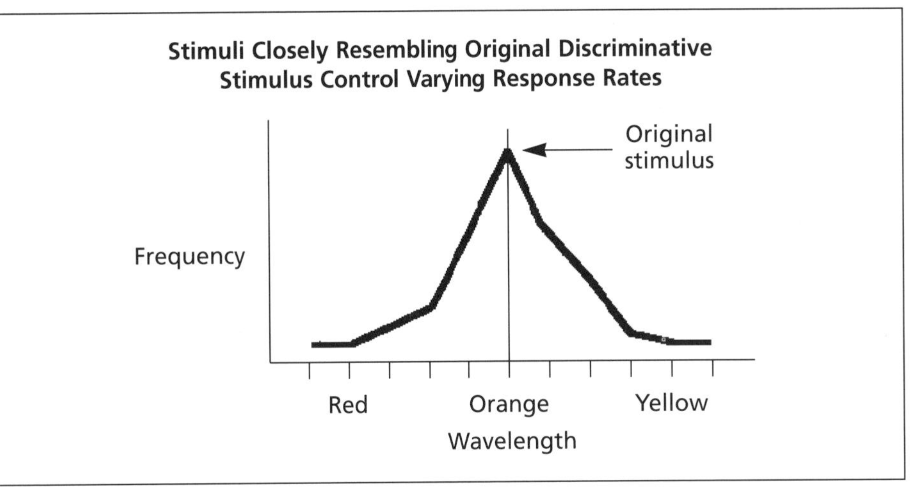

The implications are monumental. It seems as though to the extent Brand X can mimic our appearance, the consumer will buy it! I wish all our salespeople could hear this. I also think this means we have to keep our message consistent, too. If we vary, the size of the band of "wrong" responses will increase!

"More than half the people who say that they are satisfied with you will still purchase somewhere else" (Stum 1995).

You Can Make a Horse Drink

A critic once said to B. F. Skinner, "You can lead a horse to water, but you can't make it drink." Dr. Skinner replied, "You can if you deprive the horse of water for 24 hours." Observations like this irritated those who insist that everything people do is governed by free will.

"Philosophical discussions aside, it's clear that people tend not to eat when they are full. People do tend to eat when hungry. A horse tends to drink if it hasn't had water for a while. Motivational states significantly affect the probability responses will occur. Responses are highest when the response earns something needed at the moment.

"The chart here illustrates the cumulative frequency of responding for food during three conditions. Responses during the first period occurred during a period of relative food deprivation. In the second period the animal was allowed to free-feed before coming into the experimental session. Responses were still followed by the delivery of food pellets. We see that much less responding occurred. In the third period, the animal was food deprived prior to the experimental session."

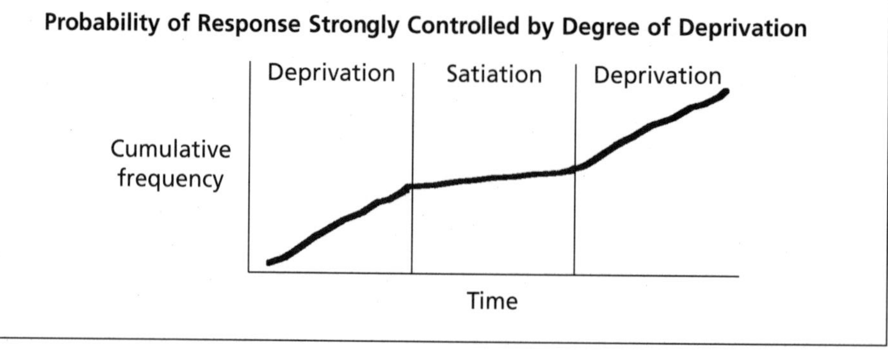

To me this looks like a chart graphing the oldest rule for business success in the book: Find a need and fill it. It looks like we will waste our time trying to sell things to people who don't crave or need them. I suppose from an engineering perspective, the lesson is that we need to implement a method for detecting who has a need and when they have it. If we try to sell too early, they won't buy. Too late, they won't buy. That gets back to the just-in-time lessons we learned earlier. We need a way to sense when our customers have a need. The more sensitive those sensors are, the more quickly they could detect shifts in motivation, and the better our chance of providing customers with a solution just in time. All these reasons point out that our lead qualification program is critical.

We also may be able to create a need people didn't know they had before. I don't think I ever "needed" or felt deprived of baking soda in my toothpaste. But once I tried it, I'd never want to go back to my previous kind.

In cases where we can't control or sense a prospect's state of motivation, I guess that means we have to be located close to wherever potential customers are most likely to experience a need. "Location, location, location," the old saying goes. Maybe that's why fast-food companies are putting versions of their products right on the grocery store shelves, in convenience stores, even in gas stations!

This also explains the importance of advertising of all types. If we can't sense a potential customer's motivational state, we'd better have a way to point a customer in our direction once the motivation does increase. And, of course, perhaps our advertising can heighten that state of motivation, if properly constructed.

The illustration about motivation also points out that unless our product line is broad enough, there are simply times when we can't sell a particular customer anything, no matter how hard we try. In those circumstances, trying would be a form of waste, I suppose.

Preference Behavior

"Most of the time customers have alternatives. They can purchase your product, purchase a competing product, or forego the purchase altogether. Scientists studying preference behavior at the level of basic research have found many things. We have time to cover one of the most important here.

"The graph here illustrates two cumulative response curves from the same subject. The experimental setup was simple. Two buttons (disks) were side by side. Each could be pressed at all times. Pressing one button would result in receiving food about 20 times an hour. Pressing the other button resulted in receiving food about 30 times an hour, a denser probability of receiving reinforcement at any given time.

"Guess which graph illustrates the response rate associated with the *denser*, more certain, probability of receiving reinforcement? [Several people say, "The top one."]

"Correct. The top chart is associated with the denser schedule of reinforcement.

"Which schedule of reinforcement are you offering your customers? Which does your competition offer? Which reinforces your client's approach and purchase behaviors the most?

"As far as repeat business is concerned, the firm offering its customers the more certain reward for purchasing is more likely to get the next purchase."

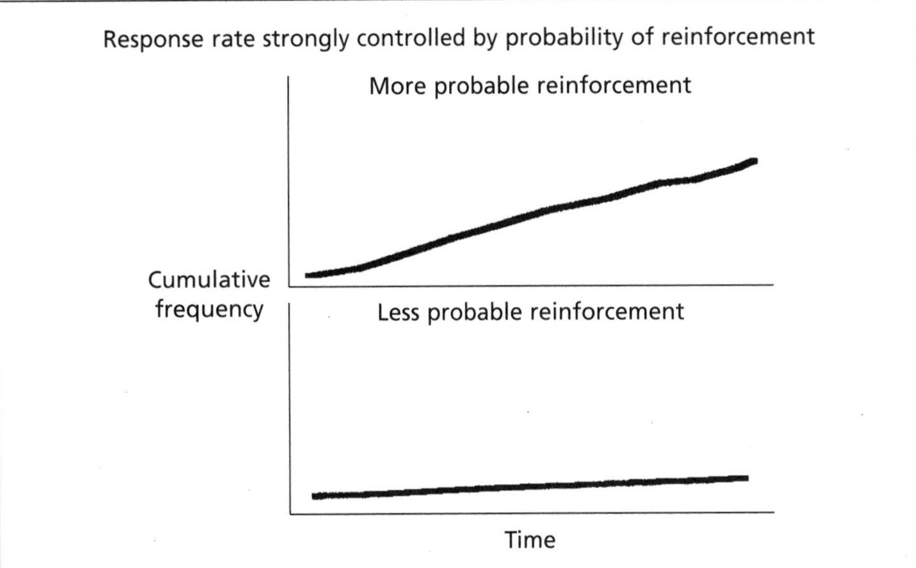

These illustrations graphically underscore the absolutely critical nature of everything we've been talking about today. The more error-free our delivery, the better-designed our products, the more closely we meet our customer's specifications and even delight them by exceeding their expectations, the more competitive we'll be. Our systems have to support this, or we're doomed to being an also-ran.

The interesting thing, too, about the graphs is that the choice was not all or nothing. Both choices were available at all times. In the setup Dr. Selden described, the consumer seems to alternate in preference. Our ability to offer the denser reinforcement schedule seems to govern the proportion of the market we receive. I wish my company's president were here today. These insights would help strengthen our resolve to follow through on some of the programs we're trying to implement.

"I started this section by stating that we need to understand what supplies the motive force in the sales process. I think we've had a good overview of just that, from a fact-based point of view. Motive force must be supplied at each stage of the process to ensure that the necessary movement or behavior occurs—we might measure that movement between stages as yield."

Tool 8: The Cause-and-Effect Diagram

"The material we just covered was rather extensive—justifiably so. We needed to balance the previous subjects by covering the human side of process mechanics. Of course, the analysis of human behavior is much richer in breadth than we've been able to cover in our brief survey.

"Returning to our agenda, let's cover another pair of process engineering tools, beginning with something called a *cause-and-effect diagram*. Cause-and-effect diagrams illustrate the relationship between an outcome—an effect—and the variables responsible for that outcome—the causes.

"In my illustration the outcome is highlighted in the box to the right: low sales or attendance. Major general factors contributing to the outcome are represented in the boxes: the five P's. In the case of service-related outcomes, the main causes usually involve the company's provisions (or tools), personnel, procedures, policies, and patrons. The language of the five P's strikes me as a bit cumbersome, but it helps to trigger useful thinking. You don't need to use the five P's if they don't seem to fit.

"The illustration maps the results of a brainstorming session in which the improvement team plotted possible factors causing recent low attendance at a circus. Attendance is not just an economic variable. It is a human behavior. Dollars don't buy tickets, people do! The team outlined a proverbial comedy of errors, much of it related to human behavior. Every business has these from time to time.

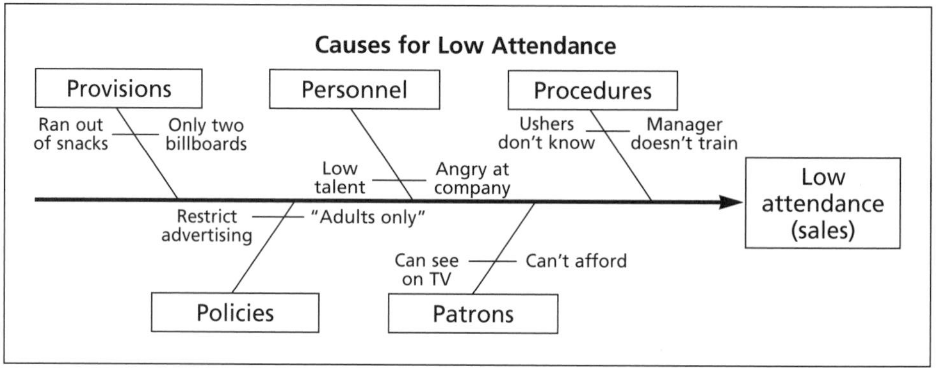

Causes for Low Attendance

Provisions
Ran out of snacks
Only two billboards
Personnel
Low talent
Angry at company
Procedures
Ushers don't know
Manager doesn't train
Low attendance (sales)
Restrict advertising
"Adults only"
Can see on TV
Can't afford
Policies
Patrons

"In terms of provisions, the concession's popcorn maker broke down, resulting in many complaints and lost sales. The marketing department could lease space on only two billboards, missing six major thoroughfares in the city instead of providing its usual ratio of one billboard per four-lane highway.

"In terms of the circus personnel, the star of the lion-taming act was ill, leaving a lower-talent understudy. Further, the clowns' comedy act wasn't funny: They went a little too far in some of their routines in which the ringmaster seemed to be humiliated. The audience wondered whether the clowns were angry with management. The negative publicity and word-of-mouth was devastating. I can think of a few businesses I've been in where I've picked up similar vibes with counter workers: They don't seem happy with their job! As a result, I didn't feel as happy to be in that shop, or hotel, or theatre.

"The locally procured temporary ushers didn't know the proper greeting and seating procedures. In general, the brainstorming team felt management didn't properly train the ushers in key procedures.

"A recent change in policy meant that the local TV and radio ad budget was cut by 50 percent; further, ads were place on adult format talk shows and news shows. Children's TV sitcoms and cartoons were deliberately boycotted because the circus owner felt that the quality of TV for children had slipped too much for his liking.

"A competing circus was televised locally, meaning that many potential patrons didn't want to buy tickets. Further, the ticket price was higher than similar events in this local market, making the event difficult to afford for the local patrons.

"A disaster! However, the diagram itself helped the team identify potential problems, and things went great in the next city. The diagram made it easier to systematically isolate the real problems and prevent them in the future. We hope all these things would never happen at once."

Cause-and-Effect Diagrams: Instructions

- Cause-and-effect diagram: diagram of relationship between outcome and potential controlling variables (from Ishikawa)
- Layout resembles "fishbone," "stream-and-river," or "branch-and-limb" appearance
- Effect is main trunk, causes are branches, main causes can be boxed at branch ends
- Does not demonstrate true responsibility between one cause and others
- Ask "five whys;" don't stop until all final root cause exhausted
- Effect, or symptom of problem, must be clearly stated or group will be confused

Cause-and-effect diagrams illustrate the relationship between an outcome and potential controlling variables. The diagram was first used by Kaoru Ishikawa at the Kawasaki Iron Works. A powerful version of this technique, called *logic trees,* is explained in *It's Not Luck* (Goldratt 1994), a book containing several good sales process improvement examples.

The layout of the diagram resembles a fishbone, stream and river, branch and limb, or trunk and root. Sometimes the diagram is called by one of these names, too, as in a *root cause* or *fishbone* diagram.

The main effect is usually drawn as an arrow pointed to the right, with the description of the main effect spelled out to the right of the arrowhead. Sometimes the main effect is highlighted by surrounding it with a box. Causes leading to the main effect are drawn as branches.

Cause-and-effect diagramming is usually combined with brainstorming to generate a set of potential causes. The effect, or the symptom of a problem, must be clearly stated or the group will be confused.

Where each branch can be categorized under one main heading, a box with the name of each branch can be drawn at the end of the branch to help organize the brainstorming. Frequently, quality engineers speak of service problems as related to one or more of five causes: provisions, personnel, procedures, policies, and patrons (the five P's). The diagram can be organized in any way that helps surface potential relationships.

The same general factor may play a part in a number of causal variables. For example, a lack of training may affect several causal streams.

The cause-and-effect diagram does not prove responsibility between a supposed cause and the observed effect, nor does it quantify the relative contribution of each variable to the outcome. Hypothetical relationships between variables may need to be quantified and subjected to experimental scrutiny to demonstrate true cause and effect. This may be a necessary next step where the relationship is potentially important and the nature of the relationship is not completely clear or obvious.

In sales, marketing, and customer service, the cause-and-effect diagram can be used to troubleshoot problems, but it can also be used to clarify potential positive relationships. The "active ingredients" leading to reinforcement of repeat buying behavior could also be diagrammed, for example.

To probe deeply for potential variables, a facilitator may try the "five-why" (5Y) technique: asking the question "Why?" five times. Start with the question, "Why did that happen?" Keep asking "Why?" until no more answers along that line come to mind. Often, the first reason offered is not sufficient to solve a problem. Asking the question, "Why?" five times (more or less) helps move beyond superficial answers.

Tool 9: The Scatter Plot

"Scatter plotting is an extremely powerful visual tool. Without setting up an elaborate empirical test, scatter plotting illustrates the potential relationship between two variables. One of these might be the cause, and the other might be an effect.

"Let's say I'm shopping for carpet. Some stores use salespeople to initially talk with the customer about the various styles and prices in the showroom. If the customer is interested, an estimator is sent to do the measurements prior to preparing a final quote. The horizontal line in the graph represents the ratio of how many job estimates follow from every 100 sales presentations. If you obtain 25 estimates out of 100 sales presentations, the yield is 0.25, or 25 percent."

The graph uses a *yield* dimension: the ratio of estimates made to presentations along the horizontal axis. Looking at outcomes in terms of yields operationalizes the measurement. The words *good presentation* can be defined in terms of the yield achieved.

The vertical axis illustrates a second variable. In this case the second variable is a factor we think might be related to the outcome, namely, the score a rep achieved on a product knowledge and sales presentation certification test. The score could range between zero and 100.

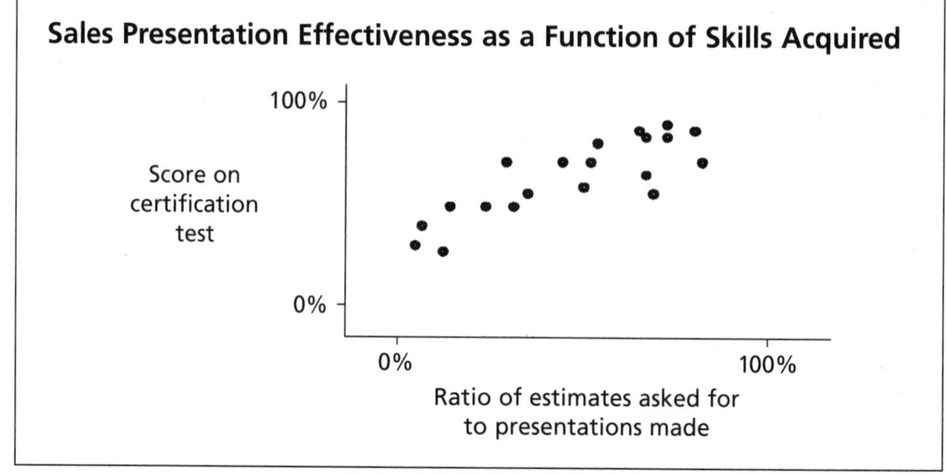

For each rep, the sales process engineer plots the intersection of certification test score against the yield. Each dot sits at the intersection of the two factors.

"Prior to graphing the results, let's say the company had no idea whether its sales training was effective, or whether the certification test really measured a skill that translated into action. As you can see, there is a high correlation between reps who did well on the certification test and their ability to turn a sales presentation into the next step of the process. The engineer can now advise the company to act with more conviction in seeing that its reps are properly certified prior to being allowed to sell.

"Not long ago I visited with the CEO of a medical products firm growing at the annual rate of about 20 percent. He told me that his firm requires its sales reps to pass a product knowledge certification test before being allowed to sell the new products. It pays to take product knowledge seriously, doesn't it?"

Scatter Plots: Instructions

A scatter plot graphs the relationship between two variables. The horizontal axis is used for one variable, the vertical axis for the other.

Collect two measurements of interest on the same item or person. For each measured subject, plot a point at the intersection of the two measures.

Points may be circled one or more times to show that two or more points occupy the same position.

Correlation does not prove a causal relationship, but it helps to narrow down the list of possibilities. For example, let's say 50 reps score high on a test that shows they can correctly fill out electronic call reports. Yet their rate of completing call reports is low. It would not make sense to conclude that knowing how to complete the report caused reps not to complete the form; another variable is probably at work. Maybe a benefit (that is, positive reinforcement) for completing the call reports is weak or absent.

Scatter plots can also be used to help isolate inert ingredients or wasted efforts.

- Scatter plot: graph of potential relationship between two variables
- Horizontal scale for one variable, vertical axis for other
- Collect two measurements of interested from same subject
- For each measured subject, plot points at intersection of measurements
- May circle points to show repetition
- Correlation does not prove cause and effect, but narrows down list of possibilities

When a relationship between an intended cause (for example, the relationship between attending a customer service training program and improved customer service) is not shown, it may be that the training program needs improvement, or it may also be that a third variable is either counteracting or responsible for the effects.

If historical data are available, correlation allows potential relationships to be explored without needing to set up special tests or experiments. For example, data may already be available from customer satisfaction surveys, sales records, employment histories, scores during training, number of new contacts made, and many other variables of interest.

Security, Motivation, and Correlation

An alarm system firm found a high correlation between purchases of home security systems and neighborhood burglary rates. The company then used public police reports to focus marketing efforts on neighborhoods with recent burglaries. Sales increased 140 percent (Minero 1995).

Checkpoint: Cause-and-Effect Diagrams and Behavior

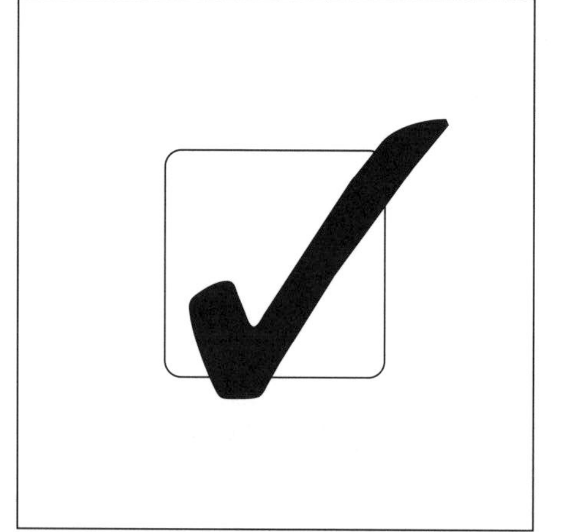

Dr. Selden challenges the group members to review their initial sales process diagram and identify a place in the process where human behavior is an important contributor to a problem they are experiencing.

He reminds the audience that when looking at a process problem in behavioral terms, an engineer must be specific about the behavior involved. For example, a sales lead is not a behavior. A sales lead is the outcome of the behavior of circling a response card in a magazine or the behavior of dialing a telephone.

As an exercise, Dr. Selden then asks each individual to quickly sketch a cause-and-effect diagram that illustrates variables he or she thinks may be causing the problem behavior. He suggests we ask the five whys as a way to generate ideas.

When Dr. Selden asks for volunteers to share their sketch with the group, I volunteer. Dr. Selden draws my sketch on the projection screen as I talk through the problem.

The problem I focused on was the lower-than-desirable market share held by our products in lines that had strong direct competition. The problem behavior I identified was that of poor product demonstrations on the part of our resellers. I mentioned that the customer's purchase behavior was probably strongly affected by the way our resellers demo'd our products.

When I asked myself why this was, the first thought I hit on was that on these particular lines we don't train our resellers well (1). When I asked myself the second "why," I concluded that the poor training was because our own trainers aren't trained by our marketing department in competitive "knockouts," that is, points that we could make to knock the competitive products out of the running (2). When I asked myself the third "why?," namely, "Why aren't our internal trainers properly trained?" my answer was that our marketing department hadn't communicated these competitive knockouts to begin with (3). The reason for them not communicating the knockouts was because the marketing staff seemed too busy with other duties (4). The reason they seemed too busy with other duties was that they were not aware this area was a priority for them to

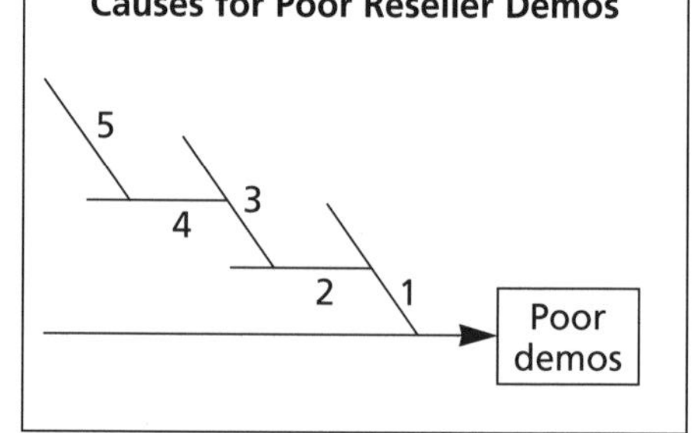

work on (5). There are probably other reasons, too, but this one seems relatively easy to correct once the priorities get reordered.

Reported causes such as "We don't have the people" or "We don't have enough time" are sometimes resolved through reprioritizing the work.

Scatter Plotting the Results

After asking for the first cause-and-effect diagram, Dr. Selden asks the class for a few other examples of sales process behavior.

One man from a consulting firm said that the volume of sales he was getting could be improved. The variables he focused on in his analysis were a relative lack of experience on the part of newly hired personnel who worked on projects, the client's lack of budget for consulting services, the youthfulness of personnel hired, and a lack of sales skills relative to technical skills.

A gentleman from a pharmaceutical firm said he was focusing on a lower-than-desirable rate of electronic call reporting on the part of the reps. He listed variables having to do with poor training, lack of clear procedures integrating the call reporting into the sales process, user-friendliness problems with the software, and inconsistent company messages regarding whether the company thought call reporting was valuable in the first place.

A woman from a food supply firm said that the reps weren't making enough cold calls. She thought variables contributing to this had to do with a lack of leads and too much time spent preparing for a call.

"Excellent! You're on the right track. Now I'd like you to share your cause-and-effect diagram with your small group partner. In turn, each of you put yourself in the role of a sales process engineer who suggests a place where scatter plotting could be used to highlight potential relationships between the variables involved. Make sure your axes are clear enough to permit real measurement. Pick an area where knowing the precise relationship would make a concrete difference in the actions you'd recommend."

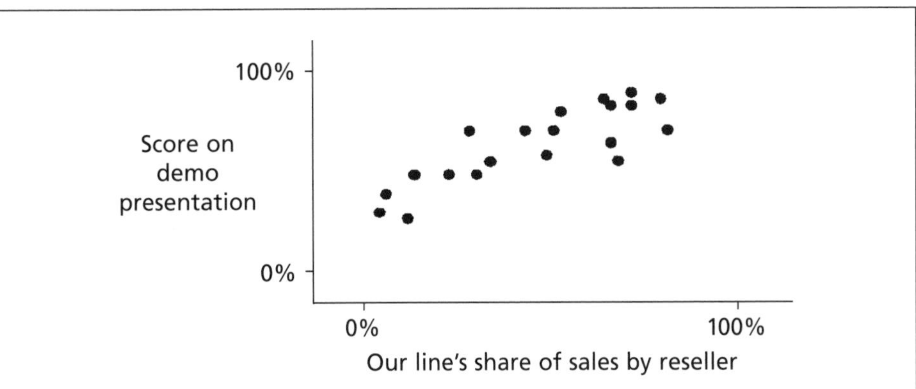

The class members go to work. After about 10 minutes, Dr. Selden asks the first volunteer to show the group what he graphed.

I feel a bit on the spot this time, being picked twice in the last 15 minutes, but I plunge ahead. I describe my horizontal axis as the share of the reseller's sales in our product line we command. The vertical axis I chose was a score we gave to dealers we would visit with mystery shoppers trained in judging their presentation. Dr. Selden complements my choice of variables.

This engineering business isn't so bad! I bet some of our sharper reps could use this to improve on a personal level, too.

Cause-and-Effect Tip

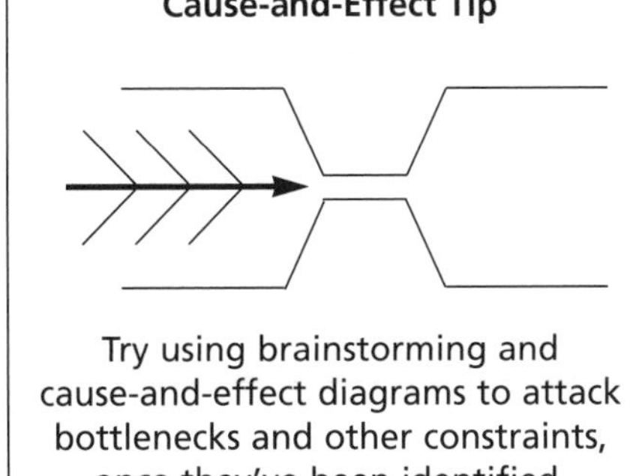

Try using brainstorming and cause-and-effect diagrams to attack bottlenecks and other constraints, once they've been identified.

Dr. Selden calls a break for lunch. The morning has passed quickly.

J. M. Juran

J. M. Juran

- Editor, *Quality Control Handbook*
- Coauthor, *Quality Planning and Analysis*
- Chairman Emeritus, Juran Institute
- With Deming, helped with Japan's recovery
- Awarded Japan's Order of the Sacred Treasure
- Most in-depth survey of quality techniques available

Joseph M. Juran (born in 1904) is the editor of the industry-standard 1500-plus page *Juran's Quality Control Handbook* (1988) and coauthor of *Quality Planning and Analysis* (1993), a text widely recommended to individuals preparing for their exam as ASQC certified quality engineers. One of Dr. Juran's lifelong pursuits was to enunciate how principles of quality engineering could be applied as a universal approach to management.

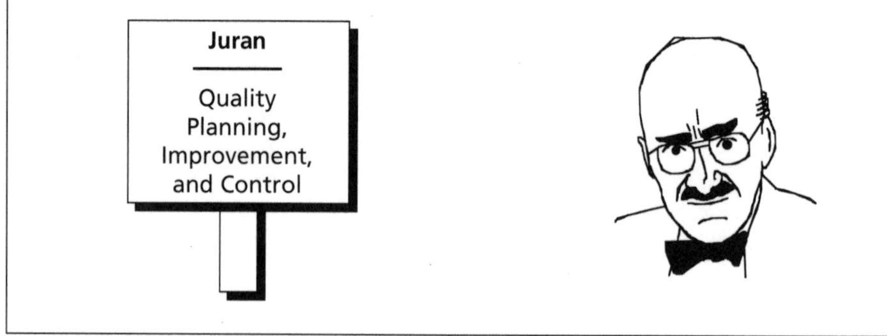

Dr. Juran achieved notoriety for teaching the principles of quality control as a tool for management in Japan during its post–World War II recovery. He was awarded Japan's Order of the Sacred Treasure for his work there, which was sponsored by the Union of Japanese Scientists and Engineers (JUSE).

Dr. Juran, while no longer active as a consultant, still remains active in the profession as Chairman Emeritus of the Juran Institute. His final series of public lectures in 1994–1995 was widely attended and extremely well received.

The breadth of Dr. Juran's work; his lifelong dedication to teaching and writing about the principles of quality planning, control, and improvement; and the influence he has achieved during his lifetime combine to give Dr. Juran a deserved place among the greatest figures in quality and process engineering.

Many of the concepts in this section are drawn directly from the third edition of the book *Quality Planning and Analysis,* which was revised by Frank Gryna, director of the Center for Quality at the University of Tampa. Together with the hundreds of published scholars, researchers, and authors whose work is cited in the text, Dr. Gryna deserves much of the credit for keeping the spirit of Dr. Juran's work alive and his message fresh in the third edition. The book is one of those rare masterpieces that combines true scholarship with practical advice.

Two Types of Quality

Dr. Selden begins the afternoon session with a story.

"There was once a self-proclaimed efficiency expert. A persuasive individual, he managed to get hired by an office furniture manufacturer. The manufacturer wanted him to reduce the cost of the firm's goods sold. This would increase profits, or so the manufacturer thought.

"After careful analysis, he recommended a way for the manufacturer to cut materials costs almost by half. 'Just reduce the size of your furniture by 50 percent,' he said.

"What a great way to save money! The only trouble was that now the furniture could only fit children. Children rarely work in offices. The company wisely decided to disregard the so-called expert's advice.

"Throughout the course so far, many of the process improvements recommended have been aimed at reducing internal costs. There is nothing wrong with this, as long as the customer still wants what you have to offer in the revised format. If the line between legitimate cost-cutting and imprudent corner-cutting becomes too fine, what engineers would like to see as a margin of safety is lost.

"Many of you may have been troubled by the emphasis on cost reduction, realizing that unless features desirable in the marketplace are maintained, the savings will be lost. The quality of what the customer wants must continue to be competitive.

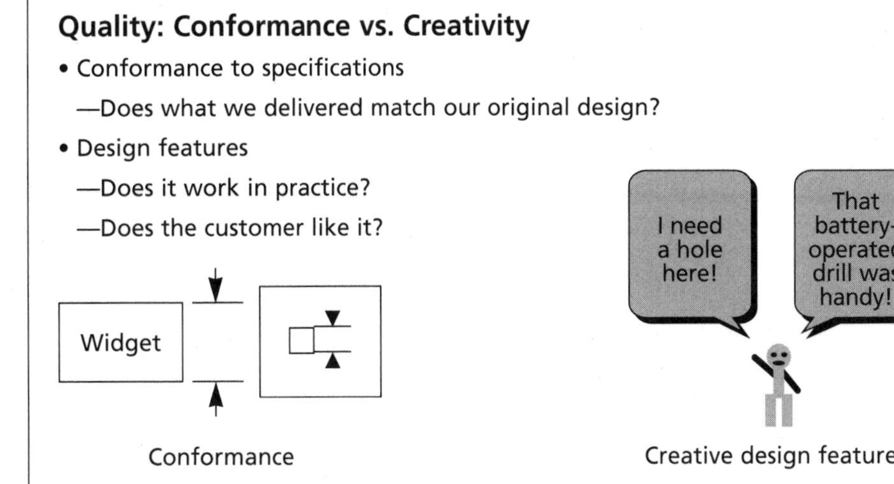

Quality: Conformance vs. Creativity
• Conformance to specifications
—Does what we delivered match our original design?
• Design features
—Does it work in practice?
—Does the customer like it?
Widget
I need a hole here!
That battery-operated drill was handy!
Conformance
Creative design features

"Dr. Juran was among the first to recognize and articulate the need for quality as a competitive sales weapon. In doing so he pointed out that quality, per se, has two aspects: conformance and design features. A sales process engineer who focuses on one and ignores the other may wind up like our friend, the self-proclaimed efficiency expert. In our field, *design features* translates into *service process features*."

One aspect of quality is conformance to customer specifications. In this sense, conformance is the degree to which original, agreed-upon customer specifications were met. Were 26 promised? Were 26 delivered? Was the color promised blue? Was what was delivered blue? Do the dimensions called for in the blueprint match up with the finished product? In this sense, quality is the absence of deviation from specifications—freedom from errors and deficiencies. In theory, freedom from error has a limit: zero defects.

Dr. Juran pointed out that conformance to specifications is just one side of the quality coin. The other side encompasses the quality of the design features. Does the design work well in practice and please the customer? Since creativity of product and service features is unlimited and since the ways to delight people are boundless, this leads to a continuous revolution in design.

Two Types of Process Cause

"Understanding these two types of quality is critical for a sales process engineer because there are usually ways for the marketing, sales, and customer service process to compensate for handicaps faced by the product itself. Two stores may sell virtually identical merchandise, but one can become more popular due to its friendlier, more helpful service.

"We can also look at the issue of how sales process engineers improve a process from the point of view of the two kinds of process problems we reviewed earlier: chronic problems (being in an unknowing rut) and sporadic problems (getting hit by attention-getting crises). The job of the sales process engineer will be to achieve desirable breakthroughs in the case of chronic problems and to develop preventive or damage-control measures in the case of sporadic problems."

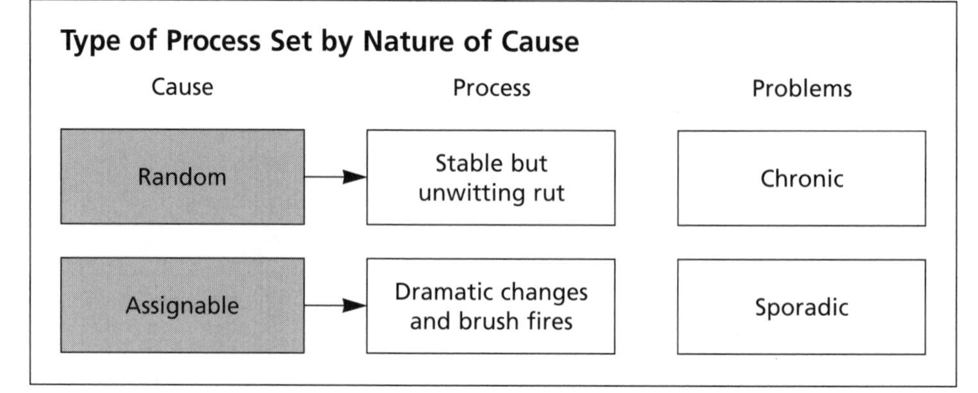

Dr. Juran articulated the difference between sporadic and chronic causes of process problems. Processes that are truly stable contain only random causes. As we saw earlier, there are usually many random causes operating at once, each causing minor variations that tend to cancel each other out. Random causes are usually built into the very nature of the process and are difficult to recognize and control because they come from the accepted "way things are done around here." Only very rarely would many random, natural variations combine to create a large difference.

Processes that vary widely do so due to variables that can usually be assigned to just one or more key factors for any given change. Brush fire management is the order of the day in such systems.

Now I see the relevance of this somewhat theoretical distinction. A sales process engineer who focuses on preventing undesirable but assignable causes such as reducing sales process errors or who can institute measures to prevent or more quickly and effectively extinguish brush fires will create a more stable process. That alone has value. I can think of many competitive advantages that would bring—we're not even close to uniformly meeting customer expectations in some cases.

A sales process engineer can also focus on increasing desirable causes. I guess this would be like trying to concentrate the active ingredients of customer satisfaction or present them in an even more attractive form. This would lead to a process characterized by breakthroughs and steady incremental steps forward. Either could make us more attractive to the consumer.

The Juran Trilogy®

Dr. Selden introduces the group to a universal progression of quality goals and process characteristics in a diagram entitled "The Juran Trilogy." The diagram shows the progression a company makes in working on one of the quality dimensions, freedom from deficiencies, in which the costs due to poor quality are hovering around 20 percent of the company's income from sales.

The trilogy shows the quality journey in three phases: planning, control, and improvement.

In the planning phase, the company uncovers and defines how much poor quality is costing. The company awakens to the need for a more systematic approach and sets about improving.

During the control phase, measures are instituted to eliminate and prevent all sporadic problems. The diagram shows how much sporadic problems can affect costs when they occur. Each time a new sporadic problem occurs, better ways to prevent or minimize it from occurring again are immediately set in place. Once this is done, the process is performing as well as it can under its current structure. Dr. Juran's illustration shows that there is still a great deal of room for improvement.

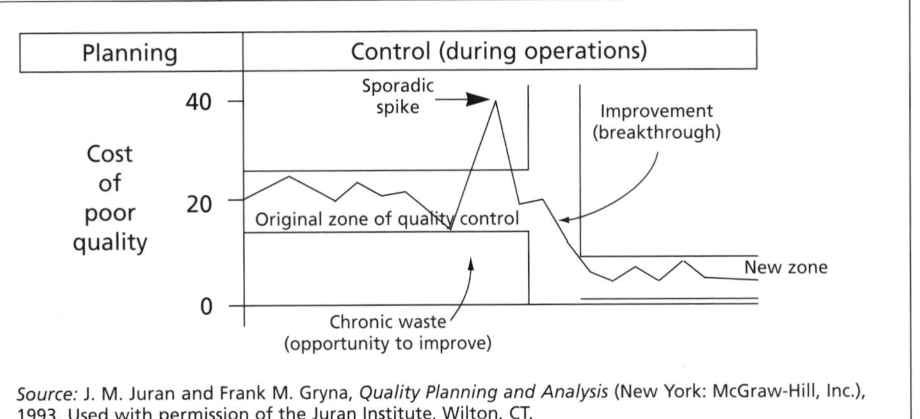

Source: J. M. Juran and Frank M. Gryna, *Quality Planning and Analysis* (New York: McGraw-Hill, Inc.), 1993. Used with permission of the Juran Institute, Wilton, CT.

In the improvement phase, innovations are employed to achieve a breakthrough in reducing the cost of poor quality. This cannot be done without changing the very nature of the process itself or its inputs. If successful, a new performance level will be obtained. The need to prevent and eliminate sporadic problems is still necessary with the new process structure. Measures for process control must be ongoing. Lessons learned must be fed back to those with planning responsibilities.

As Dr. Selden is describing the chart I find my eyes glued to the box labeled "chronic waste." That's the box that we've put ourselves into for telling ourselves that further improvement in sales, marketing, and customer service is not possible.

Quality Planning

"Most people like to have a map handy when they take a journey. It helps us get where we want to go sooner."

Dr. Juran's work provides a road map for those wishing to undertake the journey to improve quality. For each of the three main phases—planning, control, and improvement—he offers a set of specific steps.

In the quality planning phase, Dr. Juran recommends *establishing the goals* first. In sales, these goals could be related to improving any portion of the sales process, including the goal of meeting or exceeding customer specifications more systematically.

The second step is to *identify the customers involved.* A process can have internal or external customers. One customer for the material produced by a marketing department might be an external customer, someone who buys the product. But in the case of sales presentation materials, the customer is also the salesperson who must use the materials.

The third step is to *discover the customer needs.* This can be done in a number of ways, including focus groups, personal observation, and surveys.

Fourth, for each of the needs articulated, say, convenience, features of the *product* (or service) should be developed to answer the need.

Fifth, the *process* should be explicitly designed such that the desired product or service features are produced as specified.

Finally, a system for seeing that the process operates within specifications should be developed, and the process should be transferred to *operations.*

Dr. Juran was instrumental in developing a technique called quality function deployment (QFD) that systematically links customer needs, product and service features, and process characteristics.

Throughout this seminar we've been looking at our own sales process, identifying problems and goals, looking at things from our customer's point of view, and thinking of ways the process could be improved. I guess we've been engaging in what Juran would probably call the first few baby steps of quality planning.

By itself, complexity, which can be measured by the time it takes an individual to carry out work performed in an operation, magnifies the chance that mistakes will be made (Hinckley and Barkan 1995). The authors conclude that a combination of Shingo's mistake-proofing and design simplification can effectively combat these sources of nonconformities.

Quality Planning

1. Establish quality goals.
2. Identify customers.
3. Discover customer needs.
4. Develop product features.
5. Develop process features.
6. Establish process controls; transfer to operations.

Quality Control (Sporadic Causes)

"Brush fires seem to be the rule in sales, service, and marketing, don't they? For example, let's say that in a large household appliance maker, the marketing department is late in getting out press releases on a new more energy-efficient refrigerator. As a consequence, the first lot of the product is produced and sales are 18 percent less than the product manager had budgeted. This kind of thing affects careers up and down the line. Everyone suffers, including the potential customers, who are deprived of the new product until they hear about it—sooner or later. Quality control in sales and marketing will be aiming to solve problems like this."

Dr. Juran lays out seven steps for preventing quality problems due to obvious mistakes—those with assignable causes—during the quality control phase.

First, Dr. Juran recommends choosing the areas where control is most needed. In the example above, it is in the area of achieving public relations coverage: getting news stories broadcast and written about the company's newest products.

Second, units of measure should be chosen. In the example above, editorial coverage could be determined by measuring column inches devoted to a story describing the new product in a magazine.

Third, goals must be picked. In our example, the goal might be to "achieve five or more column inches of editorial coverage in magazines A, B, and C in each of three months immediately prior, three months during, and three months after a new product release, for each new product line released."

The fourth step is to create a "sensor." You must have a way of detecting the results. A routine news clipping service could take care of this, in our example.

Fifth, the performance is measured. Sixth, any difference between the specifications needs to be interpreted. Seventh, action is taken on the difference.

"The tools we've worked with so far, from brainstorming to scatter plotting, are all aimed at addressing what needs to be done in steps six and seven. The solution might be to develop a marketing checklist attached to every new product plan. If a paper checklist didn't prevent all the problems, perhaps an electronic system with automatic reminder notices and alarms could be used."

Quality Control (Sporadic Causes)

1. Choose control subjects.
2. Choose units of measure.
3. Set goals.
4. Create a sensor.
5. Measure actual performance.
6. Interpret the difference.
7. Take action on the difference.

Quality Improvement (Chronic Causes)

"Let's say a sales process engineer finds that the current closing ratio across the whole sales force is about 1 close for every eight presentations, or 12.5 percent. Further, growth has leveled off during the past few years. Competitors in business for only a few years are doubling in sales each year. The engineer works with the marketing department to design a new approach.

"The quality *improvement* engineering scenario is aimed at obtaining a dramatic change in performance, not just controlling in order to hold steady on a proven course. This is the most difficult because vested interests often want to maintain the status quo, and due to the creative challenge inherently present in achieving a breakthrough."

Dr. Juran points out that innovation is often feared by the very people it's designed to help. For this reason, the steps required to achieve a breakthrough are somewhat different than the steps involved in quality planning or control.

Step one is to prove the need. In the previous example, relevant comparisons of market share and profitability would help demonstrate the opportunities involved.

Step two is to identify specific projects. Analytic work using the tools previously discussed could help prioritize where to place the most emphasis. In this case, let's say that emphasis is placed on developing a new, more compelling sales presentation, a shift in the media used in advertising, and a change from the company's traditional cold-calling approach to one more targeted at likely buyers.

The third step is to organize project teams. Since the solution may affect many different parties, representatives who can best speak to the issues should be involved. In the previous example, marketing, sales, and a customer advisory group might be most helpful.

Step four is to diagnose the causes. Is the cause for the low growth and a poor closing ratio due to what is being offered, where it is offered, how it is offered, or other factors?

Step five is to provide remedies and prove their effectiveness. Once the new approach is developed, a pilot study can help tell whether it is just "old sausage in new casings," or something that truly increases the closing ratio. The team must be willing to try alternatives if the new "solution" doesn't work. In this case, perhaps customers are leaving due to uncompetitive credit policies, inferior products, poor service, or some other factor. Management must be willing to change old ways if necessary wherever a chronic cause is present, or no improvement will occur.

Step six is to deal with resistance to change. The benefits of the new presentation must be taught, but so must the benefit of approaching sales, marketing, and service problems in a systematic way. Many companies like to shoot from the hip when it comes to solving this type of problem.

Step seven is to institute controls to hold the gains. Quality control is still necessary, even with breakthroughs. Backsliding can still occur.

Quality Improvement (Chronic Causes)

1. Prove the need.
2. Identify projects.
3. Organize project teams.
4. Diagnose the causes.
5. Provide remedies, prove their effectiveness.
6. Deal with resistance to change.
7. Control to hold the gains.

It occurs to me that if I put all these steps together, across the three phases of planning, control, and improvement, I'll close another loop. Dr. Juran's 12-step problem-solving sequence that we learned yesterday covers them all. I feel like I have a specific direction and solid tools to support each step. This isn't just a hodgepodge set of techniques—it's a unified approach that has proven its worth for half a century in other parts of business.

What About the Human Contribution?

"What about the human contribution, the so-called 15 percent? Is a sales process engineer to forget about the individual's contribution to a process and focus only on the structure? I personally think we need to ask whether in sales, marketing, and customer service the contribution by the individual is really only 15 percent in the first place. I think we'd find that this number varies considerably depending on the nature of the specific process we are investigating.

"In sales, marketing, and customer service, orders can be won or lost by a hair's breadth. Yet the winner takes all. Every competitive advantage is important, which explains why sales process engineers must pay attention to all the variables. That's one reason why I emphasized human behavior in the section we covered not more than an hour ago. In our current sales process, people may directly control more variables than in a typical mechanical process. That adds to the complexity, which increases the sources for potential error. The individual's contribution depends on which part of the process you're looking at and how extensive your error-proofing techniques are."

Dr. Juran taught that employee errors often fall into one of three classifications.

Errors may be *inadvertent*, that is, unintentional, unwitting, and unpredictable. In customer service, an employee may try to answer a customer's question about the type of options available with a product from memory and accidently give the wrong answer. To correct this problem, aids to judgment, reference tools, and techniques to cue what to do next should be provided. Variety and rest periods should also be considered as a way to reduce inattention and fatigue when the job is more repetitive, such as in telemarketing or inside order-taking functions.

Errors may be due to *poor technique*, as indicated by errors that appear to be unintentional, specific in nature, consistent, and unavoidable due to lack of knowledge or skill. For example, a rep may repeatedly lose sales to wealthy clients because the rep has been trained to "close early and often," instead of listening to the customer and tailoring the presentation to specific needs. Cures include observing top performers and comparing their technique with those less successful, then reducing the chance for errors through training, process redesign, or by instituting mistake-proofing techniques.

Reducing Human Error

- Cause: Inadvertent errors—unintentional, unwitting, unpredictable

  Remedies: reduce need for human attention; make it easier to remain attentive
- Cause: Technique errors—unintentional, specific, consistent, unavoidable

  Remedies: find best performance; compare technique with lower performers; train, change the process, or error-proof
- Cause: Conscious errors—witting, intentional, persistent

  Remedies: explain, audit, redesign, reassign

***Conscious* errors are intentional and persistent. A marketing manager may insist on using the same ad in a certain publication in spite of a rapidly dwindling response, perhaps due to some personal relationship involved. The remedy is to explain the situation, or redesign the process, then check to see if the performance recurs. Reassignment may be the only choice left if the errors continue in spite of all other efforts to correct the situation.**

Juran and Gryna (1993, 58–73) outline a clear set of techniques on how to test whether a given problem is management-controllable or worker-controllable.

"There's a joke about the dummy who got fired from an M&M factory—he was rejecting all the candies with a *W* written on them. Now that's an example of poor technique error."

Tool 10: The Control Chart

"In sales we're used to seeing all kinds of graphs. They show the up-and-down movement that normally occurs as business takes place.

"A typical graph of sales volume doesn't tell us enough about the process that is generating it. As sales process engineers we must understand things more deeply than others. A tool that can help us do this is called statistical process control, or SPC: control charting. Using a control chart helps us see how well the process itself is performing—when it is behaving normally and when it is behaving abnormally.

"We'll be covering SPC in much more depth tomorrow; this is just a general introduction.

The example plots the mean of a sample of five orders picked at random each day for a period of 20 days. The average order size of each sample is shown, connected by lines. Three other lines are plotted. The middle line is the mean of the sample means ($\bar{\bar{X}}$). The top line is what is called the upper control limit, or UCL, and the bottom line is called the lower control limit, the LCL. The UCL and LCL are calculated using formulas explained in more detail later.

In the example, the average of the sample means is $64.60. The UCL is $85.19 and the LCL is $44.01. In a process that is under a state of statistical control, 99.73 percent of all samples drawn in the future will fall between the UCL and LCL. Such a process is stable, predictable, and performing as best it can—unless something changes. It is SPC's ability to tell the difference between random changes and unusual, nonrandom fluctuation that makes it so powerful.

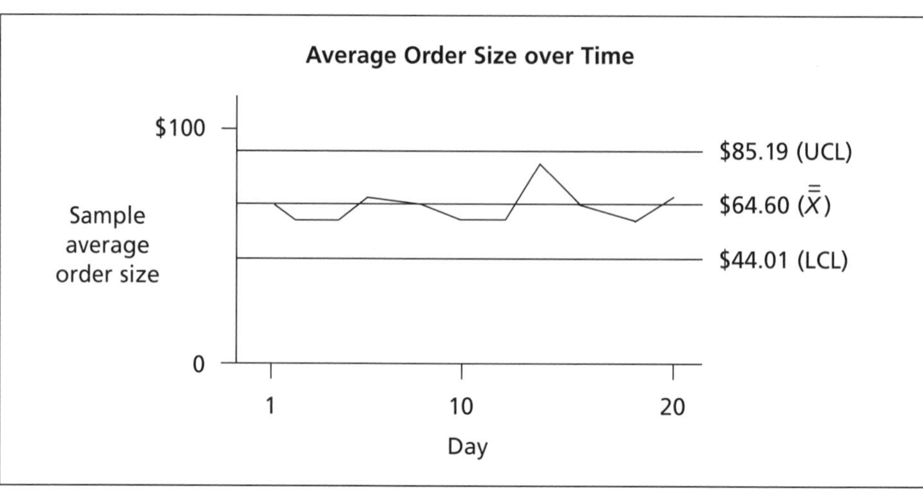

"The important thing to grasp now is a sense of what SPC means to a sales process engineer once he or she has brought a process into a state of statistical control.

"First, if the mean of the sample averages is not where the company needs it to be for business reasons, immediate action *must* be taken. The full weight of the problem-solving sequence must be initiated.

"Second, any point that falls outside the control limits must *immediately* be explored. Any undesirable special causes *must* be prevented; desirable ones *must* be made more repeatable.

"Third, and perhaps most important, results that fall within the UCL and LCL, so long as they meet the company's specifications, should be left alone. The process is performing as well as it can; nothing short of a major process design change can alter it. Any tinkering in the meantime may make things worse. The implications are enormous. We'll learn why tomorrow."

To a sales process engineer, SPC will be as helpful as a physician's stethescope.

Control Charts: Instructions

- Control chart: Run chart with statistically determined upper and lower lines drawn above and below the process mean
- Also called statistical process control chart or Shewhart chart
- Used when needing to separate naturally occurring random variation from events due to special causes
- The LCL and UCL must be calculated from tables and formulas
- Variables number vs. attributes (yes/no) require different formulas

Control charts illustrate the variability and central tendency of measurements taken. Their distinguishing feature is that statistically calculated upper control limits and lower control limits are drawn on the chart above and below the process mean.

Control charts are an invaluable means for detecting and separating results due to normal process variation versus results that are due to special causes. Since an engineer's improvements may be considered a special cause, SPC provides an operational definition of when a new approach is an improvement versus a superficial change.

The LCL and UCL must be calculated from appropriate tables and formulas. These tables and formulas are easy to follow and simply take into account factors such as the sample sizes involved. Only simple math is involved, and the calculations and data gathering can often be computerized.

As was mentioned earlier, control charts are also called SPC charts or Shewhart charts.

Different control charts are used to study different phenomena. For example, *variables* charts are used when the data can be measured on a continuous scale, such as dollars. If one is tallying how often an error occurs, an *attributes* chart is used. An *individuals* chart is used when single data points (not sample averages) are measured, such as if total order for an entire day, week, or month can easily be obtained.

Consult the bibliography for reference works on the subject, among which Hy Pitt's *SPC for the Rest of Us* (1994) and AT&T's reprint of Western Electric's original *Statistical Quality Control Handbook* (1958) are highly recommended.

Tool 11: Experimental Design

"Let's say you're a great sailor. In fact, you're so good that you're in charge of defending the America's Cup next Tuesday. If a sail-maker told you that you could cut three minutes from your sailing time by switching to his brand of sails, what kinds of questions would you ask to increase your confidence in his claims? Keep in mind that a new set of sails will probably set you back more than a million bucks." [Dr. Selden waits for an answer.]

"I'd ask what they're made of," says one person, eventually.

"Is installation included?"

"Do they come with a guarantee?"

"Can I have them ready by next Tuesday?" [The class laughs at this idea.]

"Those are all good questions. There's another you didn't ask. The sailmaker told us we could cut three minutes off our time. What we need to know is, can we expect to save three minutes *when we're in the race that counts?*

"There are a lot of sale-makers out there who promise us we can save time (or money) by using their products, aren't there? When the shoe is on the other foot, when we are the sales process engineer instead of the sale-maker, isn't there more we need to know in order to answer the question I just asked? Did the sailmaker obtain these results using our kind of boat? Did the sailmaker save three minutes one time out of 10? Ten times out of 10? What were the savings in comparison to? A boat equipped like ours? Experimental design is necessary to answer questions like the ones I've just asked."

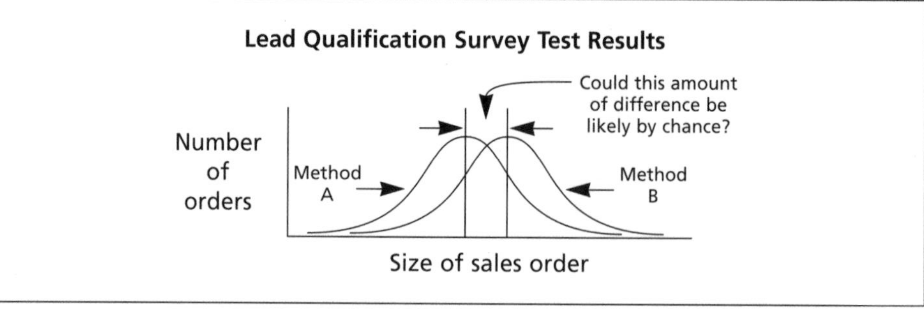

Proponents of modern industrial design of experiments (DOE) such as Genichi Taguchi suggest that SPC is good to use once the correct process "settings" have been determined. DOE can be used to find the correct parameters for a process in the first place.

"Let's say we are thinking about changing our lead qualification method from method "A" to method "B." In Method A, the field salesperson calls to follow up on typical leads received from magazine ads. In Method B, a survey firm is hired to call and ask each lead a professionally developed set of survey questions to surface the prospect's needs, motivations, and reactions to competitors. Then the lead and results of the survey are passed to the rep for follow-up, together with a computer-generated set of expert follow-up recommendations.

"The illustration shows that when Method B is used, the size of the order eventually received seems to be larger. The question becomes, how likely is it that the amount of difference is due to chance? If we tried it again, would we get the same results? With what degree of certainty? These are important questions. The role for experimental design in sales process engineering should be obvious. Even small, consistent differences between competitors can mean the difference between winners and losers."

The sales process engineer of the future will set up tests of sales process effectiveness as routinely as geologists now test for the presence of oil and natural gas deposits. Effort will be involved, but the methods will be widely known and reliable.

Experimental Design: Instructions

- Experimental design: Used to help accomplish the following:
  - —Detect presence of a controlling variable
  - —Isolate controlling variables: "active ingredients"
  - —Quantify degree of controlling variable "potency"
- Steps
  - —Planning the experiment to ensure validity
  - —Documenting steps to ensure ability to replicate
  - —Running the experiment and collecting data
  - —Analyzing the results, usually with a statistical tool
- Why the statistics?
  - —To speak from specific to general
  - —To separate normal fluctuation from abnormal
- "Significant" differences may not be enough

Experimental design involves observing important variables and their effect under conditions that allow reliable conclusions about the potential causal relationships involved.

Sales process engineers will use experiments to detect controlling variables and their effect where the relationship may not be obvious otherwise. Even when a relationship is obvious, experiments will also be used to isolate controlling variables so their role as active ingredients, including their potency, interactions, and side effects, can be more precisely quantified.

If, as widely stated, small differences can win or lose sales, then it is certainly worthwhile to use methods capable of detecting what these small, important differences are. That is where the design of experiments comes into play.

Experiments involve four major steps. Experiments are first planned to ensure their validity. The experiment's steps are then documented so that others are able to repeat the recipe and confirm the results independently in the future. Third, the experiment is run and results are collected. Finally, the results are analyzed, often using a statistical tool to help interpret the results properly.

Statistics are formulas based on the laws of mathematics and probability. For most industrial purposes, statistics are often used by people with relatively little formal education. Simple tables and diagrams can be drawn up so that work is done with an ordinary calculator. Computers can also be used to gather the data automatically and then plot and interpret the results. Using approaches such as advocated by Dr. Taguchi, statistics may not even be required.

Statistics help determine whether or not the results seen in a particular case are likely to apply in similar situations elsewhere.

Statistics are used to help determine whether a particular variable influenced a process beyond the normal amount of variation that all natural processes exhibit. Unless a variable affects results beyond the normal amount of natural variation, the variable's ability to control the effect has not been shown.

Just because a variable is shown to have a "statistically significant" impact on an outcome, the effect may not be sufficient to be economically viable. In other cases, even small improvements may be quite profitable. Costs and benefits of an approach must be considered hand in hand.

Reflections

"I know a lot of you are considering various forms of reengineering and sales automation.

"Let me see a show of hands. Is management asking you to tell whether your changes have made or will make a difference? [Almost everyone's hand goes up.]

"One more question. How many of you have had training in experimental design? [No one's hand goes up.]

"Then you are being asked to do something you cannot do. Don't feel inadequate. No one can know everything. Use your management skills to delegate the work to experts. Arrange for competent help.

"The basic technique a sales process engineer needs to master is how to separate the natural variation that occurs within all processes from variation induced by something that changes the process fundamentally. I'll teach you some very powerful ways to do this later today, and tomorrow too. As a manager of the effort, you must at least be familiar enough with the ideas involved to manage the experts. You may not become a sales process engineer yourself, but you should learn how to get what you need from one!"

I felt I had a grip on things, up until these last two tools. Now both my emotions and my head are swimming. I feel like I'm standing on the edge of an abyss. Behind me is fairly familiar ground. It was new territory, but I could grasp it. I see the relevance of SPC and experimental design; but they are beyond me for now.

Dr. Selden says that little formal training is required to apply SPC. I'll believe that when I see it. Wait. Our own manufacturing group is using it. The head of our local plant says that guys on the shop floor are using SPC to keep quality on track. Maybe if they can do it, we can too.

This experimental design stuff is different, though. It definitely sounds worth doing, but I've had no training in it whatsoever. We'd almost need a new department to handle this in our sales process. No one I know has the time or the skills to do this stuff right. I'm sure we're smart enough. It's just a matter of having the extra hours in the day.

Old vs. New

The old way to conduct experiments is to change one variable at a time and note any changes. This approach is time-intensive and often fails to surface interactions that may occur, because only one variable is being changed at a time. Modern techniques for industrial experimental design permit changing many variables at once to get an answer (Taguchi 1993; Peace 1993; and Pugh 1994). Although marketing has long been used to the concept of experimentation, that is not so true in sales and customer service.

A Personal Use of SPC

"Our exercise for SPC and experimentation is easy. First, I want you to brainstorm places where control charting might be used. By the way, there's a standard answer for that, which will serve for all occasions."

Someone immediately says, "Yeah—at work." [The group laughs at this comment.] This prompts Dr. Selden to tell a personal story.

"You're right about using SPC at work, but I'll tell you a story about how I used SPC in my personal life before we go on. I took my family on a cruise for Christmas one time. You know, the kind where they don't let you off the boat until you have eaten your weight in rich foods? I came back tipping the scales at an all-time high. I hadn't weighed that much since I free-fed on dorm food my first year in college! I was angry! Fun takes a toll, doesn't it?

"I started to chart my weight on the principle that feedback alone would cause me to lose some pounds. Knowledge of results and all that. Guess what? Plotting weight doesn't burn off many calories. After dropping a few pounds I was back to the high side of my pre-vacation weight. I still wasn't happy.

"I kept charting. The points would go up and down. I'd get excited about losing a pound or two and angry when I seemed to gain it back. Just for the heck of it, I entered the data into a spreadsheet and calculated the upper and lower control limits using the individuals charting rules I've provided in your course book. The story was clear: The fluctuations were just part of normal variation around a mean. No reason to get excited either way. Both excitement and anger were unjustified because no genuine change was taking place.

"Since no actual further change in my weight was taking place, I knew I had to change the process itself. Oh yes. The inputs, too.

"I got a Nordic Track ski machine. A structural change! I started working out 30 minutes, three days a week—just like they say in the commercials.

"The control chart showed no change. I upped it to 35 minutes. Still no change. I jumped to 40 minutes. Bingo! The control charts revealed an immediate change. Since then I've tried a sequence of changes. I'm now at 15 pounds under my high, and about 10 pounds under my pre-holiday norm.

"Without SPC, I might have prematurely given up my efforts as ineffective!"

Exercise: SPC and Experimentation

"Individuals can use SPC to keep track of their own progress in any endeavor. For example, in sales it could be used to see whether training, and further training, was having an impact on sales. A certain amount of training might have an impact. Further training may not.

"Now it's back to you. Where might control charting be used? Jot down what others say; it will help you form a list to work on when you return to your own company."

Answers start coming fast.

"Tracking individual sales performance."
"Charting errors in proposals."
"Plotting closing ratios."
"Recording the lead to appointment yield."
"Average size of sales."
"Can it be used to see whether someone in a group is outside the control limits compared to the rest of the group?"

Dr. Selden responds to this last question, "Yes. Dr. Deming says it can. One of his disciples, Bill Latzko, wrote a book in 1987 describing how this can be done.

"Now, what about experimentation in sales, marketing, and customer service? Where would you want to use that?"

"To test one brochure against another."
"Testing one ad versus another."
"To find the best magazines to advertise in."
"To check whether a new proposal format helped close more deals."
"To determine if one form of organization is better than another."
"To see if one store layout and decor pulled more business than another."

"Excellent ideas. I'm sure you can think of many more, too.

"Now I want to give you my all-purpose answer to the question I originally asked about where you'd want to use SPC. The answer is, use SPC anywhere it's economically worthwhile to detect important changes. The same answer goes for experimentation. If the potential for improvement is big enough, you can easily justify hiring someone to help you with the technical details."

Brainstorming

- Where might control charting be used?
- Where might experimentation be used?

Kaizen—Continuous Improvement

Kaizen is a Japanese word that means gradual, never-ending improvement. The word embodies an active, enthusiastic spirit that can be described as the relentless pursuit of excellence. Mouthing the words is not kaizen. Getting involved and implementing ways to do things better is kaizen.

Kaizen means setting and achieving standards that are always increasing. It is a way of life that exudes energy and interest in what you are doing and the world around you. Being complacent is not kaizen. Accepting a problem as unsolvable is not kaizen. Kaizen institutionalizes a process of measurable, ongoing improvement.

Kaizen is satisfied with, yet insists on, gradual improvement; dramatic leaps are not required. The results are often impressive, nevertheless. The approach is akin to what successful money managers call the "get rich slowly" technique. The magic of compounding small gains over time yields astonishing results over the long haul. Through small improvements over a six-year period, one major semiconductor company was able to reduce the cost of lasers used in compact disc players by 200 times its original price and increase its life by a factor of 500.

Most people are not in a position to achieve dramatic changes. Kaizen involves everyone, from the top to the bottom. It expects that those not in a position to improve matters directly will at least list their ideas for improvement as suggestions. One chemical company saved $10 million a year with its suggestion system, a 500 percent return on its investment. Kaizen provides a way for people to take pride in their efforts and ideas, regardless of where they are in the company.

The concepts of kaizen are articulated in the book of the same name written by Masaaki Imai (1986), together with many examples of its success.

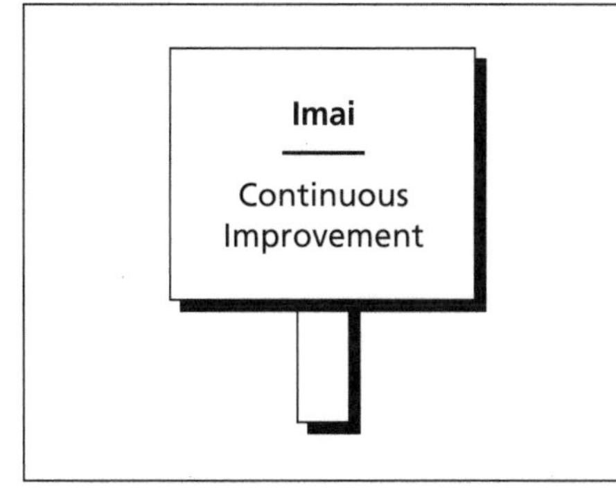

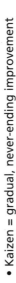

- Kaizen = gradual, never-ending improvement
- Kaizen means setting and achieving standards that are always increasing
- Improvement is gradual, not dramatic
- Results can be very impressive nevertheless
- An attitude—relentless, enthusiastic, not satisfied with problems or status quo
- Involves everyone from top to bottom

Kaizen Involves Everyone

Kaizen is compatible with reengineering or innovation. The difference is, whereas the resources required to invent, refine, and install sweeping innovative approaches are usually only available to top management, kaizen is something that everyone can employ.

The chart here illustrates that in contrast to dramatic innovation, kaizen is expected of everyone.

"In a company, most employees need to do the job at hand. The chart terms this 'maintenance and control' activity. In sales, we have goods to sell and customers to service. In marketing, we've got new products to launch and current products to support. In service, we've got orders to take and problems to solve. We've got to do those jobs or the customer stops funding our paychecks.

"With kaizen, some part of our job as frontline employees and managers must be to improve what we do and how we do it. Other companies will pass us by if we don't.

"The refreshing part about a kaizen-oriented company is that it treats all employees as thinking human beings, people who can spot problems, people who are empowered to fix things on their own and make things better.

Kaizen Involves Everyone

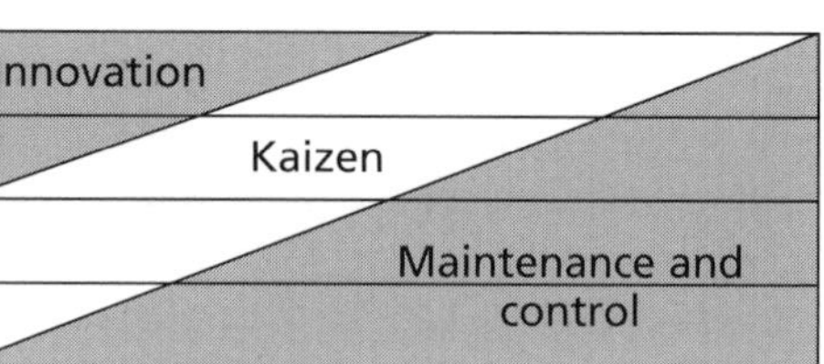

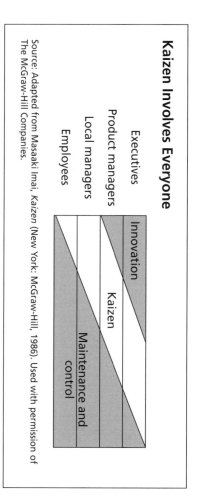

Source: Adapted from Masaaki Imai, *Kaizen* (New York: McGraw-Hill, 1986). Used with permission of The McGraw-Hill Companies.

In a classic organizational hierarchy, upper management sets the tone, strategy, and policy, and the staff implements it. In a kaizen company, top management is expected to institute dramatic innovation. However, management is also expected to aggressively pursue and encourage ways to improve without consuming expensive resources or without forcing the organization into convulsions of drastic changes. Continuous improvement and innovation are both sought.

Imai suggests that kaizen applies to sales, marketing, and service in at least five key areas. (1) All groups tighten links with customers to understand customer requirements. (2) Product surveys actively focus on where complaints exist. (3) Product failure examples are solicited. Internal suggestion systems and problem-solution logs are developed. (4) Ideas to increase customer delight are systematically explored. (5) Emphasis on short-term profitability is decreased.

"Contrast the kaizen environment with the spirit of a company that is only into reengineering its way to improvement. Kaizen energizes everyone. By comparison, reengineering is top-down."

Innovation Alone

Managers looking at a kaizen company for the first time are often surprised how much more productive it is, even though its physical tools and facilities may be older or the same age as its competitors.

Why is this? Relying on innovation alone, without harnessing human resources or encouraging an attitude of collective continuous improvement, a company often makes a dramatic leap forward in technological change, but then decay sets in. The people can feel less valued than the new machines. Often even normal and expected maintenance is not wholeheartedly pursued.

"Do you treat a leased car as well as you do your own? Do you touch up every chip in the paint? Or do you let it go, thinking, well, I'm just going to trade this in soon, anyway?

"Kaizen inspires pride in your work and a sense of personal responsibility. It encourages everyone to get in on improvement.

"So at one level, the job of a sales process engineer will be to find major structural improvements everyone can use. At another level, everyone in the sales process—including middle management and those 'in the trenches'—will need to actively employ sales process engineering at a more personal level to achieve gradual, ongoing improvement in their immediate district, department, or customers.

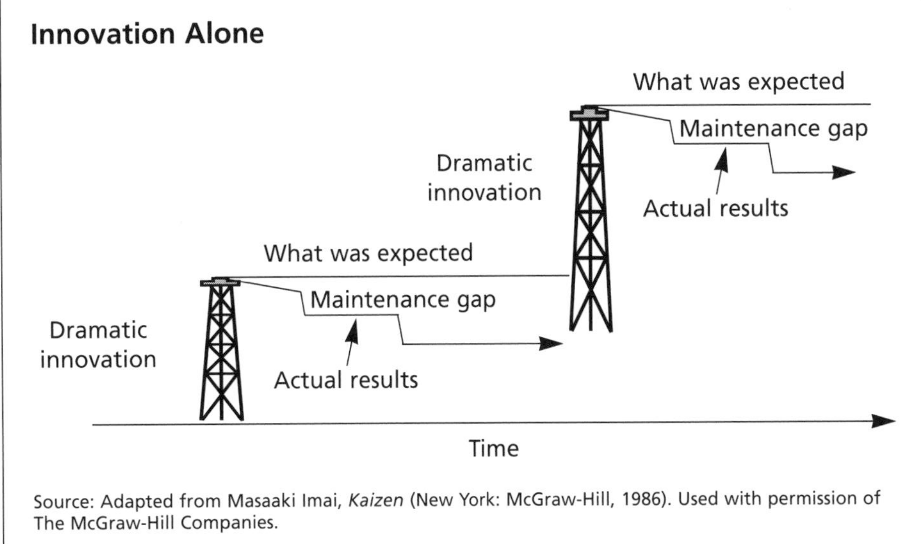

Source: Adapted from Masaaki Imai, *Kaizen* (New York: McGraw-Hill, 1986). Used with permission of The McGraw-Hill Companies.

I like the feeling I'm getting. Kaizen sounds like an approach that we could use a lot of. Many salespeople I know don't seek improvement. If they have a problem selling, they keep their head down until they are "caught." I think a kaizen approach would see salespeople actively involved in their everyday activities to see what they could improve: their presentation materials, proposals, telephone survey techniques, thank you letters, personal timeliness, attention to customer needs, everything.

What I've read of the reengineering gurus, especially the most popular, makes me feel like they are only talking to upper management. They advocate dramatic changes—going for big home runs. They say only top management can make the big decisions, and that top management almost needs to ignore the "little fellow."

I'm getting sick of all these management fads. It's almost like the writers are just publicity hounds looking at something serious engineers have been working on for a long time. They relabel it, "discover" it, and repackage it for mass consumption. There's a place for that, I guess, just like there's a place for velvet pictures of Elvis in art, or pet rocks. By contrast, this workshop is getting us to think about the basic principles in the original terms used by the inventors and professionals who have worked with the subject for years. It's not watered down. I like that. If this is Dr. Selden's answer to the "dumbing down" of America, I'm ready.

Innovation Plus Kaizen

Kaizen is complementary to innovation. Before and after dramatic breakthroughs, kaizen is continuously improving, never satisfied, always moving things even further ahead. The expectation set for everyone is that the improvement will be well above that of simple maintenance and what would normally be expected following installation of a dramatic change. All three work together: innovation, maintenance, and kaizen.

"When you've done all you can with kaizen, you still need innovation and maintenance. Innovation is hiring a company to blow insulation in the walls, where none existed before. Maintenance is restoring old caulk around the windows. Kaizen is noticing a draft and installing inexpensive weatherstripping to keep the last bits of air from blowing in. Together, they cut the most off your heating bill. Without kaizen, the savings won't be nearly as great.

"Innovation is hiring a professional firm to create a data-mining tool to exploit your customer databases. Maintenance is keeping the customer data flowing in and running the electronic inquiries to find the prospects you didn't even know you had. Kaizen is asking the sales force to be alert to new prospects and asking reps to feed back changes they are observing in the marketplace. One can work without the other. Together, they are pure dynamite. Companies that catch this spirit inevitably get ahead."

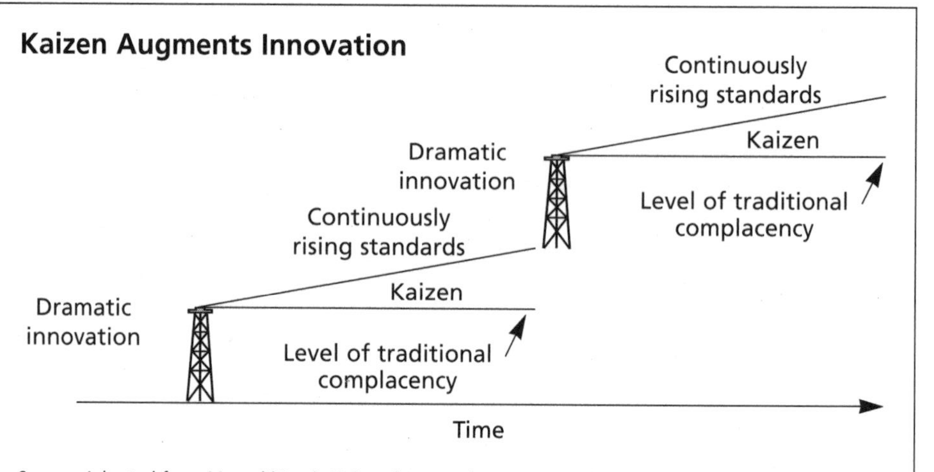

Source: Adapted from Masaaki Imai, *Kaizen* (New York: McGraw-Hill, 1986). Used with permission of The McGraw-Hill Companies.

The cover story in *Sales and Marketing Management Magazine's* November 1994 issue featured Stryker Corporation, a medical equipment maker based in Kalamazoo, Michigan (Brewer 1994). Stryker management expects that reps will feed back any problems they are having with other operations within the company. Immediate action is taken on all such problems. Stryker has grown from a $23 million company in 1977 to an $871 million firm by 1995.

I guess I've accidently followed a kaizen approach at home. I found a better way to unload dishes from the dishwasher. Instead of taking each plate out and putting it on the shelf one by one, I stay at the dishwasher and stack them in a pile in my left hand. Then I put the whole pile away. It only saves me a few minutes, but I'd rather be doing something else than stacking dishes. Same with leaves. Instead of raking a pile of leaves out to the curb stroke by stroke, I turn the rake over and push the whole pile at once. Sometimes I'll push with three rakes at once. It's a lot faster. Looks crazy, but it works.

"I wanted to teach you the kaizen philosophy last, because you'll need it as you implement your sales process engineering efforts. Not even Babe Ruth always hits a home run. If you wait for the chance at a big swing, you'll miss a lot of base hits. And if you only depend on your batters, you'll neglect your fielding. If you only work on fielding, you'll neglect the pitching and infield. Everything must be improving, all the time. It all has to work together."

Reflections on Kaizen

I like this spirit of kaizen. It's got me thinking about things I'm not sure I have the answers for. A lot of the topics we discussed earlier are coming back to me.

If everybody works on what's perceived to be problems and bottlenecks in their part of the system, I can see how the flow may smooth. But if everyone works on everything at once, won't it only increase the diameter of the pipe, bumps and all? Is there a limit on how far we should try to expand our capacity in the first place?

But if priorities are given to certain bottlenecks, so that the bumps are worked on in some sort of selective fashion to achieve a smoothing effect, doesn't that imply that somebody out there must be coordinating things? Might that coordination effect put a damper on individual initiative? Will we be telling people not to improve, in some instances? Can we avoid asking some areas to go slow, telling them that they are already ahead of the rest of us and that further improvement will be wasteful?

If we find we have overcapacity in some areas, might that mean that the improvement is to move those people to a different area? What if the people we want to move don't have the talent to work in that new area?

We've already seen that bottlenecks change. Once one has been solved, another area becomes the obstruction. That's why the improvement must be ongoing. But at some point, capacity and throughput will be relatively smooth. We've fixed the existing process so that it is running as best it can, in the way it was designed. In that sense, is kaizen only aimed at removing physical bottlenecks within our existing process? Could our internal lack of will to look at our fundamental process and the way it was set up in the first place be a constraint? Could quality become a constraint at that point? Cost? Is the physical metaphor we've been using of the wiggly lines putting blinders on us regarding other constraints we may have? Are our traditions and natural resistance to change going to limit improvement at some point? Is there any limit as to the type of thing we try to improve?

I guess, no matter what, we could all begin by talking with the customers we serve, both internally and externally, to at least size up the situation. Isn't there a lot each of us can do on our own, without waiting for a corporate permission slip?

Maybe I'm thinking too much. Some of these questions won't arise in practice for a long time. Here I am exploring the limits of improvement when I haven't even begun to scratch the surface. I don't want to talk myself into a standstill before I've started. That's a disease too many people in our company have already. That's what keeps us from taking the first step. I think kaizen means taking a step forward whenever we get the chance, without hesitation.

Tool 12: Implementation Methods

- Solid implementation techniques: vital, as cited over and over
- People must be able to use new approach: behavior is responsible for actual outcome
- Initial planning and design: to prevent as many later problems as possible
- Awareness building: to increase approach and reduce resistance to change
- Documentation: to institutionalize memory and retain intellectual capital
- Training: percent trained × percent skills needed = return on investment
- Ongoing support: to prevent natural decay

"Time and time again, great ideas for improvement fail because they are not implemented. Improvement requires change. Change is a hurdle many people resist. There are always vested interests in preserving the status quo; there are many systems in place to see that change does not occur. Many, hopefully most, are legitimate checks and balances and control mechanisms. Others are impediments.

"So as important as it is, overcoming resistance to change is just one step in a continuum of implementation steps. That's why Tool 12 is so important. Tool 12 is a kit containing five major ingredients. All are necessary to ensure smooth implementation.

"Whatever you do, don't hold back when you are launching a new approach. Passenger planes apply a huge amount of throttle on takeoff, not just the bare minimum to clear the fence. They use all their engines, not just one. Why? Higher power delivers a greater margin for safety when first getting off the ground."

***People* are responsible for the actual outcomes involved, regardless of the degree of automation or work simplification undertaken. Human *behavior* is one of the key variables in any improvement effort.**

Successful change starts in the initial planning and design phase. Make sure the true needs of the people who will be using or affected by the new approach are taken into account and that the process issues have been thoroughly thought through. This includes customers, too. New vested interests, including new checks and balances, must be thought through to offset the old.

"Everyone has hopes. Some gurus make a big deal about how happy people are with the status quo. Baloney. They are only happy with *certain* parts of the way things are. Chances are, people are *unhappy* with the current system due to its known shortcomings. They *hope* it will change in certain areas. Naturally, people have fears about what will happen to them if change takes place. Fulfill their hopes and allay their fears through sound initial design, and the rest will be easier. If you give people what they've been asking for all along and meet their legitimate concerns by modifying your own plans—not just trying to talk them into it—change is much smoother."

Internal awareness building is just as important to changing corporate behavior as an external marketing campaign is to changing consumer behavior. Newsletters, audiovisual presentations, manager's meetings, question and answer sheets—as many media as possible—should be used to get the message out. Be sure to strike the right balance. In cases where people are more in favor of the change, overpromotion runs the risk of creating false expectations of miracle cures. Where fear of change predominates, more emphasis should be placed on the benefits involved, highlighting the dangers of failing to change. Answer objections before they occur, just as in sales.

"In warfare, why do you think it is so important to capture the communications stations first? Get your message out! The grapevine will be the only network operating if you don't actively address people's hopes and fears. And the grapevine is just as likely, if not more so, to be negative. Just think how people love to gripe."

Implementation: Schedule

The third step is to document the new procedures. This institutionalizes the memory of what needs to be done and retains the intellectual capital even though personnel come and go.

"Why do we document new procedures? Because people forget. In *The Dragons of Eden,* the eminent scientist Carl Sagan (1978) writes that there are three forms of intelligence. The first type is stored in our genes, based on natural selection over generations of time. The second form of intelligence is stored in our brains through present experience. The third form of intelligence is extra-somatic—outside our body—stored in libraries, in the form of written expression. Documentation, such as job aids, flowcharts, reference diagrams, help screens, and user's guides, is necessary to preserve a consistent blueprint others can follow.

"A lot of people who don't have to implement change for a living think that all you need to do is overcome resistance to change, and everything will be rosy. Wrong. Even if someone wants to do something, they need to know how to do it well or they'll become frustrated. They need training.

Training is a necessary fourth step. Skills build over time, not overnight. Proper training accelerates the learning curve and captures the overall investment that much more quickly.

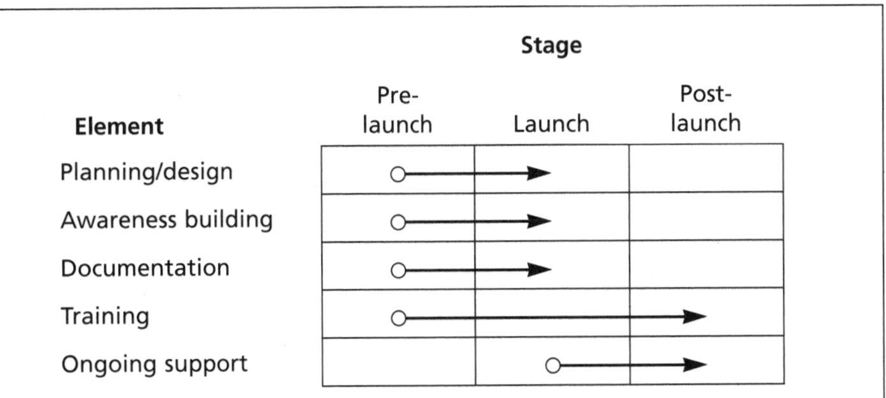

"In my experience, nine out of 10 change projects fail unless the people are properly trained. You may have calculated a theoretical ROI for your project. In reality, the ROI is a function of the percent of the people trained times the percent of the necessary skill they acquire. Think about what happens if you take a projected ROI and multiply it by 50 percent (percent trained), then multiply that number by 50 percent (percent skill acquired). This is a chained probability: The ROI is only 25 percent of what it started out to be! Even the most people-ignorant number cruncher can understand the meaning of that equation."

Fifth, ongoing support is necessary for the same reason mechanical maintenance is needed in physical systems: to prevent natural decay. This includes providing refresher training, help desk support, training resident experts, and ongoing user group discussions. Ongoing feedback about where support seems to be needed most, together with any suggestions for further enhancements, must be fed back to the planning team to facilitate ongoing improvement.

The chart illustrates when each of five main elements is emphasized as the effort to launch a new approach progresses over time. Detailed instructions on how to implement new sales process procedures are covered in the *Guide to Implementing Sales Automation* (Selden 1994).

Practical Development and Launch Sequence

"A well-known electronics manufacturer once rolled out a sales automation system. Its analysis of the initial problem was sound. It had discovered that configuring and pricing its equipment was very time-consuming and error-prone. An automated system was developed to correct these problems.

"Its implementation, however, was terrible. The system was released to meet a target date before testing was complete. In effect, the entire sales force of 75 people was used as guinea pigs.

"We don't have time to do it right the first time, but we always seem to have time to fix it later. What's the cure for this?"

Someone in the group says kaizen. *People laugh. Dr. Selden chuckles, saying that this particular company practiced a type of kaizen we'd like to avoid: release a new approach prematurely and fix like crazy.*

"I'm going to teach you a three-stage approach to testing and rolling out a new approach that minimizes risk. The approach doesn't require advanced training in anything except common sense. This approach is so widely respected that it is built into the Sales Automation Association's *Audit Standards* for improving the sales process, especially where technology is concerned (SAA 1994)."

Recommended Development and Launch Sequence

- Test in lab-like controlled settings first
  - —Modify until specs are consistently met
- Pilot with small group
  - —Modify until specs are consistently met
- Roll out one group at a time
  - —Fine-tune as needed for each group
  - —Hold up if specs aren't met

First, once the development team is satisfied the new method is sound and after traditional user testing is complete, test the new approach in laboratory-like, controlled settings. Start by using the most talented people, those who are most likely to use the new approach successfully. Do not move forward to testing with a wider, more representative group until the approach works at this level. If the approach doesn't meet your specifications under ideal settings, don't waste other people's time until it does.

Second, expand the test to a pilot setting, which includes a more representative group and more lifelike situations. This type of pilot is not like a television pilot, where audience ratings are used to extend or cancel a TV show. In a process pilot, further obstacles are surfaced and removed. The new approach is improved until it works on this scale. Stay in this phase until specifications are met.

Third, roll the approach out one group at a time to the rest of the company. Fine-tune as needed for each group. Slow down the rollout at any time if it looks like the approach needs further improvement in order to achieve a practical result.

Throughout, if your original specification called for a business result, don't accept "mechanical achievement" as a substitute for business achievement. Mechanical achievements take the form of hooking up computers or testing software until it is bug-free. Being bug-free is not the same as accomplishing a business goal.

Final Rollout Sequence Illustrated

"Look at the chart I've drawn as I describe the third step in the rollout sequence more clearly. By the way, just in case I have any purists in the audience, I want to mention that this approach is based on a class of longitudinal time-series experimental designs known as the multiple baseline approach.

"In many sales settings, territories are divided by district. Prior to introducing your change, gather baseline readings on all of them, measuring the dimension of most interest. In the chart here, the absolute volume of operating income is being charted in three districts, just to keep things simple. Remember, this is a method that has already survived the rigors of lab and pilot testing.

"Next, introduce the change in the first district or market. Do not introduce it anywhere else until you can see the effect.

"The reason for waiting is that if something worked in the pilot phase but didn't work in the first live district, you'd want to determine what was wrong before continuing. You're being paid for a rolling implementation, not a rolling disaster!

"Notice in this case that operating income went up in the East, but not elsewhere. This tends to rule out alternative explanations for why income jumped in the East.

"What might you conclude if, when the system was introduced in the East, profits went up everywhere, even without the system?"

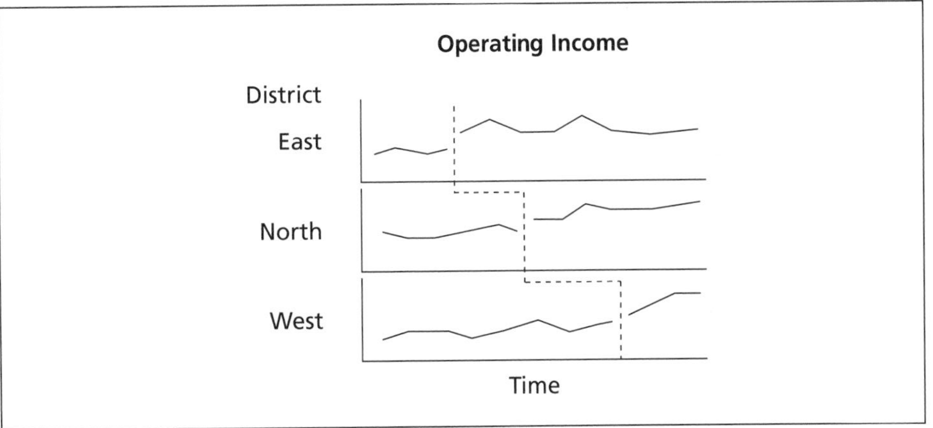

Dr. Selden pauses. Someone says that the effect attributed to the process change might actually be due to a wider change, such as a change in seasonal business or the introduction of a new product.

"That's right. If all districts' operating income went up by the same amount at the same time, when the change was only made in one district, we wouldn't really know if our system was having an impact, would we? But in this case operating income only went up in the East.

"Now the new approach is introduced in the North. What if nothing happens? It might be that the results previously seen in the East were due to the interaction of some local effect. In this case, operating income went up, and no real change was noted in the West. Again, it looks like the results were due to the new approach alone.

"The pattern is repeated as often as you need, in order to achieve what engineers such as Taguchi call a *robust* approach."

What engineers call a *robust* design is able to operate under the widest possible conditions and yet deliver an outcome that is remarkably consistent. See Taguchi 1986; Ealey 1988; and Lochner and Matar 1990.

"While not at the level of rigor demanded by other disciplines, this development and launch sequence satisfies most of the need to show practical proof—and the concurrent need to achieve success—in many process engineering settings."

Intuition vs. Analysis

Dr. Selden calls for a mid-afternoon stretch break.

A million thoughts are going through my mind. Our company tries new things in such a random way at times, it's a wonder anything turns out right. Sometimes it does, which is a minor miracle, but many times it doesn't. We accept the word of some guru with the latest theory that doing things a certain way is better and charge ahead.

The implementation method Dr. Selden is talking about makes sense. I wonder why we haven't used it before? It's probably not that we haven't tried to be systematic. But there are so many brush fires to deal with in sales and marketing that it's easy to get off track. And frankly, I don't think we've had the picture painted for us in this way, either.

Maybe we've tried this type of rollout, but on a less formal level. If you flip a switch and a light goes on, and repeat the same sequence with the same result, again and again, it doesn't take a rocket scientist to say, "Eureka!" It's easy to see the cause and effect in that case. There are a lot of relationships like that in sales and marketing. Everything doesn't need stringent testing.

But not everything we do in business is like flipping a light switch. We flip a switch, the light only flickers, and at the same time, the lights are flickering in other rooms, too. We can't really tell what's working. Just as important, we can't tell what is not working. So we wind up continuing ineffective practices, maybe on the basis of the weakest anecdotal results or isolated success stories, because we'd be embarrassed if we stopped. Or we try something that might have been effective, but its impact was masked by a momentary market swing that hit everybody else at the same time.

The development and rollout approach Dr. Selden illustrated may not be perfect. We might not use it every day, but I can think of times I wish we had followed it.

Sometimes in sales and marketing we have to go with a hunch because there is no better way to judge the merits of one approach or another. Maybe if the dollars at stake were great enough, people would take the whole thing more seriously. We use our own people as guinea pigs a lot, I'm afraid, trying out a sales theory or marketing approach without really knowing whether it's better than what we've been doing. If the approach is surefire, and the dollars at risk are small, then hey—go for it. Maybe that's the key: If the dollars at stake are large, you shelter your risk. Maybe in the future, that's where a professional sales process engineering firm would be called in, just to look things over.

Exercise: Implementation

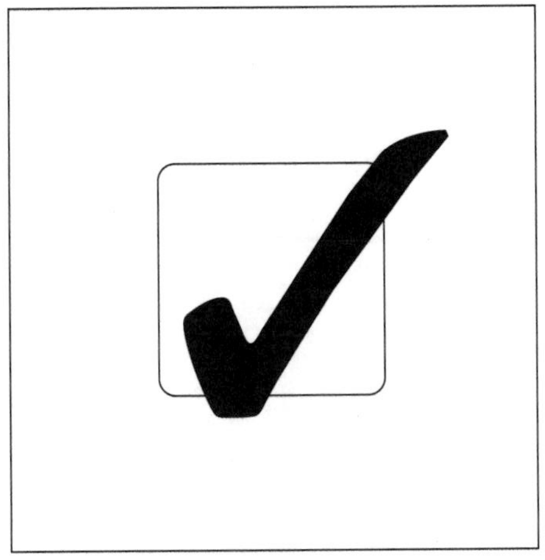

"The format for this last exercise is different. I'd like you to break into your small groups of about four people each. Most of you are thinking about specific sales, marketing, and customer service improvements, or you wouldn't be in this course. Your assignment is simply to discuss where proper implementation planning for change would be useful, using the approach we've just reviewed as your twelfth tool.

"Discuss the specific types of implementation techniques you would use to help your effort go better. Jot down your ideas and the ideas you hear that you could use."

Our group quickly focuses on a very specific implementation effort: sales automation. Most of us are thinking about using technology as a way to support the sales process.

At the planning and design stage, everyone agrees that we should interview a cross section of our customers, our reps, our marketing and service group, and our product development group to make sure we know where everyone's shoe is pinching at the moment. We also want to get a sense of positive and creative things we can do to earn more market share. We now realize we have to carefully study the process itself to see where automation could have a concrete benefit in terms of cost, quality, time, and quantity in specific places. We need to link any process change to a measurable business goal. We can get that from the executives. During the design phase, we'll be integrating the lab-test step so that we're sure of what we're doing before going further. We may hire an outside consultant to help us save time. Why reinvent the wheel?

For awareness building, the group thinks that management should serve as our internal public relations team. We'll come up with an overhead presentation that the regional managers can present to the district managers. The DMs will use that presentation with their people at a local level during a regular meeting, just to let people know the approach we're taking. We've decided not to do a slick sales job on ourselves. We're not trying to convince people that the new system is the "right" system. No system can be perfect and satisfy everyone. Instead, we'll be using the regular company media: our newsletter, info sheets, and face-to-face conversations to relay what we're doing and solicit input. If we get negative comments in response, we're going to listen very closely. After all, their objections may be right on target. Kaizen!

Discussion

- Implementation planning for change

We've also jotted down that we need much better procedure documentation than we've had in the past. How can we say we have a process if we can't document it for others to follow? Our group felt that plenty of examples of how to use the system to accomplish the sales goal, not just to get through computer screens, was important. We'll be creating paper versions to start with, including brief job aids. Not all our people are computer literate, so we don't want to confuse them with too much computer stuff at first. We'll set up electronic versions built into the system as well, so the instructions will always be handy.

Implementation Planning Continues

The group agreed that thorough training is critical, as is great support. We'll give everyone hands-on training, plus a help desk to fall back on if need be.

One person in our group had a bad experience with training where the people were trained but their managers weren't. Consequently, their managers looked unprepared, and the people lost respect for their own managers. In turn, the managers bad mouthed the system and entire districts basically just shut down in terms of automation. So we're going to train managers how to use the new approach separately, showing them ways to use the system to help and coach their people even better. We want to set managers up as one type of expert their people can call on for questions.

One person in the group even suggested that the system be set up from the start so one manager could basically let his or her people manage themselves, with some sort of alert system that would allow the manager to jump in only when trouble occurred. That might let one manager work with more reps, helping the ones most in need and leaving the successful ones to manage their own accounts with minimal formal supervision.

We felt that managers should play an active part in the rollout. They could be getting feedback and collecting data impossible to gather in any other way. Their input, together with that of the reps and other departments involved, would help shape improvements.

Our group agreed that it made sense to follow the pilot and rollout approach Dr. Selden described. Most of the people in my group felt that upper management would have to be educated as to why this approach was necessary. We agreed that upper management always seemed to use whether a deadline was met as a test of a project manager's abilities. "The way we've defined our goals in the past, nothing else is measurable except a date," someone laughed. We joked that we better bring a consultant in on that conversation, since our own credibility wouldn't be as high. "No one is a prophet in their own land," one group member quipped. Almost everyone agreed that focusing on accomplishing a concrete business goal was the best defense against deadline pressures.

Evening Exercise: Plan, Do, Check, Act Revisited

"This program is not a three-day lecture. It's a workshop. It's important you leave with a concrete action plan you can take back to your shop and get moving on. What we've covered will be much more valuable to you if you have a battle plan to refer to, so you can put one foot in front of the other and move forward. Remember, an engineer is a do-er.

"You may work on your plan alone or with others from your company if you came with your colleagues. Here's what I want you to do. Take the principles and tools we've learned over the past two days and combine them with your knowledge of how your organization operates right now. On one sheet of paper, outline the steps you will take to plan, do, check, and act on one concrete sales process improvement goal that is important to you. It will help to list these as separate steps.

"Refer to your notes and course materials for ideas to use at each stage. I suggest you start by reviewing what is included in the PDCA cycle! You may want to use this master plan as a way to link together all the other exercise ideas you've completed up to now. For example, your PDCA plan could be aimed at the bottlenecks you've already addressed with the implementation plan you just created, and so on, to make a unified whole out of the past two days.

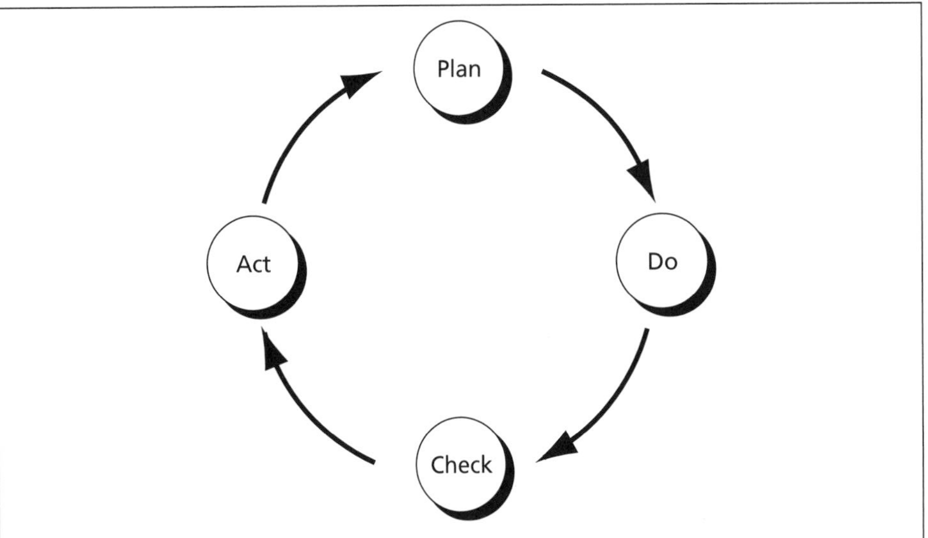

"I'll give you 20 minutes to work on it now. I'll ask you to stop at that time, and we'll conclude the first two days of our journey together.

"If you don't finish now, please work on your assignment tonight so that you are prepared to discuss your ideas in class tomorrow."

Our Journey

Dr. Selden concludes Day Two by posting the original road map again. He asks that the participants share insights they have had so far, remarking that it is helpful for people to share their views to cement ideas in place as well as to spark new ideas. There's no lack of comments.

"The point about starting with customer expectations as a specification to drive other parts of the process was excellent. If we can figure out how to get there in the shortest path possible, I think we'll be doing a lot of what you've been talking about."

"The behavioral points were a great reminder that people are involved. We can't just speed up the line in order to increase output. We must reward our customer's buying behavior. We have to distinguish ourselves from competitors in at least two ways: how rewarding we are to deal with and in the cues we give to our customers before they buy."

"Ideas and theories are important, especially if it's your boss holding them. If there's one thing I got out of this workshop so far, though, it's time to start weighing the facts more heavily."

"This workshop is exciting to me so far. It demonstrates that sales process engineering is really here. I've been in sales for some 20 years now. Much of what I read and hear about our profession is getting repetitive. This opens the door to a whole new world for me. It also ties together a lot of what I've been taught in business school and the other seminars I've attended into a more concrete whole."

Name	Philosophy
Selden	Sales process engineering
Deming	Quality is up to management
Crosby	Cost of quality
Harrington, Melan	Measurement, process selection
Shingo	Mistake-proof
Hammer and Champy et al.	Reengineering
Ohno	Just-in-time, industrial engineering
Pavlov, Skinner	Behavioral engineering
Juran	Quality planning, improvement, and control
Imai	Continuous improvement

Tool
Flowcharting
14 points
Brainstorming
Check sheets
Pareto charts
Run charts
Histograms
Cause/effect diagrams Scatter plots
SPC, systematic experimentation
Implementation sequence planning

Have the Courage to Imagine!

> One man with courage is a majority.
>
> —*Thomas Jefferson*

Dr. Selden encourages the group members to express a few more ideas before presenting his concluding remarks.

"I think we've been attacking our problems piecemeal. I like the idea that we can be systematic in our improvement efforts. I like the idea there's a path. It may not be the *path, but it's something we haven't tried before."*

"One thing I get out of this is that top managers could accelerate improvement in sales, marketing, and customer service if they put as much effort into sales process improvement as they do into our manufacturing improvement efforts."

"I'm impressed at how much a few simple tools may help us out at the start. As you said earlier, the tools may be borrowed from more established fields, but they should work fine. The tools we've covered look general enough that they can be applied. We can develop our own unique and specialized tools later, as we learn more."

"My company prides itself on being progressive. The examples you gave and the ones we came up with show me we have already successfully been applying many pieces of what you've called sales process engineering. I don't need convincing of that. The trouble is, the language and framework our firm has been using to describe our approaches is like the Tower of Babel—it's not unified. I don't sense that our old way of viewing things has the same solid, unified, and deep foundation as what you've been describing. I'm taking away the conviction that if we can put it all together, we'll get even better results more quickly."

The comments trail off, and Dr. Selden thanks the group members for their observations. Then, in a burst of energy, he addresses the audience in an enthusiastic send-off.

"I hope your insights give you courage—the courage to imagine and the courage to act! Thomas Jefferson exemplified the spirit of good old American kaizen when he remarked, 'One man with courage is a majority.' That person could be you. You don't have to wait for permission to use these principles. It's your life—use what you've learned to achieve more success at whatever you do.

"And remember, in a somewhat more colloquial piece of advice, 'You can't steal second base and keep one foot on first.' If you don't like the results you're achieving now, try something different.

"I'll see you tomorrow morning at 8 A.M. sharp. That should give you plenty of time to finish your PDCA assignment if you need to. Return rested and refreshed! Good night!"

This has been one of the most rewarding two days I've spent in a long time. As I leave the room, I think that even though some of the concepts have been hard to absorb in the time we've had, I feel like we are part of an awakening of some sort. Without getting corny, I have this strange feeling of being in a delivery room as a baby is being born. I sense a mixture of optimism at the opportunities we have, and also a sense of hunkering down in response to the realization that there's hard work ahead of us, too.

All in all, I have this tremendous feeling of an expanded horizon. I can see that many of the insights and lessons I've had in the past now have a home. I also have a sense of renewal and even a professional reinvigoration. Nope, there's nothing routine about my field. Not after these past two days. There's so much to learn. And I have been given pointers showing me where to learn more.

Day Three

Our Journey—Day Three

Class starts promptly at 8 A.M. the next day. As a few latecomers file quietly into the room, Dr. Selden remarks, "Looks like we've got some variability." The class laughs. Though a bit sheepish, most of the latecomers smile, too. The atmosphere is friendly. The goading on Dr. Selden's part is good-natured.

Dr. Selden begins the session by asking everyone to get out the evening's homework assignment. He asks a few volunteers to share their PDCA plans with the rest of the group.

A wholesaler wants to apply some of the more quality-oriented improvement principles to increase sales at the distributor level, prior to further expansion.

A service company sales vice president has a plan to survey her entire sales process to rank order the company's cost-of-quality problems to set the framework for a systematic PDCA cycle. Initially, she suspects that the needs analysis portion of the customer meetings is the bottleneck.

A manufacturing firm information systems executive wants to figure out how to automatically get better data regarding all aspects of his firm's business-to-business selling process, so the big picture can be seen more clearly in support of any improvement effort his firm makes. He isn't sure which portion of the process is most problematic, but he likes the idea of being able to measure and increase customer loyalty from an objective point of view.

The head of a small, growing chain wants to revisit the way her firm investigates the impact of different store layouts on sales in each store. She employed the entire PDCA cycle in her outline, but isn't yet sure how to test which layout was most effective.

"We're starting out the day in fine fashion! You've illustrated an important point. Basic engineering principles may be universal. But since everyone's situation is different, each application will vary. An engineering-like approach promises to help us arrive at sound solutions more quickly and with less risk than a hit-or-miss approach. We should not expect to find magic bullets, nor should we expect to be able to directly copy what others have done. The solutions will inevitably need to be tailored to each firm."

Today's Road Map

"Today you're in for a complete change of pace. The first two days of this workshop were filled with concepts, principles, examples, and tools. Very 'thought intensive.' The exercises focused on getting you to examine your own sales process, your customers, and the improvements you might make. It was probably easy to see how many of the ideas could be applied.

"But there is something you have not yet learned. If you are to understand a sales process, it is not enough just to see flowcharts. A sales process engineer must be able to do more than apply a time-saving trick here or a quality improvement technique there. A process engineer must understand the fundamental nature of the process involved and be able to measure, predict, and control the dynamic relationships within it. Today's work will introduce you to these process fundamentals.

"To accomplish our goal, our agenda for today is straightforward. First we'll review basic sales process operations and how they can be measured.

"Next we need to re-cement our understanding of process variation, and we'll learn to measure whether a process is in control or not.

Goals and Objectives: Day Three

Main Goal

Grasp purpose and begin to apply basic concepts

Day Three

- Explore fundamentals of sales process operations and measures
- Understand implications of sales process variation and control
- Use SPC to evaluate improvement
- Develop approaches to simulation and modeling
- Discuss how to foster sales process research and development

"Third, we'll implement various changes in the process and see whether they can be detected.

"Fourth, we will use a sales process simulation to systematically explore what happens when part of the sales process is changed.

"Finally, we will outline a missing structural link in our sales organizations that is holding most companies back from making sustained improvements, and what we need to do in order to fill the gap.

"Today will be filled with hands-on practice as we explore the fundamental nature of process mechanics and dynamics. How can we say we understand the true meaning of the word *process* if we don't understand how processes work, deep down inside? We'll be counting things, measuring things, and using some easy math to see how a process really performs and whether we can detect changes we make. Some of you will quickly understand how the simple models we explore can be applied to your own situation. Others will need time for the meaning of what we see and do to sink in. As you will see, today we'll be covering another deep topic in itself, worthy of years of further exploration and mastery. It will be up to you to take it to the next level in your own situation."

Measurement and Evaluation Within the SAA's Approach

The Sales Automation Association incorporates measurement and evaluation as part of its framework for sales process improvement. As with all management accounting and decision-making tools, the specific measures used need to be tailored to the specific efforts undertaken.

Measurement and evaluation views the elements of the people involved, the process changes, any software and hardware having to do with automation, and the support elements provided as a mixture that together affects the result.

Measurement and evaluation involves gathering data throughout the process, including the final results. This must be done in such a way that the knowledge gained can be used to further improve. Learning must take place.

"I was talking to a friend in a midsized company the other day. He pointed his finger at the so-called quality control guy in his firm and said, 'Yeah, that's the guy who sits back there, gathers statistics, and gives it back to the rest of us.'

"Someone who gathers data and doesn't act on it displays the symptoms of an individual who hasn't been trained to take action or someone who has been punished for taking action. Such people are Shingo's 'table,' 'catalog,' and 'nyet' engineers. We need *improvement* engineers.

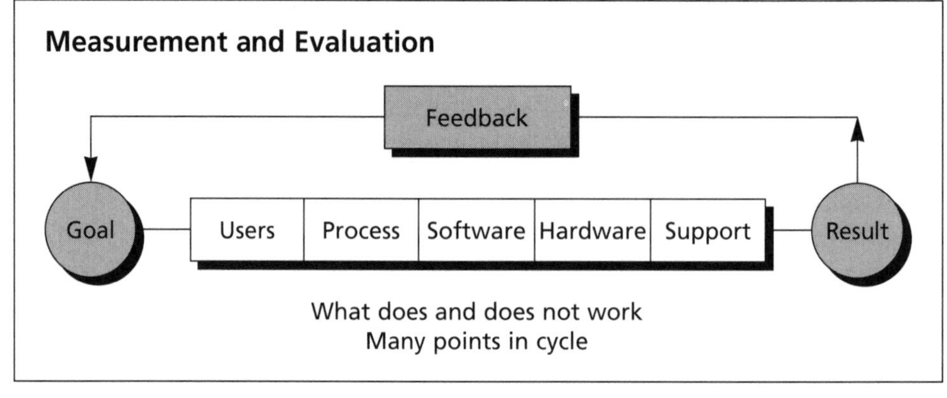

"Engineering is an *active* profession, not a passive one. Measurement and evaluation serve a larger purpose. What is that purpose? It's to help us move closer to the goal, and then once we've reached it, to figure out how we can improve even further! We need to overcome inertia by following Deming's PDCA cycle and by reducing the climate of fear in our organizations."

"There is always a premium upon the ability to get things done" (King 1944).

New Business Sales Process Model

"It helps to visualize what you are measuring. This makes the effort more tangible. Notice the new title I've given to our earlier flow diagram.

"In a business-to-business sales process, we usually obtain business from two different sources: new customers and existing clients. Let's look at the new business model separately. Of course, your model may be different.

"The process model we looked at two days ago included marketing, sales, and service operations. Many of these operations are essential in acquiring new business. For example, lead generation and cold calling are often critical when obtaining new prospects. A formal sales presentation is especially important, too. With new customers you need to clearly distinguish your product and service offering from alternatives that may be firmly entrenched. Well-executed formal proposal preparation and closing activities are likely to be highly important the first few times you do business with a customer who has not done business with your firm before.

"From a behavioral point of view, the difference between a new and existing account is that the new account has not been previously reinforced for making an actual purchase. Prospects have never bought from us before. Therefore the emphasis is on attracting new customers and reinforcing them for taking all the initial steps."

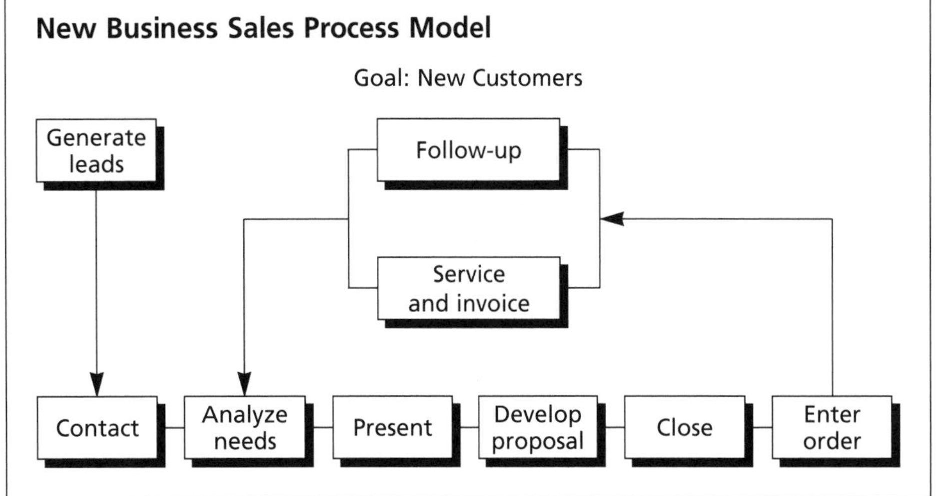

Hearing and seeing the mechanisms this way, the implications of what we need to do in marketing, sales, and service are suddenly much clearer for me. We've got to show our prospective clients why our goods and services are more desirable than the alternative at each and every step in the process, and we must be very sure we are reinforcing each small step the new client makes in coming through the process with us. To the degree we're doing this, I think we're doing all we can. The problem is, I know we have major gaps! The tools we learned yesterday and the day before should help us to identify and come up with new ways to close those gaps.

Repeat Business Sales Process Model

"Notice the difference in the model when working with existing accounts! By the way, if you study this diagram carefully, you might also see that this particular model seems to fit the consumer packaged goods sales process as well as a business-to-business model.

"In the normal process of servicing an existing account, the representative notices client needs. The steps of confirming these needs and solutions with the client are often of a different nature than when securing new business. The discussion involves exchanging advice and gaining agreement, rather than emphasizing elaborate proposal development and closing activities. From there, the order entry, invoicing, and servicing process is similar to that seen when working with a new account.

"So for many businesses, the sales process is not one process at all. It's at least two distinct processes, each with a separate goal. The one process is aimed at securing new customers. The other has a goal of retaining existing customers. Both need to reinforce the purchase decision by delivering what was promised, at the minimum, or by exceeding customer expectations."

This is a great diagram. From a behavioral point of view, I can see why it is so important to reward our customers for buying from us, each and every time. We need to reinforce their behavior of coming back to us. This must be done consistently, because we've also seen that our customers may try Brand X once in a while as part of normal variation that we may never be able to control.

Bingo! That insight triggered more connections. Yesterday Dr. Selden talked about what makes a process robust *in an engineering sense. Maybe the degree that a sales process can withstand the customer's occasional Brand X purchase behavior or ad viewing is the degree to which our process is robust. I wonder what it would take to make our sales process robust, per se, if we made that our goal?*

This diagram also shows something I've been arguing all along. Securing new business has many more steps and looks much more costly than retaining existing business. We need new customers to replace ones that don't stay with us, but we sure have to weigh the factors carefully.

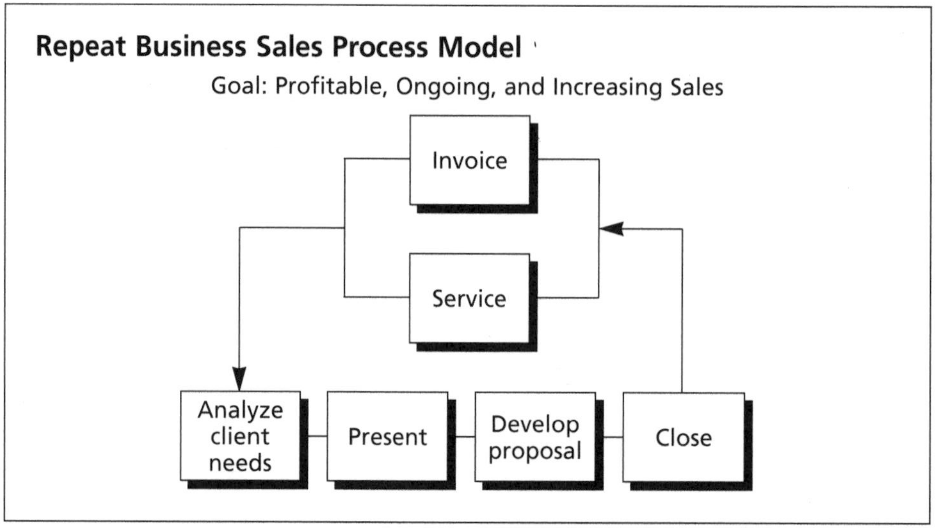

Repeat Business Sales Process Model

Goal: Profitable, Ongoing, and Increasing Sales

Invoice

Service

Analyze client needs

Present

Develop proposal

Close

It costs the average business six times more to attract new customers than to keep existing customers (LeBoeuf 1989). Retaining just 5 percent more customers from a company's current customer base can result in increases of profitability ranging from 25 percent (in credit card firms) to 85 percent (in the banking industry) (Reichheld and Sasser 1990). According to J. K. Cannie, author of *Turning Lost Customers into Gold* (1993), the average company loses 20 percent of its customers per year.

DAY THREE

Law of Chained Probabilities

"Most of us are dealing with processes that involve *chained probabilities.*"

The law of chained probability states that the chance an outcome of a series of mutually dependent events will occur is the product, not the sum, of their individual probabilities. Where we're dealing with exclusive alternatives each branch must add up to 100 percent. This law is sometimes also called the law of compound events.

"Let's say that 20 percent of all calls a rep is making at the moment are on prospects, and that 80 percent are on existing customers.

"When we call on a prospect, let's say the odds of closing the sale on that call are 10 percent. The other branch must be 90 percent.

"When we call on a current customer, let's say that the odds of closing a sale are 90 percent, and the chance of not making a sale is 10 percent.

"The law of chained probabilities means that the odds of any call leading to the sale to a prospect are 20 percent times 10 percent, or 0.2×0.1. The answer is 0.02, or 2 percent.

"The odds of any call leading to a sale to an existing customer is 0.8 times 0.9, or 0.72: 72 percent.

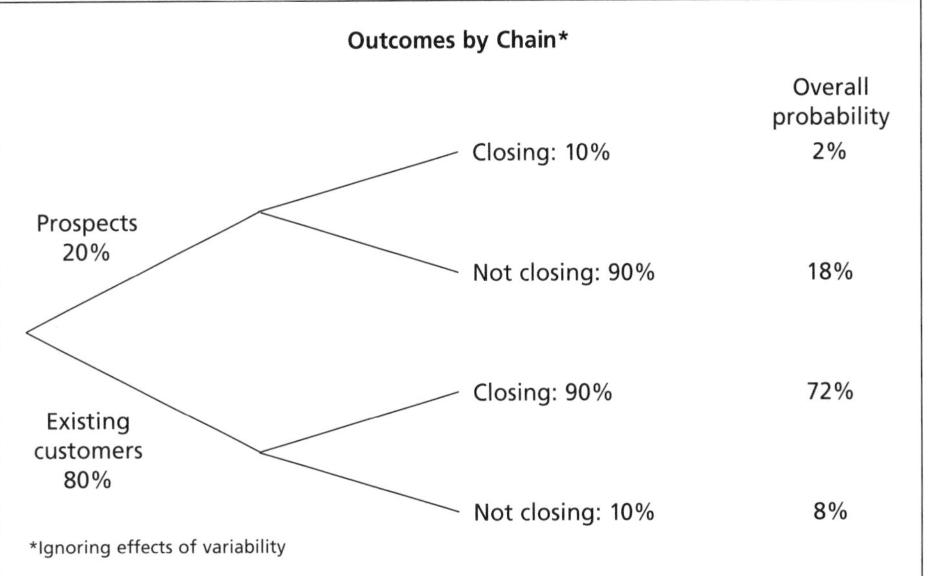

"Knowing what we learned earlier about human preference behavior, what would you expect a sales rep to do in this case? It does little good to call them lazy, by the way: We've already seen that biological organisms tend to work hardest for the most dense source of reinforcement. Appeals to moralistic constructs don't help explain the situation!"

Once reps have an established client base, most dramatically reduce the amount of prospecting. Our company assigns only heavy prospecting duties to newly hired reps, knowing that this is the only way to get reps to work on prospecting: namely, when it's their only source of reinforcement.

What seems most obvious to me is that if we knew the payoffs and costs for sales in each branch of the diagram, we could make much more informed decisions about how to manage our resources.

Process Model—Missing Elements

Dr. Selden tells a story, then challenges the class to think.

"A young fellow starting out in the printing business was sharing his frustrations with the previous owner. The young fellow said, 'I don't get it. I'm not making any money.' The old printer thought for a moment and asked the young man what he was getting for his scrap. The young man replied, 'What do you mean, what am I getting for my scrap?' 'I mean, what are you doing with it?' the old printer asked. The young man replied, 'I'm throwing it away.' 'There's the problem,' the old man said. 'In this business margins are so thin, your profit is what you sell your scrap for.'

"The young printer had overlooked something, hadn't he? In 99 percent of the sales process diagrams I've seen people draw, there are missing variables—essential for adequate understanding to engineering standards—that are not drawn. Perhaps this is because many of our symbols are inherited from other fields, such as computer science.

"You've seen this process diagram before. This one has question marks on it. Think about the story I just told. Now, point out a major process variable that seems to be missing. The location of the question marks is not critical."

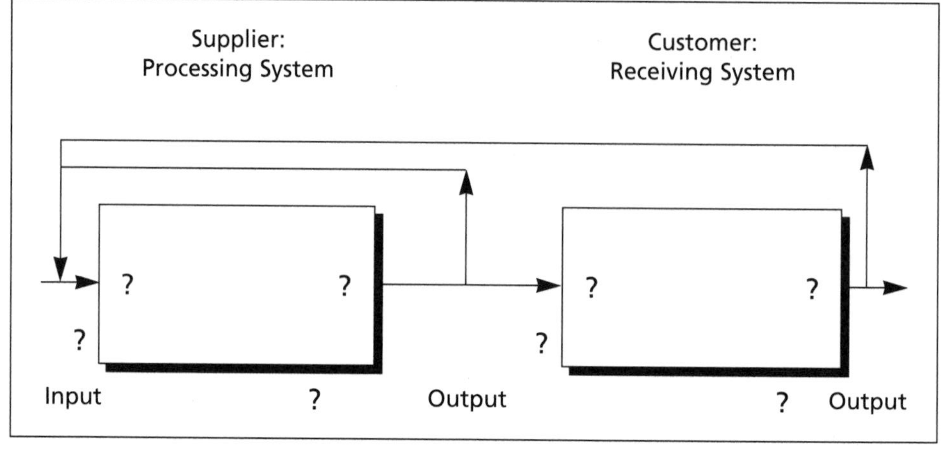

After a pause, someone says "Waste!" Dr. Selden asks the group to applaud the volunteer. He asks the group members to return to this diagram throughout the day, jotting down other missing, but important, process elements as they spot them.

"Each element offers a potential source for improvement. Take waste, for example: a natural, inescapable by-product of all natural processes. You might draw that as an arrow leading out the bottom of the boxes. Is there any scrap in our sales process that would be valuable to others? Could you sell your leads to others? To your co-marketing partners? Crazy idea? How much scrap do you have in your process? How much scrap can you help your customers save in their process?"

Part 1: Operations and Measurement

> Research is to see what everybody has seen, and to think what nobody has thought.
>
> —*Anonymous*

Objectives

By the time we finish this topic you will be able to

- List four elements comprising cycle time in any process.
- Understand nine fundamental operations found in most sales, marketing, and service processes.
- Pick measures applicable to the quantitative analysis of a sales process.
- Categorize sales measures into their two essential types.

Major Process Elements

Shigeo Shingo points out that cycle time is comprised of four elements.

- **Work—adding value to an input by transforming it in some way**
- **Inspection—comparing something against a standard**
- **Transportation—moving something from one place or position to another**
- **Waiting—pausing in a hold condition during which time no work, inspection, or transportation occurs**

Cycle time = Work time + Inspection + Transportation + Wait time

"Process time is not the same as cycle time! Process time is the time spent in work. Work adds value to something by changing its state."

Dr. Selden relays a personal observation based on time and motion studies he has conducted: Some 95 percent of the time spent preparing professional proposals consists of pure motion, versus work. He then asks the group to briefly jot down examples of the four elements in their sales, marketing, and service processes.

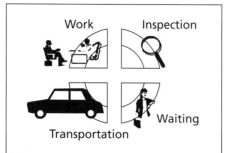

Work
Inspection
Transportation
Waiting

For me, transportation sticks in my mind as a big time consumer on a rep's part. Windshield time. It used to bother me. I've heard that some grocery stores are close to perfecting a way to grocery shop by computer. Previous efforts to offer that service were unsuccessful because they weren't profitable. The new method involves computers the customer uses to place the order. It's delivered to the customer's doorstep. Now that's a way to reduce transportation on the customer's part. I bet there would be a huge demand for that, and not just in the grocery business. I bet there are a lot of people who go shopping but who dislike it or whose time is precious enough to make the convenience worth any extra cost. Maybe video conferencing, the 500-channel TV they keep talking about, or the Internet will help solve this problem.

In marketing, the wait time between placing an ad and receiving the leads is a killer. I wish we could get an electronic feed directly from the magazines. I hear that kind of software exists right now, to capture information about who has visited Internet pages. Why should we wait until the end of the month, or even until the end of a week, just to get printed leads? Why couldn't there be a daily feed directly into our literature fulfillment center or to wherever we wanted it? Why do we have to wait for the mail and do all that data re-entry? Why couldn't we get our leads almost as soon as the magazine's reply cards are punched in?

Not that it would be desired in all cases, but I think we could use cause-and-effect diagrams to figure how to increase time spent with customers. I think that's where reps can add the most value.

Even in cases where time spent with customers is a deciding factor in sales, a firm's calculations often do not take into account time spent with the same customers *by the competition.* The relative strength of a competitor's efforts is critical. In the early 1900s the British engineer F. W. Lanchester worked out formulas describing the relative strength in military combat necessary to achieve victory in battle. Updated by Bernard Koopman of Columbia University in the 1940s, these principles are now being applied to sales and marketing, as illustrated in Lanchester's First Law (Yano 1990). Brainstorming and cause-and-effect diagrams can be used to focus on ways to increase time with customers. Tables in the *Guide to Implementing Sales Automation* (Selden 1994) suggest solutions.

Lanchester's First Law

Offensive quantity group A = E × (Average call length × Number of calls)^2
where E = Efficiency factor (Efficiency, skill, and morale)

Process vs. Cycle Time

"Increasing the work load without improving the rest of the process just increases the burden, stress, and fatigue. It forces people to work more nights and weekends. That is not an engineering improvement. That's not more productivity. Sales process engineering will build a more humane system, reducing costs associated with burnout and turnover such as lost sales, customer defections, and new hire recruiting and training cost."

Cycle time is the sum of the time it takes to move, wait, inspect, and perform work. Work in process (WIP) ties up funds in hidden inventory. The funds cannot yield a return until the inventory is converted into sales. Reducing WIP saves money. WIP in the sales process can be anything not being worked on at the moment, for example, leads, estimates, and proposals. The amount of time customers spend walking down mall aisles not examining merchandise could be considered part of their cycle time that is not spent "in process," as well. Kiosks of all sorts are moving into this void.

"In the picture I've drawn, imagine that each tick mark on the timeline represents one minute. What is the total cycle time for one item?"

Someone blurts out, "Five minutes."

"Hmmm . . . and how much time does actual *processing* occupy?"

Someone says, "Two minutes: 40 percent of the total."

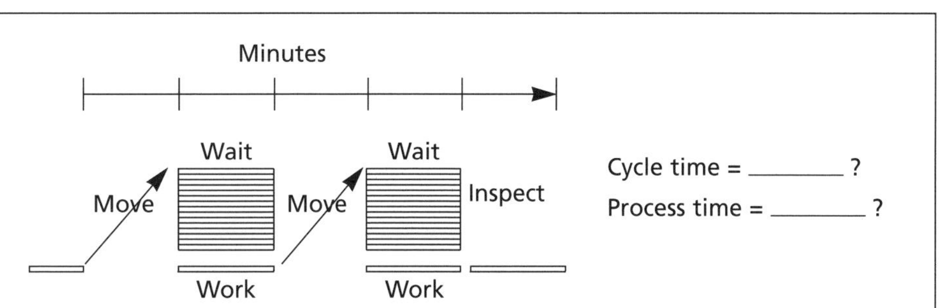

"Oops! Watch out. When you're first using math as you learn sales process engineering, use a buddy system! Mistakes are easy to make. Let's look at it more closely. Not counting the item prior to its first motion, it takes one minute to move it into line. Then what happens?"

Someone says, "It waits."

He got us. The cycle time is nowhere near five minutes. Our piece has to wait in line more than that. It looks like there are 15 items ahead of it, plus the one being processed at the bottom of the stack. If each item spends a minute in processing, our piece has to wait 15 minutes before it can be worked on.

"Without variation or unforeseen mishaps, the cycle time is 35 minutes. Total process time is two minutes, 5.7 percent of the total. That's no surprise. Prior to improvement, process time often occupies the *smallest* portion of cycle time in the entire system. I'll leave you with one last question. Where does the biggest opportunity for improvement lie? Is it in making the work more efficient?"

I'm not sure I enjoy brainteasers like this where math is involved. Hang on. Bingo—the math isn't that hard at all. If we increase work efficiency *we'll improve, sure, but if we can* eliminate *the wait time, the improvement is even greater. So many lightbulbs are going on at once. This must be why Dr. Selden talked about just-in-time and the kanban system at such length. If we speed up work, motion, and inspection by 50 percent, total cycle time drops to $17^1/_2$ minutes. If we process things* one at a time—decreasing the batch size—*the total cycle time drops to five minutes total! I think I'll add "stored work in process" to my diagram with all the question marks on it.*

Vaughan's Seed Company, a nationwide distributor of seeds and plants, has been able to reduce its average order cycle time by 95 percent, using an electronic ordering system placed on its customers' sites (Smith 1996).

DAY THREE

Examples in Sales, Marketing, and Service

Dr. Selden draws our attention to a handout, asking us to match the activities on the left to the type of process element they fit into on the right. After giving people a few minutes Dr. Selden asks for our answers.

Categorize Activity by Process Element	
Driving to a customer	
Taking orders	Wait
Credit checking	
Answering objections	Inspection
Creating advertising	
Critiquing a proposal	Transportation
Resolving complaints	
Sitting in a lobby	Work
Analyzing needs	

The exercise wasn't hard, but some of the ways I categorized things bothered me a bit. We reviewed the answers together as a large group.

I think everyone got "driving to a customer" as "transportation" and "sitting in a lobby" as "wait." We all marked "creating advertising" and "analyzing needs" as "work."

I told the rest of the group I was uneasy about marking "taking orders" as "work." And although I marked "taking orders" and "resolving complaints" as "work," something just didn't feel right about it. I believe that being a mere order-taker isn't really selling; it doesn't require as much skill. And as far as resolving complaints goes, everyone can see that mistake-proofing is the way to go. Answering objections is part of the salesperson's job, but it seems like that falls into a category mistake-proofing could improve, too.

I guess we were supposed to have at least an item or two fall into the inspection category, so I may have cheated a bit when I used some code words in the exercise to help me. I put "credit checking" and "proposal review" into the inspection category, even though they probably feel like work to the credit analysts and the managers who do our proposal reviews.

"The uneasiness you feel is your engineering instinct coming out. If we are to get large improvements, we must severely cut wait and transportation times. We must reduce to a minimum the need for separate inspection by installing preventive measures and by teaching people how to inspect their own work. We must continually try to reduce the amount of non–value-added or lesser-value work we perform."

Becoming the Best in Sales, Marketing, and Service

"Think about it! I want to tie in something we covered yesterday to what you just said. The top 20 percent of individuals in sales, marketing, and service apply a kaizen approach and their own intuitive process engineering to everything they do. They are driven, self-improvement oriented, flexible, rearrange their own process to minimize nonwork time, and they keep their eye on what works to accomplish the larger goal and avoid suboptimization. They passively—or actively—resist when management gives them more nonwork activities to do, don't they?

"Now I'd like you to tell me how the best people you know in sales, marketing, and customer service blend kaizen with the principles of engineering in their daily work."

Several participants speak up quickly.

"Top marketing people keep track of the yields on each campaign and test alternatives to maximize response. They compare costs to results and optimize the mix. When one campaign is in a lull, they work on another. They are constantly looking at their competition and to others for ideas for improvement. They time their activities so as best to support new product releases and they are always looking for feedback from the field to get a sense of customer needs. Of course, they're creative, too."

"Top sales people are fanatics about time management. They are constantly looking for the best thing they can be doing, right now, to further a sale. They keep their own records so that they can see whether their pipeline needs attention at any stage. They rehearse presentations to improve consistency and impact. They make it a point to learn the customer's specifications and make sure that what they do addresses the specifications. They don't try to force a customer; they earn the customer's trust by delivering what they promise. Everyone knows they are imaginative."

"The best customer service people are always learning what they can to improve their skills. They feed back common problems and ideas for their solution to other departments and to customers, too. They arrange their materials and other tools so they can quickly find answers. They are courteous because they know a customer who feels punished for calling on them starts to avoid the company in other ways."

Discussion: Improvement and the Engineer

"Looking at things in their pure form, in their abstract essence, helps an engineer see what needs to be done more clearly. If 20 percent of our top people produce the majority of our successes in sales, marketing, and service, what is the job of the engineer if everyone is already trying his or her best?"

Dr. Selden lets his question hang in the air. The woman next to me responds, "We should raise the performance of the other 80 percent."

"Excellent! How can we raise the performance of the 80 percent? I've said everybody is already trying their best. Let's say the reps have been to the time management and self-improvement schools. They're listening to all the tapes. So are the 80 percent!"

"I guess we'd have to change some other elements in the process itself."

She hit the nail on the head. I think in my own company I'd still like to expose everyone in marketing, sales, and customer service to these sales process engineering principles, anyway. I don't think we've used all the kaizen we can.

"We talked about this issue before. Let's explore the ramifications a little more deeply. We're getting closer to the heart of the matter."

A distinguishing characteristic of sales process engineering is that it will likely regard what characterizes the "most successful" behavior of the top performers within a sales process as fairly well explored to date (see, for example, Learning International 1983).

The emphasis on individual behavior, often put in the form of recommendations such as the "Top 10 Ingredients for Sales Success" or "Seven Tips for Excellent Customer Service," speak to the obvious importance of individual behavior in the sales process. The seductive trap, of course, is that the less obvious *structural* components found in the sales process that could help the "remaining 80 percent" may easily be overlooked when focusing solely on the most desirable characteristics of individual behavior.

"We've already discussed that a sales process engineer's first interest will usually be on the structural elements responsible for controlling a process. Lessons need to be learned from what the top 20 percent of the team is doing right so that this can be incorporated with the new structures.

"Conversely, observing the inputs, process, and outputs of the remaining 80 percent may be just as instructive and useful. Why? Because it is in the case of the remaining 80 percent that the rocks and shoals of the process are most visible. A secret of process improvement is to make problems visible! Knowing where the problems are is the first step toward fixing them! Observe what is tripping up the lower performers, and devise ways to prevent them from occurring in the future!"

Major Sales Process Operations

"To improve when everybody is already trying their best, you said it then becomes necessary to change specific process elements. Reflect with me for a moment on what would happen if we looked at the four elements comprising cycle time, and broke them down even further into specific operations."

• Motivating—using behavioral principles to affect the probability that behavior occurs. This involves doing things that cause people to gather somewhere or to avoid something, attracting them, exciting attention, and rewarding desired behavior. This is the essential "magnet" that pulls and pushes people through the process.

• Creating—shaping, combining, and forming ideas and things to make something new. Examples would include developing proposals, coming to conclusions about customer needs, and developing advertising copy.

• Packaging—containing and wrapping in such a way that it is easier to exchange and so that the contents are protected. Examples include putting a memo into an electronic note format, binding a proposal, and enclosing material in a folder.

• Sorting—separating, filtering, and screening. Examples include separating leads by type of product requested, filtering a customer database by SIC code, qualifying customers, and screening/purging names of customers who haven't ordered for five years from mass mailings.

Major Sales Process Operations: Nine Thought Starters

- Motivating: gathering, attracting, repelling, exciting attention
- Creating: shaping, combining, forming
- Packaging: containing, wrapping
- Sorting: separating, filtering, screening
- Regulating: timing, signaling, controlling
- Sensing: detecting, observing
- Measuring: comparing, evaluating
- Conveying: piping, moving, sending
- Storing: queuing, delaying, holding

• Regulating—timing, signaling, and controlling when events start and stop. Examples include setting call-back dates, prompts and alarms reminding of appointments, and release dates.

• Sensing—detecting and observing. Examples include observing customer inventory levels and listening to customer feedback.

• Measuring—comparing and evaluating. Examples include comparing sales versus a target, profitability versus the competition, or the quality of a sales presentation against a standard.

• Conveying—moving, sending, piping. Examples include transmitting data, driving to a client's office, shipping goods, and mail.

• Storing—queuing, delaying, holding. Examples include backlogs of leads, estimates, and proposals in development.

"Just as other disciplines have their own symbology to represent major operations, I can see a time in the future when sales process engineering will have its own professionally agreed-upon set. Our process diagrams will be clearer and much more helpful at that point."

The American National Standards Institute (ANSI) retains the accepted symbol sets for many industries. The gauge symbol used in the process cause-and-effect diagram during Day One is the symbol for a pressure gauge in ANSI graphic symbol set Y32.10 for hydraulic systems. In his classic work *Motion and Time Study,* Benjamin W. Niebel (1988) discusses ways to break down manufacturing work into its elemental operations.

Improving the Operations

Process engineers use terminology uniquely suited to their industries, such as the words *welding, baking, crushing, grinding,* and so forth: a standard language. These very specific words convey direct meaning. The operation names directly suggest specific metrics and even what standards to employ.

"I've surveyed a wide variety of standard engineering terms. I just suggested nine for us to think about using in sales process engineering. I rejected some terms, such as *heating* and *cooling*. They struck me as too metaphorical for direct application—even though we might currently use them in our everyday sales vocabulary. We might consider others I haven't listed."

The words other process engineers use describe what should happen during an operation. The job of a water pump is to transfer water from one place to another. The terminology also directly suggests what should not be happening. If water is not being pumped, the pump is malfunctioning, misprimed, or under capacity for the application.

"In marketing, let's say we are faced with a classic sorting operation: dividing sales leads gathered at a trade show by how interested the booth visitor is in our products. Sorting operations are supposed to *sort*—the more accurate the sort the better. In the company I'm thinking of, at the end of the expo the marketing people looked through cards dumped in a fishbowl, together with the cards the booth people had put in their pockets. Leads from companies whose names the marketing people recognized were assigned to reps. The others were just mailed a brochure. The yield from this approach was 5 percent closed deals. The company changed its approach. Now, each booth visitor that answered a specific survey asked by the booth rep was given an inexpensive promotional item. Answers were weighted and scored, and only those meeting the company's criteria were given to the field reps for follow up. Closing rates doubled.

"Sorting is supposed to sort. When it doesn't, accuracy must be improved. Motivation is supposed to change behavior. If it doesn't, the cues or reinforcements must be improved."

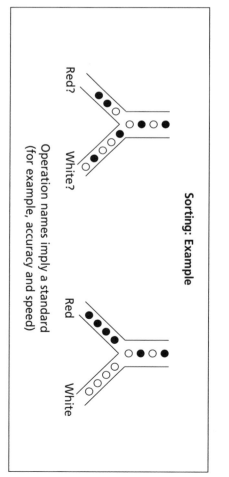

Sorting: Example

Operation names imply a standard (for example, accuracy and speed)

I just got a flash of insight. I don't know where I'll put it, but I'm going to add a pump to the diagram with all the question marks on it. I'll use a pump to represent the motivational force that has to be in the process, since we're dealing with people. If that pump isn't there, or if it doesn't pump at the right time, or if it's under capacity, or if we don't have enough of them, enough people won't move through the process.

Measuring the Sales Process

"When it comes to measuring activities, operations, and subprocesses that comprise the entire sales process, some measures are easier to get hold of than others.

"Names that come in from a magazine ad are easy to count, and dimensions pertaining to the date, type, and cost of the ad can be tracked with more or less ease. The number of signed proposals are easy to count, as are dimensions pertaining to who the customers are, what business they are in, and what was proposed versus what was accepted. The dollar value of booked orders is easy to count. Quantities, items, preferred delivery dates, and so forth can also be tallied with relative ease. Regarding service, delivery dates, back orders, returns, allowances, and services performed are all usually available. Items such as these provide a rich source of data; they comprise the bulk of what you'd expect to find in most traditional accounting systems.

"Other data are more or less available. Customer contacts might be counted, but the details pertaining to calls are often not tracked. We all know salespeople tend to resent reporting what they do, for many reasons, including fear of punishment, fear of having their territories interfered with, and protection of information that could make them easier to replace. Professional telemarketing firms probably track this information much more carefully than the typical field sales rep, who often performs a mixture of tasks.

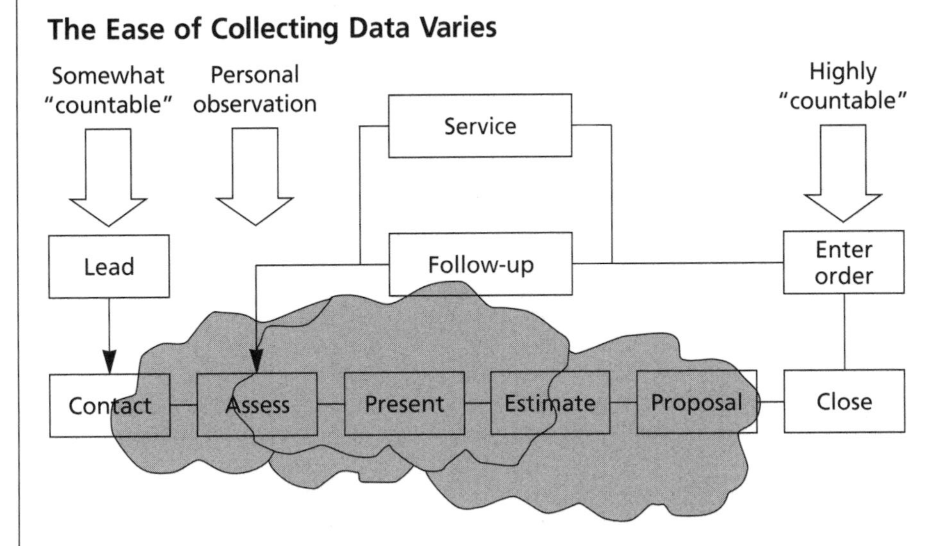

"Information surrounding the middle of the process is in the clouds. We might get a glimpse of what's going on from time to time, but the nature of sales work makes it hard to track using traditional approaches. Process engineers say *portholes* or *windows* should be opened in the process if it becomes important to do so."

I can't help it, but I find something about this notion amusing. I think many businesses develop noble-sounding explanations for why measurement isn't done. They cite respect for individual initiative, and so forth, to explain why they wouldn't do something they can't do anyway.

The concept of an audit or inspection to gather information about activities that are otherwise difficult to measure has been used routinely in many businesses. The *Sales Quality Audit* (Smith 1995) and *From Selling to Managing* (Brown 1990) contain specific lists and forms one might use to conduct such periodic sales process inspections.

Appendix A contains examples of measures that might be applied at various stages of the sales process. The book *Cost Benefit Analysis & Sales Automation* (Selden 1995) contains benchmark performance and cost data segregated by sales process stage, drawn from a variety of industry sources.

Intangibles and the Need to Operationalize

"There's another problem with some of the variables many people feel are important in sales: They are allowed to remain too ill-defined and unoperationalized.

"Professionals agree that a measure is only as good as the operation used to take it. In turn, the nature of the measurement operation depends on the intent leading one to measure in the first place—its purpose—and how much measure-to-measure variability that intent can tolerate. For example, how might we tell how hot a baby's formula is?"

The class offers different ideas, such as using a thermometer, feeling the bottle with your hand, shaking a few drops onto your forearm, and so forth.

"Shaking drops onto your forearm works for our purpose in one case. But to monitor and control a delicate chemical reaction, you'd use a thermometer. You might need to specify whether the liquid should be stirred, where the thermometer should be placed in the beaker, and so forth. If you didn't operationalize the measurement procedure your readings might vary widely even though the process itself had not changed.

"Operationalizing a measure has a way of clarifying the ill-defined. Can anyone give me an example of something we say is an ill-defined, nevertheless important variable in sales?"

A gentleman toward the back says, "Trust." Someone else adds, "Rapport." Another says, "Relationship."

"Excellent choices. Whoever is against building trust, rapport, and good client relationships, please stand up. Who has an idea of how we could get closer to operationalizing a way to measure trust?"

One gentleman says, "Maybe we can use the actions of customers as an index. Do they agree to set another appointment? Do they give us a chance to bid on their business? Do they ask us to consult with them as they are developing an RFP? Do they ask for competitive quotes? Do we make it onto their list of preferred suppliers?"

A woman up front says, "You might be able to measure trust-building activities by the number of customer calls that are returned promptly, the number of on-time shipments, the number of times a rep interrupts a customer, or whether a rep answers questions directly. Some of that you'd need to observe directly, others you could pull from records."

"If the measure becomes important to you, you'll find a way to construct an operational definition. Just don't make yourself crazy by trying to measure everything, all the time. That can get too expensive and cumbersome to maintain. A method I'm personally fond of is to do a quick once-over to find the bottlenecks and focus on those first. Just remember, a bottleneck can take many forms, some of which we may not think to look at, such as a management policy that dictates the status quo."

"The meaning of an engineering goal is expressed in how it is measured."

One sales process metric in current vogue is "customer satisfaction." Dr. A. Blanton Godfrey of the Juran Institute finds fault with typical pencil-and-paper survey approaches. He states, "What it all boils down to is that we really don't care about customer satisfaction. We care about customer retention and loyalty. . . . We need to start with the most important measurements—what percentage of available market are we getting from existing customers and what is possible from noncustomers" (Godfrey 1996a). Even in this day and age of customer focus, Dr. Godfrey recently remarked that he found relatively few companies systematically investigating the subject. There is evidence that companies that take the time to do so will benefit. In his experience, companies that operationalize their customer preference behaviors and analyze what drives those behaviors can see their profitability jump by as much as 10 percent or more in a single year (Godfrey 1996b).

The sales process engineer will need to translate many traditional but ill-defined constructs into concrete operational terms. Familiar labels such as "likely buyer" or "good customer" will likely be converted into terms of observable behavior (that is, into a behavioral definition) or in terms of other observable characteristics, such as outcomes. Only then can their meaning be operationalized.

Four Prime Dimensions

"When I was in first grade just learning to read, I glanced at some homework my babysitter was working on. She was studying a high school biology text, drawing and labeling cells in her notebook. I didn't tell her this, but to me her work looked very advanced and complicated. It intimidated me. I thought I'd never make it through high school if that was the kind of thing I had to read and write about.

"Looking back, I realize that you don't start with cellular biology when you are learning to read. Most people can make it from 'See Spot run' to 'deoxyribonucleic acid' if the steps are small—and rewarding—enough.

"That's the way it probably needs to be for most of us beginning to learn and practice sales process engineering. When it comes to measurement, we'll be best off if we start with four prime measures: quantity, quality, time, and cost as applied to whatever unit of input, process element, or output we're interested in. These basic dimensions apply to the operations and processes we've discussed so far—clouds or no clouds. Most are elemental in that they can be combined to form additional measures of importance we attach more traditional labels to, such as measures of market saturation, response rate, close rate, and so forth."

• *Quantity* can be expressed in units per time or a yield such as percent good per batch. Engineers are often interested in the capacity to perform versus the current demand or output, or current capacity versus specifications.

Four Prime Dimensions

Input, In-Process, Output

- Quantity
  —"Unit" per time
  —Capacity
- Quality
  —Outcome vs. specification
  —Satisfaction vs. delight
- Time
  —Cycle vs. process
  —Performance vs. need
- Dollars
  —Per unit: cost or income

• *Quality* is usually expressed in terms of a measure versus a specification. Conformance within a tolerance limit is the usual requirement. Exceeding specifications in a fashion desired by the customer is often referred to as "delighting the customer."

• *Time.* Process engineers often measure the time wait, transport, inspection, and work occupies in a given process. They are also concerned with the timing of events as well: when they need to occur versus when they actually occur.

• *Dollars* are often expressed as cost and/or value per unit of input, output, activities, and resources; other important measures are lifetime costs and values, and the income-generating capability of bottlenecked process elements; the costs of failure, inspection, and prevention are also considered key process engineering metrics.

Most current measurement systems only provide individual, totals, averages, and trends. A good start, but insufficient for engineering purposes.

Measure of variability (for example, range and standard deviation)

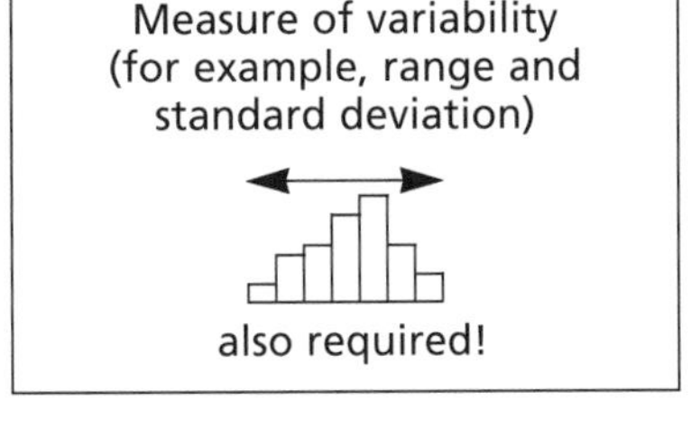

also required!

"Current reporting systems can often provide great detail on individual performance, such as a rep's sales per month, group totals, and trends. However, they do not do a good job of portraying how variable performance is, which is an index of reliability, predictability, and a host of other important goals engineers shoot for. Further reasons for depicting varaibility will become quite clear later today. As engineers, we'll have to prevail on our programmers to show us ranges, standard deviations, and other measures of dispersion that we do not now normally track."

Dr. Selden comments that George A. Smith Jr.'s *Sales Productivity Measurement* (1995) provides additional sales process measurement ideas within an engineering framework, stating that Smith has done much to advance the application of process and quality improvement principles within the sales process.

Picking Prime Measures

"Looking at our process models, who would like to suggest some measures we should start looking at when trying to detect the impact of our sales process improvement efforts?"

The group has no trouble coming up with measures. Some include: when a proposal was promised versus when it was delivered; cost per leads, including the creative cost of developing the ad, plus the cost of placing the ad; cost per proposal development, including labor of all personnel involved plus the costs for specialized analytic testing the company incurs; dollars profit per order; and cycle time for fulfilling literature requests. Virtually all aspects of the sales process seem to have an appropriate measure, though a convenient "gauge" for taking a specific measure may not be installed at the moment.

"I've already given you one tip when measuring: Start simple and practice a bit. For example, find out what it takes to measure cycle times in order processing before you try to measure cycle times for something more involved. You'll need to work with a measure a little bit in order to adjust it to your liking.

Measurement Tips

- Start simple.
- Pick something relatively easy to measure routinely.
- Pick a measure that can serve as a comparison for baseline purposes.
- Pick a measure clearly linked to the overall goal.

"A second tip is to pick a measure that can be gathered routinely as a matter of course. Measurement carries a cost. If you can use measures that can be obtained from existing systems, some of the initial expense—and frustration—can be reduced. But don't hesitate to create new measures if you need to. Sampling procedures can greatly reduce the cost of collecting data manually. Managers or your own people may already be collecting much of the 'hard to find' data you're looking for.

"Third, make sure your measure is related to the goal you're trying to accomplish. The measure should include the elements that may be affected by your improvement efforts, and not much else. Otherwise it will be less sensitive to registering the impact of what you are doing and less reliable as a direct gauge of your success.

Dr. Selden reminds the class that other management accounting approaches, such as the cost of quality (Campanella 1990), activity-based costing (Cooper and Kaplan 1988) or throughput-based accounting (Noreen, Smith, and Mackey 1995) may be more sensitive to detecting process improvement than traditional cost-accounting approaches.

"Fourth, at the very least, try to establish a pre-change baseline set of measures using the same measure you intend to track later. That way you'll at least have a way to judge pre-post comparisons."

Caution!

One agricultural products company measures its cost per order by taking its entire labor overhead per year—including the president's salary—and dividing it by the total number of orders per year.

With 200,000 orders per year and total overhead at $40 million, this firm thinks its cost per order is about $200. Such a measure offers a place to begin, but a sales process engineer needs better measures than this.

Since the company's measure includes costs like the president's salary—which may go up or down independent of how the improvement team alters the order process—such a measure poses at least two problems.

First, changes in events beyond the team's control may mask the impact of its specific improvement efforts. What if the president's salary goes up? That will increase the cost per order, either reducing or masking the impact of the improvement team's efforts.

Second, the impact of the team's effort may be minimized, psychologically. Making a $200,000 net improvement (savings less the costs associated with obtaining the savings) in this scenario "only" cuts the cost of each order by half a percent ($200,000 divided by $40,000,000).

Sensitivity and Reliability Are Important

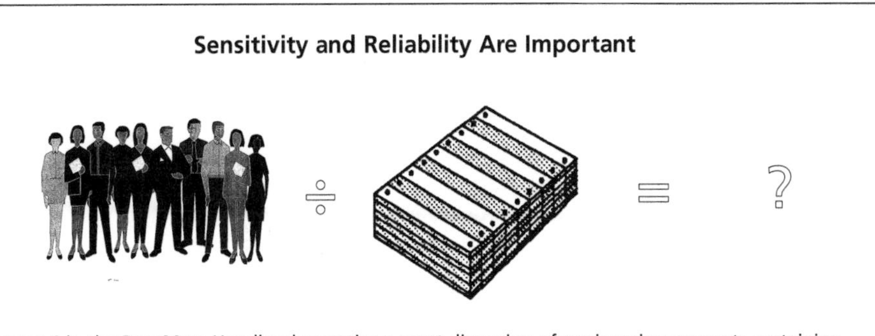

Chapter 6 in the DataMyte Handbook contains a great discussion of engineering concepts pertaining to metrology, the science of measurement (DataMyte Division 1992). Measurement techniques must conform to standards, as well as display adequate traceability, resolution, accuracy, precision, and stability for the intended use.

A better way is to focus on costs associated with the activities directly responsible for processing the orders. Using this approach, if the original combined costs of processing an order are really $400,000, a $200,000 net improvement actually saves 50 percent!

Some improvements are one time, others extend forever. A permanent reduction in costs offers tremendous payback over time. Sometimes these savings accrue in unexpected ways. When a company reduces its office space, it forever saves taxes on that property, as well.

Whether an improvement of any sort offers a so-called sustainable competitive advantage, however, is a function of how quickly competitors can mimic your improvements or come up with the same breakthroughs on their own. Developing a "sustainable" advantage is not therefore a function of any one improvement. Instead, it hinges on the sustainable *structure* an organization sets in place to develop a continuous *series* of improvements. In the twenty-first century, the *speed* with which an organization can improve may well be the most valuable—and least easy to duplicate—asset of all.

Classifying Measures: Variables

"The metrics or measurements we attach to different portions of the sales process will vary in many ways. But no matter what measure we settle on, it will fall into one of two categories, from an engineering point of view: We will either be measuring a continous variable or a discrete attribute. One provides us with more information than the other. Since the 1930s, the implications of using one or the other have been articulated quite clearly.

"The two dictate different approaches to the methods used to detect improvement. As a process engineer it's important to know the difference."

Engineers speak of two types of measures: variable and attribute. A variables-based measurement is one that can be taken on a continuous scale, such as a yardstick or a thermometer. A yardstick is used when what you are measuring could be of any length, whether two feet exactly, three feet exactly, or two feet $5^{3}/_{4}$ inches.

Variables-based measures in business usually involve money or time. A cost might be $3.76, an invoice could be sent in the amount of $16 or $430.97. The time it takes to write a proposal could be three days, two hours, 40 minutes and 6 seconds. Though not a measure of time or money, scores on an academic type of test are traditionally considered to be a variables measure, since the underlying dimension measured, such as intelligence, is presumed to range over a continuous scale.

Variable Measures

—Percent or counted measure of a property measurable in units and fractions of units

—Examples: cost, invoice amount, time early or late, score on a skills test

Classifying Measures: Attributes

Engineers define an attribute measure as a tally of whether something happened or did not happen. Like a pass/fail grade recorded on a school transcript, "shades of grey" or whether something was a "close call" is not indicated.

In the world of physical engineering, an attribute measure might be whether something passed or failed inspection, whether a color was white or not, whether a temperature passed a threshold or not (where the actual temperature and the degrees by which the threshold was exceeded are not recorded), whether the hood of an automobile is scratched or not, whether a defect occurred or not, and so forth.

Many things in sales, marketing, and customer service that we might want to measure are of the nature of a pass/fail grade in school: It either happened or it didn't. A bid was approved or not. An order form was filled in completely or not. With attribute measures, no shades of grey are counted. The attribute is either present or it's not.

A point that is difficult for beginning engineers to grasp is that one can count the number of defective items (for example, 25) in a batch (for example, of 100). This can make an attribute measure look like a continuous measure because the number of defective units could have been zero, 100, or anywhere between. Similarly, one could divide 25 into 100. This would result in a percentage, which might also seem continuous in nature. Nevertheless, if the underlying item being measured either meets some type of yes/no criteria, it is an attribute measure.

Attribute Measures

—Percent or counted presence or absence of a yes/no property; either it happened or it didn't

—Examples: whether a proposal closed or not, whether an appointment was secured or not, whether an error was made or not

Was the bid approved?

Was the order complete?

"Many of the events or items a sales process engineer might want to count involve an attributes measure. Whether a proposal was signed or not, whether an appointment was secured or not, whether an order contained an entry error or not, are all examples of important attributes measures you may wish to take."

Another loop just closed for me. The age-old observation that you can "win a sale by a nose, but you still take the whole sale," speaks to the fact that we're talking about an attribute-based measure! It's hard to believe, but this insight is sort of exciting! Now if I could just make use of this knowledge. We'll see.

Value of Data Contained: Greater with "Variables"

Some of the class members are having trouble understanding the difference between attributes and variables data. Dr. Selden points at the name tents the participants have placed to mark their seat at each table. He counts off 10 of them, knocking two on the floor, saying with a smile that he means no disrespect. The group laughs.

- "Yes/no" information doesn't reveal by how much the mark was exceeded or undershot

"Go" "No go"

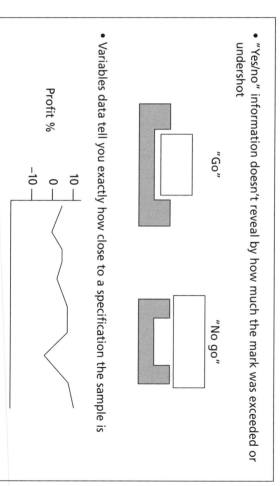

- Variables data tell you exactly how close to a specification the sample is

Profit %

10
0
–10

"The name tents are either on the table or they aren't, so 'name tents on tables' is attributes data. The number of the tents on the table can be counted: eight; a percentage can be figured: 80 percent, but it is still an attribute we are counting.

"I will try to teach you the important difference between these two types of data in the time we have; you may need further study before it sinks in. I will also teach you, by rote if need be, which measures of our sales process are attributes measures and which are variables measures. You can use the examples I give you as a crutch until you are ready to fly on your own.

"Maybe another picture will help. The slide you see in front of you illustrates the difference in the amount of information contained when working with attributes data versus variables data.

"Attributes data, which is yes/no or go/no-go in nature, doesn't reveal by how much a mark was exceeded or undershot. The 'go' gauge in the illustration shows that the part on the left fit inside the gauge. It passed inspection. Notice that we didn't measure how close the part came to failing. The part on the right failed to fit into the gauge. It failed inspection. Notice that we don't know by how much the part exceeded the required dimension. Go/no-go measures are simple and usually cheaper to obtain than variables data. On the other hand, they lack information we may need to tune our process. We may be forced to use attributes data if nothing else is available. By the day's end I think you'll understand the differences and their importance to you as practitioners at a deeper level.

"By contrast, variables data reveal exactly how close to a target we've come and how far away from it we are. In business, for example, we can tell how great our profits are. We know the amount of exact dollars and cents approved in a proposal."

Dr. Selden asks the class: "The minute I ask you, 'Did we meet our requirement for cycle time: yes or no?' what kind of data are we dealing with?" They respond, "Attributes." He asks, "Did you get the appointment or not?" The group members again say, "Attributes." Dr. Selden smiles. "You're catching on."

Classification of Sales Measures Chosen

"Let's see how well you understand. Please review the list in front of you and categorize each process measure by whether it is a variables or attributes measure. After I review the results with you, we'll take a break."

The group works on the exercise for a few minutes. It seems easy. The discussion quickly shows how far the participants have to go, however, especially related to attributes. Almost everyone correctly answered that the size of a sale in dollars, the amount of time spent waiting for credit approval, the score on a competency test, the amount of time spent preparing a proposal, and the percent a rep's sales varies from a target, were variables measures. Where a continuous measure of time and money is taken, there is little question.

Classification Exercise

- Classify the following as variables or attributes measures.

  V A Percent of leads that turn into appointments
  V A Size of sales in dollars
  V A Amount of time spent waiting for credit approval
  V A Score on competency test
  V A Number of orders containing an error
  V A Length of time spent preparing a proposal
  V A Number of leads responding to an ad
  V A Percent that a rep's sales volume varies from target
  V A Other? ________________

- The difference is critical because it determines which statistics to use later.

"The percent of leads that turn into appointments is an attributes measure. Why? Did a single lead turn into an appointment? Yes or no? We don't know how close to getting an appointment we came, but failed to get it. We don't know how easy it was to get an appointment. It's a pass/fail dimension. Converting these data into a percent gives the appearance of being a continuous measure, but it's an attribute that was measured.

"The number of orders containing an error is a tally of how many orders met a pass/fail criterion; this is attributes data. The fact that we can count a number may make you think you are dealing with variables data. If it contained one or more errors, the order went into one bin. Zero errors, it went into another. The go/no-go nature of what led you to make the tally is the tip-off.

"The number of leads responding to an ad is another example of attributes data. This is probably the hardest of all to understand. Look at the nature of what is counted: 60,000 magazines were distributed, with 60,000 reader response cards inside. Either your company's number is circled on that card or it's not. We don't know how close someone came to circling it but didn't, nor do we have any idea of how eager they were to circle it. This one displays all the characteristics of attributes data, even though when you receive the count it looks like it was free to vary over a continuous scale. A continuous scale has fractions. Your lead list did not."

Deep in Thought

The material we've covered this morning is new ground for me. Dr. Selden promised that the ideas of attributes and variables data would be relevant, but I don't see how quite yet. I understand the concepts, but I'd like to know how we can put them to work.

The measurement part of sales process engineering just seems so different. I feel like a village smithy who takes for granted that horses will always need shoes and wakes up one morning to see an automobile rumbling down the street. I guess the transition for people like me will be about the same; we'll just have to learn how to fix flat tires and punctured radiators instead of changing horseshoes and broken wagon wheels.

I'm fighting the urge to go into denial about this stuff. If this is the way things need to go if we want to be around in 10 years, so be it. A company that gets its arms around this and applies some concerted effort with some smart, dedicated people is going to find and fix problems that other companies are going to just live with. I can always hire a few bright people to take care of it for me.

I'll have to review my notes from this morning many times. One thing I do see, though. I think I've found another label to replace one of those question marks with. I'm going to label the question marks inside each box to the right, "Work in process." Our work in process is leads, contacts, estimates, and so forth that we are actively working on during any given period. I've already labeled the ones on the left inside each box, "Storage." Storage

represents brochures, prospects, "orphan accounts" in our database, and so forth that we're keeping but not actively using. The discussion about cycle and process time does seem relevant.

One thing I don't really like about our current measurement system is the fact that the numbers we receive in management are presented in an endless series of tables. If we could hook them up to pictures of our sales process, like they do in some of our customer's steel-making and chemical processing plants I've visited, the important relationships would be a lot easier to both see and take action on. I wish we could more easily see what's happening in our process.

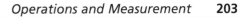

Steps for Developing a Measurement System

Hooking up an improved measurement system to our current process would give us a way to spot problems and bottlenecks more easily. Right now, most of the information about our actions is buried or invisible.

Dr. Selden said that one secret to making just-in-time methods work is to make problems visible. Linking measurements to a picture of our process would help do that.

I've sketched a couple of sales processes from a 30,000-foot-level, drawn from the point of view of the outputs the process is supposed to generate at each stage. Coming up with labels for each step that describe what's going on in observable terms is a challenge. I'd like to get Dr. Selden's opinion on what the wholesale distribution business looks like sometime.

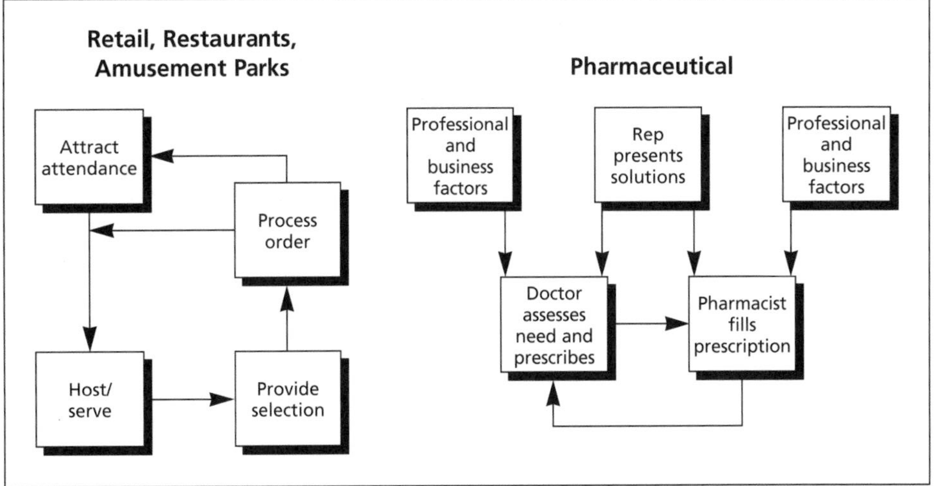

Several times people in the class have mentioned that they would like an easy-to-follow, cut-and-dried approach to measuring their sales process. With so many different types of companies and sales processes in the audience, I don't see how that would have been possible in a public workshop—our process maps are different. One of the participants said her company has had a committee trying to define what a "repeat customer" is for nearly a year, and the committee still hasn't agreed on a definition! This last section gave us lots of direction, though. I like the fact that we're getting a clear set of instructions on how to build our own approach, in much more depth than I've seen before. I think the depth is throwing people off. I've jotted down four steps that should work for me.

Obviously, whatever we do will have to be capable of alerting us to bottlenecks and problem areas, while being sensitive enough to genuine change to register it when real change occurs—without too many false alarms. Within that general framework we have to (1) map our process and (2) attach cost, quality, quantity, and timing metrics and sensors to each major step, defining them operationally in terms of dispersion as well as central tendency. We should (3) start with what we have available and work toward filling in gaps as our improvement efforts require it. Along the way we have to (4) nail down process specifications for each part of the process that is important to us. Without specifications, where do we set our alarms and warning systems? Our systems have to take into account customer use of our goods and services and certain aspects of what the competition is doing, as well. That's as much of a cut-and-dried approach to measurement as I am taking away from a general forum like this. Further customization would depend on the type of business we're in and the specific measurement systems we already have in place.

Part 2: Process Variation and Control

> If I were to reduce my message to a few words, I'd say it's to reduce variation.
>
> —*W. Edwards Deming*

Objectives

By the time we finish this topic you will be able to

- Describe the fundamental behavior of a process over time.
- Point out the difference between random and assignable causes.
- Apply the concepts of random versus assignable causes to the sales process in the context of achieving control.

Fundamental Behavior of All Processes

All natural processes exhibit variation over time. The very act of taking a measure itself exhibits, and thus introduces, subtle fluctuations from measurement to measurement.

"We started today by talking about four basic ingredients we seem to find within a process: work, transportation, inspection, and waiting. [Dr. Selden acts out his next sentence in an impression meant to suggest the deeply thoughtful and enthusiastic voice of Carl Sagan.] Today is all about understanding the *fundamental* principles that drive our sales, marketing, and customer service processes. It's time to dig deeper into how the elements behave once they are thrown together into a primorial process *soup*.

"How many of you tend to follow the same way to work in the morning? [About half the audience raises hands.] Even if you take that route because it is quickest, do you sometimes arrive five minutes earlier than normal? Five minutes later?

"If you bothered to measure the gas mileage for that trip, do you think that sometimes your mileage would be better than other times? How constant do you think mileage would be from day to day?

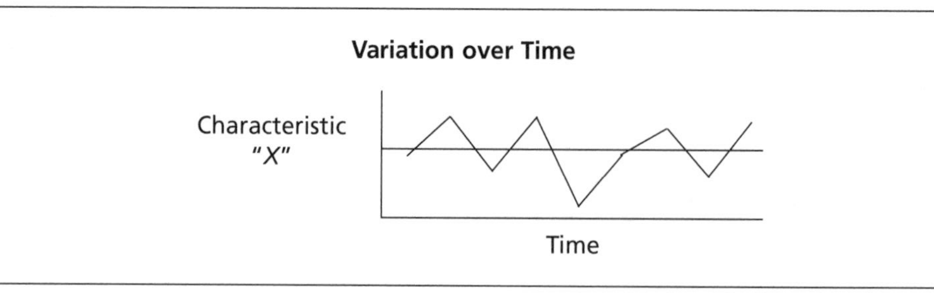

"Let's take something that's measured in the parts of a second, an event that is critical to perform smoothly each time. In television broadcasting, timing—the time a commercial is turned on, the time between TV shows, and so forth—is very important, isn't it? Yet even here we see gaps, embarrassing pauses, and dead time once in a while, don't we?

"No matter what example I choose, I cannot think of any process in nature—in the physical or biological world—that stays at an exact constant. Even if it were an exact constant, the operation that a human uses to measure the physical world varies. If you step on a scale, step off it, and step back on, are the measures the same every single time?"

Poets and philosophers have said, "You can never step in the same river twice." Natural scientists and process engineers recognize this phenomena, too. The difference between poet and engineer is that the engineer works to apply the beauty of verbal expression in additional practical ways.

From Poetic Observation to Practical Application

"The poets express deep truths in memorable language. All processes exhibit variation. Let's consider an example of how we can apply that principle in quantitative process analysis."

What happens when one process is linked in serial form to another—and each exhibits variation? What happens to their output? Engineers often use the formula

$$P_s = P_1 \times P_2 \times \ldots P_n$$

to calculate the reliability (whether the system experiences a total breakdown or not) where P_s is the probability a whole system will fail, P_1 is the probability that subprocess 1 will fail, and so on, through subprocess *n*.

"Consider an extreme form of variation—breaking a link in a chain. A chain is an example of an interdependent system composed of serial processes where outright failure in one part of the system causes the entire system to fail.

"In many ways, the sales process is composed of interdependent, serial processes. A rep who fails to assess the customer's needs properly during an initial sales presentation may not be invited back to submit a proposal. Variation is present: Sometimes the rep is invited back, sometimes not.

"Let's say that the following reliabilities apply to various stages of a sales process: leads = 0.1 (that is, 10%), contacts = 0.3, needs analysis = 0.2, and closing = 0.1.

Chained Reliability: Product of Individual Reliabilities

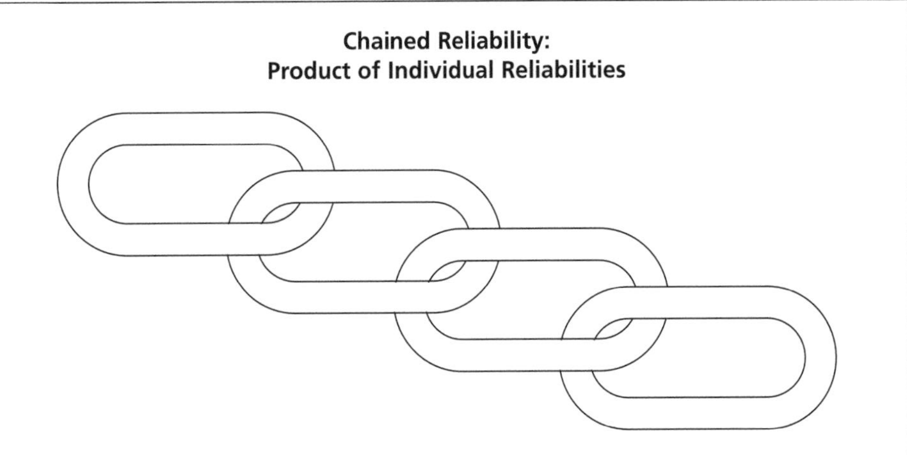

Multiply that out! The reliability of the system as a whole is an abysmal 0.0006! Most pilots would not want to trust their life to an airplane engine with that kind of reliability."

In real life, the reliability of each stage in the sales process varies around a mean—sometimes higher, sometimes lower—further degrading performance.

"We're lucky that many of our sales processes operate redundantly, in parallel; this offsets some of the negative effects of extreme variability. Even this simple example shows us that quantitative analysis underscores and helps us understand the critical role variability reduction will play in sales process engineering."

Two Sources of Variation

"The main factors responsible for process variation have been explored for many years by greats like Shewhart, Deming, Taguchi, and Juran. We recall from our earlier discussion that once all the assignable causes have been removed from a process, random causes will still be present.

"I need to decode some of this jargon for you. I don't want the terms to seem confusing or mysterious.

"*Assignable* causes of variation are those that are easy to detect; we know the reason why they occurred. They are usually preventable or correctable. They usually occur only sporadically, but when they do they often cause a big swing in the results. Some quality engineers call assignable causes *special* causes. The terms refer to the same thing.

"*Random* causes of variation are those thousand and one little things that fluctuate all the time within a process. Their effects, which are usually small, tend to cancel each other out in such a way that we never really even know they are present. On very rare occasions enough of the small changes may occur simultaneously in the same direction to produce a large effect. Normally, though, we can't tell which random causes did what. They are so transient and small that, often, trying to prevent them doesn't pay off. They are chronic in the sense they are always present in the background and that they are a built-in, inherent part of the system.

- Assignable: feedback detects, then troubleshooting, fixing, and preventing reduces chance of recurrence
- Random: ordinary feedback loop not sufficient, must change very nature of process or inputs; careful diagnosis, careful remedy testing, and implementation needed

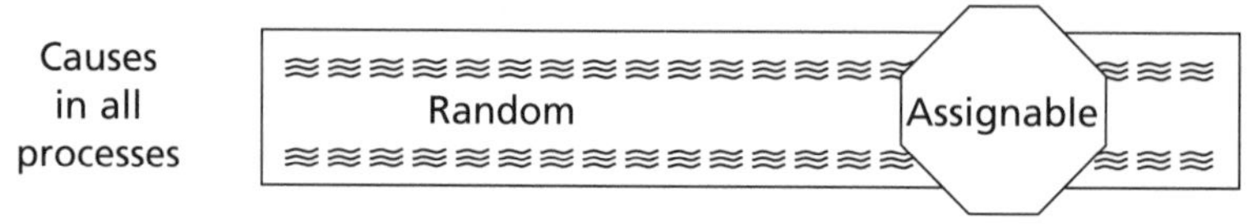

Causes in all processes

Random

Assignable

"Remember, today we're learning about the fundamental nature of all processes—in which we *must* include the marketing, sales, and customer service processes. So understanding the concept of variation and what causes it is essential. If you can control those causes, you can make the process do whatever you want: solve problems, improve performance, everything an engineer's heart desires. If you're like me, you'll need to hear this from a number of points of view before the idea really sinks in."

Causes of Variation in Sales, Marketing, and Service

In the 1980s, U.S. industry kept its ship of manufacturing afloat above rocks and shoals in the manufacturing process by using extra inventory as a safety buffer. Quality problem? Better have extra parts in stock to substitute. Labor problem? Better have extra finished goods handy, just in case. Supply problem? Better order extras. Today world-class manufacturers use a combination of related initiatives to reduce inventories: design simplification, JIT, quality improvement, new technology, and many more. As each new problem is bumped into, it is conquered. Inventory levels can drop further.

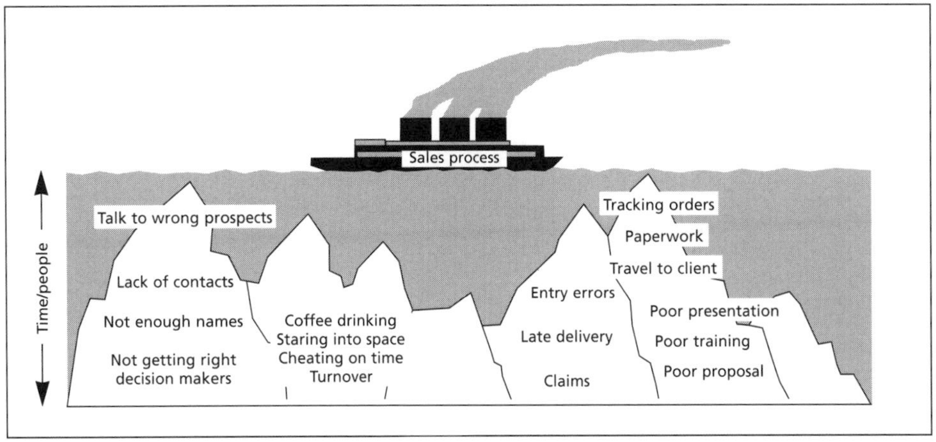

"Today, sales, marketing, and service processes are sitting in much the position as did manufacturing in the 1980s. A variety of problems lurk beneath the surface that can increase the variation in performance between reps. Instead of solving these problems one by one, many companies still buffer their ship of sales from the rocks and shoals by filling up their process with a flood of people and by accepting long cycle times as the accepted way things are done to keep the ship afloat.

"Time wasted talking to the wrong prospects? Better have more reps, so they can talk to even more prospects. Reps spending time chasing down order entry errors? Better hire more customer service people to help out. Rejected proposals? Better submit more proposals to more prospects, and that again means we need more reps. Not getting enough leads? Better have more advertising in more magazines. We'll need a larger marketing department. Simply adding quantity does not close the gap between high and low performers.

"That is the route for unimaginative managers. Process engineers need more creativity."

The Sales Quality Audit (Smith 1995) describes ways management can surface hidden problems in the sales process through the kind of systematic audit techniques practiced elsewhere in business. The _Guide to Implementing Sales Automation_ (Selden 1994) contains tables that link sales process improvement goals to specific strategies, tactics, and potential automated approaches keyed to solving the problems listed on the chart on this page.

Reflections on the Rocks and Shoals in Sales

That picture of the hidden rocks makes me think of another image. Dr. Selden used this picture before when he told us we could apply the concept of continuous improvement to our sales process problems, too. We could set a goal of dropping the amount of time we spend on a non-sales activity or the amount of "work in process" we have. Along the way, we'd bump into one of the hidden shoals. Instead of discouraging us, it would alert us to a problem. We'd then solve it, knock it down, and set a goal for further improvement. As each new problem poked to the surface, we'd tackle it in turn. We'd just keep going until the obstacles were reduced to a fraction of what they were before.

A huge insight leaps to mind. When we were talking about JIT the other day, Dr. Selden said that a secret to process improvement was to make hidden problems visible. That's exactly what happens when the water level drops and you bump into one of those rocks! Now I just have to figure out how to apply that idea. I wonder if charting and posting various process performance measures would be like making problems visible, too?

I am ashamed to admit that I've been a part of a lot of sales growth campaigns where our thinking just led us to doing more of the same instead of really improving. We wanted to double our leads, so we doubled the size of our mailing lists. We wanted to increase sales by 20 percent, so we just hired 20 percent more reps. I guess that's the easy way out when planning. Our rationale was, "We know this works. We'll just multiply it times two in order to achieve twice the result."

This is not how we have been trained to think. We are more like the military before the budget squeeze—when accomplishing the "mission" was all-important. The tax dollars were just something the public had to sacrifice. Our mission in sales has been to achieve volume at almost any cost. I heard someone say the other day that a sales manager has never been fired for exceeding expenses, as long as the sales came in.

I once heard that in the past, some auto companies' top executives never really knew the types of problems their customers experienced because as perks the executives drove top-of-the-line vehicles, then parked them in company-owned garages where they were serviced as often as needed. In ways like this the leaders of some companies are insulated, isolated, and buffered from the very process problems they are supposed to be solving! I wonder how we could put our top sales, marketing, and customer service executives more closely in touch with the processes they lead.

The picture of the rocks and shoals—the hidden causes of variation—dramatically shows that we could achieve twice the results without doubling our overhead, if we could only figure out the way to make our process problems more visible.

Exercise: Classifying Controlling Variables

Dr. Selden asks the group to classify variables that affect the sales process as either under the rep's control, under the control of management, or those that seem to be uncontrollable. He writes the results on three flip charts.

"You've thought of a long list of factors. Anyone familiar with the sales process would agree they are present. Let's explore them more deeply. Which of the uncontrollable factors are *external* to your company?

The participants observe that most of the factors they've listed as uncontrollable seem to be external.

"Look at the uncontrollable factors you've described as external. Can you think of ways their negative impact could be made smaller or prevented entirely?"

After a moment, one woman suggests that a customer's ability to afford her products could be increased by offering a time payment plan. A young man jokingly suggests that even the weather could be controlled by using umbrellas or covered walkways. The group seems to think these ideas aren't so far-fetched.

"Excellent. Traditional wisdom says many undesirable factors are *uncontrollable.* With creative thinking, we find that some of their undesirable *effects* can be reduced. Now, what about factors we've said are within the *rep's* control? Can we think of ways that these factors can be altered?"

Classifying Sales Process Variables

Rep's control	Management control	Uncontrollable
—Presentation delivery	—Payment plans	—Competitor actions
—To-do list follow-up	—Pricing	—Weather
—Product knowledge	—Product literature	—Customer budgets
—Conduct of a needs analysis	—Training	—Death
—Whether or not to call on a lead	—Lead distribution	—General economy
—Adjusting proposal to fit situation	—Advertising	—Getting answering machines
—Number of calls made	—Compensation plan	—Regulations
	—R&D	—Social climate
	—Special promotions	—Consumer's budget
	—Territory assignments	—Computer crashes

Most in the group see the point immediately. An older gentleman comments that management can see to it that reps are properly trained in many of the areas listed, including product knowledge, presentation skills, and many others. One woman points out that the tools management provides can also affect rep productivity, pointing out that the type of trade show the company chooses to go to affects the quality of leads given to a rep. Another fellow points out that hiring and compensation practices affect rep performance, too.

Specification, Production, Inspection

"Traditional managers or reps might shrug their shoulders and say, 'Nothing can be done.' The factors you've listed can change the outcome of a process. The very fact that you've been able to articulate and list them points out that many of the variables act as assignable causes. Any single one of them can have a large impact. An engineer would use the tools we learned in the previous days to tame them. Whether we are creative enough or are systematic enough in our effort to control them is another matter. I just ask you to think about whether you are confident that all your reps have a specified level of product knowledge, and that the level of knowledge specified as necessary is in fact essential and sufficient. In the face of obstacles, a manager may say, 'Well, that's just the way it is.' An engineer's job is to overcome complacency and inertia to succeed."

Process engineers learned many years ago that control is achieved by a sequence of three steps: specification, production, and inspection (see, for example, Shewhart 1939). Skinner adds the insight that a consequence—either positive or negative as appropriate—is necessary to obtain improved behavior during the next cycle—the "act" recommended in the PDCA cycle.

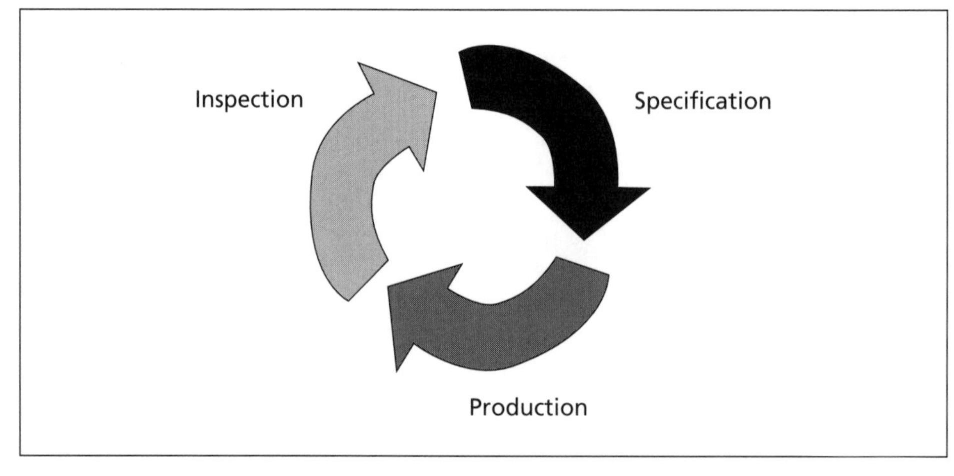

To apply this sequence in sales, let's say product knowledge was identified as an essential factor for achieving the necessary sales levels. The company would specify the extent of the knowledge required, take steps to produce that knowledge, and inspect to see whether it is present to the necessary degree. The steps taken to produce the product knowledge might include (1) training to secure the product knowledge and presentation skill, (2) changing the entire approach so less memorization and presentation skill was needed. To the extent this isn't done, extreme process variation would likely remain.

"We can overcome complacency and inertia. We can control the assignable causes. But one more set of causes will remain. When the Norse god Thor was challenged by giants to wrestle their old nurse Elli, Thor lost the match. The old nurse was Old Age, disguised in human form. No one can defeat Old Age. Like the old nurse, no one can defeat random causes. If we are to understand the sales process we must learn more about random causes. Most of us are trying to fight them all the time."

The Bid Closing (Red Bead) Experiment

Dr. Selden asks for volunteers to help him conduct an experiment made famous by W. Edwards Deming, which William J. Latzko and David M. Saunders vividly describe in their book *Four Days with Dr. Deming* (1995). Dr. Selden says he has modified the experiment to mirror how things work in the sales arena.

First, Dr. Selden asks for six volunteers to play the part of sales reps. He tells the volunteers they have the assignment of closing deals over four quarters. Bid closing will be simulated by drawing red and white beads from a container labeled "Quotes." Three men and three women volunteer. They step to the front of the room.

Next, Dr. Selden says he needs one person to volunteer as a sales manager to inspect and count the rep's performance and mix the beads to simulate a new batch of deals after they are returned to the container. A fellow steps forward. Then Dr. Selden asks for someone to serve the role of controller, recording the results on a scoresheet and calculating statistics for the rest of the company to see.

Smiling, Dr. Selden instructs the volunteers. Each rep is to draw beads from the bowl using a special scoop. The scoop has 50 holes in it, each large enough to hold one bead. Dr. Selden comments that when dealing with attributes data, such as counting whether a contract was won or lost, the sample size should be at least 50. The manager, controller, reps, and audience are asked to voice out loud the sort of observations they would normally make as they watch the year's sales unfold and to record the results in their workbooks as they occur.

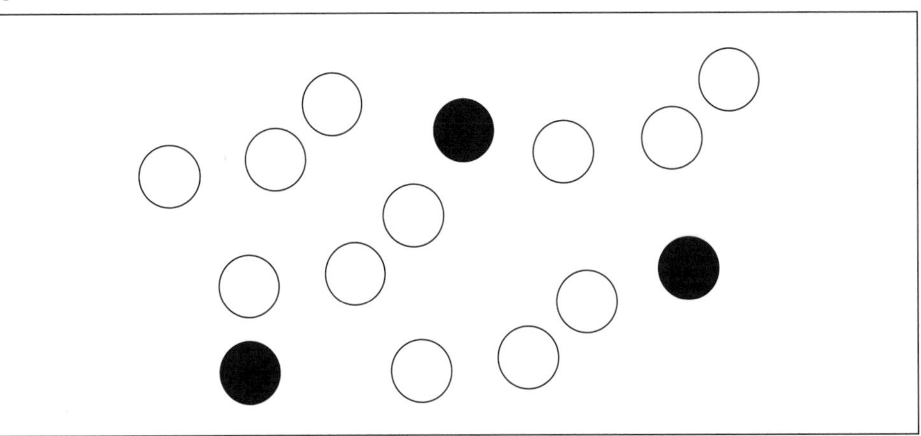

"The red quotes, you won. The white quotes, you lost. Your scoopful is a sample we'll use to measure the yield between the proposals delivered and the orders entered stages in the sales process."

Note: **In sales, the terms *bids, quotes, proposals, contracts,* and *deals* are often used interchangeably.**

Bid Closing Record

The first scoop is Jack's. He comes up with a nine. The audience is fairly quiet as Dave, the manager, examines the scoop and pronounces the result. The controller, Pete, records the result. Then Ron scoops a 17. Someone in the group says, "Go, Ron!" The rest laugh. Linda gets a 13. When Dick scoops a seven he looks disappointed. He cheers up somewhat when Mary draws an eight—misery loves company. Dave, the manager, says in a kidding way, "Hmm, you two better work a little harder next quarter," and a voice from the audience says, "You're not kidding." Again, more laughter. Emily draws a 13. The controller tallies the results: a total of 67 bids won, with an average of 11.2.

In the next round, the sales reps are reacting in spite of themselves. With their below-average results, Dick and Mary are looking a little nervous. Ron is a little cocky, bouncing up and down on the balls of his feet as if he's warming up for a boxing match. Dave makes a little speech to the effect that the group did okay, but there's room for improvement. He's taking his role as manager to heart.

Jack scoops an 11. Dave comments that he's getting closer to where he needs to be, referring to last quarter's average of 11.2. Then Ron scoops an 11. Instantly someone from the audience yells out, "He's coasting!" Dave doesn't look happy about it; Ron looks a bit sheepish, too. Then Linda draws a 15. She smiles at her improvement, and Dave tells her she did a nice job. A few people say "Ooooo."

Bids Closed: First and Second Quarters

Rep	1	2	3	4	Total
Jack	9	11			
Ron	17	11			
Linda	13	15			
Dick	7	13			
Mary	8	10			
Emily	13	14			
Total	67	74			
Average	11.2	12.3			

I can feel something happening to the group dynamics here. Everyone can see the reps are all drawing from the same bowl, but we are reacting as though we are in a real sales situation. Not only that, the reps are starting to insert their scoops more carefully. They seem to be aiming to scoop in just the right place.

Dick scoops a 13. He seems pleased. When Mary gets a 10, she actually says, "It's not my fault." A voice in the audience says, "Yes it is!" While the audience is laughing, Dr. Selden gets another laugh by observing, "This is definitely an audience of sales and marketing types. Nobody is afraid to say anything." Emily caps the quarter off with a 14. The tallies are posted. The total for the second quarter is 74, with a mean of 12.3.

Third Quarter Results

The humor continues as Tim, the controller, whispers rather loudly to Dave that there is an upward trend developing. Someone from the audience says, "You better increase the quotas." Dave looks over the totals and gives the reps a pep talk. "That was a great quarter, you guys," he says. "Now let's see what we can really do." A voice from the audience says, "Keep up the pep talks. They seem to work." The group is enjoying itself.

Jack is looking very nervous. He draws a 10 and more or less shoves the scoop back into the bowl as soon as he hears the tally. Not a happy camper. Ron starts out with a serious expression. He pulls out the scoop, but before Dave can count it, Ron actually dumps it back in the bowl and takes another try! This time he pulls a 14. That cocky grin breaks out and he says, "Knew I could do it." Someone in the back hoots, "Cheat, cheat." Dave, the manager, seems prodded into saying, "Alright, none of that," but he also observes, "Boosted my numbers, though."

Linda scoops a 13. Someone whistles admiringly. Dave comments that he's glad he can count on her. She does seem to perform consistently high. Some of the other reps say that they want to learn Linda's strategy. Dave points out to Dick, Mary, and Emily that he's counting on them to finish the third quarter better than the last one, now that the others are off to such a good start. Then Dick draws a 10, Mary draws a 11, and Emily draws a 10 in quick succession. Dick mutters something under his breath. Dave says, "That's it, he's gone. No more improvement programs." Everyone is laughing hugely. Dick is smiling too, in a way that can only be called brave. Someone in the audience points out that Mary seems to be improving steadily. Tim adds up the total as a 68. The average for the quarter is only 11.3. Now all the reps look depressed, and Dave is looking worried.

Bids Closed: Third Quarter

Rep	1	2	3	4	Total
Jack	9	11	10		
Ron	17	11	14		
Linda	13	15	13		
Dick	7	13	10		
Mary	8	10	11		
Emily	13	14	10		
Total	67	74	68		
Average	11.2	12.3	11.3		

The rest of the audience is enjoying things and getting into the act. Someone shouts out that Dick should be put on warning. Someone else says, "No, it's his *territory.*" Another says, "Now, Ron—he's got a plush territory. He just milks it whenever management notices he's falling behind." One of the reps says, "I need a stiff drink."

Fourth Quarter and Year-End Results

Before they draw, Dave points out that this is the fourth quarter. He's keeping up his manager's role as a good coach. Dave says that this is everyone's chance to finish strong for the year. He mentions something about the winner of the year's sales contest going to Hawaii.

Jack steps up, moving the scoop around in the bowl for what seems like a long time. He pulls, then dumps the scoop entirely. He finally draws an eight. Boy, does he look glum. Someone says, "Uh oh, open your next pay envelope carefully." The laughter sounds grim.

Ron pulls out a six, and he almost throws the scoop back in the bowl, too. Tim picks a couple of beads off the floor. When Tim records the six, he actually puts an asterisk by it! Tim comments, "That's a flag for random drug testing." The group howls. The asterisk is like a scarlet letter. Everyone else is roaring, regardless of how Ron may feel about it. This audience is expressive, for sure. Dave acts like he's leaving the room, saying, "I'm losing control. If I'm not back by two, it's because I'm having lunch with a headhunter buddy of mine." Linda draws an 11. It's her worst quarter, but she can see she has nothing to worry about. Dick scoops a six. He gives a quick laugh when someone says, "Get the ax," but we can tell he's just keeping a stiff upper lip. Mary pulls a 12, her fourth increase in a row. Emily finishes with an 11.

Bids Closed: Year-End Results

Rep	1	2	3	4	Total
~~Jack~~	9	11	10	8	38
Ron	17	11	14	6*	48
Linda	13	15	13	11	52 ☺
~~Dick~~	7	13	10	6	36
Mary	8	10	11	12	41 ☺ ↑
Emily	13	14	10	11	48
Total	67	74	68	54	263
Average	11.2	12.3	11.3	9.0	10.96

Tim adds up the fourth quarter finish. It's a 54, the worst of the year; the average was only nine. "I think we've got a marketing problem. They can't all be down," someone observes. The class howls.

Dr. Selden asks Tim to tally each individual's total for the year, together with the year's overall total and grand average. As he does, Tim does something totally unexpected. He draws a line through Jack and Dick's name, crossing them off the scorecard. Jack's total was 38 deals for the year; Dick's was 36. "Poor cost efficiencies," Tim remarks, and everyone breaks up laughing. "Clean out your desks," someone else says.

Then Dave takes the marker from Tim and draws a happy face next to Linda's final total. "President's Club," he says. With a 52, she was the sales superstar of the group. Dave skips over Ron's 48 and Emily's 48 and draws another happy face next to Mary's final score, a 41, with an arrow pointing upward next to it. Dave remarks, "Mary improved with each quarter. That's just as important, in my book. I may have to readjust my incentive program for next year, though."

Plotting the Performance

The class settles down as Dr. Selden points to the results.

"What did we just do? We took 24 samples of our reps' bid winning performance. Each sample consisted of 50 bids. We recorded how many red beads—bids won—we found in each sample. We recorded the results as we drew them, in sequence.

"Let's plot the sequence in a run chart and see what it looks like."

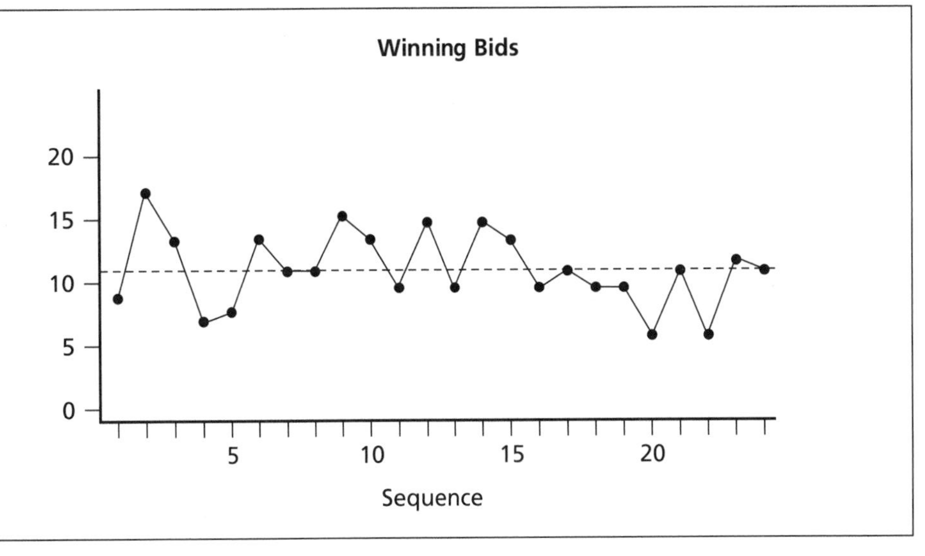

Dr. Selden asks everybody to chart the results of the Bid Closing Experiment in their workbooks. As the participants do so, Dr. Selden plots the results on an overhead transparency. When he is done, he draws a horizontal line of dashes to represent the mean (the average). The mean is derived by adding up all the individual scores (263) and dividing the total by the number of samples taken (24). The mean is 10.96; almost 11.

The Importance of Sequence

Preserving the sequence when recording results is a necessary part of a measurement operation aimed at detecting the presence of assignable causes.

Consider the following three sequences.

A) 3, 2, 4, 5, 1, 5, 2, 4, 3, 1

B) 1, 2, 3, 4, 5, 1, 2, 3, 4, 5

C) 1, 2, 3, 4, 5, 5, 4, 3, 2, 1

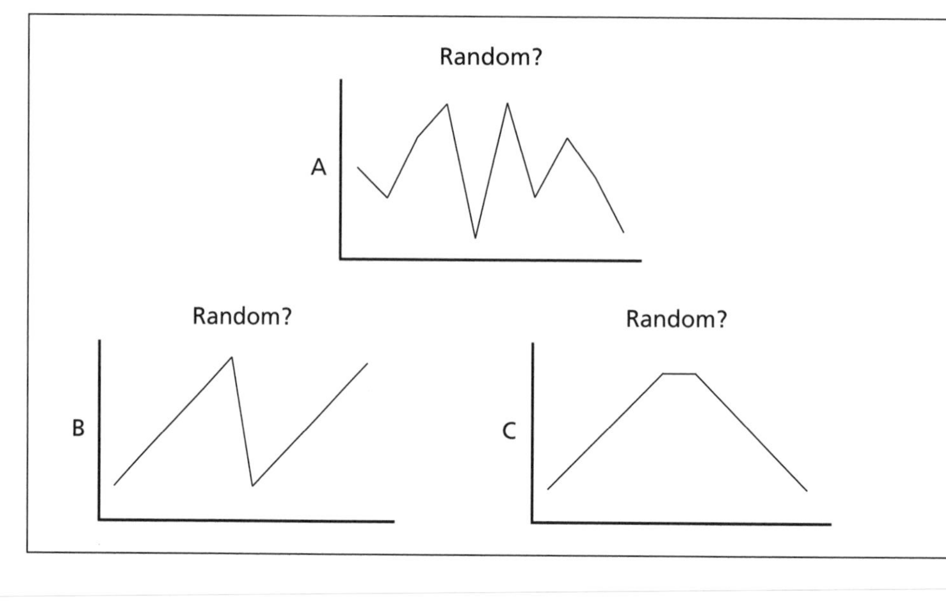

Sequence A exhibits no obvious pattern. Sequence B is an ascending cycle that resets and repeats. Sequence C ascends and descends in a symmetrical cycle.

Sequences B and C are judged nonrandom; even a casual observer would suspect the presence of an assignable cause in each case.

Judgments about the presence of assignable causes cannot be made unless the sequence of observation is preserved.

Five Observations About Normal Variation

"You were all here when we took our samples. You saw how it was done. You saw what went on in the room as we did it. You see the numbers we recorded, and you see the graph. What did you observe?"

The group has a lot of observations. One woman says that the class seemed to blame the low producers for their scores. A man remarks that the opposite was true, too: that management seemed to reward the top producer, Linda, and praise Mary for something neither of them may have had any control over. Another comments that the reps themselves seemed to act happy or disappointed about the results, even though everyone could see that everyone else's chances were about the same. A woman remarked that the mean seemed so close to 11 that she wondered whether the actual ratio of beads in the bowl was 22 red beads in every 100. One young lady predicted that the manager would probably alter his incentive plans for next year, go to a coaching school to learn better techniques about motivation, and watch Emily closely to see if her upward trend would continue. One gentleman observed that the two reps in the middle seemed to be totally ignored. Another fellow wondered whether this type of experiment simulates a process where only random variables are present. One of the reps commented that she felt she had no real control over the outcome, which was frustrating.

1. Drawing beads this way simulates a process where only random causes are present.
2. Sufficient sampling may allow theoretical inferences about actual population but we can only know the operational results in practice.
3. Single samples may vary widely from overall mean—and be quite misleading.
4. People tend to behave as though they can control both random and assignable causes.
5. Consequences experienced by an individual in this sort of system may be delivered by others involved, regardless of personal responsibility.

"I'd like to summarize your comments by offering five observations of my own. Other observations are possible."

1. Drawing beads from a container using this operation simulates a process in which only random causes are present.

2. In theory, if we took enough samples, the overall mean would tend to approach the true mean of the population as a whole. In actual practice, sampling operations experience variation that may include systematic bias and always include random variation, so our own results are operational measures and cannot be absolute in nature. Dr. Selden reveals that 400 beads out of the 2000 beads in the bowl were red, not 440, as suggested by the results. The difference may or may not have been due to reps "trying to do better," he states.

3. Any single sample or bead may vary—sometimes widely—from the overall mean.

4. People involved in a process tend to behave as though they can control both random and assignable causes.

5. Consequences faced by an individual in this sort of system may be tragic, wildly rewarding, or points between, regardless of individuals' ability to control their own results.

Two Kinds of Mistakes

Since the days of Walter Shewhart's work at Bell Labs in the 1920s, process engineers have pointed out two kinds of mistake when trying to establish the source of what is causing change in a process.

"Why must an engineer be able to separate random causes from assignable causes? I think you can *see* the answer to this question quite clearly. It may take longer to *sink in*. Unaided by special tools, the engineer may commit the same mistakes we all typically make when reacting to a process.

"We just saw how easy it was to commit the first type of mistake: treating an outcome as if it came from assignable causes, when it actually was produced by random causes. A second mistake is to treat an outcome as if it came from random causes, when it actually arose from assignable causes.

"The cost of these mistakes in the sales process must be enormous, both in human and economic terms."

Mistakes in Determining Causes

Mistake 1

Reacting to an outcome as if it came from a special source of variation, when it actually came from random causes

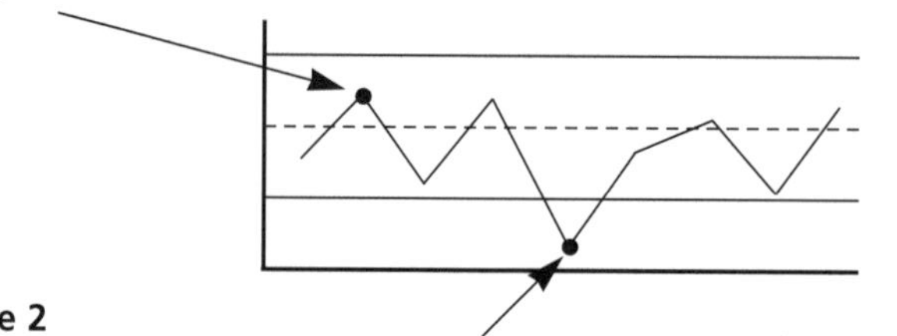

Mistake 2

Reacting to an outcome as if it came from random sources of variation, when it actually came from assignable, special sources

Simulation or Real Life?

"Is this an idle issue? How much management time is spent fighting random causes of variation and overreacting? Can anyone think of examples you've seen?"

This is hitting too close to home. Our firm just recently let the bottom 15 percent of the sales force go. We seem to go through a cycle of trimming the lowest performers every couple years. We have no idea whether their performance fell outside of normal random variation. Is this an overreaction? The number 15 percent seems totally arbitrary to me. I know we didn't spend any time looking at what Dr. Selden is calling the assignable causes of variation before we let those people go. We didn't know the concept existed.

I think the Bid Closing Experiment helped me to see that much of our current management time is probably spent trying to control random causes. It's the other causes—the assignable causes—we have to focus on to achieve real change! That kind of time and effort would be much better spent, because it's the only thing that would have a real impact.

Has anyone seen cases where management overreacts?

I know I fall into the trap myself. When sales go down even a little, I immediately put the pressure on my people to try harder. I often change a few policies or suggest new sales approaches, as well. I view that as part of my job.

My mind may be wandering off the question Dr. Selden has asked, but another point just came to me. If only there was a way to detect these so-called assignable causes with some reliability, we could use all the cause-and-effect diagramming tools, correlation tools, and everything else we've been taught over the past few days to diagnose and remedy the situation. That's the way we'd make progress!

Superstitious Conditioning

Why do people behave as though they can control variables outside of their control? Since the dawn of time people have attempted to control the weather and crop fertility through various rituals. A salesperson may wear a particular lucky tie, or a baseball pitcher may perform a special pre-game ritual in much the same way.

In 1948, B. F. Skinner found that this behavior is characteristic of other biological organisms, too. Such "superstitious" behavior can be shaped when a given behavior is coincidentally followed by an occasional reinforcer not physically caused by the behavior. The organism tends to behave as though the reinforcer was causally related even though the correlation is only temporal in nature; the superstitious behavior tends to increase, nevertheless.

The Policy Experiment

"Management is most effective when it installs innovative, corrective, or preventive measures aimed at assignable causes. What happens when policy changes are aimed at controlling *random* causes was driven home for me when I first learned about a series of four experiments that Dr. Deming called the *funnel experiment.*

"I followed directions for performing the funnel experiment provided by Latzko and Saunders. The overheads you see show the actual results of my experimentation.

"Dr. Deming called management's effort to control random causes *tampering* and *tinkering.* As I describe the experiment and the results, let's see whether you can find examples of this in real life."

The experiment was performed under the following conditions. An eight-ounce funnel was suspended four inches above graph paper by means of a rigid cage. Tightly stretched rubber bands held the funnel in a fixed position. A steel bearing measuring 3/8 inch in diameter was dropped by hand through the funnel, whose exit hole was 1/2 inch in diameter. Every attempt was made to release the bearing directly above the exit hole in the funnel. After each drop, the entire cage was rotated 90 degrees clockwise to minimize the effect of any bias in release direction and funnel location. (Prior to rotating the cage Dr. Deming's described results were not replicated.) Each experiment consisted of 50 drops.

Paradigm of Management Tampering with Random Causes

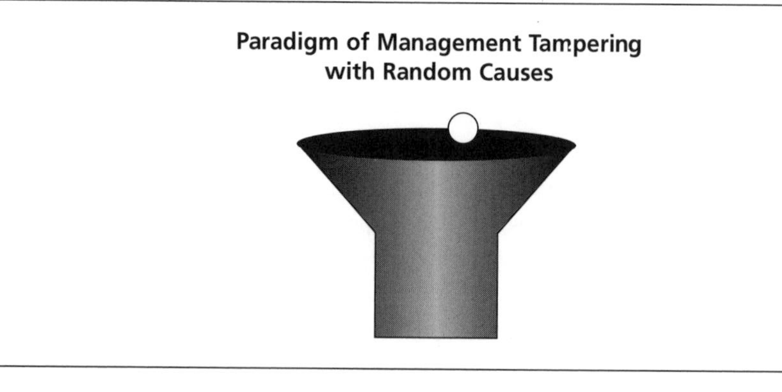

Graph paper with a cross in the center was used to mark the fall of each drop. To record the position of each drop, carbon paper was inserted carbon side up underneath the graph paper. Each drop would cause the carbon paper to mark the underside of the graph paper. An impression was made in the graph paper at this point, and the location of the impression was marked on the side of the graph paper facing upwards.

Dr. Selden tells the class that a funnel apparatus and many other process- and qualified-related instructional devices may be purchased directly from firms such as Lightning Calculator (810-641-7030) and Quantum Co. (800-574-5426).

Reaction Policy 1: Stay the Course

"One policy management can follow when faced with random variation is to *stay the course.* This is the pattern I obtained when I kept the funnel centered on the original target, regardless of where the bearing hit.

"Like a shotgun pattern, you'll notice there is dispersion. Even when trying to repeat the same conditions, not all the drops fall on top of each other.

"Notice that the center of the distribution is not the same as the center of the target. If I could list the reasons why this happened, correct these specific factors, and center the pattern, I would be working on an assignable cause. Some dispersion would still remain, under control of random causes.

"Faced with undesired variation in sales results, perhaps our sales and marketing management would also try to do something. Unless they work on genuine assignable causes, things may only get worse, as we'll see in the next three experimental runs."

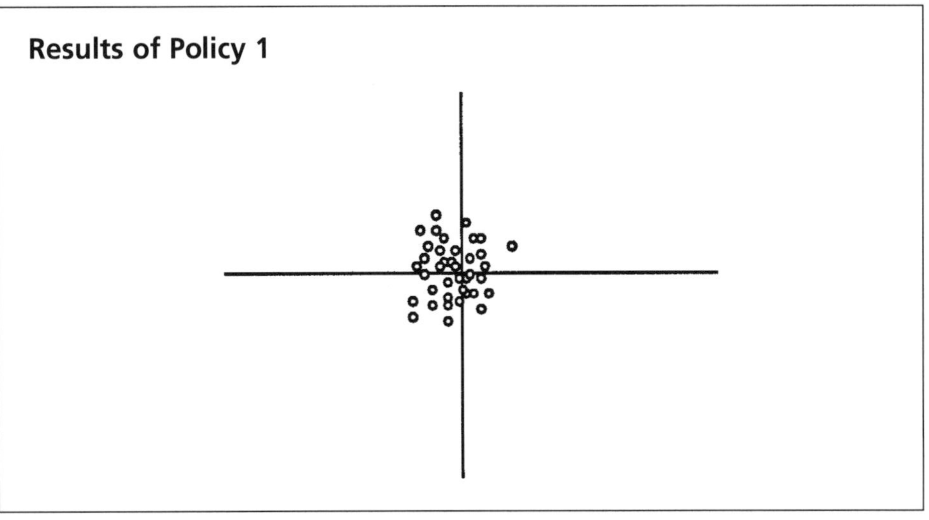
Results of Policy 1

Policy 2: Make Equal and Opposite Adjustment

"In this instance we have a management policy that could be characterized as making an equal and opposite adjustment when a drop deviated from the bull's-eye.

"For example, let's say I centered the funnel on the target. If my first drop actually fell 1/4 inch to the right, I would move the aim point 1/4 to the left from the last position. If at that point the ball fell 1/2 inch straight north from the current aim point, I would move the funnel 1/2 inch straight south.

"What do you notice about this pattern?"

Someone from the group answers quickly, "It's more widely dispersed." Another person mentions that it looks like the pattern as a whole is still centered on what appears to be the same place as before: slightly to the left.

"Notice that my new policy has actually made things worse. On the surface, my policy made logical sense. If the first shot is off to the right, adjust by moving the new aim point to the left. But I've actually made things worse."

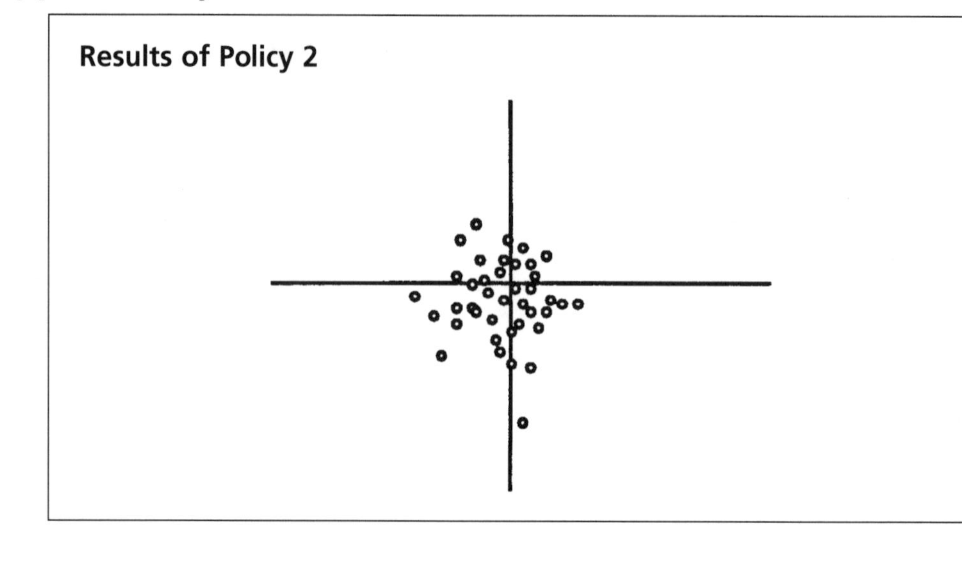
Results of Policy 2

Policy 3: Recenter and Adjust Equal and Opposite

"Well, Policy 2 didn't work out so well. Let's try another. Maybe the problem was that I wandered from my original aiming point too much. After all, I didn't consider or mention my original goal when I made Policy 2, did I?

"Okay, let's devise a third policy and try again. Policy 3 will be that we'll start with the funnel centered on the original target, as before. But from now on, if the drop is not on target, we'll *first* recenter the aim point on the original target. *Then* we'll move the funnel from the center, in an amount equal to how far off the previous drop was and in a direction exactly opposite to it.

"My first drop following Policy 3 was 7 cm north-northeast from the target. I held a ruler on the target, lined up on drop 1 and on the center of the original target. Using the ruler it was easy to put a tiny dot on the target to serve as my next aiming point, 7 cm south-southwest of the original bull's-eye. Then I moved the funnel over the new aiming point. Drop number 2 hit where you see, about 16 cm south-southwest from the original target. I lined up my ruler with drop 2 and the original target and marked a tiny dot 16 cm north-northeast of the original target. Using a ruler in this way made it easy to meet the mechanical requirement of Policy 3.

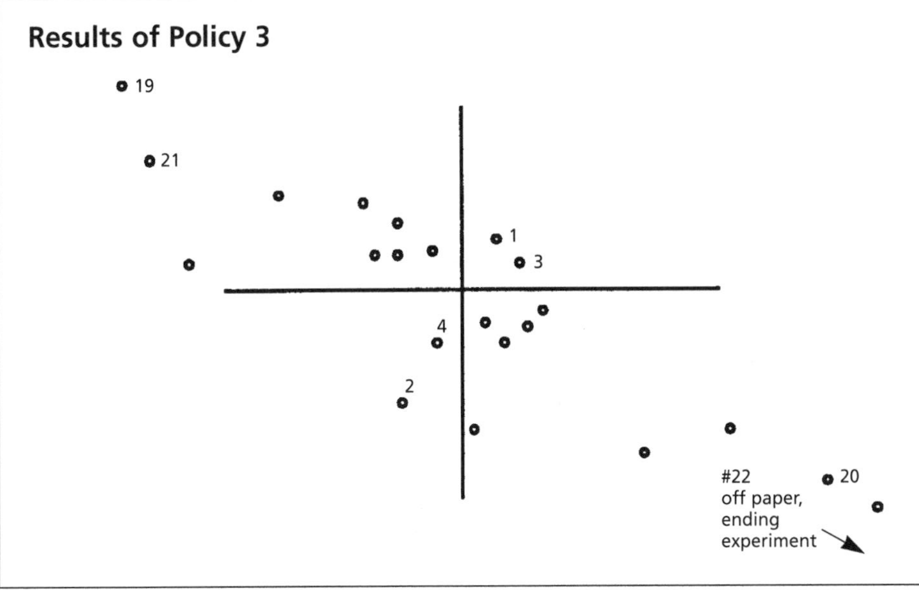

"After the fourth drop something began to happen to the distribution. An oscillating pattern developed, centered on the original bull's-eye. You see the result. I ran out of paper on drop 22.

"The pattern that developed was shaped like our Milky Way galaxy, and that's just how my experiment ended: off to the stars!"

Policy 4: Center on the Last Hit

"This is the result of my final experiment. I suppose a manager, having tried adjustment Policies 2 and 3, might be getting a little desperate.

"Other adjustment policies are possible, but this is the last one Dr. Deming shared with his classes. Policy 4 is to drop the ball, then recenter the funnel over the last hit to serve as the new aiming point.

"In my experiment I first aimed at the bull's-eye, and my first drop hit at point 1. Then I moved the funnel to aim at point 1 and dropped again. The ball hit at point 2. Point 2 became my new aim point and I dropped the ball again. When it hit at Point 3, I felt that perhaps subsequent hits would bring me closer to the original bull's-eye.

"Instead, my hits started to walk off in one direction. You see that Point 24 was almost off the paper, and I ended the experiment when drop 25 struck off the paper. Policy 4 leads you in a one-way trip off to the stars.

"If you try to replicate the experiment, make sure you are working with a huge piece of paper! And plenty of time. With all the measurement, each experiment took me 20 to 45 minutes to run.

"Lest you blame this all on a lack of marksmanship, let me assure you that I was trying to do my best the whole time and that I was quite a good shot in my younger days. In all these experiments I used the highest degree of care, as a matter of professional and personal pride. In fact, I would have loved *not* obtaining the same results as Dr. Deming. What publicity I'd get! It's hard to hide from the published results of a physical experiment that is supposed to be replicable. For better or worse, my results confirm what Dr. Deming described."

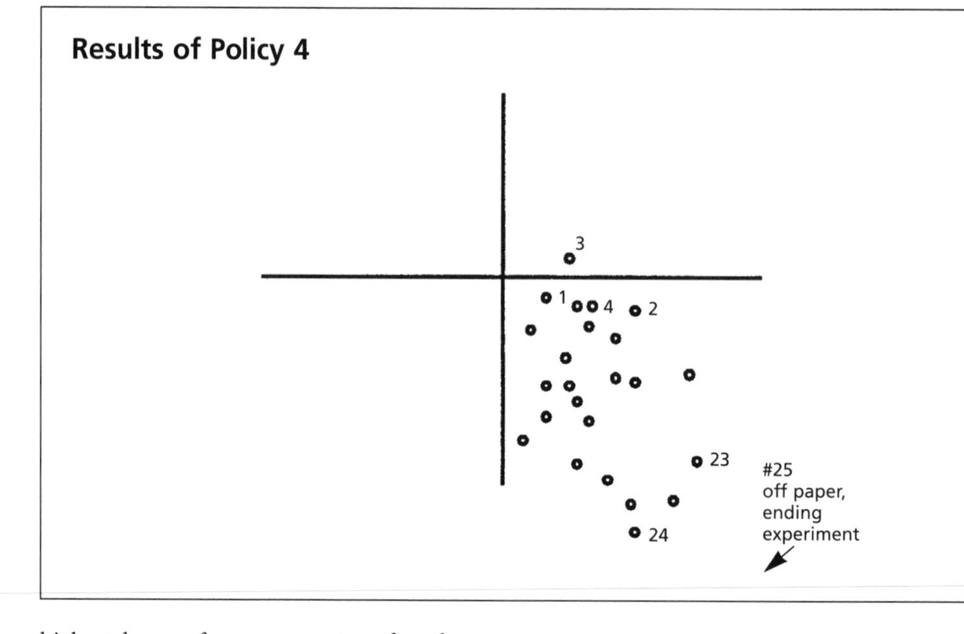

Seem Familiar?

After this thought experiment, the class has questions about whether the funnel experiment is really applicable to the world of sales and marketing. Could anyone actually get away with being such a bad manager?

"Is the experiment like real life? Have we already forgotten how we behaved during the red bead experiment? You found yourselves reacting to random process outcomes as if they were due to assignable causes, almost in spite of yourselves. What effects does our tinkering have?

"In practice, a manager who follows Policies 3 and 4 will not last too long, if for no other reason than the company would go out of business. What has the last decade taught us about mergers, acquisitions, and bankruptcies? Companies that stay in business have effective self-corrective mechanisms. In well-run companies, I imagine such managers are taught how to be more effective or tend to be replaced before damage becomes too great.

"Let's keep in mind what this experiment demonstrates. The experiment shows the results of specific well-intentioned but ineffective policies. The funnel experiment shows the effect of adjusting a process based on the result of single outcomes—single points of measure. A 'radical' change, such as structural—moving the funnel's exit hole closer to the paper—would have been better.

Examples of Tinkering

- Setting sales goals based only on last month's outcome
- Targeting or reordering merchandise based on one or two noteworthy sales
- Salesperson adjusting mixture of offerings based on last sale and personal target
- Budgets set based on variance
- Constant commission schedule changes
- Management fads
- Using last person to train next in line
- Federal deficit

The Policy Experiments show what happens when typical sorts of management "adjustments" are made to a process that is exhibiting only random variation. They do not show the result of performing normal, required process maintenance. If the funnel falls over, setting it back up is normal, required maintenance."

Dr. Selden lists a set of policies that at times may be analogous to moving the funnel. He cites the federal deficit as a case of Policy 4, pointing out that the government bases budgets on a percentage of the previous year's budget.

Need a Way to Spot Two Kinds of Assignable Cause

"The Bid Closing Experiment shows us the importance of finding a way to tell whether a change in the process is due to normal, random variation or whether the change probably resulted from an assignable cause. The experiment showed us that we tend to try controlling random causes, when in fact, we cannot.

"The funnel experiment graphically showed us that there are policies that might be mistakenly employed to try to control random causes that do more harm than good.

"For these reasons, a sales process engineer needs a way to tell the difference between random and assignable causes. It would be great if such a method could help us tell the difference between two *types* of assignable cause, as well: undesirable and desirable causes.

"Assignable causes in the sales process can be *undesirable:* failing to place an ad in time to meet a deadline, failing to check availability on merchandise as promised, failing to match a customer's needs with good solutions, and so forth. We need to tell when these factors cause undesirable results so we can install corrective and preventive measures.

"Assignable causes may also be *desirable,* causing our process to perform even better than normal. An exceptionally good sales presentation, a great answer to a client objection, or a wonderful solution for a customer's service problem are all desirable causes for change. We want to be able to tell whether a desirable change in the process occurs due to an assignable cause, so we can replicate the cause and further improve!"

Two Kinds of Assignable Cause

Desirable

When assignable variation is on the "good" side of that normally expected, it is just as important to detect it so that the factors causing it can be replicated or enhanced more consistently!

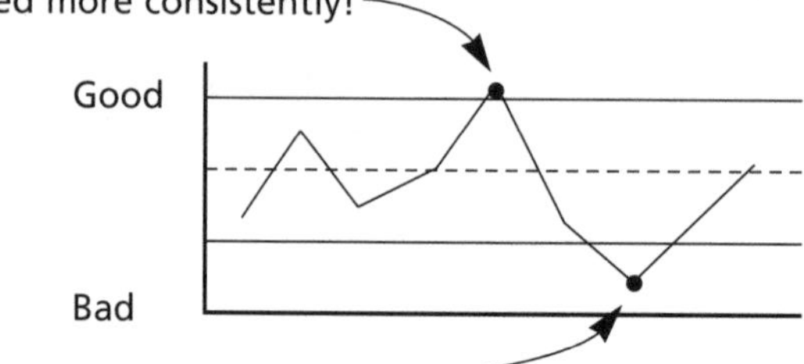

Undesirable

It is imperative to detect variation on the "bad" side, so the factors causing it can be prevented from recurring.

Aha—all this business about normal versus assignable, desirable versus undesirable, just sunk in! Now I see that a sales process engineer has to be able to sort normal from assignable variation. SPC can help us do that. I think I'm catching on!

Discussion During Lunch

Dr. Selden concludes an action-packed morning by announcing that it's time for lunch.

Several students obviously have a lot of thoughts. During the noon break they stop Dr. Selden to discuss them. It's clear Dr. Selden is not aloof. His enthusiasm, love of the subject matter, and concern that people understand really comes through. He answers each participant with respect regardless of their questions.

"All these bead examples, what do they have to do with sales process engineering?" one asks.

"An engineer needs to know how the process is performing. At each of the critical stages of the process we want to know if we are doing as well as we need to and whether we could do even better. If we don't know how our process is performing, how can we determine where to direct our efforts?

"All processes exhibit random variation, as the Bid Closing Experiment showed us. Most sales processes happen to exhibit a huge amount of assignable, undesirable variation, as well. We have to be able to pick that up. The beads help us model and understand our process more clearly and quickly."

"The way it seems to me, the only things we can really measure are the things management can control, such as how many leads come into the system. It's too hard to know what the people themselves are doing," another student comments.

"Management already measures many important outcome variables involved, that's true. The process variables also need to be studied in a way that allows us to more clearly see the relationship between key causal variables and the outcomes. If it becomes important to study the relationship between something we're not measuring currently, a talented engineer will cut a window into the process to see better," Dr. Selden responds. "It's too early in the profession to describe exactly what the nature of all these windows will be. In some large companies, each time a manager rides with a rep, a detailed set of feedback on very specific points is presented in writing. That's a great start. It will be a major leap forward each time one sales process engineer has determined the best place for new windows to be in his or her company's own sales process. That's why the work of people like Tom Siebel (1996), George Smith Jr. (1994, 1995), Cas Welch and Pete Geissler (1995), Tim McMahon (1994), and others I've mentioned are so pioneering. They're trying to suggest where some of these windows may be opened.

"The history of improvement in manufacturing also suggests that people can and should be responsible for taking their own measurements. Ultimately, the individual closest to the process needs the measures more than management does."

The Engineer's Job

"The variables management can control, such as the quality of a brochure or the ingredients they require in a sales proposal, don't really have much to do with the sales force itself, do they?" another person wonders.

"In one sense, you're right. When managers set up those variables, they set boundaries their people have to operate within. A sales process engineer will probably focus quite a bit on those variables, but variables under the control of individual reps would enter into it, too. I think it's easier to understand the degree of emphasis if I use an analogy. An engineer will be looking for ways to set up something like a bridge across the Mississippi River.

"Now, we're asking our people to swim across the river. We train them to swim the best we can. Some of them are good at it, some aren't. In hot weather, many like to dawdle in the water because it feels good. In cold weather, they don't want to swim at all. The engineer's job is to build a bridge across the water to make crossing easier for everyone. People and their need to cross the river are involved, sure. The difference is that the engineer is primarily looking for structures to support the people, not for different swimming strokes. People using the bridge then need to be taught how best to use it—not to stop in the middle of the bridge to sightsee, what types of vehicles are allowed, how fast to go, and so forth. Individual behavior still plays a role."

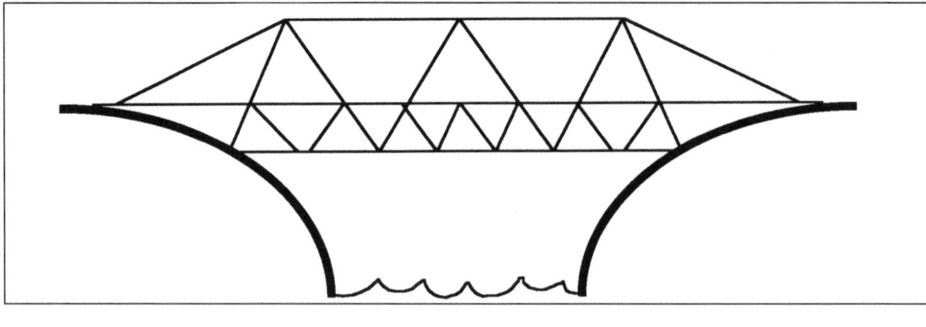

The participant responds, "The need to build a bridge is obvious. Why would an engineer even study whether to build it or not?" he asks.

Dr. Selden replies, "In the case of building a bridge across a river, the need for a bridge might seem obvious. But what if it were cheaper to install a ferry boat? A row boat? Or to issue water wings? In the sales process, we don't always know whether the need for a bridge exists in the first place. In sales, we sometimes build bridges to nowhere or we overspend or underspend on what is really needed. Does a marketing program or new technology ever fall on its face because the sales force didn't need, understand, or want it? Even in the case of bridges, an engineer needs to study the best place for the bridge, what it will cost, what capacity it must meet, what the benefit will be, and so forth."

Another member of the audience observes, "In our company, the bridge we're building has to do with sales automation. If I understand you correctly, what we need to do is explore alternative means for reaching the same goal, the costs, the benefits, whether the automation is in fact aimed at relieving a genuine bottleneck, and so forth. I might even conclude that we'd get a bigger bang for the buck by doing something else entirely, right?"

Dr. Selden smiles, and says, "Exactly. But I guarantee you that somewhere, there's a computer in the future of your sales process."

Part 3: Impact Evaluation

> Most people would rather live with a problem they can't solve, than accept a solution they can't understand.
>
> —*Lloyd S. Nelson*

Objective

By the time we finish this topic you will be able to

- Use three SPC charting techniques to detect sales process improvements.
- Use eight rules to determine whether an outcome is in control or out of control.
- Understand how to calculate simple process capability.

Bid Closing Revisited: SPC Limits

After lunch, Dr. Selden returns to the Bid Closing Experiment.

"Our engineering methodology should be able to tell us when what we're doing *doesn't* work. It should also be able to tell us when what we're doing is working exceptionally well. It would be nice if it was simple to use. We have such a tool. [Dr. Selden pauses dramatically.] It's called SPC: statistical process control.

"SPC is a common method engineers use to sort assignable causes from random ones. Recall the definitions we covered yesterday as we calculate the control limits for our bid closing process."

Appendix B contains tables and formulas for calculating six common variables- and attributes-based control charts. (1) $\bar{X}$ and *R*. The $\bar{X}$ chart formulas are used to calculate the UCL and LCL around the overall mean. The $\bar{X}$ and *R* chart is also called the *average and range* chart. [Note: $\bar{X}$ is pronounced *X-bar.*] The *R* chart is used to sense whether the variability between samples has changed. (2) *X* and R_m. The *X* and R_m chart is also called the *individuals and moving range* chart, used when charting individual scores. (3) *p* and (4) *np*. The *p* and *np* attributes charts are used when a whole item either meets or fails to meet a standard. (5) *c* and (6) *u*. The *c* and *u* attribute charts are used when a single item may contain multiple errors.

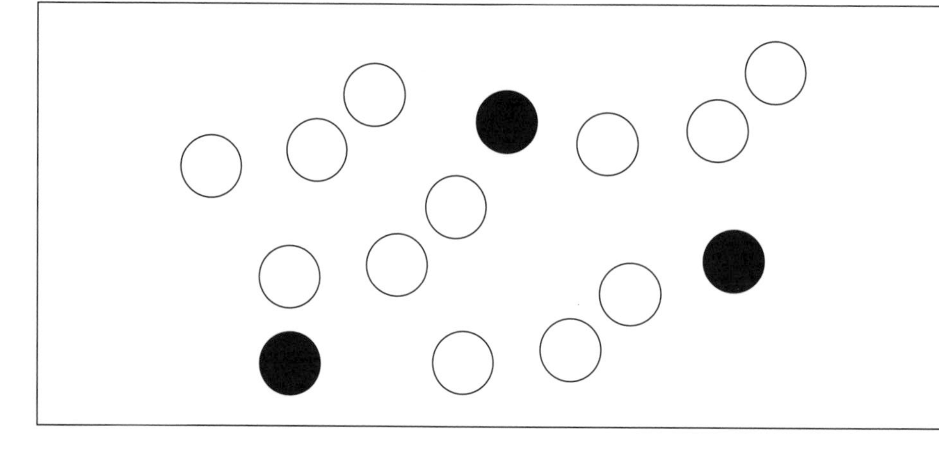

Dr. Selden works through two examples to give participants an idea of how SPC charting works. Detailed instructions for using the formulas are beyond the scope of the workshop, Dr. Selden explains. He reminds the group that his personal favorite reference works on the topic are listed in the bibliography.

Dr. Selden explains that counting the number of red and white beads to represent bid closing requires use of an attributes SPC chart called the *np* chart. The way the class measured bid closing requires an attributes measure because the class only counted whether the bid closed or not: an either/or type of measure.

Calculating the Control Limits

Dr. Selden directs the group to the formula for *np* charts, which is used in the case where a number of whole units either conforming or nonconforming to the standard is tallied. Instead of tracking the number of lost bids (nonconforming units) the class tracked bids closed (conforming units). The figures will be calculated accordingly.

The equation for upper and lower control limits on the *np* chart is

$$n\bar{p} \pm 3\sqrt{n\bar{p}\,(1-\bar{p})}$$

[Note: in this equation $\bar{p}$ is pronounced *p-bar*]

In the experiment, the sample size (n) was 50. The total number inspected was 50 times 24, or 1200. The total conforming was 263. $\bar{p}$ (conforming) is $\frac{263}{1200}$, or 0.22 (22%). Therefore, $n\bar{p}$ = 50 × .22, or 11. Substituting these figures into the equation and rounding slightly so that he can more easily display the results on his flip chart, Dr. Selden works out the equation step by step.

$$\text{UCL: } n\bar{p} = 11 + 3\sqrt{11\,(1-0.22)}$$
$$= 11 + 3\sqrt{8.58} = 11 + (3 \times 2.93)$$
$$= 19.79$$

$$\text{LCL: } n\bar{p} = 11 - 3\sqrt{11\,(1-0.22)}$$
$$= 11 - 3\sqrt{8.58} = 11 - (3 \times 2.93)$$
$$= 2.21$$

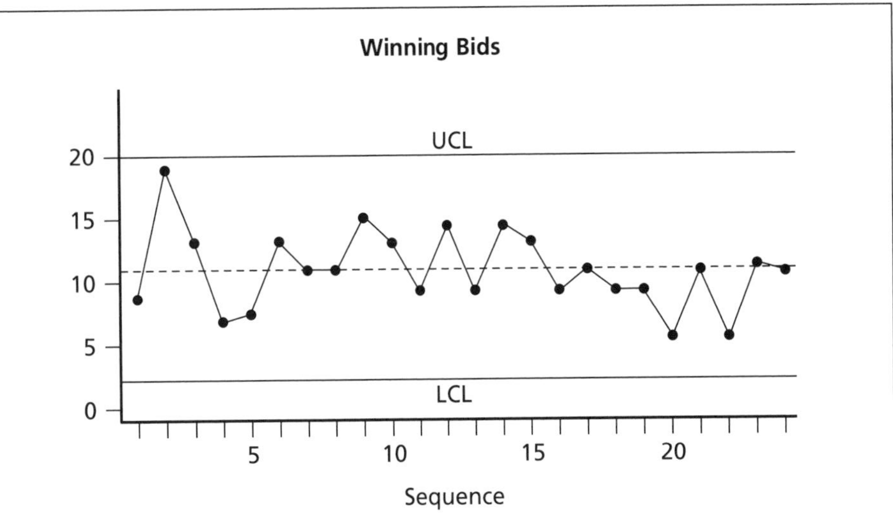

Dr. Selden plots the upper and lower control limits on the chart. The mean is the same as $n\bar{p}$, or 50 × .22 = 11, and is drawn as a dashed line.

"The upper and lower limits provide us with a pair of boundaries. If a sample falls above or below these limits, the rules for SPC tell us we should suspect the presence of an assignable cause. We saw no such assignable cause present in the Bid Closing Experiment. By definition then, this process is indeed in a state of statistical control."

Dr. Selden asks the class to independently work through the formulas for the *p* chart found in Appendix B. The *p* chart is used to determine control limits for the *percent* of closed bids. The mean bid closing rate ($\bar{p}$) is 22 percent. In this case the answer was UCL $\bar{p}$ = 39.5 percent and LCL p = 4.4 percent. Dr. Selden explains that small differences between results obtained by different participants are usually due to how they round off their calculations.

"You're learning the same tools that have already helped transform the half of modern industry responsible for producing quality goods. The trend is spreading into the health care and other industries. Our challenge is learning how we can apply these tools to the sales process."

Reflection and Discussion

One of the class members offers a comment, then asks Dr. Selden a question.

"Seeing this chart is giving me another major revelation. I can't imagine how much stress we put on ourselves as managers, and on our people, trying to control random causes.

"But just because a process is in a state of statistical control doesn't mean it's a good process, does it?" Dr. Selden's eyes shine as he hears that question.

"Excellent point! When a process is in statistical control, all you've found is that it's doing its best under the current structure. Its current performance may not be good enough. As engineers bring a process under control, however, they tend to discover and control the factors that make it behave in a way everyone would like in the first place. That revitalizes efforts to focus on finding the 'good' assignable variables. It's likely to be something within management's control. Once discovered, at least you know where to apply your effort to find the necessary improvements. Until then, it's all talk, and hit or miss."

"If you plot your process and you find points out of control, what happens to your chart once you correct the out-of-control points?"

"Another excellent question! Once you install the corrections and preventive measures, and the out-of-control points cease to occur, recalculate and replot the control limits. Do this until you can improve upon no further assignable causes. You are left with a process in control, performing the best it can under the circumstances until a breakthrough occurs.

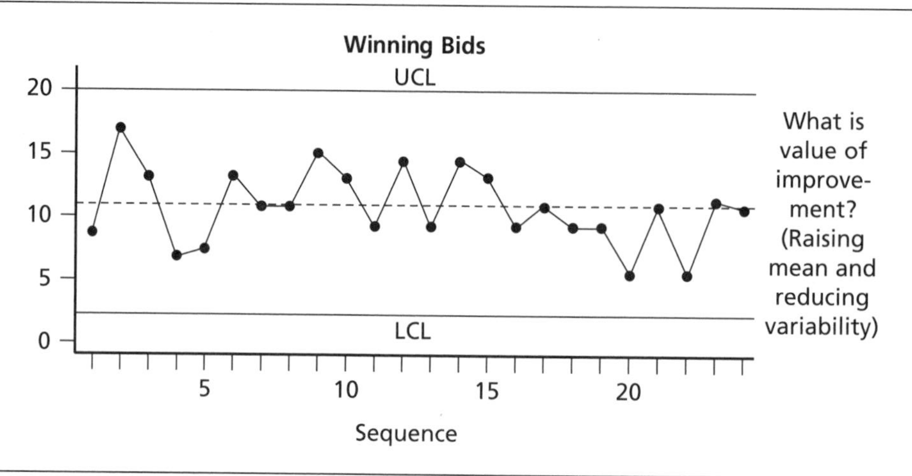

"Think! Prior to changing your process, you can look at the process performance you've graphed and evaluate the economic benefit of preventing the undesirable points or the economic gain in shifting the process in a desirable direction. The economic difference between where you are, as is, and where you would like to be can be used to justify how much it would be worth spending to arrive at the improved state of control.

"But watch out! If you can list the reasons why the process might be out of control, don't kid yourself that you can bring things into control just by thinking about them. An engineer must be a relentless do-er."

In the sales process, out-of-control points could be due to a variety of factors.

- An ad someone forgot to run
- Lateness in getting a mailing out
- Failure to do something as promised
- Launch of a competitor's product
- Using wrong pricing schedules

Troubleshooting Tips for Out-of-Control Points

"Let's say we've detected that our process is out of statistical control. The next step is to bring it into control or as close to that point as possible."

Dr. Selden displays a checklist, the inspiration for which he credits to Brassard and Ritter (1994). When an out-of-control point occurs, the problem often stems from a change in one or more of five sources: the process, policies, the personnel, the overall environment, or in the measurement methods themselves. There may be others, and the careful engineer will use his or her imagination as well as investigation to suggest assignable causes.

"Listen! [Dr. Selden raises his voice. A sudden thought has angered him and he follows his private muse.] Let's not fool ourselves. We set specifications for our sales and for many of our service people, every year, every quarter, sometimes every month or every shift, don't we? It's called a quota, isn't it? Meet a quota, or you're out.

"What did we just learn? Doesn't every process exhibit natural variation? Haven't we seen that some of these key assignable causes are within management's control, yet they affect the overall results? Whose results are they then, the reps? Management's? Both?

Troubleshooting Out-of-Control Points

- Process: nature or source of inputs, tools, materials, adjustments, feedback loop the same?
- Policies: the same procedures, policies, practices employed?
- Personnel: level of skill, fatigue/stress, fear of "looking bad" somehow different?
- Environment: process affected by weather, competition, politics, regulation, overall economy? If yes, has environment changed?
- Measurement methods: any changes, differences, variety of technique, source of samples?

"When quotas are set, do we give any thought to the natural variation that unavoidably must occur? Do we realize that if we judge people by whether they are above or below the average, half of the people will be below par, by definition? On the other hand, if the quota represents a lower specification limit, did managers set this limit because they removed the assignable causes in the sales process, and they *know* this specification can be met if the reps do their jobs correctly? Have they calculated where the predicted performance will likely be? What have we been *doing* to our people? Ask them: They'll tell you! [The group chuckles in knowing laughter.]

"One of the promises sales process engineering holds is precisely in this notion of setting practical specifications. In the 1800s, Eli Whitney learned that it was not economically feasible to hold mass-produced goods to a single exact dimension, and the notion of tolerance limits was born. Can we take these lessons and apply them to the sales process? Do you understand the implications, just in terms of the potential increase in job satisfaction and human dignity?"

Specifications for Sales, Marketing, and Service

"I want to provoke your thoughts before continuing. Let me ask you. Can you ever have too many sales, too many leads, or too much service? Many people would say '*No!* All sales are good.' Are they right? What do you think?"

Several people strongly voice their disagreement. They've all seen cases of a "bad" sale. Some aren't profitable. Some don't satisfy the customer. Dr. Selden writes some of the participants' comments on a flip chart. Some sales mean the following:

- **Accepting poor credit risks**
- **Getting high returns**
- **Inability to ship as promised**
- **Lack of service**
- **High costs**
- **High discounts**
- **Deliberate cheating and lying**

"If we're willing to say that even the most sacred of our sacred cows in the sales process—namely, the sale itself—can sometimes be bad, we can easily understand the concept that there are limits within which parts of our sales process must perform. What is the alternative?"

Several members of the group say, "Going broke."

"Doesn't this imply that specifications—engineering tolerance limits—can be set for a wide variety of variables in our sales process? [Heads nod in agreement.] Now, stick with me for the next 20 to 30 minutes or so. I'm going to be covering a more advanced topic that may sound abstract—the concept of measuring the ability of a sales process to meet specifications. The concept is far from theoretical, as we'll see.

"What things within the sales process might we be able to develop specifications for, even to the point of specifying so-called min-max tolerances? Any ideas?"

The class doesn't hesitate to voice opinions. Ideas range from setting specifications on the cost per qualified lead to specifications on how many contacts it should take before a sale is closed. One brave soul even mentions setting limits on the percentage of profitability. A few derisive snorts from other participants follow. The fellow immediately replies that the concept is hardly far-fetched. Such a firm would be less likely to go broke, more likely to teach its people how to sell by appealing to value, much less likely to be perceived by the public as a price gouger, give less room for the competition to undercut price, and lead a more stable system overall. "What do you think GM's Saturn project is all about?" he asks.

ETR = USL – LSL

There is a desirable operating range for most subprocesses: an engineering tolerance range.

The engineering tolerance range is defined as the difference between the upper and lower specification limits. Note that specification limits are not the same as control limits. Specification limits are set according to engineering *judgment,* including cost considerations. Control limits are determined by *calculating* actual process performance.

We may not know the desirable engineering tolerance range is for parts of our sales process, but we may be able to articulate our initial specifications and test the implications.

Taguchi's Loss Functions

"Once there was a wise street merchant who decided to study how much profit she could make in the bazaar if she tried really hard. She had already done everything she could to make her goods and canvas awning more attractive. Now she decided to try one last thing: to vary the price to see what difference that would make.

"First she increased her prices, hoping that the increased income would give her more profit. Instead, fewer people bought her merchandise. She now had less income to offset her expenses than before. Then she decreased her prices, hoping that she could lure more people to shop with her than before. But now she found she had less income in relation to the cost of goods she sold.

"In the end she found that a certain price, between the extremes but a little higher than what she used to charge, gave her the best overall balance. The more she deviated from that ideal, the less profit she made."

The precise relationship between costs related to poor quality and process/product specifications was mathematically defined by Dr. Genichi Taguchi in the 1950s. Losses related to poor quality escalate exponentially the further one deviates from the ideal specification, even when all the measures are falling within the upper and lower specification limits! Crossing the limit is worse, true, but as far as the consumer is concerned the difference between being just slightly inside the limit versus being just outside the limit is usually not perceptible. All the consumer experiences is a decline in satisfaction the closer one gets to the limit. A lawnmower that starts easily with one pull is more satisfying than one that starts hard with one pull and strains the back. Both mowers met the engineer's "one-pull" starting test, but which would you rather own?

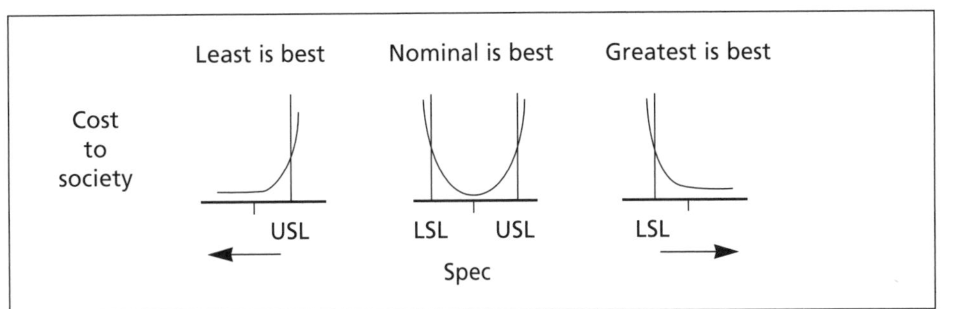

The steepness of the curves vary with the specific situation. The loss curve is determined empirically by examining actual costs to society, which may be greater than the simple cost of a broken part. The consumer's cost to fix something gone wrong is usually much greater than the cost of the broken part. Time, transportation, personal injury and aggravation, loss of use, inconvenience, and loss of time working at something more productive must all be considered. The consumer's cost must be balanced against the company's cost of achieving ever-tighter specifications.

The ideal is sometimes that "least is better." This may be the case where specifications call for the least amount of wear and breakage, fewer returns, fewer pricing and configuration errors, fewer mis-shipments, and so forth. In this case, the loss function looks like the graph displayed on the left. Costs rapidly increase the closer an item is to the upper specification limit.

The obverse of "least is better" is "greatest is better." In the sales process, the greater the yield, or ratio between outputs divided by inputs, the better. The number of sales per 100 people entering a store is an example of such a ratio.

In some cases, the nominal, or target specification called for, is best (for example, 5 cm ± 0.1 cm). In sales, a company with a well-defined market may find that an order size needs to fall within a certain dollar amount to be profitably handled by its regular sales force. The closer to either extreme within that bracket, the company finds it loses money due to increased special order work, complaint handling, idle time, and the like.

Recent studies suggest that "costs to society" taper off and probably do not rise to infinity.

Statistical Control Is Step Toward Capability

"If you agree that for a company to be profitable its sales process must be able to operate within a certain engineering tolerance range, how can a sales process engineer make use of this principle?"

Dr. Selden pauses, waiting for a response.

Somebody says, "Well, maybe we should draw up specifications for our process and each of its steps. It seems we should be able to construct all that in advance." Another person asks, "But if we're already making money, why should we go to the trouble of drawing up specifications? Isn't being profitable proof that what we're doing is working?"

Dr. Selden responds. "Engineers are practical. They don't want to make more work for themselves or the company than necessary. In fact, isn't one of their jobs to make life easier for everyone? Shouldn't they try to find ways that the company can get the same results—or better—with less work?

"Drawing up specifications would be a waste of time in at least three cases. First, where the company was making all the money it wanted to—with no competition in sight. Second, where there was no opportunity for improvement. Third, where no changes will affect the current sales, marketing, or service organization in the future.

"In all other cases, the dictum of the six P's applies: proper planning prevents plenty-poor performance!"

Some members of the group laugh. They could tell Dr. Selden had censored a popular scatological version of this saying. Dr. Selden draws a bell curve on the board with the mean marked off.

- Capability is the ability of a process to operate within required specifications.
- Most processes experience drift and sudden change.
- System must be able to detect and correct both.

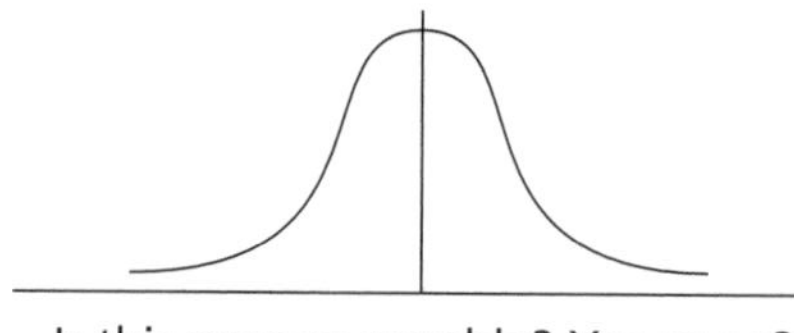

Is this process capable? Yes or no?

"You've seen this curve before. This is the output of a subprocess. Let's say you've outlined the necessary engineering specifications for a modified sales process you are planning to implement. Before you implement the change, shouldn't you know how your current process is performing, with respect to the specifications? Once you've instituted the change, isn't it mandatory that you know whether the new process is capable of meeting your specifications?

I think I'm getting the idea here. Someone can say they will institute all kinds of so-called improvements. I think Dr. Selden is asking whether it's responsible to bluster about changes that have no specifications or that can easily be predicted to be incapable of meeting intended specifications just by making a few simple calculations. Even allowing that things don't always work as planned, it makes sense that we should at least have a way of telling how close we came to meeting our specifications once the enhanced techniques are installed. I think he's also telling us that if we're going to be serious about engineering, the so-called ability to sell, or market, or deliver service is meaningless unless it's with respect to an operational standard—the specification.

- Coming up with a better way is not extra trouble.
- Improvement is the heart of obtaining a competitive advantage.
- The sustained speed with which a company can improve relative to the competition, and its ability to marshal the resources to accelerate improvement when called for, will be a key operational definition of commercial success in the coming years.

Simple Test for Capability

Capability is the measured ability of a process to reliably produce results within the required specifications, in spite of its natural variation. Part of capability is the ability to *reliably* produce results, since nearly every point measured within a process in control will fall within its statistically calculated control limits. Therefore, there can be very little or no confidence that a process producing outside a state of statistical control will be truly capable to begin with.

One of the class members asks, "Why would I bother figuring capability? From the little I know, my sales process is bound to be way out of control in the first place."

"First, you don't know whether your process is in control until you measure it and calculate the limits. Control limits are determined by calculation, not by judgment. The Bid Closing Experiment should have taught us that it can be hard to tell what is in control and what is not just by eye-balling the data. Second, consider a situation where someone presented you with a so-called sales process improvement that could not meet its specifications. How does that make you feel about the intended change? [He says, "Not too positive."] So you need a way to detect this in practice. That means examining process capability.

"Examining process capability is going to be good for you in at least two ways. On the one hand, you can save your company a lot of money otherwise spent chasing false promises! On the other hand, finding a

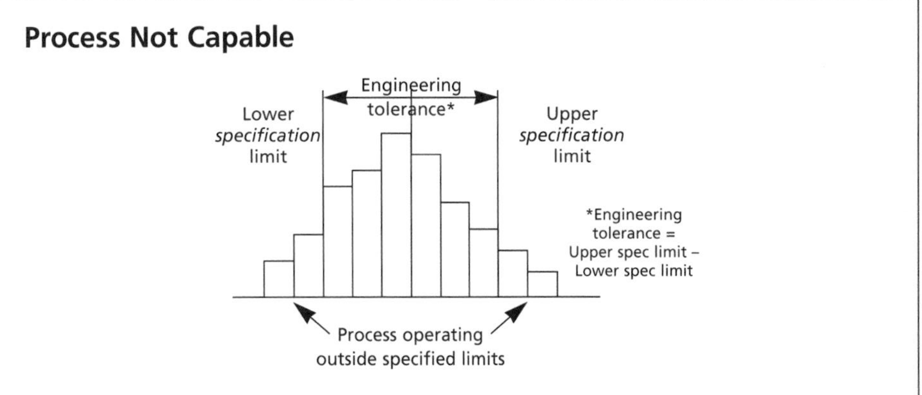

measured gap between a desirable standard and current performance points out a potential opportunity to improve! So if you are a sales process engineer, finding such a gap may make you feel great! And achieving process capability, by definition, means the process is performing *as you require.* The benefits attached to that are self-evident.

"Sales process engineers are like miners for gold. All of us are standing on mountains of opportunity! It's our job to dig it out!"

As Dr. Selden is talking, I'm translating all these concepts into simple terms I can relate to. I have an image of someone who says he can produce a round wheel for me. He installs state-of-the-art hardware in the factory with all of the latest automation. He gets all the hardware and software working great. But when I look at the wheels he ships me, they're square. That means the process is not capable. It sounds obvious. The sad part is, I have an uneasy feeling we accept this kind of practice all the time. I think we have built an entire culture around justifying continuing these practices, too. Like Dr. Selden said before, there are vested interests in preserving the status quo.

Can process capability be quantified? The simplest way to test for capability is to take a series of 100 consecutive individual measures (not averages). Chart them on a histogram (see the charted ratio of converting contacts into appointments presented earlier). Formal calculation is not required. If *any* of the individual values fall outside the specifications, the process is not capable. At that point, there are at least three alternatives: (1) improve the process until it is capable; (2) accept the performance as is; (3) change the specifications.

Process Not Capable

"Let's say you keep your specifications where they are until you feel you've really learned what makes your sales process tick. As you use SPC and perhaps a few simple experiments to help prevent or correct undesirable causes and enhance the desirable ones, you'll gradually find your results falling more and more within your specifications. As you do, you'll be finding more and more of that buried gold."

The Taguchi loss function predicts that engineers who achieve control of their processes may find that further tightening their process performance so that it stays well within specifications yields greater bottom-line results. Those in charge of internal downstream processes and customers external to the corporation may even be willing to pay more for such quality. They may be shopping around for a supplier who can deliver it. These requirements may or may not be articulated explicitly. Large corporations frequently require materials suppliers to certify a process capability with respect to physical goods; requirements such as ISO 9000 targeted at the contracting process may eventually push demand for formal process capability studies in the sales, marketing, and customer service arenas, as well.

"Even without a deliberate process change, most processes experience drift and fluctuation, if only due to normal wear and tear. Engineers need a way to detect such change. We've learned one such approach.

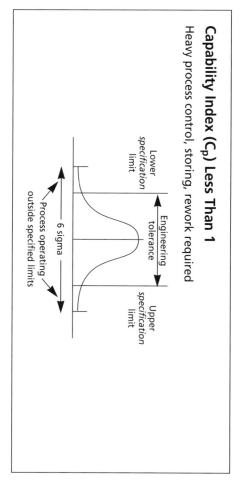

Capability Index (C_p) Less Than 1

Heavy process control, storing, rework required

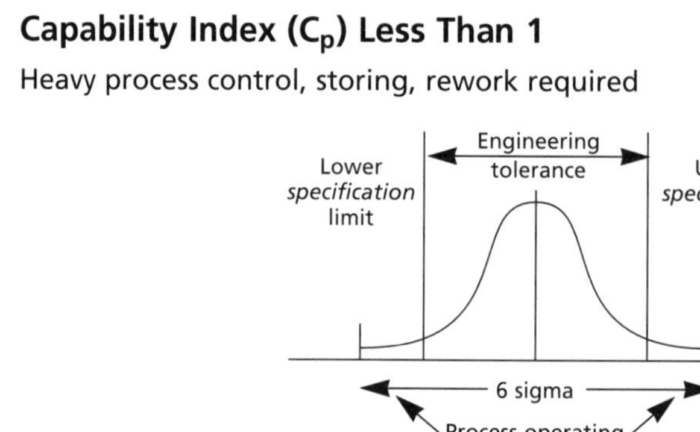

What is it? [A woman in the back of the room asks, "SPC?"]

"Excellent! SPC is a great tool. We can use automated, 100 percent inspection for detecting process drift and sudden change as well. It turns out that SPC can also help us develop more sophisticated indexes for showing whether our processes are capable of meeting specifications or not, once the process is in control. Consult some of the reference books I've cited to learn more about how this is done."

Engineers set specifications to allow for a certain amount of tolerance, or variation, while still meeting customer requirements. The illustration shows that if the ratio between the engineering tolerance and something engineers call *six sigma* is less than one, the process is not capable. In practice, this means that *more than* three out of 1000 individual data points (not the sample means) are likely to fall outside specifications. SPC can be used to estimate the value of six sigma.

Considering the economic consequences of producing the typical mistake, processes that aren't capable usually undergo heavy sorting and rework expenses by the process they feed. This is why in sales, for example, proposals must receive such close inspection. A misplaced decimal point could spell economic disaster.

I wonder if our marketing people would say their lead generation process is capable or not? But that's unfair. I doubt that sales even sets specifications around its expectations. Compared to what Dr. Selden is describing, the typical job objectives are pretty weak tea. By true process engineering practices, we have no legitimate way to judge capability in the first place.

Process Very Capable

In a very capable process, the ratio of the engineering tolerance to the process six sigma (that is, a range encompassing ±3 standard deviations, or 99.73 percent of the individual items produced) is 1.5 or greater. At this point the performance is measured in errors per million! Very little needs to be spent on the effort to stay within standards at that point, and only occasional spot checks are required to make sure unexpected change or drift hasn't occurred.

World-class companies have shown that capabilities of 1.5 or greater are far from being an unachievable standard, as far as physical products are concerned.

Marketing, sales, and service may only need to improve their process capability slightly and still achieve tremendous benefits, since the difference between winning and losing an entire contract may be slight!

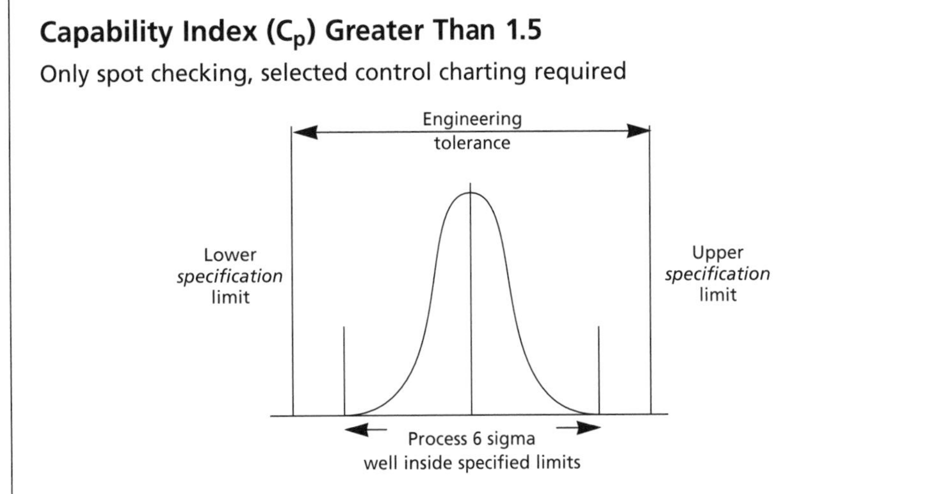

The difference between where we are and where we need to be is tough to calculate if we don't know where we are right now. So much of the data we gather in our current accounting systems is aimed at tax and financial reporting, or it's aimed at reporting only what we've already done: sales for the week, the month, the quarter. We break it down by rep, by district, and by territory; we break it down by product line and customer—but it's all just slicing the same information in different ways, and it's all looking at the past. It's like trying to drive down the road ahead by looking through rearview mirrors.

I just got an idea. What if we calculated control limits for the data and plotted them over time? That could get us a better handle on what our variability is, and we could start pursuing what's causing it.

All this is making me a little philosophical. What tremendous inertia we must have in our sales, marketing, and customer service cultures. What a barrier between manufacturing and sales, that we haven't seen how to apply manufacturing's best practices to our sales process. Oh well, I guess that was then, and this is now. I've got to play the ball from where it lies.

Calculating C_p

"I've already shown you one easy way to determine whether your process is capable or not, using the histogram. Once you are past that stage, the next easiest calculation engineers use to evaluate simple process capability is called the C_p; there are others."

At this point Dr. Selden leads the class through a technical discussion of how to calculate the C_p capability index, providing an example. He insists he is not trying to overwhelm the audience. Instead he stresses that at some point, some of the participants will need to understand the subject in a bit of depth, and he is introducing the topic against that time in their professional development.

When working with variables data, variation can be measured in a number of ways.

One method of describing variation is the range, which is the difference between the greatest and least measure in a sample. If you obtain five sales (for \$1000, \$500, \$300, \$900, and \$600), the range equals \$1000 minus \$300, or \$700.

When a larger number of normally distributed scores are available, the so-called standard deviation (sd) can be used to describe variability. In a normally distributed population, 68.26 percent of the group falls ±1 sd from the mean, 95.45 percent falls within ±2 sd, and 99.73 percent falls within ±3 sd from the mean. Modern spreadsheets and statistical calculators can calculate sd instantly, given a set of data.

Calculating C_p

- C_p = engineering tolerance range/6 sigma
- Example:
  A sales process engineer determines that to meet the company's forecasting accuracy standards, the cycle time between when a customer receives a proposal to the time a customer places the order must not exceed four weeks (longer than that increases the cost of doing business and makes it harder for reps to plan their personal budgets). The engineering tolerance range is eight weeks.

  The sales process engineer measures the company's current lead generation and qualification output and finds the six sigma is 16 weeks. Therefore, C_p = 50 / 100 = 0.50. The sales process engineer finds the process *not* capable.
- Other capability formulas are also used: C_p does not provide an index of the process center vs. specification

The standard deviation is derived from sample data. It can then be used to estimate the variation in the rest of the population, which is called *sigma*, by means of the formula sigma (estimate) $= \frac{\bar{R}}{d_2}$, where d_2 is drawn from a table depending on the sample sizes involved. C_p is equal to the engineering tolerance divided by 6 sigma.

With attributes data such as close ratios, appointment yields, and response rates, process capability is not calculated in this fashion. Instead, bring the process into control, then compare the mean for the attribute in question with management requirements. If the mean is higher or lower than desired, it is not capable and must be shifted.

For further information on calculating process capability, consult Brassard and Ritter (1994), Pitt (1994), and Pyzdek (1994).

Generally Recommended Sequence

"Do you feel you have a handle on what process capability means? It's just the ratio between your specifications and how your process is performing.

"Now that we've examined the concepts of process control and capability, let's see how they fit together in a process improvement effort. Hy Pitt (1994) and other process engineers recommend bringing the process into control first. Then work on capability. An example will help explain the rationale.

"Let's say you are looking for opportunities to improve the sales process. You've seen a number of rocks and shoals: everything from a lower than desired number of leads coming in to a sloppy method for assessing customers' needs. Let's say your system for prioritizing opportunities says that you should indeed improve the lead generation part of the process. You try some obvious improvements. The next step is to measure whether you've achieved control.

"As you see problems causing too much variation within the process—the problems due to assignable causes—you must tackle them as priorities suggest and conditions permit. Let's say that our lead generation process is out of control because in some months we've got too few leads coming in. So we brainstorm, and create a cause-and-effect scatter plot based on historical records. We find that, lo and behold, our ad rotation policy seems to be at fault. Every time we run one particular ad in one particular magazine, the number of leads dip. We never noticed this before, because this same ad worked fine in other places. To continue the story, let's say we adjust our placement rotation, and the number of leads per month becomes so steady that the points now fall within the control limits."

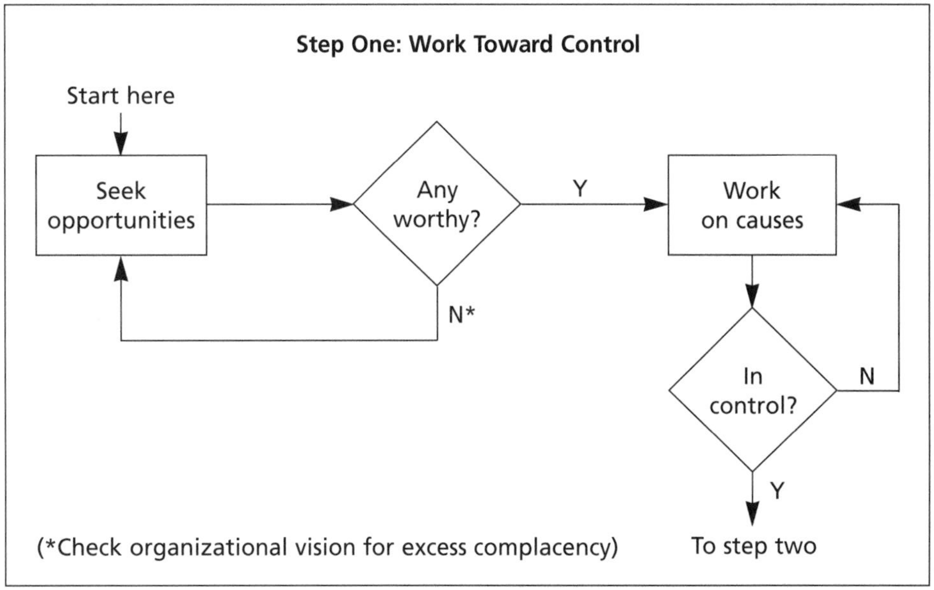

Step One: Work Toward Control

Start here
Seek opportunities
Any worthy?
Y
N*
Work on causes
In control?
N
Y
To step two

(*Check organizational vision for excess complacency)

I'm going to encounter naysayers in my company who want to throw their hands up and go back to their hit-or-miss, seat-of-the-pants approaches when I outline what I've learned here. I know that they'll say "it can't be done" on the grounds that there are too many factors beyond our control, like "the competition" or "the market." What I've learned from Dr. Selden is that of course what my competition is doing will affect my end results, but that just means my attack will have to be on two fronts: external and internal. I've got to keep in mind that the ultimate specifications are those my customer has in mind, and our ability to remember that is within our control. But I also have to keep in mind that a lot of other problems we have in our sales process are internal. I can't blame my competitor as a reason for a lack of internal improvement. By trying to bring the overall sales process into control, I'll end up working on causes external and internal to our company.

Use Existing Sources for Creative Ideas

"Do you mind if I ask a simple question before you continue?" a young fellow in the audience asks. Dr. Selden tells him to ask his question. "You said we need to control our sales process. What if the brainstorming, charting, and other tools you've taught us don't work, and we can't come up with an idea for how to improve the process in the first place?" he asks. This really gets Dr. Selden going. He uncorks an enthusiastic endorsement for all the existing sources of inspiration we have available.

"Listen! After you've tried everything you can think of, use the many sources for creative ideas we find all around us! We see them daily! This is where the world's storehouse of great sales, marketing, and service ideas and recommendations fit in! All the magazines!

"You might get your inspiration from a coworker who says or does something that gives you the solution. You might be inspired by something you learned from a great sporting coach or world-class athlete. This is where the great treasury of books comes in—the knack, the tricks of the trade, and a thousand and one great tips—all maybe waiting for you in a bookstore for less than $50! The answer may come in the next inspirational presentation you attend! It may come from former teachers, something in the news, or from your religion!

"All the tips, tricks, and classic works of know-how should be considered with the greatest respect! All the lists and bullet points of great reminders. I never said the best practices of the greatest achievers don't work or are useless, did I? No! They work! The recommendations found in the dozens of great audiotapes, lectures, and books are priceless. If you are in sales, marketing, and service, you have to expose yourself to the insights of Beveridge and Beveridge (n.d.), Carnegie (1940), Girard (1986), Hill (1960), Hopkins (1982), Nightingale (1992), Ogilvy (1983), Peale (1991), Ries and Trout (1993), Tracy (1985), Weldon (1982), Covey (1990), Zemke and Schaaf (1990), Ziglar (1984), and all the other classics. The well-tested selling systems, such as Learning International's Professional Selling Skills training; Miller, Heiman, and Tuleja's *Strategic Selling* (1985); Rackham's *SPIN Selling* (1988); Hanan's *Consultative Selling* (1985); Levinson's *Guerrilla Marketing Attack* (1989); Gallagher, Wilson, and Levinson's *Guerrilla Selling* (1992)—I've used them all. They work!

"If you're stuck on ideas for a specific part of your sales process, say, the proposal part, consult works on that subject. Do the same for all the other 'points of pain,' to paraphrase David Sandler (1996). Maybe you've tried but haven't found anything that seems to fit. Try exploring some of the systematic invention-generation software and training classes that are just now becoming available. Who knows? The engineering books I've cited might give you an idea you hadn't considered. Just don't turn yourself into a catalog engineer. Get hands on and the solution may come to you, quickest of all, when you're least expecting it!

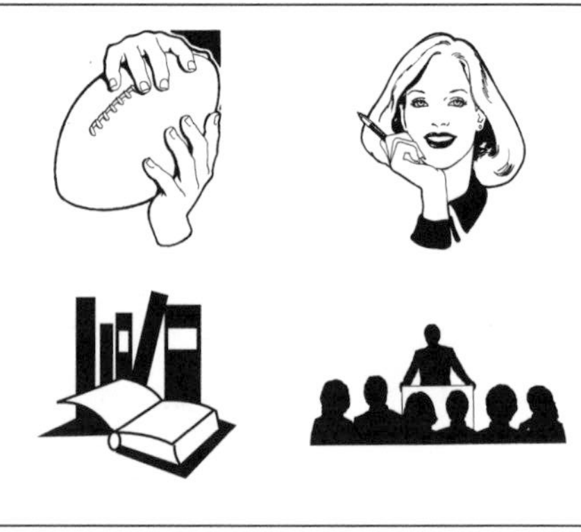

Dr. Selden's right. These books and approaches have worked for our company, too. But I think sales process engineering has the potential to breathe new meaning into and create better linkages between existing approaches, too. If we went back to all the many classic books and articles, I'd bet that most of the advice could easily be related to one of the engineering principles we've been covering. In this day and age we are being pressed to advance further. I'm here to learn new approaches.

I think sales process engineering gives us a place to hang all the good advice. What I'm seeing is that it's an effective organizing principle, just as the newer views of the universe are more useful than the old earth-centered models.

Sales process engineering strikes me as a more sophisticated way to tackle some of our age-old problems. My gut feeling is that it's more in line with where the rest of the world is headed.

Control, Then Capability

Dr. Selden resumes the discussion about improving process capability.

"After gaining control, engineers recommend working on capability.

"From time to time you'll naturally compare how the process is performing with where it needs to be. This means you'll evaluate the process mean and variability against whatever the current specifications are: evaluating its capability. In our lead generation example, assuming the quality and quantity of the leads coming in is constant and acceptable, what might you try doing if the number of leads was now quite steady, but the number was still too low? Let's say you are not permitted to increase your budget."

Someone suggests changing the ads themselves, or trying different magazines, or asking for a different location within the magazines.

"Great! Let's say that works and that now, you have a consistent number of leads generated. They are in the right quantity and quality. Best of all, you've done this at no increase in cost. Since your process is now working capably, your actual cost per good lead has fallen. Systematic experimentation may lead to further improvement. You'll also need to move on to other improvement activities, if for no other reason than something else will have become your bottleneck.

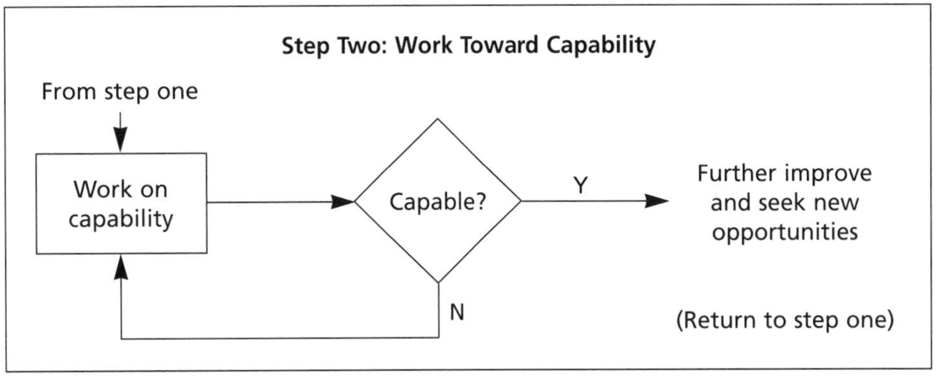

Step Two: Work Toward Capability

"Incidently, you may find that the current specifications are not economically feasible. Such high or tight specifications may not even be necessary from a practical point of view! What a shock! Someone asked for something they didn't really need in the first place. Does that ever happen? [Several participants chuckle at this understatement.] Listen to the voice of the customer! Understand your customer's true need! Does the customer need a widget or a solution? Could the specifications be altered and still accomplish the customer's goal?

"On the other hand, if the specifications are necessary and economically feasible, you have little alternative if your process is not capable. You must improve process capability—bring it into control and center the process mean inside the tolerance limits. You may or may not be able to accomplish this by changing the assignable causes. Changing the process itself through creativity, invention, and innovation may make it more robust and less vulnerable to the assignable causes! You may also be able to eliminate the process entirely!"

Choices If Improvement Is Possible

"If you can't make your process capable, yet you must deliver a result that falls within your sales process engineering tolerance limits, you have little choice: Live with what you've got and pay the price. The price of having an incapable process means you'll have to inspect 100 percent and sort to avoid passing your mistakes to someone else. Remember the cost of quality: you'll pay the price for failing to be capable in many ways. In order for a system to survive when the process is not capable, a tremendous amount of money is spent."

Being honest with myself, I have to admit we make up mistakes to our clients by taking back returns, offering heavy discounts, sending them tickets to ball games, making apologies. Those are the clients who stay with us! There's the lost business from customers who never order again. All our gyrations are just to take care of mistakes that reach the customer's attention! What about the internal mistakes the customer doesn't see? That's what most of my brush fires are all about! I could teach a great course in firefighting; I've got the experience and credentials for it. Oh well, I'm glad I can still laugh at all this. I enjoy what I do most of the time.

"If you have tight systems in place to sort out problems and scrap or rework them before they go out the door, you're still spending a ton of money. How many bungles does sales management have to sort out? How much time and effort do we have to spend on monitoring and reporting?

> **Option One: Constructive Approach**
>
> - If process *not* in control
>   —Learn what makes process tick
>   —Systematically work on assignable causes
> - If process *not* capable
>   —Understand and change specifications
>   —Bring into control
>   —Center the process
>   —Change the process itself
>   —Figure how to stop doing it altogether
>   —Live with it; come as close as possible and sort 100%
>   —Further improve through design of experiments

And the problems that make it through the net probably cost even more."

My head is reeling. This discussion isn't abstract at all. The math is something I can revisit later, but the real-world implications are easy enough to see. What does living with an incapable process do to our costs? What do those costs do to our pricing structure? What does our pricing do to our market share and profits? We've absolutely got to do everything we can to break this spiral!

Suddenly I'm feeling that yet another conceptual loop has been closed for me. Dr. Selden is speaking about the difference between paying for the costs of failure versus the costs related to prevention. Ben Franklin had it right: An ounce of prevention is worth a pound of cure. I bet we don't know how much we're spending on our current so-called cures, either. I wonder if half the money spent on sales training is spent training people how to follow a sales process that doesn't work! That's our version of the saying, "Garbage in, garbage out." I've got to find out.

"When you've done all you can, it's time to move on to the next step. Find your next bottleneck, your next opportunity for improvement, and go for it! Design of experiments may help you squeeze even more improvement out of the process. If not, it's time to try to feed back the next wave of customer and competitive information to further advance. Improvement never ends."

Options for Improvement

"We have two choices. Option one is the constructive road, which I just described. The road to survival and success. The road taken by the sales process engineer. Option two is to sit down in the middle of the road, curl up, and do nothing different. Wave goodbye as you watch your company's assets decay and go down the drain as you get run over by the competition.

"Remember, if you think you've got it nailed, you haven't understood. The job is never done. In the case of our lead generation improvement example, all those good leads coming in will create a new bottleneck somewhere else.

"So a sales process engineer will always be looking for ways to further improve. Use the philosophy of kaizen and bring out the big guns of quality function deployment—ask your quality department about that one—and use experimental design to find further creative ways to exceed your customers' expectations and improve your internal processes.

"At this point, the competition will be left in the dust. Your firm will be ranked among the top one, two, or three in your field. You will truly own a 'word in the customer's mind' as Ries and Trout (1980) say, and you'll deserve it, too—unless the competition's sales process engineering team is better than yours. The most insightful, dedicated, intelligent, and resourceful firms will make it to the top.

Two Options

- Option one: constructive approach
- Option two: watch your assets go down the drain
- Your choice

"Sales process engineering at this level will be one of the biggest thrills of your life! But don't do it because you're afraid of the competition—do it for the excitement of the professional challenge! Most of all, do it because it's the right thing to do, a form of spiritual expression and fulfillment."

Linked Sales Process Experiment

"The sequence I've just presented begs a question: How can I tell if what I'm doing is working? All your plans and good intentions will be wasted if you can't detect improvement when it occurs. You can set all those heavy thoughts about capability and improvement sequences aside now. Time to get hands-on again!

"Yesterday we saw how the systematic development sequence and multiple baseline technique could be used to increase our business confidence that what we're doing should work, and is working, in the field. That's a great approach. Very rough and ready. Practical.

"The next few experiments will show you another very powerful way to detect improvement using SPC. You look like you could use a break from heavy thinking. So let's have some fun and get the blood flowing again. You'll be running the next experiment yourselves. Welcome to my humble sales process engineering laboratory. We're going to make sales."

Dr. Selden pulls out four large signs, labeled "Leads," "Appointments," "Proposals," and "Orders," stating they represent subprocesses within the typical business-to-business sales process. He takes out three bead-filled containers and sets one between each sign. He says the containers represent the yield between each subprocess. He states that we could model any sales process this way, not just business-to-business sales processes. Then he divides the room into teams. Finally, he asks one member of each group to come forward and take a container, sheets of graph paper, and a scoop. The participants are smiling and talking. It's starting to look like fun after all the conceptual work.

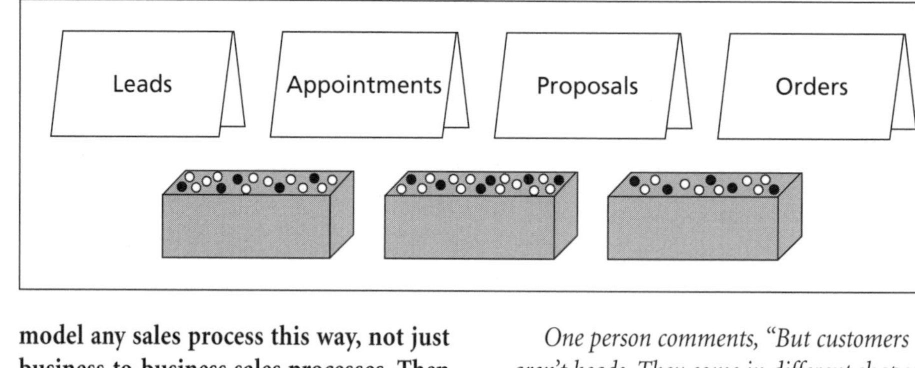

"Each group should split into scoopers, mixer-counters, and recorders. This time there are many different colors of beads in each container. They represent what could be done if we wanted to make the experiment even more lifelike. For now, count the dark beads as 'good': a lead that turns into an appointment, an appointment that turns into an opportunity to propose, or a proposal that turns into an order. Set up your graph paper as we did with the Bid Closing experiment. Switch jobs so everyone tries each job. Scoop 25 times total. Work at your own pace. Be sure to pour the beads back and forth to mix them after each scoop."

One person comments, "But customers aren't beads. They come in different shapes and sizes."

"Regardless of the customer, can you tell whether they have made an appointment with you or not? Can you tell whether they have bought or not? [Everyone agrees, yes.] That's all we're going to do. We're going to observe the process."

Letting the Process Speak

"*Control, capability, improvement.* They're all just buzzwords until you measure. Measurement is the difference between 'I think' and 'I know.'

"When you've tallied everything, work as a team to calculate your subprocess mean. Then figure your upper and lower control limits, this time using *p* charting. Use the rules in Appendix B. Remember, when plotting attributes data you can't go below zero. Use zero for your lower control limit if you arrive at a negative LCL number.

"We'll see how the entire sales process might perform after you finish. Hy Pitt (1994) calls this stage of the process improvement effort, 'Letting the process speak.'"

Dr. Selden roams through the groups, joking and answering questions as he goes.

"Be sure to mix those beads thoroughly. This experiment is so sensitive to changes in how you measure that it can even tell what color tie you're wearing."

About 10 minutes pass as everyone works to measure how each part of the process is performing.

"Okay, doctors. Let's see what you found when you listened to your patient. What did your part of the process tell you?"

Dr. Selden writes all the results on an overhead transparency. About 8.9 percent of the leads turn into appointments; 31.4 percent of the appointments turn into proposals; and 20 percent of the proposals are

Sales Process Performance

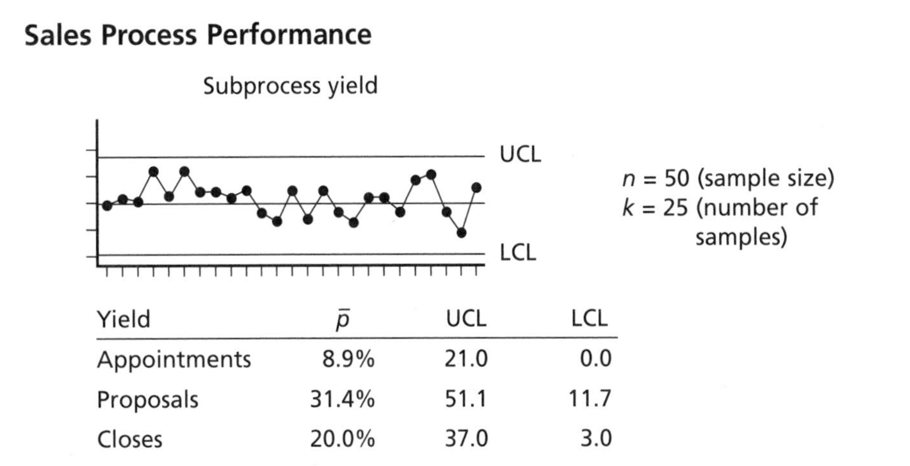

Yield	$\bar{p}$	UCL	LCL
Appointments	8.9%	21.0	0.0
Proposals	31.4%	51.1	11.7
Closes	20.0%	37.0	3.0

closed. Someone in the class uses a spreadsheet on a laptop computer to confirm the results, rounding the final control limits but not the intermediate steps. The band of normal variation for each looks fairly wide.

My mind is spinning with thoughts I can barely keep up with. There are implications for our compensation plans and incentive programs I can feel but can't really grasp. If we expect natural variation, should we save special rewards for reps whose performance exceeds the good side of their own normal control limits? What about reps whose performance is on the low side of the UCL? I guess that it would make most sense to incent people in all the sales-related departments for introducing breakthrough-type improvements as operationally defined by SPC. Whoa! This is scary. I'm talking as if I halfway understand this stuff.

Dr. Selden remarks that everybody has earned their afternoon break, after all that work.

Calculating Theoretical Output

After the break, Dr. Selden draws the group's attention to an earlier diagram.

"You remember the example of chained probabilities we looked at early this morning, don't you? Who will calculate the output we might expect out of this process for me?"

After all this work with multiplication, division, and square roots, the math is a breeze for the group members. They're actually excited to see the outcome of their sales process. Someone quickly says, "5589.2." "Hang on" someone else shouts out, "You forgot these are percentages!" "The real output is only half a percent: 0.55 percent!" "Yup, that's what I got," someone else says. The number is very small. There's a stunned silence for a moment.

The class may be quiet, but my mind is racing. I know there is an implication here about specifications in the sales process. If the total output is only 0.55 percent, our costs and income had better be set accordingly, or we'll lose our shirts! I wish I had more time to think about this, but Dr. Selden is asking another question.

"I told you that a sales process engineer could use measurement to find the constraints in a process. Knowing what you do about this process, do you see any?"

The class thinks for a bit now. "I don't think you've given us enough information to answer that," someone says.

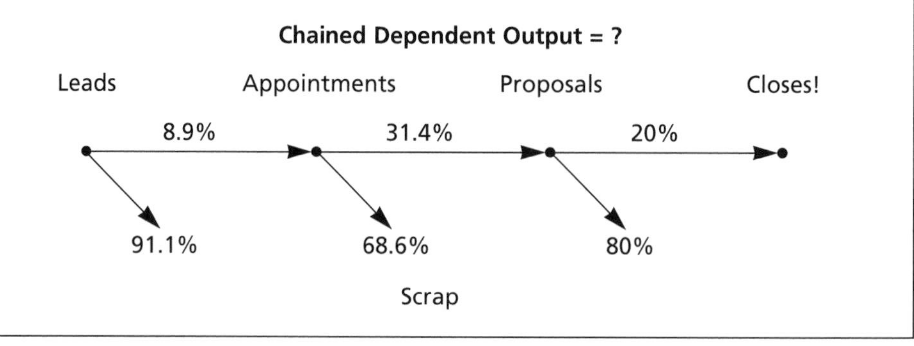

"Why is that?" asks Dr. Selden.

"Well, you told us that we should be concerned with four main dimensions—cost, time, quantity, and quality—right? We don't know the cost, and as far as time is concerned, we didn't measure that. I don't see stock piling up in front of any of the subprocesses. I don't see any bottlenecks: each process worked on everything it was given. All the *p* chart told us was the percent yield." This is a good exchange. The class is listening very closely.

"Did all the leads turn into closed deals?"

"No."

"Remember, the term *bottleneck* is a good word when working with physical obstructions. *Constraints* is a much better generalized term to use: A constraint might not always be a bottleneck in the literal sense. Try setting different yields to 100 percent and look at the impact on the overall theoretical performance we might obtain."

Ah. The light just went on. At each step, the process failed to convert 100 percent of what it was given into good output. Low quality is the constraint! Since the first step is worse than the rest, I guess the very first step is the worst.

Someone asks a final question. "This is the third time you said, 'This is how our sales process *might* perform,' and you also used the word *theoretical*. Didn't we just measure its *actual* performance?"

"You'll get the answer to that question when we conduct the last experiment today."

Experiment: Detecting Improvement

"A sales process engineer will need a reliable way to detect whether improvement is actually occurring. We've learned a lot from what you just did, but we're only halfway there, aren't we?

"All we've done so far is measure the performance of our current processes. You plotted the points and the upper and lower control limits. Did you observe any out-of-control points?"

Heads shake back and forth, "No."

"The way this process is set up, the odds of seeing an out-of-control point are about three in 1000. Not likely, but still possible just by chance. Okay. We have stable processes. Let's see how we can use SPC to detect change."

The group members with the p chart at 20 percent ($n\bar{p} = 10$) are asked to bring their bead box up front. Without telling the rest of the class what he is doing, Dr. Selden asks one of the participants to change the beads without revealing what he has done to the rest of the group. Dr. Selden announces that a professional sales process engineer has examined one of the group's processes and has indeed improved it.

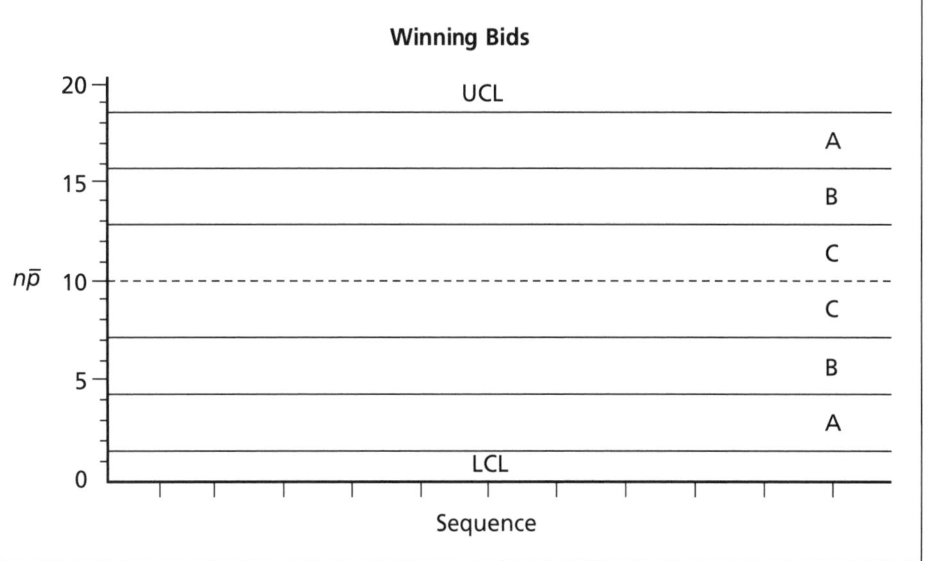

Next, Dr. Selden asks participants to draw a new scale on the back of their graph paper. The mean line is drawn at 10, a UCL at 18.5, and an LCL at 1.5. Then Dr. Selden asks the group members to look in the section titled "Tests for Special Causes" in Appendix C and divide the space between their upper and lower control charts into six equal parts, just as the charts in Appendix C are divided into zones C, B, and A.

Change Is Detected!

Dr. Selden directs the participants to the eight tests presented in Appendix C.

"Look at test one. It says that even one point beyond Zone A indicates a special—assignable—cause is present. Look over the other tests. If any of the other tests are met, the odds are very great that an assignable cause is also present.

"Your charts all look like the bid closing group's chart. Pretend for a moment that you are in charge of detecting whether our sales process engineer has made a genuine change or not."

Dr. Selden asks the bid closing group members to scoop new samples from their container and call out the results. He instructs everyone to plot the results as they are called out and look to see whether any of the tests for special causes are met. The first draw is nine.

"Plot the nine. Which zone does it fall into? Were any special tests met?"

The group answers, "No," and Dr. Selden asks for another scoop. This time it's an eight. Dr. Selden repeats his questions. Someone comments that it's hard to compare all the tests against the results. It's all too new. Dr. Selden replies that with practice it becomes easier; modern software can chart and detect out-of-control patterns automatically.

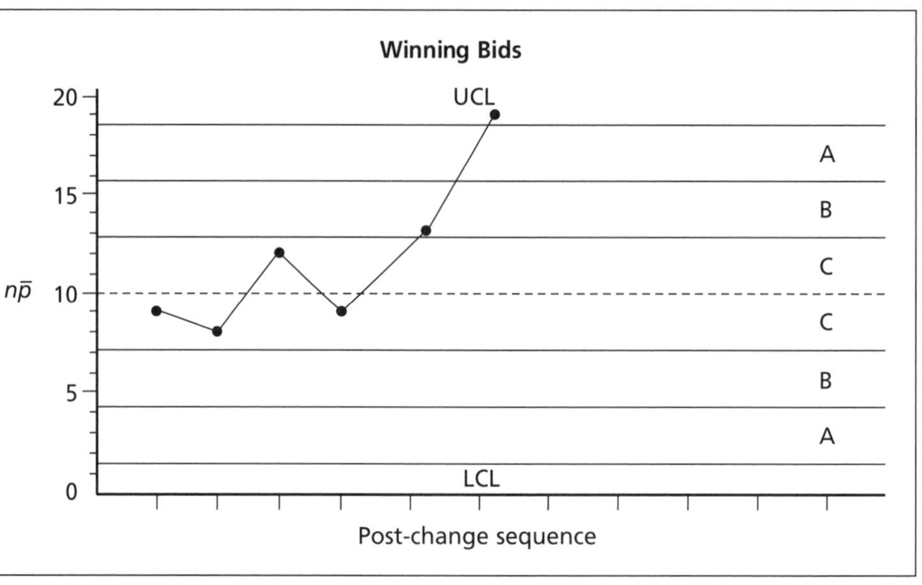

Still no tests have been met. The next scoop is a 12, followed by a nine and a 13. "The 13 is in Zone B!" someone says, "But it doesn't meet a test." Then a 19 is drawn. Someone shouts out that Test 1 has been met!

"We caught a change after six samples. Can you understand that it may take more or less trials the next time? Now, think! What if our measurement system set the time between samples at one week. It would have taken six weeks to detect a result! And what if you had promised results in three weeks? The change may have been genuine, but it took time to show it!"

Dr. Selden asks the sales process engineer to reveal what he did to the beads. The "engineer" says he removed 100 bad beads from the 1000 total beads in the container. Before the change, the container held 800 bad beads. After the change it contained 700 bad beads, for a total of 900 in the container.

Sales process engineers will be able to help their firms better plan the time spans necessary to detect change, given the specific amounts of improvement anticipated.

What Size Change Can SPC Detect?

"We just saw that using attribute measures, we were able to detect a change in the process. Percentage-wise, how great was the change for the good, pre versus post? Work it out."

Hmmm. More math. Okay. Before the change, there were 200 good beads and 1000 total in the box. The ratio was one to five, or 20 percent good beads. With 100 bad beads removed, the ratio is 200 to 900, or 22.22 percent. Dividing 22.22 by 20, that's 1.11: an 11 percent improvement. I guess it took six tries to tell that it really occurred, because natural variation was masking it. That could easily happen in any of our own improvement efforts, too, I think.

"You could try your own experiments to see how long it would take to detect greater or lesser improvements. You could even ask a statistician to help you calculate the probability of detecting a change within a certain number of tries, given a certain starting mix and ending mix, and so forth. In other classes, I've seen it take up to 20 scoops before a change of this magnitude was detected. Now, what were the results you've been promising your company?

"In my experience, when using attributes data, you'd end up wishing you could detect smaller changes sooner and using smaller samples. Why? It's less expensive! Less tedious! Who wants to collect samples when the minimum size has to be 50 or more? You'd do it if that was the only choice available. But there's an easier way.

A Quincunx

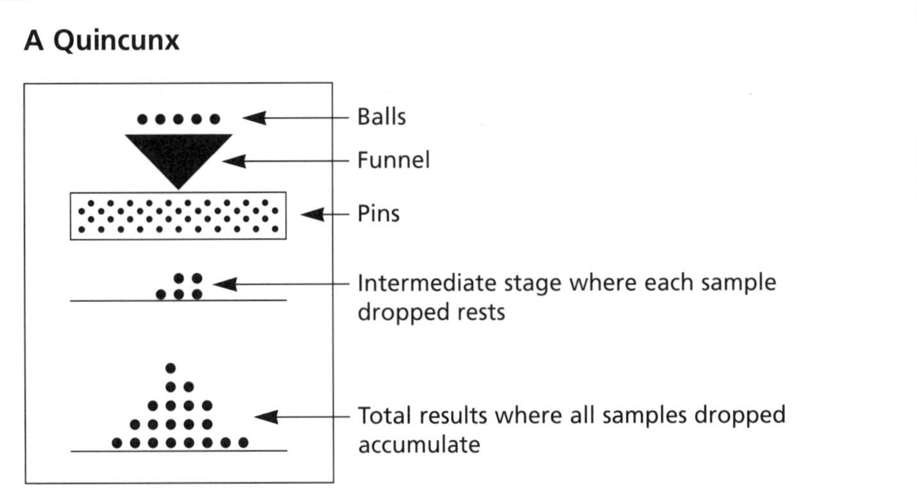

"The solution? Use variables data whenever you can. Think back to this morning. Attributes data are pass/fail in nature. Any one measure doesn't tell you how close you are to the goal, just that it passed or failed. If we lost a proposal, we usually don't know whether it was a close miss or a complete disaster. Variables data tell you in specific terms how near or far you are away from any particular specification. Now you are in a better position to understand why we need to learn the distinction between variables and attributes measures earlier.

"In this next experiment, I'll drive this point home graphically. The experiment uses a computerized version of a machine invented in the 1870s by Sir Francis Galton, the brilliant founder of biostatistics, to assist in studying probability theory. It's called a *quincunx*—pronounced *kwin-kuncks*."

Dr. Selden projects something on the screen that looks like a pokino machine. At the top, red balls are held in a funnel. Four to 10 balls can be set to drop in groups. They pass through a series of pins which causes them to bounce around. The sample rests in chutes at a center level. The way the balls stack makes it easy to see a physical histogram of their distribution. Then, the balls fall straight down to accumulate in stacks along the bottom of the device. As they accumulate they form a frequency distribution of all the balls that have fallen. Dr. Selden explains that the original quincunx used real balls, pins, slides, and chutes.

The Quincunx Experiments

"The software I am using for this experiment is called Quincunx/PC (Johnson 1993). With it we can adjust variables very easily. It automatically tracks the results and plots the control charts for us, too. [Someone says, "Good!" in a loud stage whisper. The class laughs.]

Dr. Selden sets up the Quincunx/PC to drop five balls per sample, centered on the position marked "40," telling the class to think of this as representing a variables sales process measure, namely dollars. With each sample the class can see the results accumulating and a frequency distribution forming. After 25 samples fall Dr. Selden sets the software to plot the mean, UCL, LCL, and display the A, B, and C zones for the samples that have already fallen. The chart is an $\bar{X}$ and *R* chart. The mean is $39.84, the UCL is $43.15, and the LCL is $36.55.

"That was our process before improvement. I'll move the funnel to $41 to simulate a slight improvement in the typical order size. Watch as the points are plotted on the chart. Use your test patterns. Tell me when you detect the change."

After just two samples, with means of $42 and $44.20, Test 1 is met. To make a point, Dr. Selden runs nine more samples before one of the tests is met again.

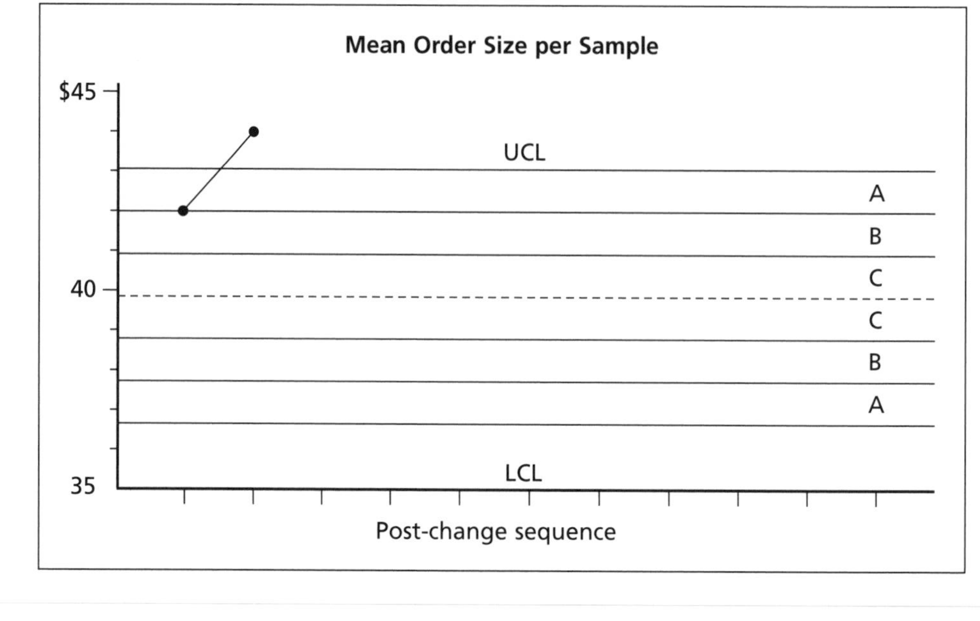

Food for Thought

This knowledge is giving me a feeling of power, like I have tools to work with that I never had before. I like this SPC business, the idea that you can use data from a process that's up and running. With the little experimental design background I've been exposed to, my understanding was that when you run an experiment you have to stop the work and control conditions received by each group very precisely. SPC seems a lot easier.

The difference between variables and attributes data really struck home with this last experiment. With sample sizes of five and 25 samples, we only needed to collect data on 125 items. When we were using attributes data we needed 150 items just for three scoops full. Variables data is the way to go, I guess. Hey, I sound like an old hand at this.

The other thing that struck me was how much tighter the control limits were when we used variables data. The control limits on the attributes data spanned a total of 20 to 40 points, depending on where the mean fell. The variables data we just took had control limits spanning a total of under seven points. That must explain some of its sensitivity, I bet.

The people who use these techniques in the sales process are going to be real pioneers. I've never heard of anyone using these approaches before in sales. Maybe I've just not been reading the right material. Come to think of it, I don't see many charts of any sort in the more popular magazines that the sales and marketing managers read.

In customer service, I've looked at our help desk operation in our computer center. They have charts up all over the place. Average call time, time on hold, number of calls per topic, and so forth. Are the employees using them in the same way a process engineer would? I don't remember seeing control limits charted. I wonder if that makes it more difficult to act on the results in the way a real engineer would?

In sales, I've seen people react as if a new, pet approach works after they only have one or two data points. We're usually told to implement a so-called improvement the minute the results seem even a little positive. It doesn't look like we're justified in doing that. Even though we met Test 1 after just two ball drops following the process change, it took nine drops the second time. Our current methods feel primitive compared to where we could be if we used the techniques we're learning today. Our current methods make me feel like I'm reading tea leaves sometimes. What I'm concerned about is that our current approaches may be even more misleading than we've considered.

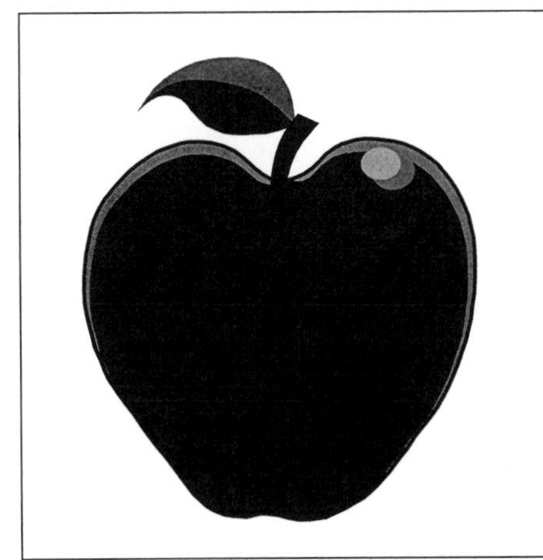

Part 4: Simulation and Modeling

> I'm a great believer in luck and I find the harder I work the more I have of it.
>
> —*Stephen Leacock*

Objective

By the time we finish this topic you will be able to

- List five basic elements of sales process modeling.
- Use a simple sales process simulation to model the effects of changing two important variables.
- Understand the role experimental design can play in helping to improve the sales process.
- Explain how variation plays a role in limiting the total output of a linked system.

The Importance of Being Able to Model

"Have any of you ever built model airplanes and buildings or set up a dollhouse with tiny furniture?

"I'll confess something. I used to spend hours and hours building models of all sorts: tanks, ships, planes, and buildings out of blocks. I never once thought that what I was building was real. I enjoyed what I was doing—it was fun—but I always knew it was play, not real. Do you know what I mean? [Heads bob in agreement.]

"When I was growing up, one of my childhood friends went to school at the Pratt Institute of Design in New York. I visited him once. In his apartment were models of buildings, complete with trees, roads, parking lots, and landscaping. He was very talented. The models were rendered in amazing detail.

"I don't think he felt that what he had constructed was just for play, do you? With those models, he could visualize the results of his real-life architectural blueprints. Ideas could be sold. Investors could see what they were getting.

"How many of you have visited a lab that uses models and small-scale experiments to test ideas before they are tried out in real life? Any examples?"

One of the group members says his firm has a test lab to try new engine designs. Another says her firm uses a miniature paper mill. Someone else says his firm uses a water tank to test different shapes of hulls. Another says her firm uses computer modeling to test how plastic will flow into molds they create. Still someone else says his firm uses a test kitchen to try new recipes.

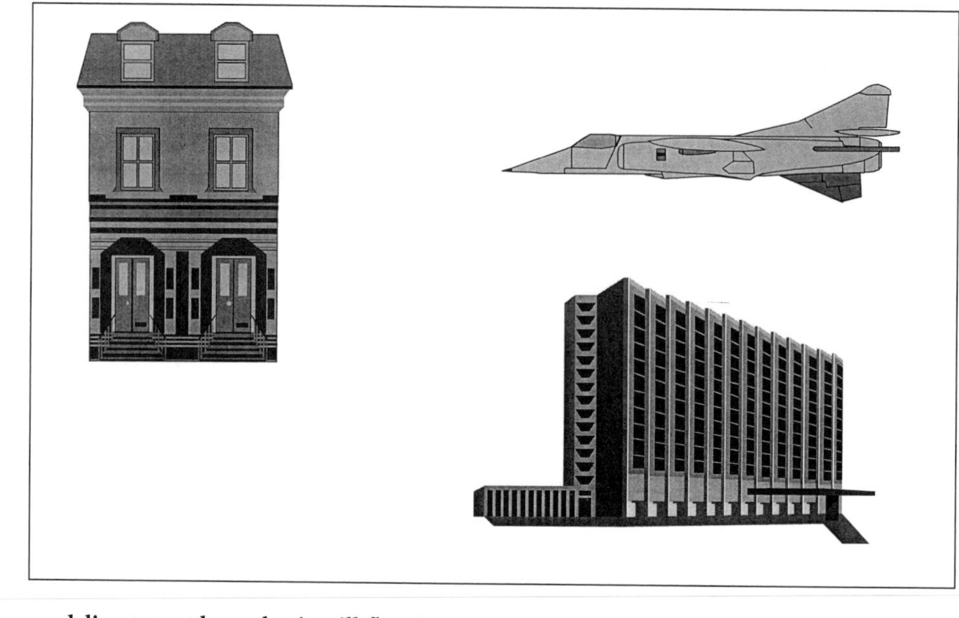

"Would you agree that models can be useful? Would you agree that to the degree a field is able to model the elements under study, that field exhibits a higher degree of professionalism and can more easily promote advancements?

"In the hands of children, models are just for play. In the hands of adults they can help change the world."

What Do We Need to Model a Sales Process?

"Using engineering to help spot and prevent problems once they occur is a step forward. That is a skill we'll all need to have. There is another form of engineering that we haven't talked much about until now: design engineering. Why not use models to help predict the effects of a change before it occurs?

"I need to ask you a question. Please be candid. Have any of you ever used a model or simulation to help design a change in your sales process? [No one answers.] But you've used word processing software to create a model of a mass mailing to customers before you sent it, right? You've used page layout software to mock up a new brochure, haven't you? Those are design tools that sales and marketing people use all the time. Even with such design tools, what type of design tool are we still missing in sales, marketing, and service?"

One of the class members says page layout tools really don't really simulate a process. She says the interaction between causes and effects is missing.

"Remember the definition of a *process?* Inputs converted into outputs, right? Do you agree that a tool that could model the *dynamic* interactions found in the sales process would be useful to a professional sales process engineer? [The class agrees. Dr. Selden is beaming.] There is so much room in this field for pioneers!

"So let's think about it. What do we need in order to simulate a *sales* process?"

General discussion follows. Dr. Selden then summarizes five points of his own. He says a modeling tool and media are needed to help visualize and build a scale model. He says a general knowledge of the subject matter, the process flow, is needed to put the parts in the right place. To proportion the dimensions correctly, relevant process data are required. The ability to view the quantitative relationships between input and output over time must also be set in place or the model will be static and not reflect the actual dynamics of how the elements interact once set in motion. Last, there must be a way to check the validity of the model against real life or the predictive value of the simulation is questionable. He comments that further exploration may reveal the need for other ingredients, but that these five provide a starting point.

> **Five Ingredients for Modeling a Sales Process**
>
> 1. Modeling tools and media
> 2. Understanding of general process flow
> 3. Relevant process data
> 4. Knowledge of quantitative, dynamic relationships over time
> 5. Way to test model against reality

The Sales Process Spreadsheet Experiment

The implications of what we're talking about now are staggering. There's a whole new profession here, unfolding before my eyes. I know industrial simulations exist, but I've never seen one applied to the marketing, sales, and service process. This session has presented a string of great ideas that obviously work in other fields. I can't wait to get back to my office and try some of them.

"At times I have invited leading makers of industrial process simulation software to speak at special sessions I host. A leading maker of such software once called me a visionary for seeing the potential such tools hold in our field. I felt flattered. It never occurred to me that such an obvious application could be characterized as visionary. He had never thought of doing it before. No one had asked him to, either. Do I hear opportunity knocking?

"For this experiment I'm going to use a primitive process simulation tool. No doubt you already own one: a spreadsheet! Analysts use spreadsheets all the time to record and model data: marketing results, pricing alternatives, cost structures, budgets, and so forth. We have the ingredients of a sales process simulation laying around the shop in bits and pieces. They just need to be hooked up."

	A	B	C	D	E	F
3					Unit Sales	Total Sales
4			Quantity	Yield	Cost	Cost
5		Leads	4000	0.25	2	8000
6		Contacts	1000	0.2	10	10000
7		Presentations	200	0.4	250	50000
8		Estimations	80	0.8	300	24000
9		Proposals	64	0.135	400	25600
10		Closes	8	1	500	4000
11						-121600
12	Value per Close		100000			
13	Sales		800000			
14						
15	%COGS	70%	-560000			
16	Gross Margin		240000			
17						
18	%G&A	15%	-120000			
19	Sales Cost		-121600			
20	GSA		-241600			
21						
22	Operating Income		-1600			
23						
24	Operating Margin	0%				

Dr. Selden directs the audience to a live spreadsheet projected on the screen. On it, the steps of a hypothetical sales process are displayed. The cost of each step is displayed, together with the yield at each stage and the quantity each step passes on to the next. The impact on the bottom line is also represented.

"Right now, this company is losing $1600. Let's experiment. What do you think will happen if we double the number of leads we're getting from 4000 to 8000? [Someone says, "You'll lose money twice as fast!"]

"The nice thing about a simulation is that we don't have to guess. We can play our hunches and see what happens in a no-risk environment."

Dr. Selden changes the number of leads to 8000. Now the company is *making* $11,300, a result some find counterintuitive.

Our Sales Process Research Program

"One nice thing about a spreadsheet simulator is it allows us to adjust different variables that might make a difference and test their relative impact. For example, instead of doubling the number of sales presentations, what if I increased the close rate from 13.5 percent to 20 percent? I won't ask you to guess. Let's just plug in the new number and see what happens.

Operating income jumps to $56,400! Dr. Selden asks people to call out different variables and numbers. He plugs in the changes, resetting the simulator each time. Participants are watching how various changes affect the bottom-line performance.

I'm getting another insight. Obviously, it's better to try changing certain variables rather than others, instead of grabbing onto the first one you think of, such as doubling the sales force. Some pinpoint changes seem to achieve huge effects.

"In real life, you usually have neither the resources nor permission to change everything at once. We'll take this fact of life into account as we conduct our sales process research program according to some simple instructions. This will go quickly. Work as individuals."

Dr. Selden first asks the class members to quickly choose one business output variable they think is important. Next, he asks everybody to pretend they are sales process engineers with limited resources. They may pick only two process variables; they may change each by a factor of only 10 percent. The participants look at the example on the screen and begin to write their choices.

When they finish Dr. Selden calls on several people. They present three cases, which Dr. Selden writes on a flip chart, calling it the company's sales process research program for the year. He simulates the results, resetting it after each case study. Everyone else is instructed to write down what happens.

Research Program Instructions

- Pick an output you feel is important

  ____

- Plan to vary two settings (up to 10% each)

  a. ______________________________

  b. ______________________________

- Which seems to be most optimal combination of settings?

  a. Set ______________________ at ______________________

  b. Set ______________________ at ______________________

Note: This experiment does not include variability as a factor.

The great marketing genius David Ogilvy so respected the power of empirical research that the Advertising Research Foundation established a prize in his honor—the David Ogilvy Award for Research Excellence (Enrico 1995).

Emotional Engineering Can Be Expensive

"First, I want to thank you for volunteering your guesstimates in public. Even in this type of no-lose, neutral situation, that takes some intestinal fortitude. It takes courage because our environment often makes people fearful of being wrong, even when being wrong doesn't matter. So I applaud you!

"In the past we've made many decisions on the basis of *emotional* engineering by playing a hunch or by following a fixed philosophy. Let's see what happens when we follow a more systematic approach.

"Refer back to the original spreadsheet and the flip chart in front of you. Can anyone spot the management philosophy behind Case 1? [No one answers.]

"Look at what we did in Case 1. We went for what appeared to be the "big opportunities." We increased the *highest quantity* item, names, by 10 percent. The multiplying effect should have been to really pour a huge number of leads into the system. We decreased the *highest cost-consumer* on the books: cost per close. That should have really helped our bottom line. The philosophy made perfect sense! We should have a tremendous impact. We did! We turned a loss into a profit!

"I gave that philosophy away. See what I am asking now? What was the management philosophy in Case 2? What emotional engineering principle did we follow?"

Someone says, "Open up the tightest yield bottlenecks first: the yields for proposals and contacts."

Results of the Group's Sales Process Research

Case 1

—Quantity of names increased 10%; cost per close decreased 10%

—Result: operating income increases to $1750

Case 2

—Yield on proposals and yield on contacts increased 10%

—Result: operating income increases to $17,600

Case 3

—Yield on proposals increased 10%; presentation cost decreased 10%

—Result: operating income increases to $17,900

"Excellent! The results we got were much, much better, relative to the first philosophy. Then along comes Case 3. What appeared to be the management philosophy there?

"That seemed to be open the tightest relative bottleneck—the proposal yield—and reduce the highest absolute cost—which happened to be in presentations."

"Very good! The last results there were best of all! Who can say with supreme confidence that we have at long last found the very *best* philosophy? [No one speaks.]

"I think you can see how expensive emotional engineering can be."

"Best Way" Found Through Careful Analysis and Empirical Study

"Why aren't you speaking? What's wrong? Isn't Philosophy 3 the best?"

One young lady says, "It's hard to know the best when there are so many other things we still haven't tried." An older gentleman says, "And we'd have to take into account the cost of making these changes, wouldn't we?"

One fellow comments, "Maybe that's part of the point. Using a simulator we could model all that before we tried anything out. The way things are working in my company, we haven't done any of this type of modeling, and we're about to spend millions of dollars giving our salespeople laptop computers and software."

Another participant observes, "So you could wind up with the worst of all worlds. You might suboptimize part of the process that wasn't any kind of cost problem or constraint at all and spend tons of money without seeing any bottom-line impact."

"That's okay," the fellow replies, "Our vice president told us to do it." The class roars with laughter.

"So what should we do instead," someone else asks, "count beads? I'd look pretty silly sitting in my office doing that." The laughter continues.

I'm deep in thought, hardly listening, I'm afraid. If the sales process research program experiment doesn't show that we have to beware of what Dr. Selden calls emotional engineering, *nothing does. The manager who pounds on the table and demands, "More leads!" would have achieved far less than a couple of well-targeted 10 percent improvements. And it looks like finding the most effective improvements is not always a matter of following apparently 'sound' or 'common-sense' management philosophy. I feel like all my props have just been kicked out from under me. I also feel like I'm being shown a better way. For sure I'm going to model some of the changes we've been talking about in my company before I spring an expensive mistake on my entire sales and marketing group. Maybe counting beads would be the best thing I could do to understand what's going on!*

"We count beads to learn about the fundamental nature of process dynamics. Once you understand the real nature of sales process dynamics, you're better equipped to start looking at the real thing. Often the best approach is found most quickly through careful analysis and systematic empirical study. Otherwise the best solution may be overlooked, drowned out by the voices of tradition and so-called common sense.

"We have time for one last experiment. In many ways, it's the most important."

The Penny Experiment

"Using a spreadsheet as a simulator has many advantages. Spreadsheets are cheap and plentiful. Everyone has one! The trouble is, like any tool, spreadsheets have disadvantages, too. One of these problems is quite serious. As a modeling tool, spreadsheets present a bit too much of a blank slate. Without the prompting and options that a true process simulator offers, it's easy to leave important pieces out. We'll see what the other problem is in the next few minutes."

We've covered so much today, it's hard to imagine what else is left to learn. I'm exhausted physically, but my adrenaline is kicking in. I can't wait to see this last experiment.

Dr. Selden points to six name tents on the table. They say in big letters *Customers, Leads, Appointments, Needs Analysis, Proposals,* and *Orders.* Each sits behind a dish. Selden pours a pile of pennies in the dish labeled customers. Someone in the room yells, "Money!" Lots of people chuckle at that remark. Dr. Selden holds up a pair of dice, shakes them, and throws them on the table. Everyone is listening closely now.

"These dice are not loaded, let me assure you. [There's laughter as he holds one die up in the air.]

This die has the numbers zero, one, two, four, five, and six printed on it. What is the average of those numbers? [Someone says, 'three.'] Very good! That's right: three.

"This die isn't loaded, but it is special. Listen closely. This represents the average *available capacity* one stage of the process has to move items into the next stage. The spreadsheet simulation experiment we saw a moment ago didn't represent the capacity of each stage very realistically. The spreadsheet made it seem as though the capacity to handle input at each stage was *unlimited.* Whatever this die rolls, that's what gets moved. That's our capacity.

"There's one other thing that was missing in the spreadsheet simulation. I'll let you think about that for a moment as I continue explaining the Penny Experiment we're about to perform."

Note that sales and marketing texts label an individual potential customer a *suspect, prospect,* or *customer,* depending on the stage of the sales process the individual has progressed to so far. For this experiment, potential customers are simply called *customers* throughout.

Downstream Capacity: Limited by Supply

"Let's say we've got a sales process where the customers have the money and they want something we've got—our goods and services.

"In the Penny Experiment we'll construct a sales process that converts those needs into sales. First, I'm going to fill the pipeline with three pennies at each of the four stages sitting between Customers and Orders. That's our average capacity.

Dr. Selden drops three pennies into each of the dishes labeled *Leads, Appointments, Needs Analysis,* and *Proposals.*

"Why did I label the third stage 'needs analysis?' [No one answers.] It fits better on the card than 'thorough needs analysis.'

"Forget about percentage yields and costs for the moment. We're simplifying this model to focus on the effect subprocess capacity has on final output. Think. Each of our subprocesses has the average capacity to pass on *three* customers per week to the next stage. The pipeline has three pennies to start with at each stage. So how many pennies should we have in the orders dish at the end of *four* weeks?

Someone in the class says, "12."

"Three pennies times four weeks equals 12 orders. Everything you've learned up to now leads you to conclude that. Listen! In real life, a downstream process can work only on what it's given by the process immediately linked upstream. But all processes

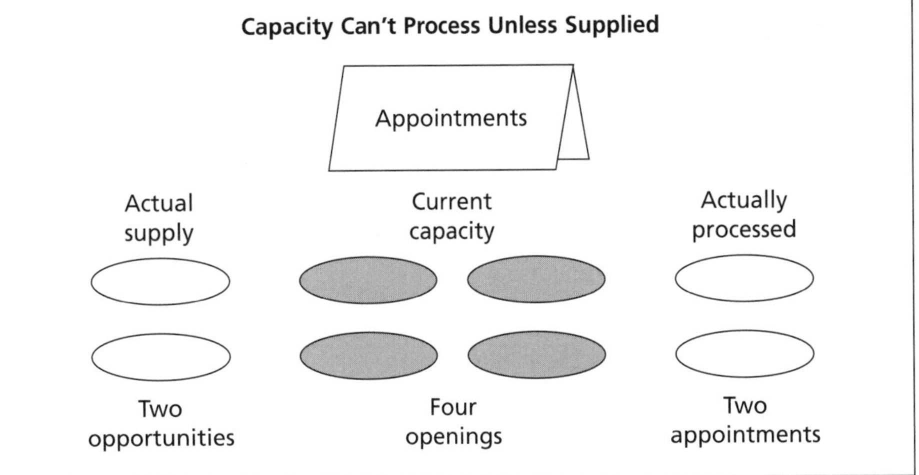

exhibit variability! I'm going to use this special die to model process variability: the other missing element in our spreadsheet simulator.

Dr. Selden points out that Eliyahu Goldratt described a similar experiment in his renowned book *The Goal* (1992), using matchsticks and an ordinary die to model a manufacturing process. Dr. Selden urges the class members to read *The Goal* if they have not already done so.

The Impact of Dynamic Variability on Output

"This little die looks helpless and innocent, doesn't it? It's not. It's vicious!

Dr. Selden calls forward five participants, each representing a stage in the process.

"Now we'll learn how variability impacts a *dynamic* system. All processes exhibit variability, don't they? If we are to simulate a live, dynamic process, the effects of that variability must be modeled, as well!"

Beginning with the proposal closer, each of the participants is given the die to roll. After each roll, the process is allowed to place that many pennies into the next dish downstream, for example, from the Proposals dish into the Orders dish. But there's a catch. Each subprocess is not allowed to move any more pennies than they have in the immediate upstream supply dish they need to draw from—just as in reality. And just as in real life, in their turn—corresponding to a week's work—the die will vary the number of potential customers they actually can work with. Dr. Selden writes the results on screen so the class can follow what happens next.

Week one begins. The first roll is a five—representing an above-average capacity to do the job. Proposals is elated at first, but then he looks at his dish. He only has three to move into the orders category, and now the Proposals dish is empty. "Come on, Needs Analysis," he says. Needs Analysis rolls a six! Way above average.

Results After Week 1: Three Orders as Predicted

Week 1	Customers	Leads	Appointments	Needs	Proposals	Orders
Dish: start	*"Tons"*	3	3	3	3	
Rolls	5	6	2	6	5	
Advances	5* ↘	3 ↘	2 ↘	3 ↘	3 ↘	
Dish: end	*"Tons"*	5	3 + 1*	2	3	3

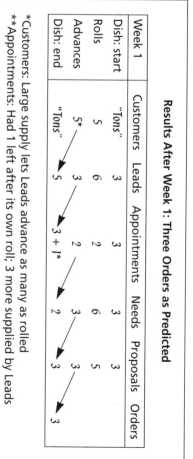

*Customers: Large supply lets Leads advance as many as rolled
**Appointments: Had 1 left after its own roll; 3 more supplied by Leads

Proposals is ecstatic, but now the Needs Analysis part of the pipeline is empty.

Needs Analysis looks on with expectation at the next roll, but Appointments only rolls a two. So the Appointments stage converts only two customers into a chance to do a needs analysis. One penny has to stay in the Appointments dish. Two pennies sit in the Needs Analysis dish. Leads rolls a six! All three leads are converted into appointments, filling the Appointments dish with four customers!

Finally, the marketing customer generator rolls her Advertising and Promotional die. It's a five!

At the end of week one, there are three orders, with three proposals, two needs analysis meetings, four appointments, and five new leads in the pipeline.

So far, the predicted outcome of three orders has been obtained.

The Process Begins to Unravel

Week two begins. Proposals rolls a two and moves two more pennies into the orders dish. Proposals groans as he realizes that he's slightly down for this week. One penny is left in the Proposals dish as Needs Analysis rolls. Proposals is clearly hopeful, but Needs Analysis rolls a zero. They both groan. No customers get moved into the Proposals stage this week.

"Oh, well," comments Needs Analysis. "Appointments are building up," he observes brightly, eyeing the dish with four pennies in it. Appointments rolls a two. Now Needs Analysis has four customers. It's as if a bulge was moving through a hose. This time Leads throws a zero.

"What are you doing to me? I need some customers!" says Appointments, who was left with two customers after the last throw. In the final throw of the week, Customers shakes the die over and over. Finally, she rolls a two. "The mighty marketing machine scores again!" someone laughs. Leads has added two more customers to the five leads they have already.

At the end of the second week there's a build-up of seven leads. There are only two appointments in the pipeline, but four customers are sitting in the Needs Analysis phase. Only one proposal sits in the hopper.

Supply Gaps Appear

Week 2	Customers	Leads	Appointments	Needs	Proposals	Orders
Dish: start	"Tons"	5	4	2	3	3
Rolls	2	0	2	0	2	
Advances	2 ↘	0 ↘	2 ↘	0 ↘	2 ↘	
Dish: end	"Tons"	2 + 5	0 + 2	2 + 2	0 + 1	2 + 3

Week 3	Customers	Leads	Appointments	Needs	Proposals	Orders
Dish: start	"Tons"	7	2	4	1	5
Rolls	6	0	5	6	2	
Advances	6 ↘	0 ↘	2 ↘	4 ↘	1 ↘	
Dish: end	"Tons"	6 + 7	0 + 0	2 + 0	4 + 0	1 + 5

Week three begins. Proposals throws a two, but only has one customer to move into the Orders category. The proposals dish is empty. Needs Analysis throws a six! All four customers in the Needs Analysis dish are moved forward. Appointments rolls a five.

"I'm wasting my talent," says Appointments, as he moves only two customers into the Needs Analysis phase. Leads shakes the die for a good 10 seconds, and blows on it for good measure. It's another zero!

"Argh!" he cries. Appointments makes his hands as if to strangle Leads. Everyone is laughing. Finally, Customers rolls. It's a six. "You stole my six," yells Leads, who is now sitting with a dish with 13 customers!

At the end of week three there are six orders. There are four proposals, two needs analyses, zero appointments, and 13 leads in the pipeline. The potential customers bowl is still chock-full.

The Devastating Effect of Variability

Week four begins. Everyone seems to feel a train wreck coming in slow motion. The effect on the volunteers is somewhat wearing, but their optimistic nature is keeping a smile on their faces for the most part.

Someone says, "Proposals, get shakin', man." The volunteers laugh again in spite of their results. Proposals rolls the die. It's a two. Two more orders are added to the total, leaving two customers in the proposal dish. Needs Analysis rolls. The die slips out of his hand and bounces onto the table in front of everyone. It's a zero.

"Let me roll that over again!" he shouts, but it's too late. Everyone sees the roll. He goes along with it, saying, "Only kidding." The room bursts into laughter. "No need for me to roll," says Appointments. His dish is empty. Dr. Selden asks him to roll anyway, "Just for the record." It's a two, but there's nothing to move.

Leads picks up the die and again shakes and shakes. You can almost see him willing the die to come up big so he can move some of that huge pile of leads into the appointments dish. Someone makes a snoring sound, and there's more laughter. When the throw comes up a zero—the third zero in a row for Leads—he just says, "I give up." He makes as if to take his seat.

The class is in stitches. Leads smiles again, remembering that it's only a simulation. Customers rolls the final throw of the week. She rolls a four and piles the pennies into the leads dish.

Hidden Variability Chokes Supply Chain

Week 4	Customers	Leads	Appointments	Needs	Proposals	Orders
Dish: start	*"Tons"*	13	0	2	4	6
Rolls	4	0	2	0	2	
Advances	4 ↘	0 ↘	0 ↘	0 ↘	2 ↘	
Dish: end	*"Tons"*	4 + 13	0 + 0	0 + 2	0 + 2	2 + 6

Finish	Customers	Leads	Appointments	Needs	Proposals	Orders
	"Tons"	17	0	2	2	8

The score at the end of week four is eight orders. The pipeline has two customers at the proposals stage, two at needs analysis, zero in appointments, and 17 in leads. There are still plenty of potential customers left.

"When I pointed out that engineers recommend bringing a process into control, how many of you doubted or didn't see the point of that advice? [Almost all of the class members raise their hands.] Please raise your hand if you better understand that advice now. [A roomful of hands goes up.] Variability can devastate a process if not controlled. Reduce variability, and you not only *learn* about your process. You *improve* it at the same time."

Dr. Selden comments that as part of his research on sales process dynamics he once continued this particular Penny Experiment out to 100 trials. The odds never "evened out." At trial 100, only 213 sales had been closed, only two-thirds of the "common-sense" outcome of 300.

The Power of Variability Reduction

"I don't want your self-sacrifice and efforts to go unrewarded. You have participated in this emotional roller coaster for the good of humanity."

Dr. Selden thanks the volunteers and asks the rest of the group to applaud them. He shakes their hands with a smile. Then he asks the entire group a question.

"What would happen if you substituted a die with less variability for the one you were just using? We know the answer: With zero variability we'd move three per throw, week in and week out. We'd have 12 sales at the end of four weeks: 50 percent more than we just got.

"Tell me one more time: How do you reduce variability?"

Someone says, "Remove or prevent the assignable causes.'"

"And how do you do that?"

"Using the 12 tools," another replies.

"Use the 12 tools. As you do, use all the tips, tricks, and knowledge of what you've learned elsewhere to improve the sales process, too. Everything else you've learned in sales, marketing, and customer service may still have great value. It's how you apply it that's different. We'll apply it in the context of systematic sales process engineering.

"Try the Penny Experiment yourself sometime. Use a die with different numbers on it, say, a four, three, three, three, three, and a two. Just put some stickers on a die you have at home. You don't even need to buy the special ones that I have. You'll find that the total throughput goes up, just by reducing variability.

"The ultimate expression of variability reduction would be a die that had all threes on it, wouldn't it? I asked this a moment ago. Again, what would the output be after four weeks with a die that had all threes on it?

Someone says, "12."

"Of course: 12. Now think back to everything we talked about not too long ago regarding specifications and capability. Do you remember the Taguchi loss functions? Remember the one that said, 'Nominal is best?' Now do you see why any variation from the target specification can produce those exponentially shaped loss functions? Those discussions aren't so theoretical after all, are they?"

"In the days that follow this workshop, think about how much money you could justify investing now to reduce the variability of the dice you throw in your own process."

An Inherent Danger in Spreadsheets

Dr. Selden pauses for a moment, gathering up the props from the Penny Experiment.

During this momentary pause I again find myself thrust deep into thought. I can see that a lot of the others are, too.

On one hand, I'm feeling a little overwhelmed—like trying to drink from a fire hose. On the other hand, I think I understand the key points. I see why it's so important to control variability. This concept was a bit abstract for me before, but now another loop has been closed. Even without changing the level *at which a process is performing, variability reduction will improve the overall output, all by itself.*

Something more subtle is rolling around in my mind, too—I'm not sure I have a complete handle on it yet. As they were rolling the die, some of the volunteers complained they were wasting their talent when they threw a number greater than they needed. Would this be like knocking yourself out to land a deal? Is this like the "too much sales" we talked about earlier? Is this like spending money on capacity we don't need? I'm going to have to think about this some more.

One thing I know for sure. We tell our reps to keep their pipeline filled. I wish some of them could have been here to see the reason why. I've never seen the concept presented in this way. I'm also pretty sure we don't define what levels a pipeline should be filled to. It seems we could create guidelines of some sort in this regard based on our sales process specifications.

"As we were conducting the Sales Process Spreadsheet and Research Experiments, I warned you that spreadsheets contain a serious inherent problem. I said they present almost too much of a blank slate.

"There is another, far more serious problem with spreadsheets as a tool for financial analysis. You have just seen a vivid demonstration of the dangers we face if we ignore variability as we come to understand and model our sales process. The Penny Experiment clearly demonstrates the need to reduce variability. As we conducted the simulations, maybe some of you were thinking that a dedicated simulation tool could overcome this problem.

"Let me ask you a simple question. How many of you have programmed a spreadsheet to incorporate dynamic variability in your financial models? [Dr. Selden's voice rises.] You haven't! That's the answer! Dynamic process modeling goes way beyond guessing at a few max-min numbers and plugging in worst-case scenarios. We've all been using spreadsheets to justify our projects. Have you ever created a dynamic model with them, one that includes variability as a truly dynamic factor? How many of you with a background in management and financial accounting even covered this concept in school? On the job? This is a serious flaw.

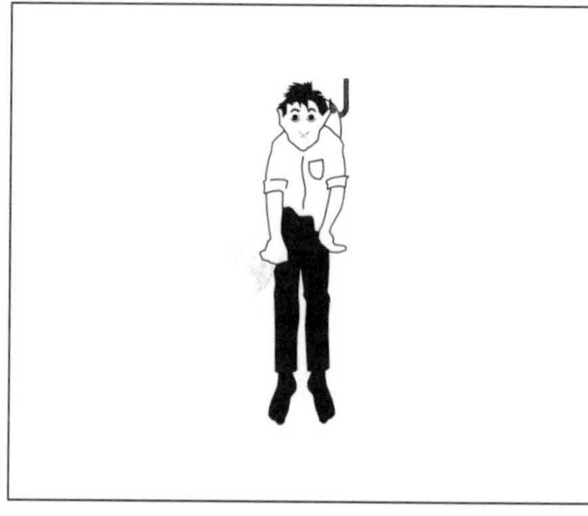

"Spreadsheets are wonderful tools. But I have my own hunch that countless project managers have been skewered by their project results because they've relied on traditional spreadsheets, set up to handle income and expense reporting, to predict events to come. This type of model has a severe shortcoming. Beware! The accounting model of income and expenses captured at a moment in time is static! Processes are dynamic! Beware!"

Conclusion

> Pleasing ware is half sold.
>
> —*Proverb*

The Customer Imperative

Following Part 4, Dr. Selden posts another quote: "Pleasing ware is half sold."

I wonder why Dr. Selden would post this particular quote, when the whole workshop has focused on sales, marketing, and customer service? This quote seems to take some of the responsibility from me and my role and give it to the products. Why is he reminding us about what the rest of the company produces?

Wait a second. Okay. Dang. Another loop just closed for me. Or maybe I just heard a note that has been playing all along, like a background theme throughout the workshop.

What I'm thinking is that Dr. Selden has been stressing that we need to know our customers to understand their specifications. To the extent we are able in marketing, sales, and customer service to uncover and communicate what customers find or would find pleasing, we can work as a team with the rest of our company to make our goods and services even more so! We have to be good listeners on a giant scale, one that goes far beyond just being a good individual listener. Our marketing people do a great job at this. I'm just thinking where we'd be if it all could be integrated better. Integrated marketing! *Here it comes, a new buzzword!*

It strikes me that this is the meaning behind the expression, "Understand what business you are really in." Thinking we are in business to sell only what we have today means we will be out of business tomorrow, when customer needs evolve. We also need to see ourselves as being in the improvement business.

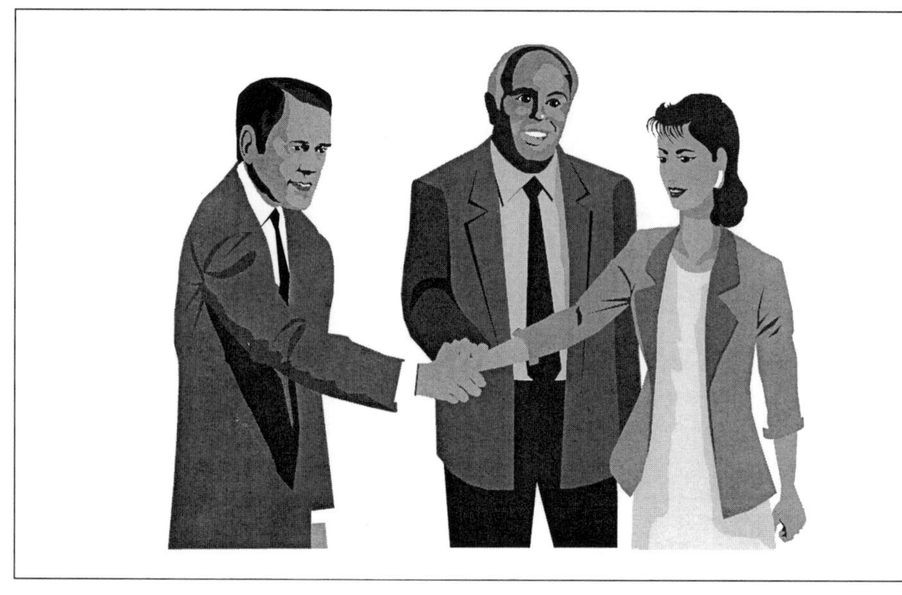

This will be another culture change. So often we train our people to sell what we have in stock and not to question the matter further. "We can't sell what we don't have." I understand that perfectly well. But it seems to me there's a longer-term view that is still compatible with short-term reality. A sales process engineer must find a way to systematically explore what the customer finds pleasing or lacking in what we have. There's no rule that says we can't readjust what we're selling to come closer to what the customer may want even more. This is a culture change our group can handle. In the meantime, I think that sales process engineering can improve the way we sell and help us better discover our customer's evolving needs at the same time. Maybe it can help us create a better structure *for ongoing improvement, too.*

Two Dimensions to Improvement

"Money is the score we count *after* the game is played. What do we have to do to achieve our profit score? As sales process engineers, what will be our focus?

"Once we truly understand our customer's requirements, the job of a sales process engineer is twofold: reducing defects wherever we find them and systematically finding new ways to exceed expectations. Some people will pursue this quest as a full-time profession. That is a matter for the future, as an agreed-upon body of knowledge and solid curriculum develop. In the meantime, many will absorb the basic principles and spirit and apply it to whatever they are doing. All of us can participate!

"Reducing defects will drive cost, waste, and time out of the process. It will cut variability and increase consistency. Defect reduction has an absolute limit: Once zero defects are reached, that's it. A low-cost, high-quality seller of widget X will sit supreme in the market for those widgets.

"Defect reduction takes many forms. I recently returned a shirt to L.L. Bean. The company not only sent me a refund check, they carefully boxed and returned an old photo of my mother I had accidently enclosed with the shirt! I was astounded such a large company would act with the *soul* and *common decency* of a real, honest person, that they would return my photo at their expense. They also had the *procedures* in place not to separate the photo from my return address! Defect reduction is not a cold, heartless goal that only efficiency experts are interested in. Defect reduction is *integrity made systematic.* It is also good word-of-mouth advertising. A company that performs at this level stands out.

Improvement: Both Finite and Infinite Goals

Reducing Defects

Exceeding Expectations

The quest is ongoing, never ending, and has at its heart fulfilling the golden rule

"On the other hand, since needs change, and since novelty itself can be a powerful attention-getter and reinforcer, the sales process engineer will always have a second goal—that of finding ways to exceed customer expectations, to create new ways of satisfying old needs, and yes, to create new needs entirely. That path is filled with more risk, since it is the path untrodden, by definition. That path has no limit. Ingenuity and creativity know no bounds. It is the future. A firm that fulfills new customer desires is a leader.

"We want sales and we want to reduce cost. Having one without the other is to go broke. Both customer focus and operational excellence are targets for the sales process engineer. Since these are also the goals of top executives, talented sales process engineers will be in demand.

"In short, there is a moral imperative to this new profession. The aim of the sales process engineer is to make it more structurally certain that we can treat our neighbors as we would like to be treated. At the heart of our profession lies the golden rule."

What will be the source of fundamental competitive advantage in the year 2000?

U.S. managers: 80 percent said "Quality"

Japanese managers: ~50 percent said "Quality"

The number one Japanese answer: "Capacity to create fundamentally new products and businesses."

Quality is becoming a base price of entry into the global market.

(Hamel and Prahalad 1994)

Our Journey Is Just Beginning

- Sales process engineering has powerful analytic tools at its disposal.
- Measurement has always been necessary. Now it is possible.
- To understand a process, we must understand its variation as well as its center point.
- SPC places impact evaluation within anyone's reach.
- Simulation and modeling the sales process helps visualize opportunities and reduces risk.
- Further learning and success require systematic application.

"I've reached some personal conclusions regarding the topics we've covered today and about this fledgling profession of ours. I'd like to know whether you agree with me as I share them with you.

"I contend that sales process engineering has powerful analytic tools at its disposal, as well as many well-tested philosophies to guide our initial explorations. Would you agree with me?

"I contend that we've felt measurement has always been necessary. Now I believe it is possible. In the future, we may be able to develop tests for changes in quality, cost, quantity, time, and variability that far surpass our traditional methods. With automation, auditing, sampling, and charting techniques at our disposal, I feel a new era in sales process measurement is dawning. Do you agree?

"I contend that to understand a process, we must understand its variation as well as its center point. To our dimensions of cost, quality, quantity, and time we must add a fifth: variation. Are you in agreement with me?

"I contend that setting up the sales process measurement system of the future will be a creative act requiring talent and imagination. Creativity is difficult. But it is also my belief that statistical process control is simple enough to use so that, once set up, the ability to detect changes in the sales process will be within almost anyone's grasp. Would you agree?

"I contend that, by simulating and modeling the sales process, we can visualize opportunities and reduce the risk inherent in our improvement efforts in ways not otherwise possible. Are we in agreement on that point?

"And finally, I contend that these skills hold tremendous potential for our organizations, but that, as with any other engineering thrust, success will come most quickly through a program of systematic application. Do you agree?"

The class agrees vocally with each of the points.

The Real Structural Breakthrough Required

"Our three days together are almost at an end, but I have a few more questions for you. If your experience agrees with my research, your own comments will point out a hidden element, which is silently impeding serious progress in sales process improvement. This is one of the most dangerous rocks and shoals we face, because it is inherent in our traditional corporate structure and hence unseen and unnoticed as a constraint. This is the last main point I'll cover with you today. Here are my questions.

"First, do you know what our largest companies currently spend on R&D? [People voice various answers.] It's between $3 and $4 out of every $100 in sales.

"Let me ask you something else. Who brings that money into the company in the first place?"

Someone shouts, "Nothing moves without the sale!"

"Right! Nothing moves without the sale.

"Now think about the way our R&D teams go about finding improvements and breakthroughs for their end of the business. [Dr. Selden pauses.] How much of your company's funding is dedicated to systematically improving the sales, marketing, and service processes with the same degree of professionalism and care? ["Ha. Not a dime!" shouts another voice from the back of the room. Everyone laughs.]

"How many of your firms are embarking on tremendous spending programs in the name of sales automation, integrated marketing, database mining, customer data warehousing, the Internet, or similar efforts, right now? [Almost everyone's hand goes up.]

"So let me get this straight. Your firms spend tremendous amounts of money on new product R&D, but they certainly aren't spending this kind of money on sales process R&D. Yet millions of dollars are being spent on changes: automation, restructuring, you name it. Many of these efforts are led by people who are either working at it as a temporary assignment or who won't even be with the company when the anticipated benefits are projected to accrue. And this is all in the name of improvement. Would you say that much of this spending is riding on emotional engineering, somewhere between a hunch and a hope?"

Dr. Selden holds out his hands in front of him.

"In the one hand we have millions of dollars of investment. In the other, our goal of improvement. Keeping the two apart, there are structural obstacles. What are they?"

The class mentions many: a lack of knowledge, training in the right concepts, a cadre of internal experts, information, the right culture, improperly allocated budgets, sufficient cross-company communication, the means for R&D-like testing, and others.

Current structural constraints . . .

- Lack of knowledge
- Lack of training and real expertise
- Lack of measurement information
- Culture
- Budget
- Cross-departmental influence lacking
- Limits on controlled testing

. . . have a structural solution.

"I sum up the required structural breakthrough for making serious progress in sales process improvement in one last recommendation: Corporations need a full-fledged, structurally endowed sales process engineering R&D department. Without it, progress will continue to be slow, characterized by hit-or-miss efforts, and filled with danger."

Recommendations for Management

- Personally lead creative vision
- Promote general orientation to sales process engineering
- Train staff of genuine sales process engineers
- Sponsor pilot connected to key goal
- Fund systematic sales process R&D effort

[Dr. Selden adopts a drill sergeant–like bearing.] "Class! We have obstacles! You are potential sales process engineers of the future! What does a sales process engineer do when facing an obstacle?"

From the middle of the room, with obvious enjoyment, rises a stage voice. "We eliminate or prevent the obstacle. Sir!" The class breaks out in laughter.

"You guys are great. You must have had a good teacher. [More laughter] Okay, when faced with a structural problem, an engineer builds structural solutions. What would you recommend that management do to overcome the obstacles you've mentioned. Any ideas?"

In the back of the room, a silver-haired gentleman stands. He speaks in a resonant, self-assured voice. Everyone turns to face him.

"Dr. Selden, I am a senior vice president in my firm. My organization is one of those Fortune 500 companies that happens to respect the value of research and development a great deal. We know that R&D is where our next meal comes from. What you've presented has struck a responsive chord. Someone has to lead the vision and plant the seed; that will start with me.

"Throughout this workshop I've been taking notes on a course of action. My plan starts tomorrow. I've already set up an appointment with our president to outline my ideas.

"First, I'm going to brief our entire top management on a sample of the sales process principles you've covered. It seems to me that many of the sales process engineering principles we've learned are similar to natural laws: we can ignore them, but it would be extremely disadvantageous to do so. We'll also spread these principles through the ranks so that people can put them to immediate use at their own level.

"Second, I'm going to fund an ongoing, systematic sales process improvement R&D function within our company. Your pictures of the rocks and shoals and bottlenecks makes it clear that we'll fail if we adopt a one-time 'project' mentality. Once one problem is eliminated, others will pop up; that's why our efforts must be endowed to be ongoing, as you say. In the past three days it's become clear to me that the typical 'project team' approach lacks follow-through and long-term goals. My vision is that this new department parallel our more established engineering and R&D efforts. In my field the rate of advancement is directly related to well-targeted R&D spending. I'm betting that relationship will hold true in the sales process arena, too.

"Third, to staff this effort, we need to find and train an internal group of sales process engineers. Perhaps you could recommend a good workshop? [He says this with a smile. Several of the class members laugh quietly, in spite of the feeling of gravity in the room.]

"Fourth, we'll lay out a course of systematic exploration and pilot tests, just as we would with any other R&D program. We'll get our experience and hopefully make progress at the same time. I'd like to get your thoughts on this concept when we have more time."

The rest of the class offers further comments. The general consensus is that improvements will be hit or miss in nature unless the effort to improve is more systematic and sustained than in the past.

A rationale for establishing a sales process R&D function is further discussed in Selden 1996.

DAY THREE

Personal Efforts at Any Level

Someone in the class comments, "Those steps are fine for people who are in authority already. Frankly, I'm not in the position this other gentleman is in—yet, anyway. I'd like to hear some practical suggestions that anyone can use. Some kaizen ideas, I guess you'd say."

"Class, what do you think? I'd like to draw on your thoughts and insights. We've got an excellent cross-section of corporate insiders here. Let's brainstorm, with the one proviso that these are ideas you could put to use immediately."

Dr. Selden jots down the ideas as they are mentioned. The flip chart fills quickly. Some of the ideas include the following:

• *Continue to advance personal knowledge.* Books, tapes, public or in-company workshops, and similar resources can be used to gain further insights and depth. This workshop has included many such citations.

• *Set personal sales process R&D goals.* A personal R&D goal to determine and control cause and effect in one's own sales process is virtually the same as learning how to consistently meet sales productivity improvement targets in the first place.

• *Paint a process picture; chart data on hand.* A big problem becomes smaller if one chips away at it. By using personal data on hand and the techniques learned, it is easier to isolate and control assignable causes. This is a necessary step no matter what the goal is.

- Continue to advance own knowledge
- Set personal sales process R&D goals
- Paint a process picture; chart data on hand

No Limit on Kaizen!

The ideas continue to flow. Comments from the group pour out.

• *Gather financial justification data to institutionalize.* Personal data can be gathered to show that the cost of sales process defects is much greater than the cost of preventing them. A case can be made to upper management that institutionalizing a systematic effort on a larger, long-term scale will be just as rewarding in the sales process arena as in any other area of business, as has been shown in the product development arena.

• *Use personal pilots for prove-out; learn by doing.* An institutionalized sales process engineering effort would use small-scale pilots to prove out sales process changes. There is nothing to stop an individual from doing the same thing on a personal basis. The more systematic the approach, the quicker what works would be sorted out from what doesn't work and the quicker personal success would be achieved.

• *Use qualified consultants to accelerate the effort.* A qualified, reputable consultant may be able to accelerate efforts on a departmental, divisional, or wider operational scale by helping to outline approaches that would otherwise take months or years to figure out internally.

- Gather financial justification to institutionalize.
- Use personal pilots for prove-out; learn by doing.
- Use qualified consultants to accelerate progress.
- Share information with other professionals.

Marketing professionals, sales process automation and improvement team leaders, and mid-level managers in sales and service management often have access to consultants that individual sales and service personnel do not have.

• *Share information with other professionals.* Joining a national professional association or participating in local chapter meetings and sharing information with others faced with similar problems is an opportunity available to anyone. The investment in participation is slight compared to the value of the insights often available just for the asking.

Professional Certification and Personal Enjoyment

Dr. Selden offers a couple of his own recommendations to wrap up the list of things an individual can do to use the principles of sales process engineering, regardless of position.

"Not everyone is interested in becoming a professional artist, musician, or engineer. But anyone can make a hobby out of a field, develop his or her skills at his or her own pace, and learn to enjoy, understand, and appreciate it!

"Whether a professional, amateur, or a member of the audience, we can all approach this subject with the same degree of zest and enthusiasm we display for anything else in life!

"Whether you use this knowledge as a way to fulfill professional, personal, or moral goals, I urge you to enjoy the journey, regardless of your aims and aspirations!

"People just entering a field are often not aware of efforts already underway to support advancement. I'd like to tell you about two professional societies in particular. After working in the field for some 20 years, these are the two I've come to feel are at the absolute center of this developing field. They have affiliates and members in many countries around the world. Of course, there are many other fine organizations. To my way of thinking, the others specialize in topics you'd want to become involved in once you have a solid grasp of the fundamental principles."

The nonprofit Sales Automation Association was founded in 1991 for the purpose of promoting and advancing improvements in the field of sales and related areas involving automation, information management, process improvement, and the philosophy of sales, marketing, and customer service. Today, improvement in the sales, marketing, and customer service process frequently involves a component of automation. The SAA currently has chapters in many U.S. cities and publishes a Chapter Starter Kit for those interested in advancing the purpose of the Association elsewhere. The SAA has developed a body of knowledge that will eventually serve as the basis for certification as sales process engineer. For more information, call 978-470-8608.

ASQC was founded in 1946 as a nonprofit organization with a mission to serve as the leading source for quality-related information. It too publishes a body of knowledge; this outline is available to anyone who asks. For more information, call 800-248-1946 or 414-272-8575. A well-established organization, ASQC offers many different certifications to persons meeting requirements, including that of the certified quality engineer, certified quality auditor, and others. In the past, the focus of ASQC's application has been in the area of manufacturing. In the last few years the society has encouraged applications in education, government, service industries, and most recently, in marketing, sales, and customer service.

Persons designating themselves as a sales process engineer or quality engineer may or may not be certified by a professional body or society. When in doubt, check credentials. The purpose of certification is to help professionals interested in developing their own skill and to help organizations wishing to employ such professionals gain a further measure of confidence in their capabilities.

- Get involved in certification efforts.
- Make a hobby out of improvement! Have fun with the tools!

What Are You Taking Home?

Dr. Selden runs down the list of expectations people had for the workshop, making sure all have been covered. Then he asks the same question he raised the day before, asking people what ideas they are taking away that they find most meaningful. Many in the class speak out.

"I feel I'm taking away some valuable models," says one fellow, "but would you believe that, in my company, one of this continent's largest insurers, we have absolutely no clue as to what values we should plug into the model? My take-away is the realization that we have to get our arms around that data."

"I came to this workshop with my sales performance improvement team leader and top information systems executive. They insisted we come here together. I fit your profile of a top executive who heard about what our competition is doing with automation and wanted to jump right on the bandwagon. We'll automate, all right, but I see now that our first approach would have been seriously mistaken. I'm taking away the need to target improvements and to size up expectations in light of reality, not opinion. I'm also taking away the feeling that your ideas will save us a lot of money."

"My take-away is that our company can adopt both a kaizen approach and an innovative one. Sometimes the best we can do is fix things one at a time. I believe in individual effort and responsibility, and I think our reps will be eager to adopt some of the ideas we've discussed. But my eyes have also been opened that we're dealing with an entire system and that many factors are at play. It may take a mix of approaches to yield the best results. So my take-away is actually the interest to learn more about what you've called the modern design of industrial experiments, since you mentioned they can be used to study the impact of many variables at once. My personal background is in chemical engineering; I'm not frightened by the concept."

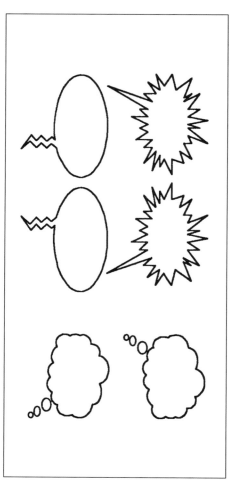

Reflections from the Group

Dr. Selden asks for a few more observations.

"I'm getting the idea that the first step is understanding your current process. The minute we back away from that, we're sliding into the rut we've always been in."

"As I've gone over the lists you provided, I'm thinking that I know where to get this type of data. I'm already making plans to do so."

"I'm feeling there is a way to move what we're doing into a more scientific approach. I'm not going to throw away anything we know to be working. But you can be sure we'll be using the elements of this approach to look for further improvement.

"I'm taking away the conviction that what you said before is true: that there can be a discipline called sales process engineering."

"I'm taking away more than just concepts. This workshop has helped me to identify of few of my own sales process bottlenecks. I can use this information for a project I have to get underway quite quickly. I've also got a lot of good ideas for the type of measurements we'll be needing."

"My manager has read many of those books by the people you've presented. But we've only applied the ideas and techniques in our machine division. That's our business. This workshop will make it easier for me to put together a proposal for improvements in our sales, marketing, and customer service departments."

"None of us might be the person doing this work. But any of us might need to manage that function. Now I've got more confidence that I can do so."

"When I signed up I was looking for the ability to measure the intangibles. I started out by thinking that the way to improve sales is by improving the salesmanship. After going through all of this I think we can can save ourselves a lot of effort by measuring objective results instead of focusing on psychological or personal issues and still make a lot of headway. Speaking as a lifelong leader of sales organizations, that's completely different than how we've been approaching this."

"I have two final questions for you. First, judging from your own experience and the examples you have heard over the past few days, have you confirmed the merit of the sales process engineering techniques we've covered? [People are nodding in agreement.] Second, can anyone find logical fault with the assumptions upon which this discipline is based? [No one does.] Then I say to you, ladies and gentlemen, welcome to a new field and a new era in marketing, sales, and customer service."

Personal Insights

As the others are talking, I'm thinking that in general this type of approach will appeal to the kind of person who isn't afraid to be analytic. Intuitive approaches may be just as effective, but they are so tough to communicate to others. They have a boundary, and that limit seems to center around personal success. If you have the right intuitive moves it helps you as an individual, sure. But a company needs something more the minute it contemplates a structural change such as new technology or a whole-scale shift in the way we sell that everyone else is supposed to follow. The people working out that new approach had better be more systematic.

My company has some data, but we work through independent agents as well as our own reps. We may never get all of the data we'd like. But I'm intrigued by the concept that we can use what we do know to triangulate our current position or interpolate what's happening inside a process, even if we can't measure it directly.

I'm still wrestling with this concept that management holds the keys to overall process improvement, just as much or more so, than any individual does. It's a radical concept because our culture puts almost all the responsibility for success on individual reps. The money we spend just on motivational speakers to pump up the sales force is incredible. I'm thinking that once we isolate a sales or service problem, we may be able to achieve improvement in many different ways. None of them may involve changing individual "attitudes." Some of the best sales trainers say that the best way to change attitudes is to change results. If we can give our people better ways to achieve results, their attitudes should improve, too.

As I think about sales in the past, we've all known that there are a lot of gaps and process inconsistencies. I think that's why we've been content to let our salespeople do their own thing and see where they end up. That quote—"living with a problem you can't solve, rather than using a solution you can't understand"—applies to us. I don't think we've looked into this deeply enough. We'll talk about fixing a few bottlenecks. A week later everyone forgets what we talked about. We're very creative in coming up with ideas. We can brainstorm all day long. But we've never tracked the history of our ideas to see what really works and doesn't work.

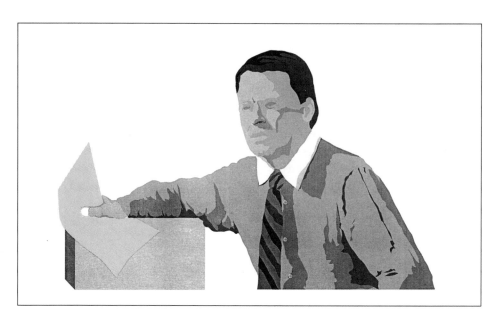

I'd like to get my top management's commitment to start on this road in our company. I'm afraid that until we institutionalize some of this effort, we'll slip back into our hit-or-miss approaches all over again. We can't afford that. The price tag on some of the new approaches we're dreaming up is too high to approach things the old way anymore. Dr. Selden may have hit on something with his point that the lack of a structurally empowered sales process R&D function is the missing ingredient in a lack of strategic progress.

Regardless of the level we approach this on, I think a fact-based approach to management can work in the sales process. If people tell me an engineering-like approach can't work, they are going to have to show me some evidence!

Let the Spark Start with You!

> To raise new questions, new possibilities, to regard old problems from a new angle requires creative imagination and marks real advances in science.
>
> —*Albert Einstein*

"Ladies and gentlemen, the hardest part in any new journey is often taking the first few steps. Sometimes once we learn a general principle, the greatest difficulty is in finding the first place to apply it to a specific situation.

"I hope we've been able to share enough examples with each other over the past few days that you can take the next steps on your own. I've given you plenty of ideas for resources you can draw on if you need help. Perhaps I'll see you in one of my seminars in the future.

"As you set out, perhaps you can take personal inspiration from this quote by Albert Einstein, as I do. I need that inspiration as much as anyone, because this is an unending quest. In spite of the distance I've come, I look at the road ahead with as much trepidation, respect—and yes, a sense of reverence and awe—as anyone. As soon I reach one vantage point, I see new mountains ahead that must be climbed. I know very little, but what I've learned excites me with the promise it holds. Those who follow will know more.

"I have been blessed with the freedom to explore this mountain on my own and with my clients, as Sir Edmund Hillary said, 'Because it is there.' My fondest wish for you is that all of you reach a point where you can undertake such exploration in a way that means the most to you. I believe you all have the potential. You have the potential to help others, too.

"In the near term I see a time when we can create a visual image of our sales process, complete with ongoing, dynamic measurements both at the individual level and at departmental and corporate levels so that we can all use these facts to do our jobs more effectively.

"In the long term, I see the creation of a whole new field: that of sales process engineering, with departments structurally empowered and dedicated to sales process research and development, and to ongoing improvement in an exciting, fertile territory.

"In the future, I see this knowledge being disseminated through our colleges and universities so that our young people can be of even more direct assistance when they enter their careers.

"Let the spark that ignites someone else's imagination start with you!"

Thank You!

"Thank you for your kind attention and gracious participation during the time we've shared together. Thank you for letting me take these few steps on your own journey—with you—together.

"I wish you good luck on your own journey—but after today, I urge you to find ways so that we don't have to rely on our luck as we've done in the past. Think what good we can accomplish! This path offers spiritual, not just professional, fulfillment.

"God bless you and, when in doubt, always remember the golden rule."

Dr. Selden bends at the waist in a brief bow. The class breaks out in long applause.

This has been one of the most interesting—and moving—workshops I have ever attended. It has opened my eyes to a whole new way of looking at the world and has acquainted me with the philosophies and works of so many great minds. It has certainly revitalized me on a professional level.

As Dr. Selden mentioned in a side comment to me, this is indeed a subject about which much will be said and written in the years to come. I feel lucky to have been introduced to the subject in such a genuine, gentle, and inspirational way.

Appendixes

Appendix A

Typically Available Numbers (Records and Receipts Exist)

—Gross sales records by internal groupings
—Lead lists and costs
—Rep tenure records
—Rep earnings
—Number of reps
—Quota attainment by rep, district, etc.
—Customer lists
—Product sales by territory, rep, other
—Delivery timing
—Certain sales expenses
—Order department cost info
—Service department cost info
—Claims info
—Inventory related info: stock outs, turns, over/shorts
—Other
—Order process time/cost
—Lead follow-up information
—Billing accuracy info
—Discounting practices: quantity, costs
—Returns/cancellations
—Other

Number That May Be Available Now (May Require Data Analysis)

—Competitive info: sales volume by company, product, etc.
—Competitive info: market share
—Profitability by specific sales, reps, products, etc.
—Customer purchases and service history
—Contact/call logs
—Order size
—Proposal issue/close logs
—Change order data
—Other
—Fine grain sales cost items: samples, marketing program, telephone, etc.
—Comparisons of costs to results: assignment of cost accounts to specific proposals/orders

Numbers That May Not Be Available Now (Not Tracked/Receipted)

—Conversion ratios
—Time selling vs. non-selling
—Cycle time for process or operation steps
—Time spent on specific activities
—Specifications for sales-related outputs
—Customer/prospect: demographics, psychographics
—Intellectual property: calendars, meeting notes
—Other
—Problem logs
—Complaints
—Customer survey info
—Repeat order data
—Customer retention, jeopardy account data
—Service related: warranty work, service calls
—Quality
—Intangibles: value of timely info, distributed expertise
—Other

Note: The source for these lists is *Cost Benefit Analysis & Sales Automation* (Selden 1995). This book also contains specific values for many costs found in the typical sales process and a summary of quantitative benefits companies have found in their sales process improvement efforts.

Appendix B

Variables Formulas: $\bar{X}$ and R (Average and Moving Range)

Use when you can measure variables and must sample.

$$UCL_{\bar{X}} \text{ and } LCL_{\bar{X}} = \bar{\bar{X}} \pm A_2 R \qquad UCL_R = D_4\bar{R} \qquad LCL_R = D_3\bar{R}$$

Useful for checking size of sale in dollars, training scores, time spent in activities, costs. Check range chart first, then means. If LCL < 0, set LCL to 0.

k = number of samples taken (best if 25 or more)
n = sample size (usually 3 to 6)
$\bar{\bar{X}}$ = mean of sample means
$\bar{X}$ = mean for each sample (total $\bar{\bar{X}}$'s / n)
R = range for each sample (max. X – min. X)
$\bar{R}$ = mean of sample ranges (total R's / k)

$\bar{X}$ and R Chart Table of Constants

Sample size n	A_2	D_3	D_4
2	1.880	0	3.267
3	1.023	0	2.574
4	0.729	0	2.282
5	0.577	0	2.114
6	0.483	0	2.004
7	0.419	0.076	1.924
8	0.373	0.136	1.864
9	0.337	0.184	1.816
10	0.308	0.223	1.777

Variables Formulas: X and R_m (Individuals and Moving Range)

Use when you can measure variables and have individual measures

$$UCL_{\bar{X}} \text{ and } LCL_{\bar{X}} = \bar{X} \pm 2.659\,\bar{R}_m \qquad UCL_{R_m} = 3.267\bar{R}_m \qquad LCL_{R_m} = 0$$

Useful for checking size of sales in dollars, training scores, time spent in activities, costs, when the total of all individual items of interest is known. Check range chart first, then means.

Sample size = 1

k = number of samples taken (best if 25 or more)
$\bar{\bar{X}}$ = mean of samples (total X's / k)
R_m = moving range (abs $[X_{i+1} - X_i]$); where i is an individual score
$\bar{R}_m$ = mean of moving ranges (total R_m / number of R_m's)

Attribute Chart Formulas: $\bar{p}$ and $n\bar{p}$

Use when a whole unit either meets criterion or not

$\bar{p}$ chart — Percent of whole units nonconforming — $\bar{p} \pm 3\sqrt{\dfrac{\bar{p}(1-\bar{p})}{n}}$

Note: If UCL > 1, set to 1; if LCL < 0, set to 0.

np chart — Number of whole units nonconforming — $n\bar{p} \pm 3\sqrt{n\bar{p}(1-\bar{p})}$

Note: If UCL > n, set to n; if LCL < 0, set to 0.

n = sample size (best ≥ 50)
$\bar{p}$ = total nonconforming / total inspected (i.e., mean nonconforming)

Population should be ≥ 10 times sample size. Collect 25 samples or more; $\bar{p}$ charts may have sample sizes that vary; use mean sample sizes for samples with ±20% of mean sample size; calculate separate limits for samples beyond ±20%. $n\bar{p}$ charts must have constant sample sizes.

Appendix B (cont'd.)

Attribute Chart Formulas: *c* and *u*

Use to count errors when a single whole unit may have multiple errors

u chart	Mean nonconformities per unit or measure	$\bar{u} \pm 3\sqrt{\bar{u} / n}$

Note: If LCL < 0, do not plot

c chart	Number of whole units nonconforming	$\bar{c} \pm 3\sqrt{\bar{c}}$

Note: If LCL < 0, do not plot

n = sample size

$\bar{u}$ and $\bar{c}$ = total nonconformance / total units inspected (i.e., mean nonconforming), either per unit ($\bar{u}$) or per sample ($\bar{c}$). Sample size must be at least 16, but best when at least 4–5 occurrences expected in sample and probability of occurrence on each trial is < 0.1. *u* charts may have sample sizes that vary, use mean sample sizes for samples within ±20%. *c* charts must have constant sample sizes.

Appendix C

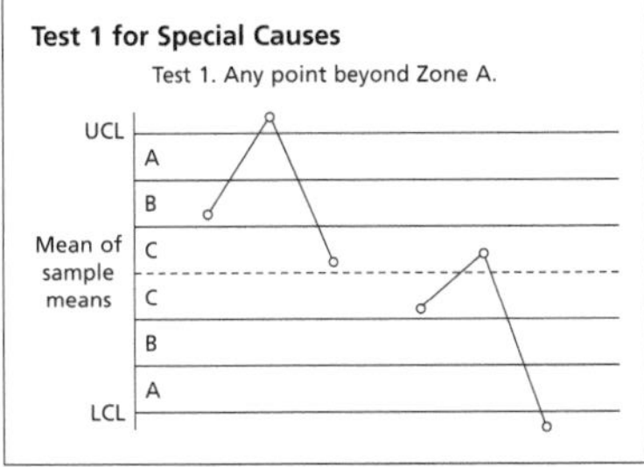

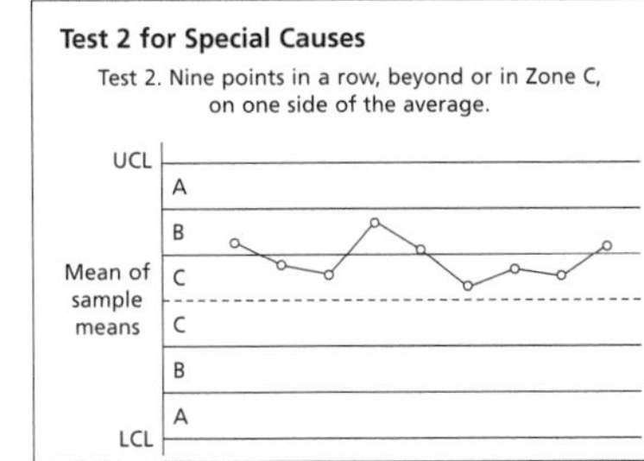

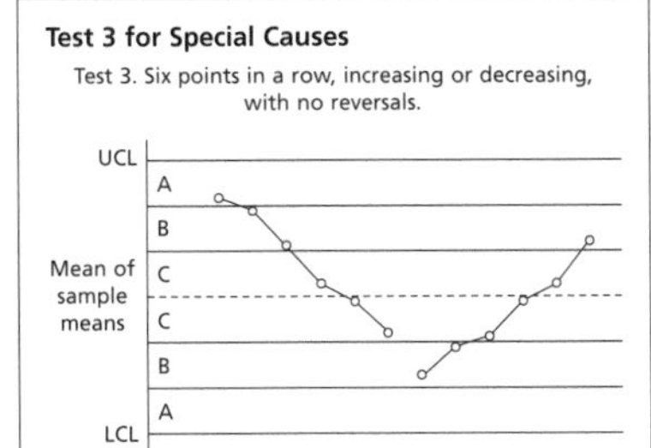

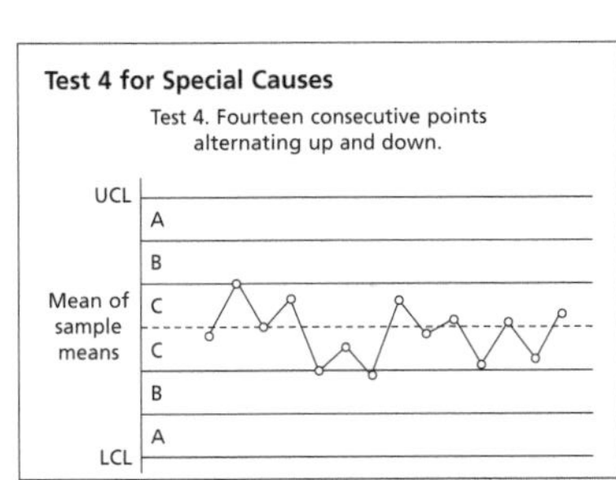

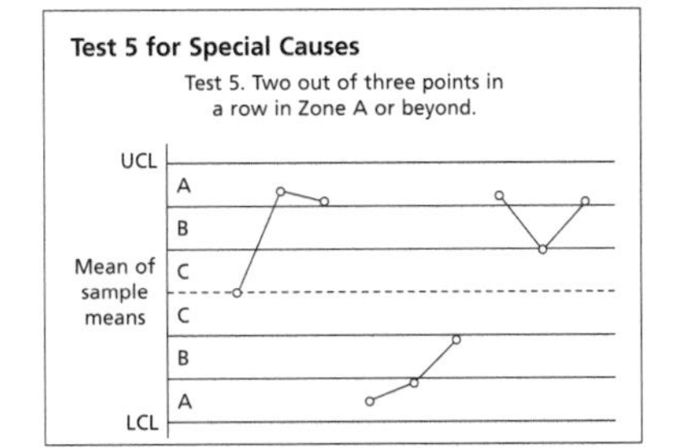

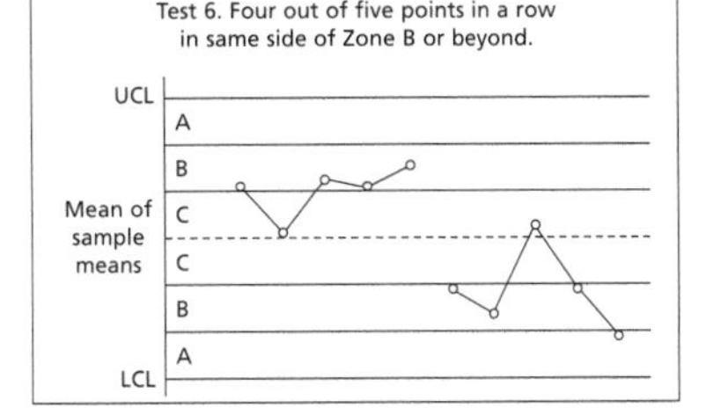

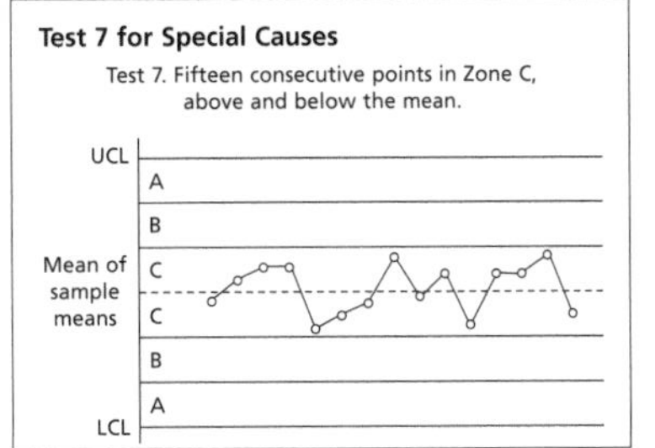

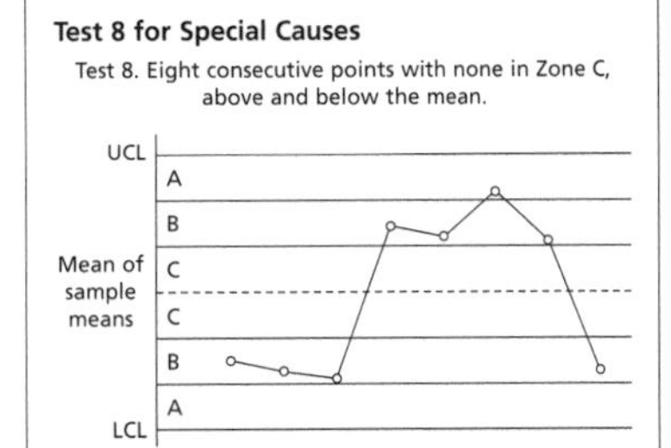

The size of zones and the SPC formulas were originally determined with regard to manufactured products. The tables, formulas, and tests do, however, provide guidance to properly trained individuals and are well proven in other fields. Student of sales process improvement will find ample opportunity for further research in this area.

Engineering is a conservative field. Keeping in mind that even though thousands of personnel use statistical process control on a daily basis, supervision is strongly recommended until your own skill in using SPC is developed through further study and practice. Mathematical mistakes are always easy to make. Double-check all computations made and always use careful judgment when acting on the results, especially related to matters where health, safety, and human welfare are concerned.

Bibliography

Asimov, Issac. 1989. *Asimov's chronology of science & discovery.* New York: Harper & Row.

Associated Press. 1996. Poll: College graduates lack basic knowledge. *Kalamazoo Gazette,* 1 June, C8.

AT&T. 1958. *Statistical quality control handbook.* 2d ed. Reprint of Western Electric's original. Indianapolis, Ind.: AT&T Technologies.

Baer, Donald M., Montrose M. Wolf, and Todd R. Risley. 1968. Some current dimensions of applied behavior analysis. *Journal of Applied Behavior Analysis* (spring): 91–97.

Beveridge, Dirk, and Don Beveridge. n.d. *New call selling* (audiotape). Chicago: Dartnell Audio Library.

Big pickups for serious hauling. 1996. *Consumer Reports* (September): 50–54.

Brassard, Michael, and Diane Ritter. 1994. *The memory jogger II.* Methuen, Mass.: GOAL/QPC.

Brethower, Dale. 1972. *Behavioral analysis in business and industry.* Kalamazoo, Mich.: behaviordelia.

Brewer, Geoffrey. 1994. 20 percent—or else! *Sales & Marketing Management* (November): 66–72.

Brown, Paul L. 1982. *Managing behavior on the job.* New York: John Wiley & Sons.

Brown, Ronald. 1990. *From selling to managing: Guidelines for the first time sales manager.* Rev. ed. New York: AMACOM.

Burke, James. 1995. *The day the universe changed.* Rev. ed. Boston, Mass.: Back Bay Books.

Campanella, Jack, ed. 1990. *Principles of quality costs.* 2d ed. Milwaukee, Wis.: ASQC Quality Press.

Cannie, J. K. 1993. *Turning lost customers into gold.* New York: AMACOM.

Carlton, Jim. 1995. Marketing plays a bigger role in distinguishing PCs. *Wall Street Journal,* 16 October, B4.

Carnegie, Dale. 1940. *How to win friends and influence people.* New York: Pocket Books.

Champy, James, and Michael Hammer. 1993. *Reengineering the corporation.* New York: HarperCollins.

Columbo, George. 1994. *Sales force automation.* New York: McGraw-Hill.

Computers capture capital spending. 1996. *Business Week,* 3 June, 8.

Connellan, Thomas K. 1978. *How to improve human performance.* New York: Harper & Row.

Cooper, Robin, and Robert S. Kaplan. 1988. Measure costs right: Make the right decisions. *Harvard Business Review* (September/October): 96–103.

Corcoran, Kevin J., Laura K. Petersen, Daniel B. Baitch, and Mark F. Barrett. 1995. *High performance sales organizations.* Burr Ridge, Ill.: Irwin Professional Publishing.

Covey, Stephen. 1990. *The seven habits of highly effective people.* New York: Simon & Schuster.

Crosby, Philip B. 1979. *Quality is free.* New York: McGraw-Hill.

DataMyte Division. 1992. *DataMyte handbook.* 5th ed. Minnetonka, Minn.: Allen-Bradley Co.

Davenport, Thomas H. 1993. *Process innovation.* Boston: Harvard Business School Press.

———. 1995. Why reengineering failed. *Fast Company* 1, no. 1.

Deming, W. Edwards. 1986. *Out of the crisis.* Cambridge, Mass.: MIT Center for Advanced Engineering Study.

Ealey, Lance A. 1988. *Quality by design.* Allen Park, Mich.: ASI Press.

Enrico, Dottie. 1995. Ogilvy: Ad research opens creative avenues. *USA Today,* 20 March, 6B.

Farnum, Gregory. 1995. Configurators go from smart to smarter. *Managing Automation,* October, 45–49.

Fleschner, Malcolm. 1993. Out of the ashes. *Personal Selling Power* (July/August): 37–41.

———. 1996a. Prescription for success. *Selling Power* (January/February): 24–29.

———. 1996b. Copy this. *Selling Power* (March): 22–26.

Fukuyama, Francis. 1995. Trust: *The social virtues & the creation of prosperity.* New York: Free Press.

Gallagher, Bill, Orvel Ray Wilson, and Jay Conrad Levinson. 1992. *Guerrilla selling.* Boston: Houghton Mifflin.

Galloway, Dianne. 1994. *Mapping work processes.* Milwaukee, Wis.: ASQC Quality Press.

Gibson, Richard. 1993. Poor handling turns leads into no-sales. *Wall Street Journal,* March 31, B1.

Gilbert, Thomas F. 1978. *Human competence: Engineering worthy performance.* New York: McGraw-Hill.

Girard, Joe. 1986. *How to sell anything to anybody.* New York: Warner Books.

Gleick, James. 1987. *Chaos: Making a new science.* New York: Penguin Books.

Godfrey, A. Blanton. 1996a. Beyond satisfaction. *Quality Digest* (January): 15.

———. 1996b. Personal conversation with author. 7 June.

Goldenberg, Barton. 1996. *Guide to sales, customer service, and marketing automation.* Washington, D.C.: ISM Inc.

Goldratt, Eliyahu M. 1990. *Theory of constraints.* Great Barrington, Mass.: North River Press.

———. 1992. *The goal.* 2nd ed. Great Barrington, Mass.: North River Press.

———. 1994. *It's not luck.* Great Barrington, Mass.: North River Press.

Hamel, Gary, and C. K. Prahalad. 1994. *Competing for the future.* Boston: Harvard Business School Press, 1994.

Hammer, Michael, and James Champy. 1993. *Reengineering the corporation.* New York: HarperBusiness.

Hammer, Michael, and Steven A. Stanton. 1995. *The reengineering revolution.* New York: HarperBusiness.

Hanan, Mack. 1985. *Consultative selling.* 3rd ed. New York: AMACOM.

Harrington, H. James. 1991. *Business process improvement.* New York: McGraw-Hill.

Hill, Napoleon. 1960. *Think & grow rich* (revised). New York: Fawcett Crest.

Hinckley, C. Martin, and Philip Barkan. 1995. Variation, mistakes, and complexity in producing nonconformities. *Journal of Quality Technology* (July): 242–249.

Honig, Werner K. 1966. *Operant behavior: Areas of research and application.* New York: Appleton-Century-Crofts.

Hopkins, Tom. 1982. *How to master the art of selling.* New York: Warner Books.

Hunt, V. Daniel. 1993. *Reengineering.* Essex Junction, Vt.: omneo/Oliver Wight.

Imai, Masaaki. 1986. *Kaizen.* New York: Random House.

Japan Management Association. 1989. David J. Lu, trans. *Kanban: Just-in-time at Toyota* (revised). Cambridge, Mass.: Productivity Press.

Johansson, Henry J., Patrick McHugh, A. John Pendlebury, and William A. Wheeler III. 1993. *Business process reengineering.* New York: John Wiley & Sons.

Johnson, Barney. 1993. *Quincunx/PC.* Knoxville, Tenn.: B. Johnson Software.

Juran, J. M., ed. 1988. *Juran's quality control handbook.* 4th ed. New York: McGraw-Hill.

Juran, J. M., and Frank M. Gryna. 1993. *Quality planning and analysis.* 3rd ed. New York: McGraw-Hill.

Kankus, Richard F., and Robert P. Cavalier. 1995. Combating organizationally induced helplessness. *Quality Progress* (December): 89–90.

King, W. J. 1944. *The unwritten laws of engineering.* New York: ASME Press.

Latzko, William J. 1996. Personal conversation with author. 12 May.

———. 1987. *Quality and productivity for bankers and financial managers.* New York: Marcel Dekker.

Latzko, William J., and David M. Saunders. 1995. *Four days with Dr. Deming.* Reading, Mass.: Addison-Wesley.

Lazere, Cathy. 1995. Spotlight on SG&A. *CFO* (December): 39–49.

Learning International. 1983. Success factors in selling. White paper. Stamford, Conn.: Learning International.

LeBoeuf, Michael. 1989. *How to win customers and keep them for life.* New York: Berkley.

Levinson, Jay Conrad. 1989. *Guerrilla marketing attack.* Boston: Houghton-Mifflin.

Lewis, Bill. 1996. The wealth of a nation. *Wall Street Journal,* 7 June, A12.

Lochner, Robert H., and Joseph E. Matar. 1990. *Designing for quality.* White Plains, N.Y.: Quality Resources and Milwaukee, Wis.: ASQC Quality Press.

Magrath, Allan J. 1993. *How to achieve zero-defect marketing.* New York: AMACOM.

Mazie, David. 1995. Where it pays to have a great idea. *Reader's Digest* (June): 100–104.

McCloskey, Larry. 1995. *Selling with excellence: A quality approach for sales professionals.* Milwaukee, Wis.: ASQC Quality Press.

McGrath, Roger Jr. 1994. Organizationally induced helplessness: The antithesis of empowerment. *Quality Progress* (April): 89–92.

McMahon, Timothy. 1994. *Selling 2000.* N.p.: A Signature Book.

Melan, Eugene H. 1993. *Process management.* New York: McGraw-Hill.

Miller, Robert B., Stephen E. Heiman, and Tad Tuleja. 1985. *Strategic selling.* New York: Warner Books.

Miller, Lawrence M. 1978. *Behavior management.* New York: John Wiley & Sons.

Minero, Thomas. 1995. Personal comments delivered during the Sales Automation Association workshop, 28 February, New York.

Monden, Yasuhiro. 1983. *Toyota production system.* Norcross, Ga.: Industrial Engineering and Management Press.

Morris, Daniel, and Joel Brandon. 1993. *Re-engineering your business.* New York: McGraw-Hill.

Niebel, Benjamin W. 1988. *Motion and time study.* 8th ed. Homewood, Ill.: Irwin.

Nightingale, Earl. 1992. *Earl Nightingale's greatest discovery* (audiotape). Los Angeles: Audio Renaissance Tapes.

Noreen, Eric, Debra Smith, and James T. Mackey. 1995. *The theory of constraints and its implications for management accounting.* Great Barrington, Mass.: North River Press.

Paulos, John Allen. 1995. *A mathematician reads the newspaper.* New York: Anchor Books/Doubleday.

Peace, Glen Stuart. 1993. *Taguchi methods®: A hands-on approach to quality engineering.* Reading, Mass.: Addison-Wesley.

Peale, Norman Vincent. 1991. *Positive imaging* (audiotape). New York: HarperCollins.

Peppers, Don, and Martha Rogers. 1993. *The one to one future.* New York: Currency/Doubleday.

Pitt, Hy. 1994. *SPC for the rest of us.* Reading, Mass.: Addison-Wesley.

Plsek, Paul E., and Arturo Onnias. 1989. *Quality improvement tools.* Wilton, Conn.: Juran Institute.

Pugh, G. Allan. 1994. *Industrial experiments without statistical pain.* Milwaukee, Wis.: ASQC Quality Press.

Pyzdek, Thomas. 1994. *Pocket guide to quality tools.* Tucson, Ariz.: Quality Publishing.

Rackham, Neil. 1988. *SPIN selling.* New York: McGraw-Hill.

Reichheld, Frederick F., and W. Earl Sasser Jr. 1990. Zero defections: Quality comes to customer service. *Harvard Business Review* (September/October): 105–111.

Rice, Don. 1996. *Sales success—When the price is right.* Kalamazoo Gazette, 20 March, A5.

Ries, Al, and Jack Trout. 1986. *Marketing warfare.* New York: McGraw-Hill.

———. 1993. *The 22 immutable laws of marketing.* New York: HarperBusiness.

Sagan, Carl. 1978. *The dragons of Eden.* New York: Ballentine Books.

Sales Automation Association. 1994. *Sales automation excellence program and audit standards.* Chicago: Sales Automation Association.

Sandler, David. 1996. *You can't teach a kid to ride a bike at a seminar.* New York: Dutton/The Penguin Group.

Scofield, Todd C., and Donald R. Shaw. 1992. *Sales automation: Concepts, justification, planning, and implementation.* New York: AMACOM.

Selden, Paul H. 1994a. Applying TQM to the sales process. *Sales Process Engineering & Automation Review* (December): 23–31.

———. 1994b. What is sales process engineering? *Sales Process Engineering & Automation Review* (December): 3–6.

———. 1994c. *Guide to implementing sales automation.* 2d ed. Chicago: Sales Automation Association.

———. 1995. *Cost-benefit analysis & sales automation.* Kalamazoo, Mich.: The Paul Selden Companies.

———. 1996. The next structural breakthrough in sales isn't more automation! *Sales Process Engineering & Automation Review* (March): 3–7.

Senge, Peter. 1990. *The fifth discipline: The art and practice of the learning organization.* New York: Doubleday & Company.

Shewhart, Walter A. 1986. *Statistical method from the viewpoint of quality control.* Originally published in 1939. Mineola, N.Y: Dover Publications.

Shingo, Shigeo. 1986. *Zero quality control: Source inspection and the poka-yoke system.* Cambridge, Mass.: Productivity Press.

Shuffleburger, Carlton. 1993. Presentation at the Power Selling Conference, 12 October, Chicago, Illinois.

Siebel, Thomas, and Michael Malone. 1996. *Virtual selling.* New York: Free Press.

Skinner, B. F. 1948. *Walden II.* New York: Macmillan.

———. 1953. *Science and human behavior.* New York: Macmillan.

———. 1971. *Beyond freedom and dignity.* New York: Bantam/Vintage Books.

Smith, Frank. 1996. *How will we know it's working?* Presentation at the Sales Automation Association 6th Annual User's Conference, 13 June, Chicago, Illinois.

Smith, George A. Jr. 1994. *Sales productivity measurement.* Milwaukee, Wis.: ASQC Quality Press.

———. 1995. *The sales quality audit.* Milwaukee, Wis.: ASQC Quality Press.

Stum, David. 1995. Capturing customer loyalty: What everyone in the organization needs to know. *Corporate University Review* (November/December): 11.

Sulzer-Azaroff, Beth, and Dwight Harshbarger. 1995. Putting fear to flight. *Quality Progress* (December): 61–65.

Taguchi, Genichi. 1986. *Introduction to quality engineering.* Allen Park, Mich.: ASI Press.

———. 1993. *Taguchi on robust technology development.* Allen Park, Mich.: ASI Press.

Tehrani, Nadji. 1995. Direct mail vs. telemarketing vs. the Internet. *Telemarketing* (October): 2–4.

Thurow, Lester C. 1996. *The future of capitalism.* New York: William Morrow & Co.

Tracy, Brian. 1985. *The psychology of selling* (audiotape). Chicago: Nightengale-Conant Corporation.

———. 1995. *Advanced selling strategies.* New York: Simon & Schuster.

Voss, Bristol. 1996. Inside the Spiegel/Eddie Bauer distribution center. *Operations & Fulfillment* (March/April): 10–81.

Walton, Mary. 1986. *The Deming management method.* New York: Perigee Books.

Welch, Cas, and Pete Geissler. 1995. *Applying total quality to sales.* Milwaukee, Wis.: ASQC Quality Press.

Weldon, Joel. 1982. *Sell it! With the million dollar attitude* (audiotape). Scottsdale, Ariz.: Joel H. Weldon & Associates.

Yano, Shinichi. 1990. *New Lanchester strategy.* Sunnyvale, Calif.: Lanchester Press.

Zemke, Ron, and Dick Schaaf. 1990. *The service edge.* New York: Plume/Penguin.

Ziglar, Zig. 1984. *See you at the top.* Gretna, La.: Pelican Publishing Co.

Index